VASILIY PAVLOVICH AKSËNOV:
A WRITER IN QUEST OF HIMSELF

VASILIY PAVLOVICH AKSËNOV

VASILIY PAVLOVICH AKSËNOV: A WRITER IN QUEST OF HIMSELF

Editor
Edward Możejko
The University of Alberta

Co-Editors

Boris Briker
The University of Alberta

Per Dalgård
The University of Alberta

Slavica Publishers, Inc.

Slavica publishes a wide variety of books and journals dealing with the peoples, languages, literatures, history, folklore, and culture of the peoples of Eastern Europe and the USSR. For a complete catalog with prices and ordering information, please write to:

Slavica Publishers, Inc.
P.O. Box 14388
Columbus, Ohio 43214
USA

ISBN: 0-89357-141-5.

Each contribution copyright © 1984 by its author; all rights reserved. This book was published in 1986.

All statements of fact or opinion are those of the authors, and neither the Editors nor Slavica Publishers assume any responsibility therefor.

Text set by Sheila Wolohan and Randy Bowlus at the East European Composition Center, supported by the Department of Slavic Languages and Literatures and the Center for Russian and East European Studies at UCLA.

Printed in the United States of America.

TABLE OF CONTENTS

1. Aksënov's Photograph — 2
2. Editors' Note — 7
   B. Briker, P. Dalgård, E. Możejko
3. Introduction — 9
   Edward Możejko

PART I
THE MAN AND THE WRITER

4. Interview with V.P. Aksënov — 14
   I. Lauridsen and P. Dalgård
5. A Conversation in the Editorial Office of *Kontinent* — 26
   V. Maksimov, È. Kuznetsov, N. Gorbanevskaya
6. V.P. Aksënov: A Literary Biography — 32
   J.J. Johnson, Jr.

PART II
GENERAL ARTICLES

7. The Exotic in the Early Novellas of Aksënov — 54
   R.L. Busch
8. Some Literary Roots of Aksënov's Writings: Affinities and Parallels — 68
   P. Dalgård
9. Notes on Aksënov's Drama — 87
   K. Kustanovich
10. Beautiful Ladies in the Works of Vasiliy Aksënov — 102
    I. Lauridsen
11. Basketball, God, and the Ringo Kid: Philistinism and the Ideal in Aksënov's Short Stories — 119
    P. Meyer
12. The Function of Conventional Language Pattern in the Prose of Vasiliy Aksënov — 131
    A. Vishevsky and T. Pogacar

PART III
ARTICLES ON SPECIFIC TOPICS

13. *In Search of a Genre*: The Meaning of the Title and the Idea of a "Genre" — 148
    B. Briker
14. Mystianic Prose — 165
    E. Ètkind

15. Aksënov as Travel Writer:
    'Round the Clock, Non-Stop   181
    D.B. Johnson
16. *Our Golden Hardware* as a Parody   193
    N. Kolesnikoff
17. *The Steel Bird* and Aksënov's Prose of the Seventies   205
    E. Możejko
18. Aksënov's "'Victory'": A Post-Analysis   224
    A. Zholkovsky

APPENDIX

19. Tianstvennaya proza (Russian version of
    "Mystianic Prose")   241
    E. Etkind
20. A Bibliography of Works by and about
    V.P. Aksënov   253
    Compiled by B. Briker and P. Dalgård
21. Contributors   269

For Vasiliy Pavlovich, who "shël po Liteynomu na bul'var St. Michel i dal'she na Manhattan".

EDITORS' NOTE

The idea of compiling this volume about Vasiliy Pavlovich Aksënov was originated by three of his admirers. It was intended for the occasion of his fiftieth birthday in 1982, but as so often happens in our profession, the idea is one thing and its realization another. We significantly underestimated the time required for discussing, writing, editing, typing; and for gathering in the papers and their critical assessments. Consequently, the process of preparing the manuscript for print stretched over a longer period of time than we had initially anticipated, so that we decided to dedicate the book not to Aksënov's anniversary, but simply to Vasiliy Pavlovich. Nor, indeed, do we need a special occasion to honor him: the emphatically positive responses of invited contributors from the continents of Europe and North America bear witness to this.

A few explanatory remarks about the editorial guidelines follow. The system of transliteration used in this volume is that of the Library of Congress, with some modifications. The changes are, indeed, minor, and affect the two Russian vowels *e, ë*, which we decided to transliterate as *ye* and *yë* after vowels and ь or ъ, and Russian *ü*, which we transliterate as *y*. Quotations from texts using different transliteration systems remain unchanged; likewise, the names of authors whose surnames retain the ending *-sky*, hence "Vishevsky" and "Zholkovsky." Single Russian or foreign words in general are in italics and followed by an English translation within single quotation marks. Shorter quotations (not indented) and longer quotations (indented) are followed immediately by an English translation. Whenever an author wanted to emphasize a point, we used quotation marks, although italics, reserved mainly for foreign words, are not entirely excluded.

Our foremost intention has been to facilitate the reading of the text. Thus, only Mr. John J. Johnson's biographical survey carries the Russian titles of Aksënov's works. Russian titles of works not mentioned by Mr. Johnson but which appear in other articles may be found by the reader immediately after this editorial note.

Professor Ètkind wrote his article in Russian and requested that it be published in the original. Whoever reads his contribution will understand his motives. It is a kind of homologue of Aksënov's experimental prose: marvellous but hardly translatable. As such, it constitutes an experiment within literary criticism itself. While complying with Professor Ètkind's request, we also considered it necessary to include an English translation. From its inception, the volume was intended to be a collection of articles written in English and we did not wish to waive this principle. We believe that Mr. A. Reid's translation renders justice to Professor Ètkind's text, thus making this analysis accessible to a much broader readership.

A few words ought to be said about the bibliography. It was compiled through a great effort and we are particularly grateful to Professor Priscilla Meyer for her generous suggestion that we incorporate the bibliography which she published on Aksënov in 1973. The present bibliography contains more than twice as many items—an indication of the growing popularity and importance of Aksënov as a writer. Unfortunately, it was beyond our human and financial resources to obtain and check each item, so that publication details, such as pagination, could not be recorded in every instance. We cannot vouch for the completeness of the bibliography, yet despite its shortcomings, we have every reason to hope that it will serve well those who are interested in Aksënov.

We would like to thank all the contributors who agreed to participate in this project, as well as the Department of Slavic and East European Studies and the Department of Comparative Literature at the University of Alberta for financial and technical assistance. Our special thanks go to Dr. Robert L. Busch, Chairman of the Department of Slavic and East European Studies for his kind cooperation. We wish to acknowledge our indebtedness and gratitude to Mrs. Doreen Hawryshko, who, with patient dedication, typed the manuscript and greatly facilitated its completion. We would like to express our appreciation to Mrs. Sheila Steinhauer and Dr. Francis Macri for reading the manuscripts of non-native speakers of English and to Miss Margaret Bradley, Mrs. Inger Lauridsen, Dr. Michael Bigins and Mr. Allen Reid for translating some of the Russian texts.

A final debt of gratitude is owing to Vasiliy Pavlovich, who kindly opened his home to us and cooperated significantly in the realization of this project.

Additional Russian titles not mentioned by Mr. John J. Johnson:
1. *Aristofoniana s lyagushkami* — Aristophaniana and the Frogs.
2. "Gibel' Pompei" — The Destruction of Pompeii.
3. "Mechta taksista" — A Taxidriver's Dream.
4. *Tsaplya* — The Heron.
5. *Vash ubiytsa* — Your Murderer.

INTRODUCTION

Edward Możejko

This collection of articles is devoted to Vasiliy Pavlovich Aksënov, one of the most outstanding writers in contemporary Russian literature. Despite all changes, turn-abouts and zigzag developments so typical of Soviet cultural life in the past quarter of a century or so, his presence in the literary process has been felt throughout the whole post-Stalinist era. Aksënov gained his reputation not through opportunistic bows to party demands or official critics, but through understanding literature as a spontaneous response to reality and through fidelity to his own creative principles. In their conversation, which is included in this collection, V. Maksimov, N. Gorbanevskaya and È. Kuznetsov rightly observe that Aksënov has become a symbol not only of the "Thaw" and the hopes associated with it, but also of human integrity.

Since his debut in 1959, Aksënov's literary output has grown rapidly in volume, so that today he may be considered by any standards a prolific writer. Even those who are interested in modern Russian literature have difficulty in keeping pace with his literary activity, which includes short stories and novels, plays and novellas. If we take into account Aksënov's tendency to include in his narrative entire poetic units of rhythmic and even rhymed prose, then we may be led to the conclusion that no literary genre has escaped his attention. The writer makes skillful use of a variety of literary devices in almost all his works published after 1965, thereby furthering significantly the innovative, experimental tradition of Russian twentieth-century literature. This variety of forms is matched by thematic richness. Roughly speaking, he has gone through an evolution from describing the anxieties of his generation in the late fifties and early sixties to expressing criticism of the Soviet system and a search for new spiritual values (*The Burn* and "The Village of Sviyazhsk"). Yet his metaphorical style is of such associative power, his prose and plays contain so many allusions to various spheres of human existence that one could not rest with such a limited statement about his "periodization." Essentially, Aksënov has never abandoned his social responsibility as a writer and has remained a sensitive observer of his time. To him, the principle of experiment for experiment's sake is entirely foreign. In fact, as is the case with any great writer, form with Aksënov becomes part and parcel of the content and vice versa. It is thanks to the form that we are able to grasp, or rather sense, the importance of the critical message which he tries to deliver. Its parabolic metaphorical nature compels the reader to reflect upon the works he reads, and to find answers to and interpretations of what he or she has experienced. It would be difficult to find another Russian writer in whom content and form find such a strong dialectical interdependence and yet retain, as a whole, ambiguity.

Aksënov, more than any other Russian writer, needs a commentary. This book is not only a tribute from its participants to Aksënov's talent as a writer, but also a modest attempt to respond to this need, that is, to provide a commentary. This explains, of course, why so much attention in the present volume has been given to specific works such as "Victory," *Our Golden Hardware*, "The Steel Bird" and others. The same is true for the articles of a more general nature: they not only formulate an issue or question, but attempt to explain it, too.

In his shrewd and penetrating "post-analysis" of "Victory," A. Zholkovsky strikes at the central question of Aksënov's writing when he asks "whose and what kind of victory is it?" *Per analogiam*, one may ask a similar question in more general terms: what is the meaning of Aksënov's short novels, stories, plays and novellas, especially those published after the mid-Sixties? Without being encouraged to do so, many contributors have addressed this question either directly or indirectly. In this context, E. Ètkind's masterly critique of *Our Golden Hardware* deserves special attention. By trying to define the specificity of Aksënov's prose, he points to its two most important characteristics: its polysemic essence and ambiguity.

In the section which includes more general articles, their authors analyze either specific periods or problems predominant in this prose. Thus, P. Meyer examines the conflict between the material temptations which Soviet life may offer (mainly the wish "to be like others") and the idealistic dreams of the protagonists to try to obey or to follow their own consciences. In Aksënov's latest works, this conflict seems to be resolved in favor of religious spirituality.

I. Lauridsen formulates the essence and the role of "femininity" in Aksënov's writing; if discussed against the background of Russian literary tradition, the theme of "femininity" acquires in Aksënov essential innovative features. Lauridsen's final conclusion, that she prefers to see the image of woman in Aksënov as the first non-depressing image of the "good person," is preceded by other penetrating observations about his works in general.

By mentioning some of the contributions to this volume, my intention is to demonstrate the underlying tendency of our collective effort. In doing so I would also like to draw attention to an interesting comment made by K. Kustanovich in his notes on Aksënov's plays. He suggests that all his works could be read as variants of one and the same text. If so, what dominant, then, lends unity to such a "text"? The answer is not difficult to find: the author of *The Burn* has always been fascinated with the fantastic. It is present even in the earliest novellas (see the article by R.L. Busch) and achieves particular significance in the later period of his writing. Aksënov's literary world is composed of dreams and fantasy on the one hand and reality on the other. This blend leaves an indelible mark on the whole of his literary oeuvre. The grotesque, the absurd, his irony and ambiguity, in short all the constituents of what we may call "modernity," find their origins in the use of the fantastic. It comes, then, as no surprise that in one way or another all the contributors address this fundamental question in their analyses.

In preparing this volume the editors did not intend to impose any preconceived ideas, but tried to pursue one general goal: to cover the widest possible range of topics so that the reader might be guided through various aspects and stages of Aksënov's evolution as a writer and thereby develop some insight into his work. Although at times some topics may seem to overlap, their interpretations do not (compare the articles by Ètkind and Kolesnikoff on *Our Golden Hardware*), owing to the contributors' varying critical attitudes to the subject. Furthermore, in our call for papers we avoided suggesting any unified methodological approach. We left it entirely to the discretion of the contributors. Surprisingly, however, the result is a quite consistent critical whole which has been defined, probably most aptly, and not without irony, by Zholkovsky's subtitle, "a post-analysis." It is a sort of common methodological denominator for the articles in this collection. The prefix *post-* stands, of course, for the "post-structuralist" period, which seems to put emphasis on interpretations by using the tools provided by the preceding theoretical achievements of structuralism. The current hermeneutical bent in criticism is understandable: it is not only a reaction against exaggerated and pure "theoretizing," but rather a response to the growing complexity of modernist and post-modernist literature. Aksënov's prose belongs definitely to this category of literature. As has already been observed, the bulk of his literary corpus and the criticism about it have grown to such an extent that they call for ordering and classification. It is to be hoped that this volume of essays may contribute to this goal and serve not only as a point of departure for further studies on Aksënov, but as an impetus for the discussion of modern Russian literature in general.

PART I

THE MAN AND THE WRITER

INTERVIEW WITH V.P. AKSËNOV
Washington, D.C., December, 1982

by Inger Lauridsen and Per Dalgård

CHILDHOOD
What do you remember about your childhood in Kazan'?
Hardly anything; in 'thirty-seven, something happened—something which, in a child's life, is a serious change: our home was wrecked. At first, they [NKVD—eds.] arrested my mother, then my father; and I remember that the rooms were sealed.

The apartment was a large one, with many rooms, I think there were five of them because my father was a big-wig in Kazan'. After the search, the NKVD closed these rooms, and, as a result, there was one room left in the whole apartment: my little room, where I lived with my nurse; and my paternal grandfather also lived there, in the kitchen.

You had a brother?
I did—a halfbrother, by Mama. His father took him away to Leningrad—unfortunately, as a matter of fact, because he died in the blockade there. And my sister (my father's daughter) was taken by her mother to Moscow. Her mother was also arrested in 1940, and my sister was left all alone as a little girl. She teaches now in Moscow University—she's my elder sister. My younger sister is an actress: she was adopted as a child in Magadan.

For how many years did you live in Kazan'?
Until I was sixteen. The NKVD had taken me when I was four years old: they had special homes for the children of those who had been arrested; and there were a lot of them. I was quite a tiny kid (*ya kroshkoy byl*) then. I was put with two other boys into a separate compartment of a train going to the town of Kostroma. With me came a female security officer (*chekistka, baba*) who was in charge of us; and we were not allowed to leave the closed compartment. We were four-year-old child-prisoners.

I was in the children's home for about six months, until my relatives found me. The NKVD gave no information of my whereabouts, but my uncle, my father's brother, came to Kazan': he was unemployed because as my father's brother, he had lost his job at the university, and he spent his days simply waiting to be arrested. Since he had nothing to lose, he very bravely went there, pounded his fist on the door and shouted: "Give me the boy!" He then entered, boldly reclaimed me, and took me to the home of my aunt (my father's sister) in Kazan', where I was brought up until I was sixteen—and at sixteen I went away to Mama in Magadan.

You went to school there?
Yes; I graduated from Magadan's high school. It was a very good school, even by those standards.

Was it all like it is in **The Burn***?*
Similar, but not entirely, of course.

You had a stepfather there? . . .
Yes, Mama married again in the prison-camp. [Aksënov's mother, Evgeniya Ginzburg, was released from the camp itself after some years but was not allowed to leave Magadan; see Biography—eds.] He was a concentration camp-hospital doctor, she a nurse; and, in the final analysis, she no longer had any hopes whatsoever of a meeting with my father. Ten thousand kilometers separated them from each other, the whole of Siberia was between them; and furthermore, apparently no letters came from my father for the first three years. When the war began, many people were killed by the *chekists*, and it was generally believed that my father had already died. Mama also believed so. To make a long story short, she met Anton Yakovlevich Val'ter. He was a remarkable man, a Russian German from the Crimea, a doctor. He'd already served three terms in prison: as one term neared its end, they'd give him an extra term while he was still inside the camp, to make sure that he would never get out. To make matters worse, he was a German in wartime! The fact that he was a very good doctor saved him.

RELIGION

And what about religion?
That was the man who somehow introduced me to religiosity—not to religion, but to belief in God. I had a religious instinct—but at the same time, of course, I was just a boy: frivolous, and uninterested in these matters.

How do you feel about religion now?
Now, for lack of time, I'm not a church-goer. I am, of course, a strong believer—not simply a believer. Belief and prayer gives some kind of very powerful support.

You're half-Jewish?
Half-Jewish, yes, but I'm a Christian. I'm formally a member of the Russian Orthodox Church, I was christened in an Orthodox church as a child: as described in the short story "The Village of Sviyazhsk," but I'm likewise close to Catholics also, because Anton Yakovlevich was a Catholic.

Once freed, they both went to live in L'vov—although there was nothing there—for the simple reason that L'vov had Catholic churches.

Svirsky writes . . . [Na lobnom meste, London, 1979. Also translated into English; see bibliography—eds.]

Svirsky exaggerates and underestimates a lot in his book, he tries so hard to show that he knew everyone and was at the center of events. He really helped Mama with the apartment, but in general he distorts a great deal . . .

Did the fact that you are half-Jewish influence your life?

I've never had a sense of being Jewish, and Mama, strangely enough, never did either, even though she's a full-blooded Jewish woman. But nevertheless, Jews in Russia are a certain element of cosmopolitanism; on the whole, the presence of Jews in Russia somehow united Russia with the world.

In your recent works, there are a lot of . . .

You're talking about Jewry?

Yes, let's say, Monogamov **[The Heron—eds.].**

With him, it is simply a secret, the apothecary Epštein pops up in his family tree. In *The Crimean Island* there is also a *chekist* who has a Jewish mama, a fact which he hides.

UNIVERSITY

Then you moved to Kazan', to medical school. Why were you expelled from there?

As is now becoming clear, they were already then, in 'fifty-three before Stalin's death, planning to arrest me—and they'd already gathered material on me—simply because my "coming of age" had drawn near. After their twentieth birthday, all children of important "enemies of the people" were arrested and sentenced. I was a student in Kazan', where my father had been the chairman of the city executive party committee—that is, everyone knew me, I was in the public eye. In my student years, our crowd was of such a kind that, if we had known that the phrase "Beat Generation" existed, we would have called ourselves the "Beat Generation"—but we considered ourselves to be the successors of the Russian Futurists. We lived absolutely like *Beatniks*, with all the elements of *Beatnik* life which they had in San Francisco. We went round in torn clothes, listened to jazz, we lived in a commune, we painted abstract pictures, we had this notebook, where we wrote all kinds of hooliganish poems, we drank, danced the "boogie-woogie," and at that time girls used to come to us, creeping into the commune by the window. It was altogether amazing—we even used to stroll naked around the city and the main street.

How did "they" react to all that?

They were worried. The apartment landlady painted over the walls, which were covered with drawings. I was expelled from the university after Stalin's death; they expelled me because I had not indicated in the questionnaires that my parents were "enemies of the people." That was the official reason. However, in 'sixty-six I returned to Kazan' and got together with my old friends, some of whom had been *beatniks*. We got very drunk, and it suddenly transpired that they had all been called for questioning by the KGB. They were all questioned about me and it is evident, I think, that had Stalin not died, I would probably have been in a prison-camp within a month.

You entered Leningrad university without any problem?

It was with the ministry's help. Different times had already come, the change was obvious. Likewise in the department in Leningrad. I simply felt immediately that I was among different people in 'fifty-five.

What was student life in Leningrad like?

Very stormy. It was a totally new time. Literally every day, something new was revealed; a window to the west was opened in Leningrad. There was the development of *stilyazhestvo* [often compared to the hippies in the West—eds.]; the *stilyagi* were Soviet society's first dissidents. It expressed itself only in clothing, manners, and tastes, but it was an esthetic dissidence. At first it went on through dances: each Saturday and Sunday, unofficial dances for young people were organized, attracting huge crowds (*valili tuda*). They had interesting haircuts! There was only one place in Leningrad where it was possible to have one's hair cut fashionably, and enormous lines of young people used to form at this hairdresser's. But, besides that, there were continued satirical student shows (*kapustniki*), and, moreover, with a great deal of humor—humor which was even dangerous. All the time, youthful, musical groups were springing up. Exhibitions began to appear; they brought out Picasso from the Hermitage's storerooms. The first touring artists from outside the Soviet Union appeared. I remember that the Everyman Opera from America came with *Porgy and Bess*—we stood in line for a week. It was an endless line of young people; campfires burned and everyone had a terrific time (*zhutko razvlekalis'*)—it was very cheerful. Literary groups sprang up. I began, at that time, to go to a youth club in the Petrograd quarter. It was my first such literary association. There I met those with whom I would be friends and working alongside for long years afterwards: Evgeniy Reyn, one of the "Metropolitans," for example. The club was directed by the writer Dar, who died in Israel when he was already an old man. Brodsky used to go there while still just a boy, and Tolya Neyman was there—a brilliant young poet. We called them the "Akhmatova boys."

MEDICAL DOCTOR

You became a doctor?
Yes, I became a doctor in 'fifty-six.
Why did you choose such a profession?
Because Mama advised me to, and so did my stepfather—for they had hardly any doubt that I was destined to find myself in a prison-camp. It's easier for doctors in prison-camps.
Then you began to work?
Yes, at first I worked in a Leningrad quarantine-station.
As in Colleagues?
Yes, I and a group of my companions assigned ourselves to sail in ships as naval doctors—but to do so it was necessary to obtain a visa. After spending more than a year without an answer, I went first to a village and then to Moscow.
Was it good, working as a doctor?
Not bad in general, but I never had a special vocation, to be honest. However, I did everything that I was supposed to do. In the country, especially, I had to work as a real doctor. That settlement is called Voznesen'ye, it's on the bank of Onega Lake. And there I had to work and sometimes even perform minor operations alone, particularly after criminal abortions. Many women, too, became the victims of this illegal activity, because abortions were forbidden in the Soviet Union. And I treated all kinds of old women and drunkards. Fights were going on there all the time; the mutilated were treated. I worked in a tuberculosis clinic in the environs of Moscow for six months, and then I began to work in Moscow itself.

WRITER

When did you write Colleagues?
I began to write *Colleagues* in the north, in that settlement; I finished it as long ago as 'fifty-nine, and two more of my stories appeared in *Youth* in 'fifty-nine. It was thanks to Vladimir Pomerantsev, the author of the famous article "On Sincerity in Literature," an article typical of the "Thaw"; which had the impact of a bomb. "Stop lying" (*khvatit vrat'*) was the idea. And he told me: "Come on now, bring me what you're writing there!" I brought it, and he immediately began shouting, terribly enthusiastically, that it was good. He took a packet of my stories to *Youth*, and

Katayev—after all they did tell him that it was from Pomerantsev—somehow more or less began to read. He too, evidently, wanted to wave it all away, but he also liked it, and thus in 'fifty-nine I was published for the first time. In 1960 they took me into the navy for three months, and we were in Tallin as naval doctors.

Did you begin to write **A Ticket to the Stars** *there?*

I didn't begin writing it yet, but this was definitely the reason why *A Ticket to the Stars* came to take place in Tallin. Tallin made a very deep impression upon me, it was such a remote little place—sad, desolate, but Europe!

When did you give up working as a doctor?

After *Colleagues*, in the autumn of 1960.

Was it possible to live on that money?

Well, even after that I kept on living. The thing is, it was very difficult to live on a doctor's income; a young doctor's salary is so paltry. It was almost impossible to live. My wife [Kira—his first wife—eds.] was a student at that time, and receiving one hundred and twenty roubles on account of her father, who had been shot. I was receiving eighty roubles, I believe. Then she finished, and overall nothing was left; it was simply very difficult.

FAME

But it probably became better when you were a famous writer?

I never had a great deal of money. Never. Of course, it's difficult in the literary world: sometimes there is a great deal of money, and then no money for a long time. But it's more pleasant, nevertheless, if only you know that you can hope, fantasize. That's how it was for me during all my twenty years of work in Soviet literature. Although I was very well-known, there was generally no money—I was always in debt. And not only I, but many people—Akhmadulina for example, or the late Yuriy Kazakov or Gladilin and Voznesensky—were also always without money. Only a few people . . . Evtushenko, for example—he always had an enormous amount of money, wherever he got it from.

But you were a member of the Writers Union—didn't you receive anything from the Literary Fund?

You get nothing from there: you can only borrow from the fund, and pay it back later. They give vast amounts of money to their generals, the union secretaries, for apartments, *dachas* ['summer cabins'—eds.]—but a writer in Russia receives no wages whatever.

*Neizvestnyy says that you were a socialite (***svetskiy chelovek***).*

Neizvestnyy said that about me? . . . Well, to a certain degree, yes, of course—but it was a rather bohemian life.

A great deal of vodka, and of cheerful, drunken get-togethers. The sixties were very upbeat, despite all those "crackdowns" [Aksënov uses the English word "crackdowns"—eds.]. A new generation came into literature— daring, a bit hooliganish, and defiant. It was such a provocative generation—there was a Renaissance-like, carnival spirit. And there were constant fiestas, under the direct impression of the Hemingway *Fiesta* (*The Sun Also Rises*)—fiestas, fiestas around the town all night long, from one house to another, and from Erik Neizvestnyy's studio besides; this was the permanent meeting-place for every kind of bohemian crowd. In the middle of the night they would appear, and, in short, drink; they'd all loll by the canal and swim in it, at four in the morning. Suddenly in the morning you'd wake up and it would turn out that you'd flown over to somewhere during the night. It was generally very jolly. But in 'sixty-eight, the "hangover" began.

What was happening in your personal, family life in those years and in the seventies?

My first family virtually began to disintegrate. Maya [now his wife—eds.] and I met each other in 1970. At first it was simply a health-resort affair—afterwards, it became clear to everyone; everyone knew about our relationship. My first family was, for a long time, merely formally a family—although I did have a warm relationship with my son.

AKSËNOV'S FATHER

Your mother died in 'seventy-seven—everyone knows her, they know her splendid book; but as for your father . . .

My father lives in Kazan' to this very day; he's eighty-four years old. When he returned from the camp, he again made his home in Kazan' and got married at that time. His wife died only this year, and he was left completely alone.

How are your relations with him?

Very good indeed.

He's not a writer?

Well, no—he's a typical party man, but he did write, and now he's even writing some very interesting memoirs. That also frightens "them." Once, while they were shadowing me in Moscow before my departure, I was sitting with an Italian friend of mine in the kitchen there [in Moscow—eds.]; and I told him that my father was writing memoirs—and he said: "It would be good to have a look at these memoirs somehow." But everything around us there was, evidently, bugged—therefore they found out immediately.

Two days later, when we went to my father in Kazan', an entire sub-unit of the KGB met us; there had been four men in civilian clothes, one friend told me. They had summoned my father to the regional party Committee (*OBKOM*) during the day before my arrival, and had said to him: "The imperialist press is hunting for your memoirs," and "Why have you brought up such a bad son?" But he said: "I didn't bring him up—it was you who brought him up. I was in a camp." And that's correct, incidentally.

AUTOBIOGRAPHY
How is your personal life reflected in your work?
What happened to me is, of course, always reflected, but never exactly. Even in "The Village of Sviyazhsk"—which is about an experience I had—I all the same detach myself from it as far as possible. "Emigration," for example, is a theme in itself, and I am going to write a novel about it. It will again be an autobiography—but not really, of course. In today's world, writers very often write about writers—it's the easiest way of writing novels: John Updike, Philip Roth and Max Frisch write about writers. I at least try to detach myself somehow. I'm now writing a novel about photographers, if only to avoid writing about writers. It is based on the history of *Metropol'*—it's solely a reflection of *Metropol'*'s internal condition. The "photographers" are metaphorical.

FALSE RENAISSANCE OR "BEAT GENERATION"
Was the "New Wave" at the beginning of the sixties the Soviet "Beat Generation"?
Well, they called us the "New Wave." We were closest to the *beatniks*, when we didn't know about their existence—but, all the same, it wasn't quite like the "Beat Generation." I would call all of that literary and artistic activity of the sixties a "False Renaissance"—but, nevertheless, a renaissance. After Stalin's death, confusion arose amongst communists—as though they didn't know how they could live without Stalin. Thanks to that confusion, our generation appeared. We were interesting for the very reason that we appeared in a brief, untypical period of Soviet society's development.

All the same, there were a great deal of similar elements between the "New Wave" and the "Beat Generation."
Of course, of course, such rebellious processes also happened in America to a significant degree. Here, when I arrived, I saw an old Elvis Presley film, a film about him—how he began to sing, and what indignation this music provoked in the fathers of the town—how it was all prohibited!

The works of Kerouac . . .

Yes, yes, of course, not to such an extent as in the Soviet Union, but nonetheless there is a lot—in common.

The McCarthy period—that was also an untypical American period . . .

There was a great deal which was similar to those English "Angry Young Men."—To their psychological structure—a protest against caste society (*kastovaya sistema*). I remember that, in a festival in 1957, I saw Osborne's play, *Look Back in Anger*: I understood not one scrap (*ni khrena*) of English at that time, but I felt so much that they were somehow like our people in the way they went about and in their style.

What united all types of art forms at that time?

There was great unity and everyone was looking for the possibility of uniting with others, of uniting efforts—everyone was looking for friendship, artists were trying to be together with writers, "jazzmen" . . . it was a source of inspiration, in the spirit of jazz sounds—that is, it was as if everyone recognized everyone else. . . .

Was a synthesis created?

A synthesis not in the literal sense. I recall such a moment after Khrushchëv's attacks on young art in 'sixty-three. They decided at that time to exert an influence upon the development of young art; they organized a seminar for 'creative youth' in the sports camp *Trud* 'Labour'. Cinematographers, writers, artists and musicians were there. At the end, when the seminar was closing, they, so to speak, formed us into a square and shoved speeches at us. Gladilin came out from the writers and said: "Dear comrades . . . we have worked very fruitfully. We have sought, and found, a positive hero of our time, and now we want to present him to the delegates of the cinematographers." And Lësha Zaurikh, a poet, totally drunk, was sleeping in the tent at that time—the poor fellow was sleeping in his shorts, and we pulled him out and carried him across the whole field to the cinematographers. There was such a terrible guffaw (*zhutkiy khokhot*), everyone was falling about, that whole idiotic "square" fell apart, and an improvised *kapustnik* began—the whole of which went on in a mocking tone.

ON WRITERS

Which writers do you feel close to?

As before, I like Updike best of all the Americans—although now, living here, I see weaknesses which I did not see before. Of our writers, Bitov is more interesting than anyone, and the late Kazakov was a brilliant writer; I like Trifonov's prose very much. But now, you know, reading isn't particularly useful—it affects your writing. I was very keen on Nabokov at one time—I read and read him, and suddenly began to notice that *Nabokovshchina* was flowing from my pen, and I stopped reading Nabokov. Perhaps it's better to read English books now . . .

AMERICAN LITERATURE

. . . But it seems to me that there is little of interest in American literature nowadays. There are some brilliant figures still remaining from the sixties, there's a general high-level literary "school"—but besides these there's nothing outstanding. A colossal provincial graphomania exists here in American literature generally. Take the periodicals, all these *Atlantics*, it's such shit (*govno*).

Have you read The White Hotel (D.M. Thomas)?

I like it very much. This novel is begun in the spirit of a pornographic metaphor, and then there's such an unexpected development—it all sinks into such a deep layer of traditionalism. It made a very strong impression on me.

CRITICISM

What is your attitude towards literary criticism?

You know, that structuralist work of yours . . . I like it very much. Structuralism has its kernel, a fruitful tendency—if, of course, this method isn't used very truculently (*esli, konechno, ne ochen' svirepo pol'zovat'sya ètim metodom*).

Do you yourself work as a literary critic?

Yes. That is, I teach from the point of view of my personal experience—as a participant in events.

EMIGRÉ LITERATURE

There is absolutely no such concept. And Carl Proffer is right, there: emigré literature sprang up before the arrival in the West of new people from Russia—when everything here was already dying. I don't feel myself to be an immigrant in a literary respect, and our literature here is not emigré literature but genuine *Russian* literature. A border runs between Russian literature and "paraliterature," even inside a separately-taken book: take one of Aytmatov's books and see this border. Here, also, are both hacks (*grafomany*), who profit by an anti-Soviet theme, and "real" writers.

AKSËNOV'S LITERATURE

We have already talked about Russian and American literature—but where

is Aksënov going? Will there be a synthesis of American and Russian?

I don't think so. I have no intentions whatever of penetrating American literature—only in translations, as usual. In the first novel, which I began and completed in emigration [*Paperscape*—eds.], the entire narrative goes on in Russia; only the final chapter takes place in America. Some people—those who have read it—say that some things won't be understood by the Russian reader. But surely it isn't necessary that he should understand everything—everything doesn't have to be understood without fail. A sense of atmosphere has to arise; some kind of corresponding thoughts . . .

Style?

In *The Burn*, I wanted to obtain everything, to whirl it around in all possible ways: formal, philosophical, historical, political. Now, a more peaceful, "piano" work is present—*Paperscape*. Earlier, I wanted to conclude a thing with a kind of "surrealistic spiral"; to take off from the earth's surface—and that, evidently, shall also happen later on, though always with an emphasis on the earth.

What do you think of translations? Belyy said that it was impossible to translate his things; what about yours?

I liked the last translation, *The Crimean Island*, translated by Michael Heim. I think that it is possible if some kind of ideal variant arises—when a kindred soul translates you, a writer—one, moreover, who knows the language. Such variants hardly ever occur.

About the role of the grotesque?

Without the grotesque, I just can't work.

Where does it come from?

From folklore, of course. One beloved thing, I unfortunately couldn't take out of the Soviet Union—I simply lost it, in the end: a film-scenario called "Oh, that flighty, restless youth" (*O, ètot v'yunosha letuchiy*), made according to the motifs of Russian satirical folklore. When I was writing it, I had become very absorbed in folklore, and I saw where that spiral, that taking-off from the world, came from.

From folklore via the avant-garde?

Yes; the avant-garde is connected with folklore. What is considered to be a basic, realistic trend—it's just a thing without roots, a thing out of the practical nineteenth century of cheap, superficial positivism. Avant-garde arose as a reaction against that positivism of the sixties of the last century—it holds out its hand to the genuine roots of human art.

How do you regard poetic prose?

In what seems to me to be "real" prose, it becomes so closely united with poetry that it's indistinguishable: take such prose as Belyy's or Mandel'-

shtam's. I have very often wanted to use rhyme and rhythm, especially when pieces are so electrified, and it arises according to strange circumstances. In prose, it is as though you are freer—but in actual fact you're not—because, rhyming, you enter an unexpected metaphorical world, and remarkable finds are made there.

The motif of the road . . .

It is escapism; it's a metaphorical crossing over into another state, a widening of your horizons.

Birds?

I love them.

Where do they come from?

The devil knows . . . The heron [cf. the play *The Heron*—eds.] is simply a personal impression from the Baltic. I saw such a heron—it made a very strong impression on me then—a very strange bird, so amusing . . .

*Finally, miracles (*chuda*): should one believe in miracles?*

Yes—the only thing on which it is possible to count is a miracle; there are no logical bases for hope.

America—is it a "miracle" for you?

America is no longer a miracle for me. I live here as a local inhabitant; as a member of the "ethnic minority" [Aksënov uses the English phrase—eds.] —Chinese, Malaysians, black, yellow, white . . . I do a lot, I'm earning money—you see, in America the earning of money is a socially-useful labor; in Russia the earning of money is your own affair, and not very good with respect to the state or society. Here, the earning of money is a useful, respectable and socially-beneficial business.

Translated by Margaret Bradley
The University of Alberta

A CONVERSATION IN THE EDITORIAL OFFICE OF *KONTINENT*

Vladimir Maksimov, Èduard Kuznetsov, Natal'ya Gorbanevskaya

V. MAKSIMOV: Each of the three of us sitting here had some connection with the so-called "Thaw" era of the late 50s and early 60s. This is so clear in the memory; the atmosphere was such that we all thought that now our country was going to become freer, better, warmer. This era seems so close still that it is hard to believe that a man who was then one of the symbols of these hopes is now already fifty years old. You can have different opinions about Vasiliy Aksënov as a writer, but when it comes to the man Aksënov, it seems to me that his admirers and his antagonists are of the same opinion. As a writer, I personally feel closest to the man Aksënov. Whatever he said at the time, whatever happened around him—he was always at the center of the critics' attention: some defended him, some attacked him with equal zeal—but, having risen to those heights, he remained the same Vasiliy Aksënov whom he was—as I know now from his mother's memoirs—even in his youth, before his fame, and whom we now know here, already in emigration. This is a man of amazing integrity and amazing human reliability. The two of us have different life experiences, different human and literary allegiances—on the whole, we are almost opposites. And yet, when he emerged, even I, feeling not close to, but perhaps even antagonistic towards his prose, clearly understood that a man of fantastic talent had entered into literature. Knowing him, you, my interlocutors, cannot but agree with me.

N. GORBANEVSKAYA: Certainly. And, just as certainly, Aksënov's name is for us bound up with this era of hope, with the so-called "Thaw." As a matter of fact, I think Aksënov's example shows very well how times have changed, how hopes have been shattered and what a state our country and the literature in our country are in at the present time. The position of those writers who began to be published during the "Thaw" was in most cases associated with a certain success and flourishing, and this kind of success could very easily break a man. In this sense, Aksënov's example is doubly significant. Above all because of what you said about his human qualities: because he didn't break, didn't get carried away by success when this no longer meant following one's own path, but rather being led along an "alien path" or, to be blunt, selling oneself. And as for the fact that he was forced or, looking back now, we should perhaps rather say that he managed in time—to emigrate, this shows the almost absolute impossibility today of working with a minimum of sincerity outside the Samizdat. I am talking about the minimal sincerity of a writer who remains a member of the Writers' Union, who agrees to the censor's cuts, but who all the same would like to publish without betraying himself.

È. KUZNETSOV: What we are saying is that Aksënov's name can be seen as a symbol, along with those names which were associated with the flourishing of hopes—yes, I remember it, the euphoria that was, in fact, there, the arguments that were going on as to whether or not the liberalization process had any future. In these youthful arguments, his name was always mentioned as, as it were, one of the *first*. Now that Aksënov has been expelled—this may be regarded as a symbol of the expulsion of all hopes from the country. Besides, I simply like him as a writer—I read him in one go. Stylistically he is rather remote from me too—from me personally, that is—but pick up any of his books—*The Burn*, for instance—and you simply can't tear yourself away from it. And yet I too feel more compelled by his human fate. He is, of course, one of those people who were first run over by the wheel of Soviet history already in early childhood, he has been through it all. In a certain sense, the fate of a man like Aksënov might serve as the model for a history of Soviet society. His parents were subjected to repressions, and because of this he himself was from childhood on a *persona non grata*; then he lived with his mother in exile, and afterwards there was his literary coming of age, his success as a writer and the fact that, when the hard times came, he did not let himself down, but kept his human face, and then, as a result of all this together, he was expelled. This is a complete index of the life of an honest, Russian intellectual . . .

V. MAKSIMOV: . . . who was able to stay true to himself under those circumstances. I am not going to mention names, in order not to offend anybody living over there, but we know that there were many of his generation who, when faced with the choice between the "magic crystal" and the bank account, chose the latter; that is, cooperation with that pernicious system. This is a crucial choice for a writer. And Aksënov could have made the same choice, he had every opportunity. Because, although he was criticized, and at times even severely, he was, on the whole, riding on a wave of success. He had an enormous readership, which the authorities had to take into account. Aksënov is a very typical figure of the new literature—he lived with this literature from the day it appeared to its logical end within the country, and then he became an exile. You know, in contrast to the three of us, me in particular, he really had something to lose personally when making the decision whether to stay or leave. I, for one, had nothing to lose. I would like to qualify what I said before about my attitude to his prose. It is true that his world is not mine, but I do love his short stories and I often read them again, both "Halfway to the Moon" and "Comrade Smart-Hat," and many others. As for *The Burn*, I read that novel with enormous interest, and although it is not quite my kind of thing, the book shed light on a lot of things for me. I feel much closer to Aksënov after this novel; in it, he has explained a lot of things about himself. And I want to stress one more time that Aksënov is a man of absolute reliability. I know that from my own experience, but he has always been that way to everybody around him: always generous, broad-minded, extremely honest. And under the conditions of life over there—especially when everybody is sniffing around everybody else's doorstep—it is very difficult to be yourself. Vasiliy Aksënov has remained himself, his development as a writer is promising and we can still expect a lot from him.

È. KUZNETSOV: Yes, and a lot is expected by a lot. He was always eagerly read, and by the widest possible public. But he not only writes himself—do you remember, he had that translation of Doctorow's *Ragtime* in *Inostrannaya Literatura*? I was in the camp then. He has an incredible feeling for Western life. A translation of an American writer, about life at the beginning of the century and, even without knowing anything about it, you can feel the adequacy of the apprehension and rendering in Russian of American life: the atmosphere is communicated. He turned out to be a marvellous translator, something which is, generally speaking, fairly rare under those circumstances. He is a versatile fellow.

V. MAKSIMOV: This is what is defined by the term "European" in Russia today. Aksënov is a cosmopolitan in the best sense. This shows even in his appearance, in the way he dresses, in his tastes and in his love for jazz, which he has written about like a connoisseur. At the same time he has always remained a thoroughly Russian writer. That is exactly what is meant by the term "European." A true Russian is always a European, in the cultural sense. Isolationism, isolationist motives have never lent great quality to Russian literature. The concern of the great Russian literature, which has now conquered the world, was always first of all universally human.

N. GORBANEVSKAYA: I want to continue the discussion about Aksënov's prose. It seems to me that in those days people overlooked one thing about this prose. When it began to appear, first in *Yunost'* (Youth), then in separate books, it was always received as "youth prose" and there were heated debates about the "youth problem" in it. This gave me a strange sensation as a reader: when his novels and stories first appeared, while they were still surrounded by raging discussions about this very "problem," I would find his prose rather irritating. And I don't know by what miracle, but somehow I always had the patience to return after a year or two and read each of these stories again, this time in the book edition. And each time I would discover, to my astonishment, that I felt akin to this prose. To such an extent that, for instance, I brought with me to Paris *It's Time, My Friend, It's Time*, by then already a tattered old volume. Suddenly it would turn out that the stories were something completely different from what you had read in the heat of the discussion, from your first, superficial reading. First of all, this is not "youth prose" at all; the fact that the protagonists are young is a detail. It is equivalent to classifying *Romeo and Juliet* as a play about the problems of adolescence. It would turn out that the stories were "simply about people," and, returning to them after the critical battles had been fought out, you would find that they were far better, far more subtle and filled with an all-pervading compassion, with something very deep and urgently human which was perhaps what later prevented Aksënov from taking the easy way out, as it would seem, by selling himself. Now we sit here and say: "What a man, he was true to himself, he didn't take the easy way out." But probably there simply was no easy way for him, since for this he would really have had to stop being the man he was. As for his later works . . . I have to admit, as I said also to Aksënov himself, that *The Burn* is alien to me—apart from the Magadan scenes. But obviously I can't judge the novel by some scenes torn out of context: if Aksënov made them part of the novel and used them to string together the rest of the action, then they must not only have an independent meaning, but also an important compositional function. Maybe I shall have to return to *The Burn* too in a year or two . . .

È. KUZNETSOV: *The Burn* really is a complicated work. There is a lot there that I didn't quite agree with either, especially on first reading it. But then, when what you have read has been allowed to settle, you find yourself left with a certain feeling: Aksënov has the ability to create, to impose a certain atmosphere, a kind of indirect sensation of Soviet life, something of the order which is communicated above the level of the written word. I feel that he is trying to communicate something which cannot be expressed in words, and he heaps up words that come close, circling around his theme, and as a result of this the atmosphere is created after all; the horror and sadness of that Soviet existence reaches you like a breeze from over there, beyond words. Each word seems at the same time to be the right one and not quite [it]; and, taken together, this works. I couldn't explain it accurately, but in the beginning I too read with a strange feeling—well Magadan is, of course, simply fantastic—but now it has settled, six months have passed and I feel that I did get something out of it, a kind of a whiff.

N. GORBANEVSKAYA: Literally the other day* I was talking to a friend of mine and I was just saying that Magadan—that is remarkable, but as for the life of the Moscow elite, all these trials and tribulations of theirs, that makes me want to say "Would I had your troubles, Mr. Teacher . . ."

È. KUZNETSOV: Well, maybe that is the reaction he was counting on.

N. GORBANEVSKAYA: That is exactly what my friend said: that perhaps Aksënov wanted to evoke just that feeling in the reader. And that may be the reason why the Magadan scenes did not come together in one separate beautiful, but unequivocally comprehensible story, why Aksënov interspersed his dreadful Moscow drinking tale with the Magadan story.

È. KUZNETSOV: He was indicating the scale. Magadan is simply the scale, the criteria according to which the rest should be judged. That is how we all live. You often get lost in this difficult life, all kinds of misfortunes fall on your head when you lose sight of the past; but when you keep the scale of the past in mind, everything falls back into place and you judge things completely differently.

N. GORBANEVSKAYA: I think it was the presence of this or a similar scale which helped Aksënov in *The Island of Crimea*, which I like very much. Here it would have been very easy to collide with all kinds of sunken rocks, you know. Maksimov is right in saying that Aksënov is a naturally European, naturally universal and at the same time thoroughly Russian writer. *The Island of Crimea* combines a genuine knowledge of and feeling for the West with a free, critical perception of it—on Russian criteria, but without provincialism. Note that this was not written after Aksënov had already lived in the West for a while: the visual and the, so to speak, ideological aspects of his novel are the results of his travels while he was still living in the USSR. What does the Soviet tourist, even the Soviet writer usually see in the West? He sees freedom, he sees prosperity, he sees only the good side, when we exclude those who see only "the unemployed dying under the bridges." Aksënov, however, saw what we see, after years of life here: how the West, like a rabbit, is gazing at the Soviet boa constrictor which has hypnotized it. In *The Island of Crimea* Aksënov built a model of the West in one separate country. The question is whether the West is able to survive. In Aksënov's fictive, "local" West there is not only the fascination with the bars and the cocktails, including the cocktail of political parties; there is also the visible decay stemming from this: the envy, the neurosis, the longing for wholeness, for a beautifully monolithic world—even if we have to

---

* The conversation took place in the beginning of 1983—eds.

enslave or be enslaved, let's become beautiful and whole, the way the communist world is beautiful and whole. This you will find in the real West too and not only right next to the Soviet border; but it is not all that easy to see, let alone to describe so precisely, in prose rather than in journalism.

V. MAKSIMOV: If I was asked to pick an epigraph for all of Aksënov's life and work, I would choose a phrase from the scene in *The Burn* where mother and son meet in the apartment of a prison-camp commandant: "Mum, don't cry in front of them . . ." This explains a lot about Aksënov, if not all.

Translated by Inger Lauridsen

V.P. AKSËNOV: A LITERARY BIOGRAPHY

J.J. Johnson, Jr.

Aksënov was born in Kazan' on August 20, 1932 as the shadow of Stalin's purges dimmed the lights of the literary experimentation of the nineteen-twenties. His father, Pavel Vasil'yevich Aksënov, was a Russian and a dedicated communist well-known in the region. His mother, Evgeniya Semyënovna Ginzburg, was a Jew from Moscow, teaching history at Kazan' University at the time of Aksënov's birth. From 1932-1937, he lived with his parents, his paternal grandmother, his older brother Aleksey, his sister Maya and a nurse. Avdot'ya Vasil'yevna Aksënova, the grandmother, was an illiterate peasant woman with a strong philosophical bent and a proverb for each and every one of life's troubles. Aksënov's sister Maya now teaches at Moscow University. His brother Aleksey died in the blockade of Leningrad during World War II.

When Aksënov was but four-and-a-half years old, his mother was arrested and sent to a labor camp in Yaroslavl'. Two years later she was sent to Magadan and Elgen, which are in the frozen deadlands of the northern Far East. Her memoirs of the period, *Krutoy marshrut*, have been published in several languages, including English, where they are known as *Journey into the Whirlwind*.[1] By the time Aksënov was five, his father had been arrested and put into forced labor in central Siberia, along the Pechora River. Eventually his father remarried and gave Aksënov a half-sister named Antonina, presently an actress in the Leningrad Comedy Theater. Both his parents survived the camps and moved back to European Russia after they were rehabilitated by Khrushchëv in the nineteen-fifties. Evgeniya Semyënovna died on May 25, 1977 in Moscow.

Orphaned by the purges, Aksënov was raised from 1938-1948 by his father's sister Kseniya and her family in Kazan'. From 1948-1950 he lived with his mother in Magadan, where he completed school. By eighteen he was attending the Pavlov Medical Institute in Leningrad and became a doctor in 1956. As is customary for professionals in the Soviet Union, Aksënov was required to dedicate his first two years of practice to state-assigned post-graduate work situations. He spent part of his first year as a port doctor in the quarantine service near Leningrad, coming into contact with foreigners in a period when that was unheard of for most Soviet citizens. The rest of the first year, he worked in a hospital for water-transportation workers on Lake Onega, north of Leningrad.

In 1957 Aksënov met his first wife, Kira, at a dance in Leningrad. They were soon married and relocated to Moscow, where he worked in a tuberculosis clinic. While a medical student, Aksënov had developed an interest in writing and had been a member of a group called the Petrograd Side Youth Club.[2] In July of 1959 *Yunost'* (Youth) magazine used two of his earlier stories: "Nasha Vera Ivanovna" (Our Vera Ivanovna) and "Asfal'tovyye dorogi" (Paved Roads). "Our Vera Ivanovna" is set in a hospital much like Aksënov would have known on Lake Onega and Vera Ivanovna is a doctor who is dedicated, idealistic and above reproach. When she refuses to cater to an important official or to use his aid in getting a preferable reassignment, she acts as a representative of the true Soviet man, filled with the duty to bring into life the promises of the Party. A variant of this story was later released as "Poltory vrachebnykh edinitsy" (One-and-a-Half Medical Units).

It is no surprise that the youthful and idealistic Aksënov would draw on his experience and write moralistic stories about a young doctor like "Our Vera Ivanovna." What distinguished Aksënov and became more significant in the long run was the application of this point of view to the materialistic, westward-oriented generation infiltrating Soviet reality but ignored by Soviet realism. "Paved Roads" is the story of a conflict between the way the establishment says to succeed and the shortcut the less socially conscious might utilize—the black market. Army veteran Gleb Pomorin returns to his neighborhood and finds his old friend Gerka living with his girlfriend. Their goal is not the building of socialist society but living for the present. Gerka is a blackmarketeer able to live well off of his illegal earnings, and his existence in a Soviet story was a radical admission. The fact that Gerka is portrayed as evil and an outcast did not mitigate the offense of letting the truth out. Aksënov was seen by some as expanding Soviet literature in unapproved directions.

The problem the authorities had was in identifying the parameters of literary expression in a changing political environment. In the decade following Stalin's death, "between 1953 and 1963, Soviet social, economic, political and cultural life underwent a thorough revision."[3] What was permissible in socialist realism during the period was unclear. There were conservatives, traditionalists, hardliners, liberals, revisionists, and experimentalists all forming their own ground rules for literature. Aksënov and others pushed on the limits of content and characterization, not yet actively varying form and style. It becomes instructive to compare "Our Vera Ivanovna" with "Samson i Samsonikha" (Samson and Samsonikha), a short story of the period published several years later. In this story the young doctor abandons service to the community and takes a better job in the big city. The moral compulsion to serve society is still there, but this time the decision is to live for personal goals, not the Soviet future. The girl jilted and left behind by the doctor is symbolic of the current Soviet saying, "obman rabochego klassa" (deception of the working class), which expresses the disappointment of relying on Soviet promises.

Differenzqualität in characterization is stronger and clearer still in Aksënov's first novel, *Kollegi* (Colleagues). Three young doctors begin their post-graduate assignments in locations quite familiar to Aksënov—two as shipboard doctors and one in a small northern village. They encounter bribery, poverty, alcoholism and criminal violence in the land of socialist utopia. They do not act in the religious tradition of the Soviet man, but read Western books, listen to Western music and exhibit a cautious approach to the platitudes of Party rhetoric. A generation gap becomes clear between those who serve society by selfless sacrifice and those who serve by rational compromise. Soviet youth had a direction to go distinct from their parents and now they had an author who argued their side of the issue in the public forum of literature. This particular youth movement attacked the *esprit de sérieux* in the socialist camp: "miniskirts against apparatchiks, rock 'n roll against Soviet Realism."[4] Thus was born what was later called "young prose" or "New Wave" writing. *Colleagues* was published serially in June and July of 1960 and by September, 1960 Aksënov had resigned his medical position and dedicated himself to writing full time. The play version of *Colleagues* was performed by Moscow's Maly Theater at an international festival in Paris in 1962.

Aksënov soon stood for faith in youth as the future of his society. "These kids deserve to be written about as well as possible and as much as possible," he said.[5] Aksënov's approach to the socialist utopia was to deal with problems openly and honestly. "Ne otstavaya ot bystronogogo" (1961; Keeping Up with the Fleet of Foot) is an essay about literature's responsibility to accurately represent contemporary youth. "Printsy, nishchiye dukhom" (1960; Princes, Poor in Spirit), about drug dealers and blackmarketeers, and "Gerbariy" (1961; The Herbarium), about a Casanova turned rapist, are attempts to deal with reality responsibly.

Up to this point, Aksënov's characterizations had been innovative but safe. Young doctors cannot be said to be social parasites, twenty-five-year-olds cannot usually be said to be immature and naive. However, new ground was broken in *Zvëzdnyy bilet* (1961; A Ticket to the Stars, or as a British translation reads, A Starry Ticket), where seventeen-year-olds with no certain career prospects make the same arguments as the doctors. The possibility of teenagers taking on the establishment is not a radical concept in other places in modern times, but was extremely radical in the Soviet Union in 1961. Polemics arose and Aksënov's fame was increased by the controversial exposure.

The heroes of *A Ticket to the Stars* head for the beach for the summer, working only as need be, to survive. Their language and interests are turned decidedly westward to the corrupt land of rock 'n roll. Leonid Il'ichëv, chief propagandist of the Central Committee of the Communist Party, complained in *Pravda*: "A characteristic feature of the young people described by V. Aksënov [. . .] is skepticism. [Aksënov] did not dethrone it, but took a sympathetic attitude towards it."[6] Doubting the socialist future is not a forgivable act in the Soviet state and Aksënov would eventually have to pay for his indiscretions, but for now he was the darling of the intellectual elite, the rave of the reading public. So popular, in fact, that a movie version of the novel was released after a long fight in the censorship committee in 1962 as *Moy mladshiy brat* (My Younger Brother).

During 1962, Aksënov travelled to Poland and Japan, returning by way of New Delhi, India. International travel and domestic recognition bolstered his challenge and his first experimental prose was published. "Zavtraki sorok tret'yego goda" (1962; Lunches of '43) is the story of a humiliated man certain that he has recognized his childhood tormentor on a train. The tale is spun in descriptive colors laid impressionistically out of sequence. Like many of the humiliated men in Russian literature, the hero twists reality to compensate for personal shortcomings and creates a supposed extraterrestrial out of his opponent. Consistently, he suffers through this entire scene of self-torture, only to realize that it is not the same man. This toned-down version of self-abasing psychology is more directly related to Babel' and Platonov than to Dostoevsky, a direction that seems to have appealed to Aksënov in his search for new genres.

By 1962, his son Aleksey was two years old and the thirty-year-old Aksënov began to feel the responsibilities of fatherhood more closely. In "Papa, slozhi!" (1962; Papa, What Does It Spell?), the thirty-two-year-old hero seems to resent the intrusion of his wife and young daughter on his time out with the boys. A series of events leading to implications of adultery cause him to awaken from his immaturity and recognize that what is important for him is this little girl.

In the same period, Aksënov wrote his most famous story, translated into dozens of languages and praised worldwide. "Na polputi k lune" (1962; Halfway to the Moon) was based on a backwoods character whom Aksënov watched board a flight from Khabarovsk to Moscow.[7] This worker immediately fell in love with the stewardess because of her polite mannerisms: "'What is your name?' he asked, with the same feeling he always had coming down the mountainside on his tractor—a mixture of fear and a feeling that the worst was over."[8] In the story, the worker spends his entire vacation flying back and forth the length of the Soviet Union in search of his fantasy woman. Such a journey was easily the distance half-way to the moon physically and psychologically.

Aksënov's popularity was now of such a magnitude that he began to have power in the literary world. That November, Aksënov, Evtushenko and Rozov were made editors of the magazine *Youth*, where he had first been published three years earlier. Solzhenitsyn had recently been published and expansion of the parameters of socialist literature seemed in progress. However, the move outward may have been too quick for the old school and the reaction became brutal. In December, Khrushchëv attacked the works of abstract artists on display near the Kremlin. By the beginning of the year, poetry readings to large gatherings were forbidden.

In February and March of 1963, the literary journals were filled with attacks on the "young prose" movement which Aksënov was a leader of. Writers, artists and musicians were summoned to the Kremlin on March 8, 1963, where Il'ichëv and Khrushchëv lectured the artistic assembly on Party ideals and expectations. Simonov, Shostakovich, Neizvestnyy, Rozhdestvensky came forward to confess the error of their ways. Aksënov, who was called to the stage to speak, resisted for a while longer.

The Writers' Union, the only channel for writers to be officially published in the Soviet Union, held a similar meeting and threatened Evtushenko, Bella Akhmadulina and Aksënov with withdrawal of privileges if they did not fall into line. This loss to Aksënov would not only mean inability to continue publishing but release from the editorship position he had recently gotten and inability to travel abroad. On April 3, 1963 in *Pravda*, Aksënov recanted and promised to create more acceptable characters. A similar statement appeared as an editorial in *Youth*. It is difficult for those who live in the West to understand a Soviet writer's need to be published and remain in the public eye. Our religions have liberalized and the lessons of Galileo are mostly forgotten. Much later and in an entirely different context Aksënov wrote these words:

> Maybe I should make something up? More simply maybe I should lie?
> For a writer such a life-saving idea can be reassuring.[9]

Aksënov continued to be published after his promise to change, but the fire seemed dimmed in his pen. His best works were written for private perusal or reworked into acceptable variants for publication and sustenance. A novella of the period, *Apel'siny iz Marokko* (1963; Oranges from Morocco), was far from his most brilliant work. The story emphasizes the importance of unobtainable consumer goods to the common man. Its point is a continuation of the "deception of the working class" theme found in earlier and later works, that the promise of a better life should include basic supplies like oranges without great effort.

Aksënov's recantation protected his privileges and when the movie version of *Colleagues* was shown at a film festival in Argentina in 1963, he was allowed to go with the delegation. A fictional account of his travels was published under the title "Pod nebom znoynoy Argentiny" (1966; Under the Skies of Sultry Argentina). After his second trip to Japan, an account was brought out called "Yaponskiye zametki" (1963; Japanese Jottings), which is a "safe content" piece that utilizes a radical, impressionistic style. Such a work is of minimal interest except to show that innovation was working its way back into his writings. In a speech in Leningrad in August, 1963 to an international audience of writers, Aksënov said that contemporary Soviet literature (by this he meant the new wave) was in harmony with the Russian past (citing Solzhenitsyn as an example) and that the European novel could be a means of expanding the progress of Soviet literature to world importance.[10]

In an attempt to placate critics, moralism crept back into some of Aksënov's works of the period. "Syurprizy" (1964; Surprises) is a return to the character of "Paved Roads" five years later. Appropriate life achievements are provided for the former heroes depending on their proximity to the Soviet ideal. Gleb Pomorin, the "good guy," is now an exemplary industrial worker and night school student, married to his former girlfriend. Gerka, the blackmarketeer, was convicted of robbery and is in prison. There is a playfulness to this neat package that Aksënov provides, suggesting that his critics of 1959 did not understand the direction of his work and its harmony with prescriptive Marxism.

A further reaction to the polemics was the novel *Pora, moy drug, pora* (1964; It's Time, My Friend, It's Time, or as another English translation is titled, It's Time, My Love, It's Time). The plot centers around a driver working with a movie crew on location in Estonia. Throughout the novel the hero questions the inherent conflict between an individual and the collective socialist society and in the end leaves to search for truth in working the land in Siberia. In a sense the entire novel is a contemporary fleshing-out of the Pushkin poem from which the title derives:

> It's time, my friend, it's time! the heart seeks peace--
> The days fly one after the other, each hour brings
> A piece of life, and you and I together
> Propose to live, then watch, how soon we shall die.[11]

Although Aksënov's characters tended to be less youthful and rebellious as time went on, his stylistic innovation still caused him to be regarded as a dangerous writer by the hard-liners. His work was often described as "bad" writing by those who saw "good" writing to be official socialist realism. Aksënov and others who were of similar bent began to refer to their school of writing as "mauvism," derived from the French *mauvais* 'bad'. Examples of this trend appear more colorful and creative than standard official writings or even "young prose" works. Fantasy, exaggeration and literary grotesque invaded the concept of reality and "mauvism" became a movement.

The story "Dikoy" (1964; The Odd-Ball) tells the tale of a returning victim of Stalin's purges in conversation with his childhood friend, the odd-ball. The odd friend complains that he never managed to go very far from home or do anything important. The irony comes clear when the odd-ball shows the returning friend his life-long secret work—a machine that has been running without power for many years, the elusive *perpetuum mobile*. In the story "Tovarishch krasivyy Furazhkin" (1964; Comrade Smart-Hat), a taxidriver plots to get the local constable married to his daughter, foreseeing clear sailing on his illegal activities. Ironically, the new relative works twice as hard to shut down the operations, in order to keep his father-in-law out of trouble.

Irony also plays a role in "Mestnyy khuligan Abramashvili" (1964; Local Hooligan Abramashvili), where a naive local boy is seduced by a married tourist from Moscow. When she later ignores his love for her, he gets understandably angry, starts a minor ruckus and is thereafter labelled a hooligan for life. This story is interesting in its open approach to sex, a subject taboo in Soviet literature. For many years some of the original manuscripts of Aksënov's works carried sex scenes which were routinely deleted by the censors. As a result, later works printed abroad surprised some critics with the appearance of such scenes, but the phenomenon was not new, only new to the public.

The history of philosophy tells us that the concept of reality may be both objective and subjective, concrete or abstract. Aksënov never commits himself to any school of reality but consistently rejects the idealistic realism of socialist literature. Critics of the Soviet school of realism sometimes refer to it as religious faith,[12] medieval romanticism,[13] or, in humor, as the varnishing of reality. In this light the story "Malen'kiy Kit, lakirovshchik deystvitel'nosti" (1964; Little Whale, Varnisher of Reality) is a study of reality from varying points of view, in this case three generations of Aksënovs: the rehabilitated father, the "dreaming" author, and the imaginative young boy, "Whale." This story was returned to in "Lebyazh'ye ozero" (1968; Swanny Lake), published for the first time in 1976, which made more clear the variable or situational basis of reality. It is notable that in his 1963 recantation Aksënov wrote that there was no generation gap between his generation and his father's: "We are the flesh of their flesh."[14] In this 1968 work, he has his father say about him: "[. . .] there was no way I felt that he was 'flesh of my flesh,' as they say."[15]

In 1965 *Vsegda v prodazhe* (Always for Sale) became Aksënov's most popular play [staged in 1965—eds.]. Although it was never published, the manuscript carried in apposition: "a satirical fantasy," which is consistent with the "mauvist" direction of his work. "Pobeda" (1965; Victory), one of Aksënov's favorite short stories, is full of irony as the intellectual chessmaster loses a chess game to the worker in a symbolic capitulation to the system. "Ryzhiy s togo dvora" (1966; Ginger from Next Door), about the reunion of childhood friends, stretches the limits of fantasy and exaggeration as "Ginger" juggles dishes and bounces without the use of a trampoline up to the second floor of a restaurant. The *maître d'* recognizes this all as typical behavior for childhood friends meeting in restaurants.

In "Na ploshchadi i za rekoy" (1966; On the Square and Across the River), the end of World War II is celebrated on the square with images of reality (a circus troop) that seem fantastical and are contrasted by an image of fantasy that seems real: a man appearing to be Hitler flies off as a metallic bird and disappears. This image appearing in the Soviet press in 1966 was a reference to a work called *Stal'naya ptitsa* (1965; The Steel Bird), which was never published in the Soviet Union, except in the form of a meaningless excerpt. Steel birds in this work are the breed of tyrants that run the world, destroy art, change history, and basically defile humanity. The novella is a biting satire of power and corruption of ideals, one of the best in any language.

Aksënov's hatred of inhuman dictatorship carried over to his feelings about Stalin and when a bust of Stalin was unveiled near Lenin's mausoleum in 1966, Aksënov was among the protesters arrested. The effects were not as serious as one might suspect and he was allowed to travel abroad an eighth time in that period. In 1966 a movie based on "Lunches of '43," "Half-way to the Moon" and "Papa, What Does It Spell?" was released with Aksënov playing himself, i.e., the author. There were a number of articles and stories published in this period but little of lasting consequence.

Of significant literary value is a *povest'* 'story' released in 1968 called *Zatovarenaya bochkotara* (The Tare of Empty Barrels) which was subtitled "a tale with exaggerations and dreams." This work is a fine example of the matured style of this innovative writer, easily in the class of Bulgakov, Olesha or Gogol'. Superficially the story is about a group of people travelling to the county seat on a truck loaded with barrels. The truck seems to represent Soviet society with its barrels of socialist promises. The collective dream of the group for Good and the personal dreams of the individuals are presented as fantasies. Still, like the society they move in, the truck keeps getting off course. The barrels are treated with great respect but they do little more than provide a purpose for the trip.

"V svete podgotovki k predstoyashchey vesne" (1969; In Light of the Preparations for the Coming Spring) is a playful piece of experimentation in that it combines phrases from a regional newspaper into a readable story. It is interesting to compare this to Burroughs' cut-up technique:

> Somebody is reading a newspaper, and his eye follows the column in the proper Aristotelian manner, one idea and sentence at a time. But subliminally he is reading the columns on either side [. . .] That is a cut-up.[16]

Another experiment was "Opyt zapisi letnego sna" (1969; A Dream for a Summer's Night), which Aksënov then called "rhythmical prose." The "story" is actually an excerpt from *Ozhog* (The Burn), discussed later, a novel otherwise kept secret by Aksënov due to the great political danger involved in its message. If a dream is considered to be a series of images, concepts and fanciful dialogue that occurs while in a state of sleep or rest, then this disconnected story can be considered an accurate attempt to record such a dream in a comparable written form. In Soviet psychology, dream recall originates in a paradoxical, fast-wave sleep, characterized by rapid eye movement. Aksënov, a medically trained writer, seems to run his verbal sequence through a prose equivalent—a fast-moving rapid visualization, in the form of a paradoxical dream sequence. Professor Robert Stacy has noted the interest of psychiatrists in dream 'defamiliarization' *ostraneniye*, and one might expect a similar interest by a writer with a medical background.[17] Although not well received in its period, the story may have significance in a historical literary sense because Aksënov has recently defined his current writing style as "rhythmical realism."[18]

About this time a new character was introduced who was to play a large part in seven or eight later works by Aksënov. In "Vyvod nezhelatel'nogo gostya iz doma" (1969; Getting an Unwanted Guest Out of the House), the public first meets Memozov, the anti-author who keeps causing problems for Aksënov in a psychic war of good and evil. As is somewhat clearer in "Schast'ye na beregu zagryaznënnego okeana" (1970; Happiness on the Shore of a Polluted Ocean), Memozov is always associated with materialistic, Western ideas corrupting or polluting Aksënov's Russian soul.

In the same period Aksënov began two children's books, probably to entertain his son. *Moy dedushka—pamyatnik* (1969; My Granddad, the Monument) and *Sunduchok v kotorom chto-to stuchit* (1976; The Box in Which Something Thumps) are the stories of a young Soviet boy as competent and adventurous as a James Bond type hero. An interesting anecdote followed the publication of *The Box in Which Something Thumps* when Aksënov was lecturing in France. Aksënov had arranged a meeting with Marc Chagall at St. Paul-de-Venc and since Chagall was mentioned in passing in the text, he decided to present Chagall with an autographed copy. Chagall surprised Aksënov by saying that he knew his works quite well. Unfortunately, subsequent discussion showed that Chagall was confusing Vasiliy Aksënov (born 1932) with Ivan Aksënov (1884-1935), who was a futurist poet of the Centrifuge group and the author of the first Russian book on Picasso (1917). An adult James Bond type is found in a spoof Aksënov co-authored called *Dzhin Grin—neprikasayemyy* (1972; Gene Green—The Untouchable), a novel highly sought on the blackmarket in its day.

Following *Gene Green*, there was a scalding review by Evtushenko criticizing Aksënov's emphasis on violence and corrupt Western mannerisms.[19] The previously close relationship between Evtushenko and Aksënov became a bitter and hateful rivalry of accusations as editors began to reject Aksënov's works, citing the article. Some have noted that the break of friends had begun in 1971 with the printing of "Randevu" (1969; The Rendezvous), which is about a famous poet often resembling Evtushenko.[20] There are a number of points that could be made showing that Aksënov did not mean Evtushenko, but the fact remains that the public often thought he did and Evtushenko might have been angered by that. It is clear, however, that Aksënov was not published for three years and that Evtushenko did write a poem responding to Aksënov's accusations relating to this matter.[21] The irony is that Aksënov might have been referring to himself in "Rendezvous," a possibility which is bolstered by comparing the accomplishments of the hero there with those of Tolya (Aksënov) in "Swanny Lake," written in the same period. It is Aksënov who must choose between a rendezvous with Soviet banality or death and prefers to die. Fortunately, another choice became possible.

A rendezvous with Soviet banality became a creative challenge for Aksënov in *Lyubov' k èlektrichestvu* (1971; Love for Electricity). At the time, a relatively new form of literature called the Documentary or Chronical Novel was extremely popular in the Soviet Union. It is a form of historical novel in which actual documents from a given period are interwoven with a fictional account of a historical figure. Overall it gives a "living," although not extremely accurate, account of history. The editors of a series of books about dedicated revolutionaries commissioned Aksënov to write in this style about the life of Leonid Krasin, a bolshevik and electrical engineer who was involved in both political and electrical changes in his homeland from 1890-1909.

Although it was not a genre that Aksënov repeated after this effort, it was nevertheless one which he must have approved of. He once wrote that "true prose should give the reader that which he cannot find in a single chronicle—the single life of the facts."[22] Most critics were quite happy with the way he did just that in *Love for Electricity*, one saying that he "clarified history" by his style.

The novel begins with the rejection of Krasin from engineering school in 1891 and follows his subsequent career as the builder of an electrical station near Baku. Krasin was, it is related, an important bolshevik activist and a close friend of Lenin during the 1905 uprising. Throughout the novel interesting newsclippings are cited and daily history is reviewed in a personal way. For example, Aksënov brought a touch of human realism to his portrayal of Lenin. In *Love for Electricity*, Krasin strolls through the cockney streets of London with Lenin, who proclaims a strong love for fish and chips. Originally Aksënov attempted to describe Lenin drinking Guinness stout in a pub, but that was rejected by the censor as unbecoming behavior for such a personage.

Other characters, "Englishman Vasya," who is a fictional revolutionary of romantic capabilities, and the "experienced gardener-beekeeper," who keeps trying to find out what it all means, pose questions about what people want, what they need, why they start revolutions. The answer is not forthcoming from Aksënov. There are only hints that the answer is disappointing, that the revolution is in the end a tragedy. However, it is not only this tragedy that Aksënov hints at, it is the tragedy of the entire revolutionary process for the Russian intelligentsia, who started the ball rolling but were the first to be crushed by its motion. Krasin's love for electricity blinds him to the needs of humanity. In the end, the story is the history of the idealistic bolshevik revolutionaries who were silenced by the mechanized levers of Party bureaucracy. Apparently this meaning is not clear to all readers of *Love for Electricity*, for the novel was included in the 1976 list of recommended books for school children.

From this period on, official publication became more difficult for Aksënov and the major works he completed in these years were only published years later in the West. One of these is *Zolotaya nasha Zhelezka* (1972; Our Golden Hardware), which is about the imposition of disharmony on harmony, metaphysics on physics. A section of this work did appear in the

Soviet Union in 1973 as if a short story, but the full text publication appeared only in 1980 in the U.S.A. The mysterious powers of the chunk of iron are related to the unknown energy source of a spaceship which had possibly crashed in the region, leaving the chunk of iron as the only physical trace of the incident.

On June 30, 1908, an explosion which was felt thousands of kilometers away actually did occur in Central Siberia and to this day has not been satisfactorily explained. Officially, a meteorite, called the Tunguska meteorite, exploded upon hitting the ground due to "a very considerable geocentric velocity."[23] The fact that no one investigated the remote area until 1921 has allowed for speculation from several scientific and non-scientific sources. For example, since the subsequent air waves travelled around the world twice, and bright, possibly radioactive clouds lit the skies over Europe for several nights thereafter, many ufologists today feel that the event was no meteor, but a nuclear explosion probably caused by the crash of an extra-terrestrial ship. It is with this theory in mind that Aksënov developed the plot of *Our Golden Hardware*.

Great-Salazkin is drawn to an island in the swamps of Siberia where fir trees have flourished since the crash and establishes his scientific research center for the elusive material *Dabl'-f'yu*. The center is honored and revered as the path to the future, a future where chance has disappeared and science reigns. When the mesons "dance" and thus activate their cosmic rays, *Dabl'-f'yu* will appear and the energy source will rejuvenate. The scientists are drawn to the center and live their lives for it alone. But the scientists are sons of Apollo (Apollinariyevichs) and thus are lovers of music (jazz) and poetry. They continually call on Prometheus, the benefactor of mankind, to guide them in their progress, the revealing of the secrets of the gods.

Certain characters who appear in others works by Aksënov balance out these scientists' formulae for progress by adding metaphysical and human symbols to the meta-analysis. Sabler, the jazz image Aksënov prefers, is music ("Life Is Short but the Music Is Beautiful"). Sirakuzers is the millionaire capitalist who can buy whatever he wants and thus place externalities on logical expectations. Teleskopov is the symbol of the trusting masses and therefore a burden that attaches to scientific responsibility for social preservation, the saving instinct. Lastly, but most importantly, there is Memozov, the anti-author and black magician who brings disharmony to the center. Memozov takes over Morzitser's apartment, hints to Morkovnikov that his wife is having an affair with Sabler, takes Kitousov's poetry to his wife, suggesting they are for another woman, and to Pavel Slon, suggesting the other woman is his wife, tells Krafaylov that these latter two wives are actually enamored of him, and tells Agafon that soon all goods will be priced at one ruble, driving him insane with greed.

In the final dream sequence, Memozov, who now controls all the characters, attempts to destroy the power of the chunk of iron only to see it reactivate and fly off back to its mother star. With Memozov broken, Great-Salazkin finds another chunk of iron and the characters grab shovels to begin again.

In the fall of 1974, Aksënov was invited by the University of California at Los Angeles to be Regent Lecturer and visiting professor. His application for an exit visa was delayed, having been bounced around by bureaucratic mismanagement until well after the intended starting date of January, 1975. At one point Aksënov was even asked for a verbatim transcript of all the lectures which he intended to deliver in the six months that he would be in California. The decision of responsibility went all the way to the highest levels of the Kremlin, and according to rumor, Brezhnev himself intervened, saying that he considered the lectures to be in the interest of détente. Shortly after this intervention a visa was issued and Aksënov appeared in the United States in March, 1975.

This trip was the source of several short stories and one long literary travelogue about America: *Kruglyye sutki, non-stop* (1976; 'Round the Clock, Non-Stop). The latter is important in that he talks much about himself in it as well as about his earlier works. Somehow bored with the usual notebooks and travel journals on America, Aksënov constructs a complicated mixture of fact, fiction and fantasy to present the America of his unusual perception. The antics of Aksënov's nemesis, Memozov, mentioned above, are here counterbalanced by a good hero, who is called the Muscovite, who is involved in a search for Truth in the form of a woman dressed in white. The novel episodes his experiences at U.C.L.A., Los Angeles, San Francisco, Monterey, Las Vegas, Calico City (a ghost town), New York and London. It also serves as a forum for discussing his views on reality and fantasy, totalitarianism, sculpture, the hippie culture, the establishment, American prose, American–Soviet relations and the supposed influences on his work by other writers.

In general, Aksënov is uncomfortable with the very concept of literary influence. He seems to feel that everything in his world is an influence and is not an influence to the same degree. He lists in this work some of his favorite foreign writers at the present time and confesses to their influence affecting him "almost as much as the pines, the sea, the mountains, gasoline, speed and city blocks."[24] Instead he prefers to speak of writers whom he admires, respects or to whom he feels spiritually closer: Tolstoy, Chekhov, Babel', Platonov, Hemingway, Faulkner, Böll, Salinger, Sillitoe, Ionesco, Beckett, Albee, Bulgakov, Brotigan and Vonnegut.

In 1976 two short stories by Aksënov had been published as if separate entities when in fact they were intended to be sections of a single, larger work. The first story was "Vne sezona" (1976; Out of Season) and the second, "More i fokusy" (1976; The Sea and Tricks). The longer work which includes these stories is called *Poiski zhanra* (1978; In Search of a Genre), which begins with the hero, Pavel Durov, having his car rammed from behind by a street-cleaning truck which is driven by a drunken hooligan. The local police are impressed by this famous master of an undisclosed genre of art. Short of hotel space, the police allow Durov to sleep in his car in the compound designated for cars involved in fatal accidents. The reader gets the first hint of the artist's unusual powers when Durov begins to communicate peacefully with the fatalities themselves.

As Durov drives on, various unique scenes from his trip are episoded. First there is an encounter with a hitchhiker in search of her husband who had run off. The next episode is the story which was printed separately as "Out of Season." In this section, rock musicians at a seaside resort, out of season, are shown acting in a manner blatantly disrespectful of others. In sport they kill a helpless duck. However, Durov's girlfriend brings the duck back to life through the help of the supernatural. Each of these episodes, it seems, brings Durov one step closer to his perfected genre. His earlier discussions with the fatalities taught him that death is an illusion, now he learns that life is illusory as well.

Just as Tolstoy interspaced his philosophy of history between the scenes of action in *War and Peace*, Aksënov here splits each of the episodes with philosophical commentary about his own genre. However, Aksënov has no intention of formally stating his thoughts in a precise and clear philosophical way as Tolstoy did. Instead the reader is given five magical scenes which fit together with random hints from the episodes to create the real message. By closely observing the text, the reader assembles the outline of the intended message. For Aksënov, the writer is an illusionist, a magician of sorts, and so the tale of Durov in search of his genre can be interpreted as Aksënov's search for truth in literature. Aksënov, as a writer of "young prose" or as an experimenter with "mauvisim" or fantasy and overstatement, belongs to that small group of artists, symbolized by Durov, who are searching for the truth of their genres and for the answer as to what degree it is illusion, buffoonery or actually serious.

The interspersed scenes of magic and commentary referred to above highlight Aksënov's own search, not Durov's. Scene I concerns his search through the rhythm of prose (cf. "A Dream for a Summer's Night," 1970). Scene II is about Aksënov's use of yoga to relax his mind and to separate himself from the world, in order to become an observer. Scene III is about the murder of Professor and poet Konstantin Bogatyrëv in Moscow, which occurred in 1976 and deeply affected Aksënov. The murder story in this version is placed in Indiana in order to pass the censors. Scene IV is an appeal to the trees, the core of Mother Russia. The last interruption, Scene V, is about Aksënov's work in Venice. In his 1976 work, *'Round the Clock, Non-Stop*, Aksënov had used Venice as a paradigm of changing realities. In this work, he first explained that he had earlier had an imaginary view of Venice, then he went there and attained a new, "real" view. The synthesis of imagination and reality, he concludes, is a new, higher reality.

The last publication Aksënov had in the U.S.S.R. was a short story called "Superlyuks" (1978; Top Class), the tale of a young physicist who takes the top class room on a cruise ship, and by passing out hundred-ruble notes as tips, is able to get whatever he wants, whenever he wants. He seems able to buy friends and even love by his free-spending generosity. Some of his success comes from "networking" his accumulation of friends.

Eventually it comes out that he is under official observation. His money comes from selling "foreign" goods actually made in the U.S.S.R. He is told to disappear and not to return to Moscow, which upsets him not as much for the loss of material goods as for the loss of friends. Aksënov, claiming to be tired of literary clichés, supplies three possible endings then quits writing. In the first, the hero is arrested with his friends dancing in the background. In the second ending, he is arrested but his friends are there and lovingly supportive. In the third, he is washed overboard and ends up on an island to be judged by the philosophers.

At this time an interview Aksënov had given in the West was published and the Soviet establishment angrily cut off all publications by and about Aksënov. For years he had been toying with the idea of publishing a book of works rejected by the censors for artistic, rather than political, reasons. Many of his friends had been interested in contributing and encouraged him to take advantage of the freeze-out to begin the effort. Publication in the Soviet Union is a monopoly of the government and previous attempts to offer an alternative press were quickly closed down. This effort utilized the best techniques of *samizdat* 'the illegal, underground press' and Western technology. Twelve large copies were to be made and kept in several places, two of which were to be smuggled abroad for publication. Twenty-two writers contributed to *Metropol'*, as the journal was called. The completed version was ready in January, 1979 and a press party was called with the intention of remaining within official procedures. The state came down hard on the group and one non-participating author publicly demanded execution by firing squad.[25]

The Soviet Union wanted to punish Aksënov for his editorship but was afraid of the foreign reaction. All books by Aksënov were removed from the libraries and in the end he was strongly advised to go abroad. Knowing the finality of the situation, Aksënov divorced his wife of twenty-three years and married one of the non-literary participants in *Metropol'*, Maya Karmen. His deepest regret was leaving behind his son, now a student in Moscow's Cinematography Institute.

By the summer of 1980, he was in Paris and making new plans for the future. He taught classes at the University of Michigan and U.S.C. over the next year. In January, 1981 the Supreme Soviet took away his Soviet citizenship and he became stateless. In 1981 Aksënov was a guest scholar with the Woodrow Wilson Center in Washington, D.C., where he has now chosen to reside.

Several of Aksënov's earlier unprintable works have now been published in the West. *Chetyre temperamenta* (1967; The Four Temperaments), an absurdist play, was published in *Metropol'*. *The Steel Bird* has already been mentioned. The major work *Ozhog* (1968-1975; The Burn) came out in 1980 and *Ostrov Krym* (1977-1979; The Crimean Island) came out in 1981. In 1968, in "Swanny Lake," Aksënov, under the name Tolya, meets with his rehabilitated father and reviews his past accomplishments. One notable event is his authorship of a novel, *Muzhskoy klub* (The Men's Club), which at the time seemed hypothetical. In fact, that was the title of Book One of a novel Aksënov had begun at the time. The novel, *The Burn*, is the story of Aksënov's past and present presented in the guise of several characters all based on bitter experiences of Tolya Von Steynbock, a child of the purges, an adult of the "Thaw" refrozen.

Tolya, like Aksënov, followed his mother to the labor camps of Magadan still praising the system and hoping to be a normal Soviet youth. In time, with an education, he hoped to become a mathematician, a sculptor, a musician, a doctor or even a writer. Each of these possible futures then becomes a character in the novel, all sons of Apollo, all with different experiences but with the memories of Tolya. There is a nearly factual description of Aksënov's life when the writer Panteley is called before "his excellency" (Khrushchëv) to account for his dangerous writings. This was the event of March 8, 1963, described above. Panteley is unable to publish a work called "Rzhavaya kanatnaya doroga" (The Rusty Funicular), which was a work Aksënov wrote in 1970, starring Alice, a major character in *The Burn*.

The sculptor Khvastishchev is the author of an apologetic article, "Otvetstvennost' pered narodom" (Responsibility Before the People), which was the title of Aksënov's recantation of April 3, 1963 in *Pravda*. He, like the real Aksënov, had an American cowboy painted on the bathroom door of his apartment. Other aspects of Khvastishchev resemble the sculptor Ernst Neizvestnyy, a friend of Aksënov and the object of similar artistic persecution in the U.S.S.R. The scholar, Kunitser, refers to Tolya's mother as *his* mother and talks about what *he* saw in Magadan. Mal'kol'mov is a doctor and did service in a tuberculosis clinic, like Aksënov, though this clinic is placed in Africa. He, like Tolya, and to a degree Aksënov, is of the Catholic faith [see Interview—eds.]. Sabler is a saxophone player in a jazz-rock combo, an image Aksënov often used as a variant of himself. The group, in a symbolic resistance to party "gods," is called the Giants and Aksënov spends a great deal of time describing the mythological field of battle as portrayed in the National Museum in East Berlin, a theme elaborated on in his *'Round the Clock, Non-Stop*.

Several women of his life are merged into the good, but defiled, images of Alice and Mashka. Foreign friends become Patrik Tanderzhet (Thunderjet), a doctor, an astronaut, a professor of Slavic Languages and Literatures and deserter from the U.S. Army who wants to defect to the U.S.S.R. Sanya Gurchenko, *a/k/a* Ringo Kid, is an outsider who came back to the land of his parents with a naive feeling of duty. His beating by the state police is a central theme repeated throughout the book. The story of Ringo Kid, an early movie characterization of John Wayne, is discussed more thoroughly in the short work "Promezhutochnaya posadka v Saygone" (1969; "Layover in Saigon"), which is roughly equivalent to Mailer's *Why We Are in Vietnam*.

Martin is the German doctor who taught Tolya, and Aksënov, Roman Catholicism. The police agent, Cheptsov, who beat Sanya in front of Tolya, is the evil of the modern KGB in its timeless continuity. As a retired officer he rapes his stepdaughter then tries to turn her in as a political criminal. In a drunken state of remorse, he bangs his head on a wall and dies in the care of Dr. Mal'kol'mov (Tolya), who felt he had saved him.

The novel is full of scandalous revelations from the Magadan labor camps to the social elite of Moscow. There is a group of nonconformists trying to live free of the Soviets in a fog-covered pit, but they are shot. People have their conversations taped from food vans nearby. Deficit goods are sold on the blackmarket. The best shoes are found on the feet of the store manager, never for sale. Racism and anti-Semitism are high at the men's clubs of Moscow, the beer stands. The tourist bars are operated by KGB officers, down to the whores. The coat-checkers demand a bribe to "find lost coats," preferring foreign currency in an effort to save for a new car. (Compare Aksënov's "Fenomen 'Puzyrya'" (1969; The Phenomenon of Bubble).) Conditions in the sobering tanks were bad enough to elicit a spontaneous demonstration. A court does not listen to charges or defenses and metes out the same sentence to defendants of disparate crimes. Modern dissenting political groups are so highly infiltrated that they are practically controlled by the KGB. Finally, there is a group of elite artists in Moscow treated specially by the police as they drive with abandon in their Mercedes-Benz.

The crowning touch is the shame of Aksënov in relating his nation's movement into Czechoslovakia. The novel, like its parts, carries above all a political message. From VW's imported by mail to cheating women, life in the U.S.S.R. is portrayed as a lie.

As literature teaches us, political commentary is often much more potent when subtly developed in a fictional fashion. Whereas *The Burn* was about life in the land of the lie, *The Island of Crimea* is about the naivete of outsiders willing to believe that lie. The Crimea, a peninsula lying inside the Soviet Union, is transformed into an independent island outside Soviet borders. The island is Russian, capitalistic, technologically advanced, democratic and basically everything today's U.S.S.R. is not. The hero of the book, Luchnikov, is an auto-racing playboy and newspaper editor whose dream is to unite the Russians of the island with the mainland communists. With the characteristics of a James Bond, or more likely Gene Green, he survives numerous attempts on his life and succeeds in unifying most of the political functions and nearly all the population into his "Union of Common Destiny." No one seems to appreciate the necessary debasement of their lifestyle; no one wants to believe that the Soviet Russians consider them anything but brothers, temporarily cut off from their historical motherland. On the other hand, the Kremlin has no desire to openly welcome millions of free-thinking, comfort-loving dissidents, so their response to the negotiating proposal is to move in the troops and take over the island. The emphasis is on the results of trusting the Soviets. They cannot help but lie, it is the only way they know of ruling.

The publication in the West of works formerly hidden in drawers is important, but perhaps more important will prove to be the publication of works, yet unwritten, hidden in Aksënov's mind. Works entirely written in America have begun to come forward. While Aksënov taught at U.S.C., he wrote a short story called "Sviyazhsk" (1981; The Village of Sviyazhsk), which has a decidedly religious emphasis. The main character, Shatovskiy, is a national champion basketball coach. When one of his favorite young players dies, he is ashamed that he cannot pray for him because he does not know how and does not feel as if he has the right. He begins trying to find a new life by reconstructing his memories of his family roots and his childhood. Most vividly he remembers his pioneer camp on the Volga, where he discovered in the village of Sviyazhsk an old, beautiful "working" church. Through a series of events he learns for the first time as an adult that he had been baptized by his nurse and his father's official chauffeur when he was a baby and that the ceremony took place precisely in this church of his childhood memories.

Full of religious emotions at the championship match, he crosses himself and blesses his starting line-up. The five then cross themselves, followed by the bench, the assistant coach and trainer. Interestingly, this unexpected behavior was carried live to millions of Soviet television sports fans before the cameras were shut off. In its most basic form, the style of this story recalls the ironic methodology of Aksënov's earlier stories, before the stylistic experimentation.

Aksënov's first "American" novel was written while he was with the Kennan Institute for Advanced Russian Studies in Washington, D.C. *Bumazhnyy peyzazh* (1982; Paperscape) is the story of Igor' Velosipedov, a naive Soviet engineer who dreams of revolution as if it were just a cinematographic exercise. With a distaste for paperwork, he allows his mail to accumulate: bills for electricity, gas and sewer, a warning from his cooperative, a calendar from Lenin University, even a notice for an army physical. On the weekends he balls up what he can and tosses it away. Unable to understand why he should not be allowed a garden plot, a car and a trip to Bulgaria, he simply writes to Brezhnev explaining how the U.S.S.R. should not be a land of paper replies, especially negative ones. When he agrees to sign an open letter condemning Solzhenitsyn and Sakharov, he is granted all his wishes.

The letter causes him to be shunned by all his friends. Aksënov seems to be poking fun at the superficiality of the pro-West-anti-Soviet fad in Moscow. As Velosipedov's social education evolves, he begins reading underground authors. His next letter to Brezhnev is full of praise for Party leadership but suggests minor improvements, such as returning the Crimea to the Tatars, allowing Solzhenitsyn and Sakharov to work creatively, leaving the Czechs alone, stopping psychiatric treatment of political dissidents and putting an end to rigged elections. A copy of this letter is smuggled to the West and Velosipedov becomes a hero in Moscow. He is subsequently dismissed from his job and sentenced to ten years at hard labor.

When he is released in 1983, he is allowed to emigrate to the U.S., where he finds practically everybody he knows has already gone. Aksënov uses this section to poke fun at the predictable behavior of Russian emigrés in America. His analysis of American television, especially commercials, computerized paperwork and junk mail makes his disappointment with "freedom" obvious. Human rights organizations are treated as comical; emigré newspapers, as myopic and reactionary; emigré journals, as deceptive. His American paperscape includes a social security number, memberships in AAA, Blue Cross/Blue Shield, Book-of-the-Month, credit cards and an IRA account. The paperwork involved dwarfs the Soviet version. Yet in the end a new life seems to be dawning in America, the door is closed on his Soviet life.

Currently Aksënov is working on a novel about photographers, tentatively called *Skazhi izyum!* (1983; Say Cheese!).[26] His plans for the future include an unending string of books, as fast as he can write them.

FOOTNOTES

1. E.S. Ginzburg, *Journey into the Whirlwind*, trans. P. Stevenson and M. Hayward, New York, 1967.

2. V.P. Aksënov, "Molodyye o sebe," *Voprosy literatury*, No. 9, 1962, p. 18.

3. M. Slonim, *Soviet Russian Literature: Writers and Problems 1917-1967*, Oxford, 1967, p. 293.

4. H. Marcuse, *An Essay on Liberation*, Boston, 1969, p. 26.

5. V.P. Aksënov, "Goryachiy sneg v rukakh," *Literaturnaya gazeta*, December 1, 1960, p. 3.

6. Cited by T. Whitney, *The New Writing in Russian*, Ann Arbor, 1964, p. 21.

7. V. Roslyakov, "Nedostovernaya dostovernost'," *Literaturnaya gazeta*, No. 12, March 20, 1974, p. 6.

8. V.P. Aksënov, "Halfway to the Moon," trans. by R. Hingley in the collection *Halfway to the Moon*, P. Blake and M. Hayward, eds., New York, 1965, p. 95.

9. V.P. Aksënov, "Kruglyye sutki, non-stop," *Novyy mir*, No. 8, 1976, p. 107. My translation.

10. V.P. Aksënov, "Mne dorogi sud'by romana," *Literaturnaya gazeta*, August 27, 1963, p. 3.

11. A.S. Pushkin, *Izbrannyye proizvedeniya*, Leningrad, 1968, p. 207. My translation.

12. A. Camus, "The Artist and His Time," *Myth of Sisyphus and Other Essays*, New York, 1959, p. 148.

13. A. Gladilin, *The Making and Unmaking of a Soviet Writer: My Story of the "Young Prose" of the Sixties and After*, Ann Arbor, 1979, p. 144.

14. V.P. Aksënov, "Otvetstvennost'," *Pravda*, April 3, 1963, p. 4.
15. V.P. Aksënov, "Lebyazh'ye ozero," *Literaturnaya Rossiya*, June 4, 1976, p. 13.
16. "William Burroughs: An Interview," *Paris Review*, No. 35, Fall, 1965, p. 49.
17. R. Stacy, *Defamiliarization in Language and Literature*, Syracuse, 1977, p. 1.
18. Letter to this author, February 28, 1983.
19. E. Evtushenko, "Tresk razryvayemykh rubashek," *Literaturnaya gazeta*, January 31, 1973, p. 5.
20. P. Meyer, "Aksënov and Soviet Literature of the 1960's," *Russian Literature Triquarterly*, No. 6, Spring, 1973, p. 454.
21. E. Evtushenko, "V lesu," *Ottsovskiy slukh*, 1975, p. 34.
22. "Shkola prozy," *Voprosy literatury*, No. 7, 1969, p. 85.
23. E. Krinov, *Giant Meteorites*, New York, 1966, p. 125.
24. V.P. Aksënov, "Kruglyye sutki, non-stop," *Novyy mir*, No. 8, 1976, p. 119.
25. V.P. Aksënov, "The Metropol Affair," *The Wilson Quarterly*, Special Edition, 1982, p. 158.
26. The literal translation of this title would be "say raisins."

PART II

GENERAL ARTICLES

THE EXOTIC IN THE
EARLY NOVELLAS OF AKSËNOV

R.L. Busch

The exotic is prominent in Aksënov's early fiction and is by no means confined to his longer works. However, in order to keep the material for analysis homogeneous and manageable, we will confine our study to Aksënov's four novellas from his "early period": *Colleagues* (1960), *A Ticket to the Stars* (1961), *Oranges from Morocco* (1963), *It's Time, My Friend, It's Time* (1964).

The exotic is here understood as the unconventional and strange. In the works at issue it is manifested most saliently in: speech elements alien to the standard literary language, including both foreignisms and sub-dialects, e.g., the language of the Soviet "beat generation" (ca. late 1950s, early 1960s); remote, unusual settings; subjective flights into fantasy.

Aksënov's earliest novella, *Colleagues*, is his most conventional, one that most reflects certain norms of Socialist Realism. This undoubtedly contributed both to its being translated by the Soviets for distribution abroad and to its being made into a film. *Colleagues*' ties to conventional Socialist Realism also help to explain its relative paucity of the exotic, for Socialist Realism embraces the normative and has not condoned much exoticism, which is inherently non-normative and can suggest dissatisfaction with Soviet conditions.

In *Colleagues* exotic speech elements are numerically modest. Foreignisms are often routine. They may reflect the most rudimentary acquaintance with a second language: "Khello komrids" (Hello, comrades; 89),[1] *Orevuar* 'Au revoir' (29), "Gud bay" (Good-bye; 29), "Veri vell!" (Very well!; 56). Others often involve foreignisms already assimilated in Russian: *biznes* 'business' (12), *nokaut* 'knockout' (111), *èkstaz* 'ecstasy' (145), "chas kokteyley" (cocktail hour; 165), etc. This presumably extends to such foreign cultural referents as *Tarzan* 'Tarzan' (53), "Mikki Maus" (Mickey Mouse; 149), "Dzhon Sil'ver" (Long John Silver; 96), etc.

Foreignisms are predominantly connected with Aleksey Maksimov in that they either emanate from him or from the milieu in which this young doctor moves—Leningrad intelligentsia circles and work in the port as a medical inspector. Thus, Maksimov first hears about rock and roll while on assignment. Having been asked *pro forma* whether any rats were seen dancing during the voyage, a befuddled chief officer replies:

— Izvinite, doktor, pervyy reys delayu starpomom, ne znal ètikh voprosov. Znachit, plyashut? Umora. Chto zh, rok-n-roll oni, chto li, plyashut?

> — Chto za rok-n-roll?
> — Ne znayete? Èto novyy tanets. V Anglii vse s uma poskhodili.
> — Nechto vrode bugi-vugi?
> — Ustarelo. Vy by videli rok-n-roll—psikhiatrichka nastoyashchaya. (p. 55)

> ("Sorry, Doc," he said, "this is my first run as Chief Officer, I just didn't know. So they dance, do they? But that's killing! What do they dance? *Rock-an'-roll*, I suppose?"
> "And what might *rock-an'-roll* be?"
> "Why, that's the latest dance, man. All Britain's gone mad on it."
> "What, is it something like *boogi-woogie*?"
> "That's out of date. You should see *rock-an'-roll*—it's a regular bug-house.")[2]

At Vera's birthday celebration, Maksimov temporarily joins forces with a hairy hippy to give "slavnuyu batal'yu [. . .] obskurantam" (glorious battle to the obscurantists; 147) over the question of abstract art, an essentially western, "exotic" phenomenon. Foreignisms and foreign cultural referents frequently occur during the debate. What matters most is not the particular stylistic coloration of these elements, most of which are not used by Maksimov himself, but their indirect characterological use to associate him with an alien, non-Soviet outlook. This extends beyond the arts to his hatred of official high blown "cant" (17), his dislike of establishment values and his desire to "break away" by getting assigned to duty on the high seas:

> Chelovek v drap-velyurovom pal'to, slovno volshebnik v detskom spektakle, otdërnul shtorku, za kotoroy otkrylas' sverkayushchaya vodnaya glad'. Proplyl mirazh—pal'my, neboskrëby, kupola, piramidy. Vy mechtali o zhizni neobychaynoy, nasyshchennoy, interesnoy? Vy dumali, mechty ne osushchestvlyayutsya? Naprasno. Poluchayte vkhodnyye bilety i begite v budushcheye, uvlekatel'noye i lëgkoye, kak kinofil'm. Indiya! Argentina! Dvoynoy oklad! Dissertatsiya! Shtormovyye usloviya. (12)[3]

> (Like a magician in a children's play, the fellow in the velour overcoat had plucked a curtain aside, to reveal a glittering expanse of water. They saw mirages of palms, skyscrapers, oriental domes and pyramids float before their eyes. You had dreamed of a life out of the ordinary, a full life, an interesting life? And thought your dreams would never come true? Well, you thought wrong. So take your entrance tickets and off with you into a future that is as attractive and easy as a film. India! Argentina! Double pay. Write a thesis. When the stormy winds do blow. . . . 15)

This ardor for the exotic appears to be undermined by its association with childish fantasy and by the incursion of pragmatic considerations about a dissertation and double pay. This is quickly reinforced by Gor'kushin's indignation: "durni, polezli v èkzotiku" (the twits are into the exotic; 12).

Indeed, within the confines of the novella, Maksimov's exotic aspirations are confounded. Sanitary inspection in Leningrad becomes humdrum and demeaning:

> Krestiki i nuliki, — dumal Maksimov. — Zamechatel'no! Znachit, ya uchil fiziologiyu, biokhimiyu, dialekticheskiy materializm, pronikalsya pavlovskimi ideyami nervizma dlya togo, chtoby schitat' tarakanov? Zdorovo!! (129)
>
> ("Crosses and noughts," said Max to himself. "Wonderful! So I've mastered so much physiology, biochemistry, dialectical materialism and Pavlovian neurology merely to count cockroaches? Marvellous!" 155)

Ironically, it is Zelenin, the novella's positive hero, and in many ways Maksimov's opposite, who finds both professional fulfillment and personal happiness by dutifully going off to backward and "grey" Kruglogor'ye. His lot is not to count roaches, but to save lives, rehabilitate the sick and serve as a *Kulturträger* for the local rustics. The natural setting for Zelenin's activities, while not patently exotic in most regards, is frequently shown as scenically attractive and vital. In one instance, in particular, its effect on Maksimov, who has come to visit Zelenin, has strongly moving exotic overtones:

> Na sosednem kholme stoyala tserkov'. Vysokiye belyye steny eyë s prostupayushchey koye-gde krasnoy setochkoy drevney kirpichnoy kladki strogo podnimalis' vverkh gladkimi polosami i lish' na samom verkhu ukrashalis' skupymi razvodami. U Maksimova zakhvatilo dukh. On oshchutil maloznakomyy gul v dushe, kakoy-to drevniy prizyv [. . .] (185)
>
> (On the next hill-crest stood the church. Its tall walls, with only here and there a line of ancient red brickwork, reared with severe, smooth lines, only at the top being ornamented with more fanciful ridges. Max caught his breath. A quickening which was most unfamiliar, a sort of voice calling from the past, suddenly stirred his heart [. . .] 222)

Maksimov feels weak-kneed at the sight of the church, which represents the exotic not just through its exterior physical form, but through a chronological distancing which vividly summons forth to him traditional spiritual values. Ironically too, it is the usually cynical Maksimov who objects to the blots on the scene caused by adjacent construction, while the normally idealistic Zelenin is untroubled.

Zelenin is quite simply comfortable working for innovation in a backward setting that offers much that is relatable to the exotic: beauty, adventure, romance and a return to the primary values of the Revolution—the latter being emphasized by his occupying the former residence of a revolutionary doctor. As the novella's positive hero, Zelenin pursues these values clumsily and naively, occasionally falling into the sort of cant Maksimov cannot abide. Shortly after extolling the virtues of contemporary man, he is nearly killed by a local hood, only to be saved by Karpov and Maksimov, whose opportunities to experience the exotic on the high seas lie beyond the confines of the work.

A Ticket to the Stars was Aksënov's first novella to depict a "westward flight." To be sure the action is confined to the Soviet Union, but the bulk of its characters seek adventure and self-understanding in Estonia, a part of the USSR that by tradition and culture serves as a surrogate for the West. The actants in this flight are not university but high school graduates dissatisfied with Soviet "bourgeois" establishment values.[4] Thus, they resist the standard routes to social acculturation—institutes, universities, factories, etc.

The western leanings of these youthful mavericks are again reflected characterologically in their speech, or in western associations attributed to them. Thus Alik Kramer, the aspiring writer and "ubezhdënnyy modernist" (convinced modernist; 27), is associated with western cultural referents: *syurrealizm* 'surrealism' (21), Fellini's *Sladkaya zhizn'* (*La Dolce Vita*; 21), *èkzistentsializm* 'existentialism' (65), etc.[5] Galya, the aspiring actress, is compared to Lolita Thorez (9) and Brigitte Bardot (15). Yurka, the basketball star, is associated with international sports terminology and is urged to play like the "vsemirno izvestnyy negr Uilt Chemberlen" (the world-famous black, Wilt Chamberlain; 3). Dimka Denisov, arguably the novella's central character, is also linked to sports. While there are few salient westernisms in his speech, he is the one who instigates the trip west. Furthermore, he wears jeans (a blatant sign of westernism in the early 1960s) and likes Moscow haunts where "Fords" and "Pontiacs" can be seen.

More striking than the westernisms is Aksënov's use of slang to characterize the speech of the new generation. These "hip" expressions of a subculture are intrinsically exotic. In *Colleagues*, patently substandard usage had been essentially limited to the thieves' jargon of the villainous Fed'ka Bugrov. Now a substandard idiom is given to likeable characters, especially to Dimka and Yurka, who use expressions like: *kon'* for 'old man'/'father' (3); *nakiryat'sya* for 'getting pickled' (7); "molotki rebyata" for 'real cool dudes' (11); "zakidony glazkami" for 'rolling one's peepers' (20); *kodla* for 'gang' (26); etc.

An example of the charming, affective quality of this subdialect occurs when Yurka is announcing his departure to his Estonian girlfriend:

— [. . .] chto èto ty, brat? Chto ty *zasmurela*, Linda? [. . .] seychas my s toboy voz'mëm *motor*, pokatayemsya, poydem v restoran, potom v klub *pobatsayem* na proshchaniye . . . skhvacheno?

— Znayesh', Yurka, kogda my snova s toboy vstretimsya, ya nachnu uchit' tebya pravil'nomu russkomu yazyku. Skhvacheno?

— *Zakon*! — radostno zavopil Yurka [. . .] (38, emphasis mine— R.L.B.)

("[. . .] Hey, what's wrong, pal? Why so down? We'll get some wheels right off, ride around a bit, then for good-byes we'll go off to the club and jive to some tunes. Got it? [. . .]"

"You know what, Yurka, when we meet again, I'll start teaching you how to speak correct Russian. Got it?"

"Right on," roared Yurka joyously [. . .])[6]

As a group, Dimka and company, modern "Argonauts," head for the sea, a traditional source of exoticism involving beauty, adventure and freedom:

"Vot èto zhizn'! Goryachiy pesok. Sosny, chayki. More [. . .] I nikto, ponimayete li, ne davit na tvoyu psikhiku." (22)

("This is the life. Hot sand. Pines. Seagulls. The sea [. . .] And, you know, there's nobody getting on your case.")

Dimka's and Galya's first moments of physical intimacy are closely bound up with the sea and its immediate environs. Shortly before they become intimate, Dimka views Galya in relation to Aphrodite:

Afrodita rodilas' iz peny morskoy i ostrova Krit.
A Galya?
Neuzhto v roddome Brauèrmana vblizi Arbata?
V sushchnosti, Afrodita—dovol'no tolstaya zhenshchina, ya videl eyë v muzeye.
A Galya?
Galya stroyna, kak kartinka Obshchesoyuznogo Doma modeley.
Chto by ya sdelal seychas, esli by byl ya grekom?
Drevnim, konechno, no yunym i moshchnym, tochno Gerakl.
O Galya!
Ya by skhvatil eyë zdes', na pustuyushchem plyazhe.
Na mototsikle promchalsya by s ney cherez Tallin i Tartu.
Snyal by glushitel', chtob bylo pokhozhe na grom kolesnitsy.
Ya by unës eyë v gory, v khram Afrodity.
Knigu lyubvi my prochli by tam ot korki do korki. (23)
("Aphrodite was born from out of the sea foam on the isle of Crete.
"But Galya?
"Was it really at the Brauerman Maternity Hospital near Arbat?
"Actually, Aphrodite was on the fat side, I saw her in a museum.
"But Galya?
"Galya's svelte, just like a picture out of the All-Union House of Models.

"What would I do now if I were a Greek?
"An ancient one, of course, but young and powerful, like Hercules.
"Oh, Galya!
"I'd grab her right here on the deserted beach.
"We'd race through Tallin and Tartu on a motorcycle.
"I'd take the muffler off so that it would sound like a thundering chariot.
"I'd take her off to the mountains to Aphrodite's temple.
"We'd read the book of love from cover to cover.")

Exotic elements from ancient mythology are intermixed here with discordant ones from contemporary life—the motorcycle and its muffler, contemporary fashion models, the museum Aphrodite, etc. This is typical of Aksënov's handling of the exotic Tallin setting within the novella. The sea is beautiful and inspiring, but is not without its modern-day scum and litter, and Tallin's cafés, with their exotic drinks, expresso machines, "starry" decor, Charleston and calypso, can be cluttered with cigarette debris, etc.

The relatively minor discordant elements for the exotic in the early stages of the "Argonauts'" Tallin experience, and in Galya's and Dimka's love relationship, increase drastically as the real world impinges upon the group's existence. By the end of Part Two of the novella, the prose of real life has taken over—a shortage of money brings hunger, the lads are exposed to graft and exploitation as they become day laborers, Galya breaks with the "feckless Dimka" to pursue in vain her cinematic dreams by living with an aging actor from a bohemian film circle. The male Argonauts will really get to know the sea—no longer as sunbathers or deep-sea divers armed with a harpoon, but as members of a fishing collective where routine, numbing toil and seasickness become their lot. This represents an adjustment to the norms of real life, movement along a path to maturation and constructive self-development through work, that fundamental value among canonical Soviet values.[7] For the escapist Argonauts, the exotic, although attractive, proves to be illusory, unsubstantial and unfulfilling.

In *A Ticket to the Stars*, another important character connected with the exotic, one who, in fact, is at the source of the novella's exotic title, is Dimka's older brother Victor. He can go into ecstasy over a Soviet satellite:

> Kusok zemnogo metalla, polnyy lyubvi, polnyy geroizma, i schast'ya, i stradaniya. Ves' on nash, plot' ot ploti . . . On odin tam, v chuzhoy srede, okruzhënnyy chuzhimi metallami, ozaryayemyy kostrami chuzhikh zvëzd, letit i gudit i drozhit ot muzhestva i trogatel'no signalit: "Bip-bip . . ."
> — Chërt vas voz'mi! — krichu ja svoyemu brattsu i ego druzhkam i raspakhivayu okno. — Slushayte!
> — Nu, slyshim, — govorit Dimka. — Kosmicheskiy avtobus.

(A piece of earthly metal full of love, heroism, happiness and suffering. It's all ours, flesh of our flesh ... It's alone out there in an alien environment, encircled by alien metals, and lit by the fires of alien stars, it flies and booms all aquiver with courage as it sends its touching signal: "Beep-beep ..."

"Damn you!", I yelled at my little brother and his buddies as I threw the window open. "Listen!"

"So, all right, already, we hear it," said Dimka. It's just a cosmic bus." 11)

This disparagement of the exotic connected with cosmic conquest and scientific advance is conceivably consonant with Victor's ultimately tragic fate. Victor is the novella's positive hero. His "YA CHELOVEK LOYAL'NYY" (I'M A LOYALIST; 1) begins the novella. He embraces many Soviet values and serves as an emulative figure for the recalcitrant Dimka. Curiously, however, Victor, unlike his strait-laced colleague Boris and others, is largely tolerant of the rebelliousness of Dimka and company, in whom he can still see himself a decade earlier. Their penchant for the exotic is not foreign to him. He just channels it differently—more acceptably and constructively by Soviet standards. Victor even shares in the younger set's rebelliousness as he stubbornly and successfully goes against the *collectively* established practice of nearly a whole scientific institute to prove the false premises on which his own and many other dissertations had been based. Near the end of the novella Victor dies while doing field work. Viewed from one perspective this may just be, to paraphrase Andrey Sinyavsky, another in a line of tragic endings that are really for the good since Victor's heroic example endures, and his starry ticket is passed on to a much reformed and searching Dimka. From a very different perspective, one can discern a progression in Aksënov's ambivalent treatment of the positive hero.[8] He almost destroyed the "wide-eyed, goody-goody" Sasha Zelenin. Victor does not survive, but falls victim to his scientific strivings whose ultimate applications are so double-edged in their potential.[9]

The positive hero is unambiguously denigrated in Aksënov's third novella, *Oranges from Morocco*. The only remnant of this mainstay of Soviet fiction is a "heroine," Lyudmila Kravchenko, a puritanical Komsomol activist, who dreams of a statue to Lenin one day embellishing the new Far Eastern town where she has settled. Lyudmila prefers not to think about the puzzling prison camps that once dotted the environs, questions her personal desires out of duty to the collective, reads Gorky for relief from depression, etc. However, she is prominent in the work not for her Soviet virtues but for her good looks.

It is no surprise that Lyudmila's speech is devoid of the westernisms and other substandard elements that tend to characterize youngsters in early Aksënov. However, these are found in the speech of other important characters. Westernisms are most notable in the speech of Nikolay Kolchanov and Victor Koltyga.

Kolchanov, a reserved young architect, uses terms broadly connected with Western culture: "Rokuèll Kent" (Rockwell Kent; 139); *Brodvey* 'Broadway' (141); "Garri Bellafonte . . . pel 'Kogda svyatyye marshiruyut'" (Harry Belafonte was singing "When the Saints Go Marching In"; 148); "Siksten tons" (Sixteen Tons; 219); etc.

Koltyga, much less the intellectual, tends to be associated with sports and also with a slang that is common to his crowd: "[. . .] basketbol! Voprosy taktiki ya beru na sebya. Lichnyy drug Reya Meyera iz universiteta De-Pol' [. . .]" ([. . .] basketball! I'll handle the tactics. Ray Meyer of De Paul University is a personal friend [. . .]; 210); "Togda mne kranty" (If so, I've had it; 134); "zhala maslo" (was boozing it up; 206); to one of his friends importuning him: "Vit', ya na tebya nadeyus' v smysle titi-miti" (Vic, I'm banking on you for bread; 129), Victor eventually responds: "— Konchay, — govoryu, — svoyu tyagomotinu" (Like, don't bug me man, I tell him; 131).

Racy language is even more prominent in the chapters devoted to Koren', a social outcast who served time in Magadan for an outlandish Moscow breakin dating from the 1930s. The pungency of Koren's lingo is likely derived from a combination of recent slang and thieves' jargon: "zdes' nam ne oblomit'sya" (we can't get smashed here; 185); *khanuriki* 'the nurds' (185); "vstrechat' mne svoyego papashku s khoroshim fingalom na fotografii" (I'll have to meet my old man with a nice shiner on my mug; 231); "[. . .] iz vsekh nashikh fezeoshnikov ya byl samyy priblatnënnyy" ([. . .] I was the thievinist of all the lads in our gang; 188).

Oranges, the "produkt of Marokko" (product of Morocco; 205) as it says on the crates, the "marokkanskaya kartoshka" (the Moroccan spud; 196) as Kolchanov puts it, are most prominently representative of the exotic in the novella. These two phrasings express the potential for ambivalence with which the exotic is so often infused in Aksënov's early novellas. On the one hand, one has an analogue to the common potato; on the other, a product from distant parts which, under Far Eastern Soviet conditions, triggers a human stampede from hundreds of miles around and street brawls over its possession.

It is clearly the exotic attributes of the orange that Aksënov foregrounds. The description of its first appearance is indicative:

> Èto byl bol'shoy, ogromnyy apel'sin, velichinoy s prilichnuyu detskuyu golovu. On byl bugrist, oranzhev i slovno svetilsya. Evodshchuk podnyal ego nad golovoy i podderzhival snizu konchikami pal'tsev, i on visel pryamo pod gorbylëm nashey palatki, kak solntse, i Evdoshchuk, u kotorogo, pryamo skazhem, matershchina ne skhodit s gub, ulybalsya, glyadya na nego snizu, i kazalsya nam v ètu minutu magom volshebnikom [. . .].
> (It was a large, no, enormous orange, roughly as big as the decent-sized head of a baby. Its skin was very grainy and bright orange, as though it were lit up. Holding it from underneath on his fingertips, Evdoshchuk raised it above his head just beneath the topmost reinforcement slab of our tent, where it hung like the sun. And Evdoshchuk, who, to be honest with you, was never without a four-letter word on his lips, stood there smiling up at it, and to us at that moment he seemed like a real wizard [. . .]; 129)

The transfixing power of this piece of exotica is variously evident for all the main characters who narrate the story themselves. Their initial narrations always end with references to the oranges which mobilize them to converge on the town of Talyy.

The ensuing enchantment and carnivalesque atmosphere is conveyed by Nikolay Kalchanov:

> Tantsy v strane Apel'sinii, takimi i dolzhny byt' tantsy pod lunoy,— ekh talyanochka moya, mat' chestna, gopak ili tvist—ne vsë li ravno, razudalyye tantsy na Apel'sinovom plato, u podnozhiya Apel'sinovykh gor, u kraya toy samoy Apel'sinovoy planety, a sputnichki—apel'sinchiki svistyat nad golovami nashimi sadovymi.
> (Dances in the land of Orangeium—just the kind that are meant to be beneath the moon and stars, ah, you sweet accordian, you're really something else, makes no difference if we're doing the twist or a good ol' country dance, we're romping and stomping on Orangeium's Plateau, at the foothills of the Orangeium mountains on the edge of the planet itself, the planet Orangeium, while dear sweet orange sputniks whistle above our spaced-out heads. 217)

Oranges as exotica bring people together and provide an embellishing, uplifting, other-worldly touch to the romantic relationships which are paramount to most of them. Unlike Aksënov's other early novellas, *Oranges from Morocco* contains a fundamentally and unequivocally positive manifestation of the exotic. It has a short-term effect on Katya and Nikolay Kolchanov, whose love flourishes under its spell, but must give way to the return of Katya's husband. It has far-reaching effects on the other major characters. German does not get Lyudmila, but finds Nina, with whom a close relationship is clearly underway. Victor Koltyga gets the much-coveted Lyudmila, whose cerebral and puritanical Komsomol precepts succumb to the power of love. In the sole instance in the novella where Aksënov pays tribute to the Soviet work-ethic value,[10] Koren' seizes on the opportunity provided by the exotic to get back into the collective aboard the *Zyuid* from which he had been removed for misconduct.

The last of Aksënov's early novellas, *It's Time, My Friend, It's Time*, brings one approximately full circle to *Colleagues* in that the exotic is shown to be fundamentally hollow. It essentially lacks even the transitory appeal it had in *A Ticket to the Stars*, and certainly does not have any of the positive effects with which it was associated in *Oranges from Morocco*.

It's Time, My Friend, It's Time is basically lacking in the "starry-boy lingo" that one had come to associate with Aksënov's works. However, foreignisms and foreign cultural referents are still significantly present. These are prominently associated with Kyanukuk, an exaggerated foil for the central male character, the writer Valentin Marvich.

Kyanukuk likes Oscar Peterson and Ella Fitzgerald. He is the first known reader of Marvich's stories, and he favors avant-garde literature, which is an implicit western connection. The same connection is perceivable in his attraction to Estonia. This extends beyond cafés and high-tone hotels to an intensive study of Estonian history, culture, etc. However, Kyanukuk prefers an imaginary world, one that allows him to fantasize about being sought out for a scientific exchange with the University of Michigan, one that has a rich and devoted Lilian totally concerned about his happiness, one that allows him, like Marvich, to nurse an impossible love for the film actress Tanya, Marvich's estranged wife. Kyanukuk is both a likable and pitiful misfit whose exotic leanings are symptomatic of his alienation. They may provide a modicum of escape, but they do not bring him happiness. One finds him wishing his life were behind him before his death pursuant to partying with Tanya and her "beatnik" friends.

On the whole, foreign cultural referents are semantically negative. This is clearly the case with Mario Cinecetti, the "con artist" m.c. at the "trendy" Bristol Hotel, who turns out to be not Italian, but Russian. At one point Mario, i.e., Kolya, does a few steps of the twist and to a transfixed audience announces a number from his international repertoire: "— 'Ochi chërnyye' tak, kak ikh ispolnyayet velikiy Armstrong, moy drug!" ('Black Eyes' like my friend, the great Armstrong, does it; No. 5, 67). Cf. the mindless namedropping at the première of Tanya's film:

> Razgovor shël neskol'ko strannyy:
> — Godar, — govoril odin.
> — Tryuffo, — otvechal drugoy.
> — A Benyuèl'? — ekhidno podkovyrival tretiy.

— Antonioni, — rezko pariroval chetvërtyy.
(The conversation was going somewhat strangely:
"Godard," said one.
"Truffaut," replied a second.
"And Bunuel," jabbed a third maliciously.
"Antonioni," parried a fourth sharply." No. 5, 97)

The film première, which should be a thrilling experience for Tanya, ends up disenchanting her and leads her to doubt her career: "Tak vsyu zhizn' ya budu igrat' 'krasivykh devushek.' Vesëloye amplua! Chto tolku?" (So my whole life I'll be playing the pretty-girl roles. Some job! What's the point? No. 5, 99).

Tanya's disenchantment with her acting career is symptomatic of the negativism surrounding the exotic in the novella. Her profession, which is construably synonymous with the exotic, is shown in a prosaic, behind-the-scenes fashion. After-hours in the Estonian resort town of Pyarnu are characterized by soulless revelry. This is emphasized by Kyanukuk's death at the end of Part Two, which is ironically entitled *Razvlecheniya* 'Amusements'.

Similarly to Tanya, Valentin Marvich is beginning to find success in his own exotic career as a writer of supposedly innovative stories. His fondness for the works of outstanding representatives of Russia's literary past (Esenin, Blok, Bryusov) suggests that he is sensitive to high literary value. Part One constitutes his own autobiographical narration. However, the example of his "belletristic" writing which appears in Part Three offers no indication that Marvich possesses exceptional literary talent. The writer, Guryayev, finds him sub-professional and, after what the reader has already seen of the Soviet film world, a studio's seeking Marvich out to sign a scenario contract is hardly proof of the contrary.

Whatever Marvich's claims to artistic recognition, it is clear that he has rejected his wife Tanya's cinematographic Bohemia and shows no attraction to a writer's Bohemia. His problems are more personal than professional. Like all the major characters of the novella, he suffers from acute isolation, which he attempts to overcome in good Soviet fashion by striving to build a better world through working in the collective as a heavy-machine operator. Consequently, his writing to Tanya from Siberia: "My tut s druz'yami-tovarishchami so strashnoy siloy 'kuyëm chego-to zheleznogo'." (My good comrades and I are putting enormous effort into 'forging something super here'; No. 5, 94.) Upon being reunited with Tanya, Valentin recites to her lines from Blok's verses to his Beautiful Woman and connects this forthwith to pathos involving the Soviet work collective:

> — Mne zdes' nravitsya, — medlenno zagovoril on. Zdes' nasha obshchnost', zdes' nasha tsel'naya dusha. My zanyaty odnim delom i chuvstvuyem teplotu drug k drugu, khot' i ne vse znakomy, no my vse vmeste—svarshchiki, kranovshchiki, shofëry, traktoristy . . . Ponimayesh'? Vse vmeste . . . Poètomu ya i privël tebya syuda. Ty ponimayesh' menya?
> — Ya tebya lyublyu, — skazala ona.
> ("I like it here," began Valentin slowly. "Here we've got a communal spirit, here our souls are unified. We're all working on the same thing and we feel a mutual warmth for each other. While we are not all acquaintances, still we're all together—the welders, the crane operators, the truck drivers, the tractor drivers . . . You understand? We're all together . . . That's why I brought you here. You understand me?"
> "I love you," she said. No. 5, 124)

Aksënov appears to be heading for a trite Socialist Realist "happy ending": After exemplary efforts in construction (Marvich is on the "honor roll"—*doska pochëta*), tractor driver gets girl. However, such is not the case. Marvich and Tanya are brought together briefly at the end of the novella, but only to discover their need to separate again, and this is fully consonant with the spirit of Pushkin's poem from which the novella derives its title. One could conceivably ascribe the outcome to an orthodox Soviet placing of socially useful work above an individual's need for emotional fulfillment through love. However, it is more appropriate to see the ending as being in keeping with the work's presentation of pervasive alienation in affairs of the heart. Try as he might, Marvich cannot recapture the exhilarating romantico-exotic moments from the past when he used to possess Tanya in a medieval Estonian tower. Concerning this he states in the novella's opening chapter:

> A ya-to uzh byl khorosh: nedouchka, nachitavshiysya Grina; mne grezilas' beskonechnaya nasha obshchaya zhizn', ty da ya ot Severa do Yuga, ot Vostoka do Zapada, dvoye brodyag, lyubyashchiye serdtsa, dvukhmestnaya baydarka, dvukhmestnaya palatka . . . Nelegko prostit'sya s yunosheskimi grëzami, no zhizn' oblamyvayet tebya, ona tebya "uchit," [. . .]
> (As for me, well I was really something: I was shallow and my head was stuffed with Grin's romantic notions; I dreamt of our interminable life together, you and me from North to South, East to West, two vagabonds, two loving hearts, a canoe for two, a tent for two . . . It's hard to part with adolescent dreams, but life breaks you down, it gets you to "wise up," [. . .] No. 4, 51)

Thus, from the very outset the romantico-exotic appears in the hostile context of Marvich's dismissing his adolescent dreams. Still, the difficulty of parting with these dreams is borne out by his desire to reiterate them in the same vein at the end of Part One. He keeps these thoughts to himself, but Tanya lowers them nevertheless by denying his reconciliation proposal: "[. . .] i nikakoy idillii u nas ne poluchitsya" ([. . .] and we won't be able to live any sort of idyll; No. 4, 92).

Tanya's sober-mindedness precipitates Marvich's departure for Siberia, where he will outgrow his romantic notions of love with its exotic embellishments. In this regard, it is significant that their re-emergence during his Siberian reunion with Tanya is expressed not by Marvich but by Serëzha Yugov. By the novella's end, Marvich has outgrown his adolescent dreams, and he can draw on his sense of belonging to a supportive collective to maintain his overall well-being. However, the mutual need which he and Tanya have experienced while apart would suggest that the collective will not altogether suffice.

It is conceivable that the considerable devaluation of the exotic in *It's Time, My Friend, It's Time* can be explained, at least in part, by pressures on Aksënov to conform to traditional Soviet literary canons.[11] In this respect it is noteworthy that the novella was published in the orthodox journal, *Molodaya gvardiya* (The Young Guard), rather than the bolder *Yunost'* (Youth). However, the devaluation could be attributable to Aksënov's own doubts concerning the exotic, whose value during his early period peaked in *Oranges from Morocco*, but figures nowhere during that stage without some degree of ambivalence.

In the early novellas of Aksënov the exotic functioned especially: (1) to reflect a burgeoning, destalinizing interest in western phenomena among Soviet youth; (2) to show a need to escape the humdrum of daily routine; (3) to achieve stylistic expressiveness through a substandard idiom which was symptomatic both of organic developments within the Russian language and of disaffection with overall conformity to Soviet "prescriptiveness;" (4) to capture the transporting power of love.

While Aksënov's early novellas culminate with a marked tendency to downplay the exotic, this can be misleading in that it will be strongly reincorporated in his later writings. Particularly noteworthy here is his marked turn towards subjective fantasy and the fantastic which will, as in the case of exotic features examined herein, continue to be variously intermixed with realistic depiction.[12]

FOOTNOTES

1. Vasiliy Aksënov, *Kollegi* in *Zhal', chto vas ne bylo s nami*, Moscow, 1969, p. 10. Subsequent references in Russian to *Colleagues* are from this edition and will directly follow quotations. The same holds for Aksënov's other novellas.

2. Vasili Aksenov, *Colleagues*, London, 1962, p. 67. Longer translations are from this edition, shorter ones are the author's.

3. Cf. pp. 60, 64 in the Russian; pp. 73, 78 in the English.

4. *Zvëzdnyy bilet*, Aarhus, 1970, pp. 14, 18.

5. Cf. p. 15 for his reading material: *The Daily Worker, L'Humanité, Junge Welt, La Paesa Sera, L'Ecran, Unesco Bulletin* and also *Yunost'* (Youth), the bold Soviet journal in which Aksënov's novella first appeared.

6. *Skhvacheno* is highly colloquial for *ponyatno/ponimayesh'*, and in repeating it, Linda is aping Yurka.

7. One can fully agree with P. Meyer who, in her Ph.D. dissertation, sees this novella as celebrating the work ethic just like *Colleagues* before it. See *Aksënov and Soviet Prose of the 1950's and 1960's*, Ann Arbor, 1971, pp. 32-33.

8. On this, see *ibid.*, p. 37.

9. The destructive side of advanced scientific technology is referred to very openly and negatively in Aksënov's next novella, *Apel'siny iz Marokko*, [in *Katapul'ta*], Moscow, 1964, pp. 136, 222-23. Cf. *Pora, moy drug, pora*, in *Molodaya gvardiya*, nos. 4-5, 1964, p. 61 (no. 4). Further references to these works are from these editions. Ambivalence towards the scientific, together with a tendency to give it a fantastic and exotic embodiment, is characteristic of Aksënov's later works. See Per Dalgård, *The Function of the Grotesque in Vasilij Aksenov*, Aarhus, 1982, pp. 58-59, 91-93.

10. P. Meyer, *op. cit.*, p. 45, argues that *Oranges from Morocco* marks Aksënov's final rejection of the work ethic.

11. See "Otvetstvennost'," *Pravda*, April 3, 1963, p. 4.

12. See P. Meyer, *op. cit.*, pp. 123, 142, also Dalgård, *op. cit.*, p. 18, *passim*.

SOME LITERARY ROOTS OF AKSËNOV'S WRITINGS: AFFINITIES AND PARALLELS

Per Dalgård

1. Introduction

The ability to synthesize is perhaps the most striking feature of Aksënov's creative genius. His mature works always link the most different levels of speech—from archaisms to ultramodern slang—and they are always interspersed with numerous hidden and direct allusions. Yet, it never becomes too lofty and exclusive as in the novels of some modernist writers. Aksënov's never-lacking irony, self-irony and humor always take the lead and destroy any kind of academic pomposity. In this respect he can be compared to two other great contemporary writers—Günther Grass and Gabriel García Márquez.

When speaking about the literary roots of Aksënov's writings, one must take the following into account. Firstly, that the relationship between a writer and his possible literary antecedents does not necessarily imply "imitation," but rather "parody" or "use of other's word" (in the Bakhtinian sense) in order to enrich the text. Secondly, that one cannot clearly distinguish between "influence" and "parallelism." In this connection it is worth noting that Aksënov has always been open and sensitive to influence from what he has been reading, which is why he rather bombastically declares that reading is bad for the mature writer (cf. Interview). Finally, by analyzing some of Aksënov's literary roots one should be careful not to underestimate his own contributions, nor should one put him into schemes which would preclude other affinities and possible parallels.

However, it is reasonable to see Aksënov's works as a synthesis of two elements—the Gogolian tradition in Russian literature and the influence from Western, mainly American, literature. This assumption is based on my own reading of Aksënov, on discussions with him and on his own statements. When asked to name the important sources of influence, Aksënov placed Belyy's *Peterburg* (Petersburg) and Hemingway's *Fiesta* (The Sun Also Rises) at the top of the list.[1]

Aksënov is part of the revival of the Russian tradition of Gogol' and Belyy (and other Russian writers of the avant-garde) which took place in the sixties. At the same time he is one of the leading representatives of the "New Wave" in Soviet-Russian literature, which was very similar to and influenced by contemporary developments in American literature.[2]

2. Aksënov and the Tradition of Gogol' and Belyy

> I love Vasiliy Aksënov's prose. Come to think of it—is that prose at all? He rapturously inserts pieces of poetic text into his works, sometimes he rhymes, his speech is many-voiced as in drama. It is the choral monologue of that spontaneous being called the city of today, the concrete music of the bus-crowds, of the overheated carburators of Moscow in July. Come to think of it—is that a city at all?
>
> Andrey Voznesensky

Aksënov places himself in the Gogol'-Belyy tradition, as in this interview given to Priscilla Meyer in 1972:

> The dislocation into unreality and grotesque in my fiction leads to greater depth. This shift in my writing corresponds to my enthusiasm for the avant-garde, especially for Belyy's prose [. . .] a reinstatement of an interrupted tradition, that of the prose of the 1920's which represents a continuation of the fantastic tales of Gogol'. I bow before Dostoevsky; but for me he is less important than Gogol'. Dostoevsky is a prophet, a Messiah, but Gogol' is a writer, and literature is impossible without play, without stylistics.[3]

The most striking similarities between Aksënov and Belyy are to be found in the area of style, both have their roots in Gogol's prose. Like Aksënov, Belyy considered Gogol' more important that Dostoyevsky. Talking about Dostoyevsky's unmusicality and "false notes," he wrote: "The bad taste of Dostoyevsky can be overcome in two ways: (1) forward to Nietzsche, (2) back to Gogol'."[4] Belyy took the influence from Gogol' so seriously that he wrote a book about it, *Masterstvo Gogolya* (Gogol's Craft), in which he openly admitted that his prose—from the sound level to plot structure—is a renewal of the Gogolian tradition in the twentieth century.[5]

What exactly is it in Gogol' that Belyy considers so important?—He gives the answer himself, and here I think that we have the key to our comparison. For Belyy, Gogol's contribution to Russian literature consists of Gogol's "putting into his prose the whole range of the lyricism given in rhythms, from which Pushkin distanced himself in his prose, and thus made his outstretched lines tremble like strings and give off the sound of assonance and alliteration." (MG, 5) The renewal and enrichment of prose by poetical-lyrical elements is, according to Belyy, the prime distinctive feature of Gogol' as compared to Pushkin. Such a lyrical quality of prose (prose-poetry) implies basically the following structural changes:

1. use of poetical devices: play with sound, rhythm, alliteration, repetition, etc.
2. retardation of the epic narrative; lack of the conventional, logical-causal development of plot, character and action, replaced by

3. development of a lyrical theme shown in its various aspects, from different points of view, creating a mosaic of motives, symbols, themes, etc.⁶

2a. Poetical Devices in Belyy and Aksënov

A very clear parallel between Belyy and Aksënov is the use of "triple repetitions" (troinoy povtor), which Belyy admits he has taken from Gogol'. It is a very common phenomenon in Aksënov, as for example: "zamechatel'nyy, zamechatel'nyy, (zamechatel'nyy!)," "prekrasnyye, prekrasnyye, (prekrasnyye!)," "bryukhatyy, bryukhatyy, bryukhatyy," "gaz, gaz, gaz."⁷

The accumulation of verbs, nouns or adjectives is a typical feature of both Belyy and Aksënov. Belyy: "Doma, domy, domiki, prosto domchënki, i dazhe domchënochki," or "ulitsa skladyvalas' stolknoven'yem domov, fligeley, mezoninov—kirpichnykh, korichnevykh, belykh, tëmno-pesochnykh, zelënykh, kisel'nykh, olivkovykh, fistashkovykh, kremovykh;"⁸ and Aksënov: "pauza i molchaniye, khoteniye i vozhdeleniye, sheburshaniye i oskverneniye, omerzeniye, gniyeniye, vozrozhdeniye i samozarozhdeniye [. . .]," or "mozhno vsë-taki privyknut', mozhno, mozhno, mozhno vsë-taki privyknut', privyknut' mozhno, mozhno, mozhno, vpolne mozhno privyknut';" or "pakhuchiy, sifonnyy, sifonno-vodorodnyy, sifonno-vinegretno-kotletno-khlebnyy, kul'turnyy, osvezhayushche-oduryayushchiy napitok."⁹

And we have already reached another common feature of Belyy and Aksënov—the rhythmic prose based on wordplay, repetition, alliteration and rhyme. In Belyy: "Pan Yan, ne geroy, uspokoytes' zh: èto za oknami, v okna,—bryatsalo, babatsalo, tsokalo, kokalo! Konnitsa! Koka, kornet, pered neyu prokokal konëm gnedorozovym: iz nochi v noch';"¹⁰ and Aksënov: "Lilo, lilo po vsey zemle . . . Lilo il' lilo? V lilovyy tsvet na pomele menya vnosilo. Kogda metët, togda 'melo' otnyud' ne 'melo.' Vesnoy teryayesh' remeslo. Takoye delo."¹¹ This leads to the phenomenon of play with names and sound-leitmotifs. With Gogol's Akakiy Akakiyevich, Bashmachkin and Chichikov in mind, it is interesting to find such "symbolic" names as Sporyshev, Lippanchenko, Shishisanov, Pepp Peppovich Pepp, Dudkin, and Shishnarfiyev in Belyy's works. In Aksënov: Patrick Thunderjet, Marina Kulago, Yan Strudelmacher, Fruktozov, Slon, Morzitser, Velikiy-Salazkin, Buryak Fasolevich Borshchov, Monogamov, Teleskopov, Popenkov, Fuchinian and Kulachenko. These names display clear similarities between Belyy and Aksënov. Belyy's heroes in *Petersburg* are Apollon Apollonovich Ableukhov and his son, Nikolay Apollonovich; some of Aksënov's names are only slightly different from these: Pavel Apollinariyevich Durov, Vadim Apollinariyevich Kitousov, and the five heroes of *The*

Burn all have the same patronymic: Aristarkh Apollinariyevich Kunitser, Panteley Apollinariyevich Panteley, Samson Apollinariyevich Sabler, Radiy Apollinariyevich Khvastishchev, and Gennadiy Apollinariyevich Mal'-kol'mov.

The use of refrain, repetition and sound-leitmotifs is frequent in both Belyy and Aksënov, but I shall only give a few examples. Belyy: "Zashurshalo, zatrepetalo, zabilos' . . . pisknula mysh'" (MG,306), which is very similar to Aksënov's: "Zatovarilas' bochkotara, zatsvela zhëltym tsvetkom, zatarilas', zatyurilas' i s mesta stronulas'."[12] This is repeated throughout *The Tare of Empty Barrels*, and becomes not only a refrain but a sound-leitmotif related to the main image (the tare of barrels) of the work. The sound-leitmotifs, as observed in the sounds related to the names, are discussed by Belyy himself; everything related to the Ableukhovs is full of the sounds '*pll-pll-bl*' (Apollon Apollonovich) and '*kl-pll-bl*' (Nikolay Apollonovich); for instance: "Senator pitayet strast' k figure parallelepipeda" (*pr-l-llp-p*; MG, 306-7). Also, the provocateur Lippanchenko has a sound motif—'*pp*': "Pepp Peppovich Pepp budet shirit'sya, shirit'sya, shirit'sya; i Pepp Peppovich Pepp lopnet: lopnet vsë," which according to Belyy even has the exact meaning of sounds related to the destruction of the prison. He concludes that the content of the plot is, as in Gogol', hidden in the sounds (MG, 307). In Aksënov we find a similar tendency to express content through sound and to characterize protagonists by their play with words and sounds. In *The Steel Bird* the dictator, Popenkov, is described through his absurd computer-language: "Rurrro kalitto Zhizha Cuiza Drong! Chivilikh zifafa koblo urazzo [. . .];" the sly old Mamanya in *In Search of a Genre* is characterized by her play with words and sounds: "Velikiye Luki . . . Luki-Luchiny-razluki-izluki," or "Trëshechka trëshechka moya trefovaya trëshechka, shishechka, shishechka [. . .];" and in *The Tare of Empty Barrels* Stepanida is characterized by the same feature: "Okh, babushka-krasovochka, [. . .] zakruchu tebya, babul'ka, bul'ka, yayki, mleko, buterbroter, tantsem-shmantsem."[13]

In the following I shall try to investigate the main principle of "prose-poetry" in Belyy and Aksënov, keeping Belyy's statement in mind: "Moya proza—sovsem ne prosa; ona poèma v stikhakh" (My prose is not prose at all, it is a poem in verse).[14]

2b. Retardation of plot, action and characterization

The plot of *Petersburg* is extremely simple and short. A young man (Nikolay) has promised a political terror organization to kill his own father (Apollon), a well-known senator. When the time comes, the organization reminds him of his promise and brings him a time-bomb. The bomb explodes, but nobody is hurt by it. This kind of short and simple plot reminds one of Gogol's and Dostoyevsky's plots, a fact that Belyy was well aware of. Similar simple plots are to be found in Belyy's other novels *Moskva* (Moscow) and *Maski* (Masks). In all cases it is clear that the plot development is of minor importance.

The same could be applied to the characters. The depiction of the heroes is not given in order to create "real" characters, real human beings, but the protagonists are bearers of "ideologies," they become "independent" voices thrown up against each other. In this respect Belyy followed Dostoyevsky rather than Gogol'.[15]

Apollon and Nikolay Apollonovich Ableukhov are the protagonists and the antagonists of the novel. Apollon is a 68-year-old senator, a small person with a face like papier–mâché. He is characterized very simply through his gestures, blowing his nose, breaking pencils, and through his speech, which consists of never completed sentences. Nikolay is a student, he hates his father, Apollon, although from time to time he also feels love for him. When he detonates the time-bomb he makes the excuse to himself that there will be plenty of time to throw the bomb into the Neva. He is false and almost schizophrenic, his eyes are elusive and his movements are vehement, he talks to himself. Sof'ya Petrovna Likhutina is perhaps the best example of the puppet-like characters in the novel. She is unhappily married to the officer Sergey, and has a romance with Nikolay. In a quarrel she calls him a "Krasnyy shut" (Red clown), to which he replies: "Yaponskaya kukla" (Japanese puppet).[16] She is the beautiful *femme fatale* of the novel, has dark hair, the color of her face is pearly, and her eyes: "ne byli glazkami, a glazami: glazishchami tëmnogo, sinego-tëmno-sinego tsveta (nazovëm ikh ochami)"; her red lips are too big, but her teeth ("zhemchuzhnyye zubki") shine when she smiles her childish smile.

One can only agree with S.D. Cioran when he points out that all the major characters in *Petersburg* are grotesque exaggerations of earlier symbolist concepts.[17] Sof'ya is obviously a parody of Solov'yëv's divine Sophia and of Belyy's own "Woman Clothed in the Sun." The Ableukhovs represent two major streams of thought: Apollon is a grotesque exaggeration of Comtean positivism and Nikolay represents the metaphysical idealism of Kant.[18]

The main emphasis is neither on the plot nor on the development of characters as representing "real" persons; instead the author reveals an "idea" or a lyrical theme through a network of subthemes, motifs, symbols, through the character's hallucinations, symbolic dreams and metaphysical discussions, to which I shall return.

Aksënov uses the same principle as Belyy. His plots are almost always extremely simple. In *The Tare of Empty Barrels* a group of people gathers to drive with Volodya Teleskopov to the nearest town, where he is supposed to deliver the empty barrels. From this town the people are expecting to continue their journeys. They arrive only to discover that nobody wants the barrels. Then they continue the journey together. In *In Search of a Genre* there is practically no plot, except for the various episodes, in which the hero Pavel Durov becomes involved during his endless journey around Russia. In *Our Golden Hardware* a group of scientists gathers in a scientific town in Siberia searching for the "Dabl'f'yu," but the whole thing is destroyed by the demonic Memozov, and the novel ends with their starting all over again.

In all these works the heroes are like puppets and marionettes, we get the impression that they are nothing but masks. Their psychology is described in their dreams, inner monologues, nightmares, hallucinations, etc., in which they become aspects of mankind; their dreams often mix and often one cannot determine who is dreaming. A good example of this is *The Tare of Empty Barrels*. Here Aksënov has assembled a selection of his earlier characters—the drunken rolling stone, Volodya Teleskopov, who has drifted around for several years; the fighter, womanizer and sailor, Gleb Shustikov; Vadim Afanas'yevich Drozhzhinin, the intellectual, who is one of the world's few experts on the Latin-American country of Khaligaliya; *ded* Mochënkin, a retired colorado beetle inspector, who has never seen such a beetle, and who is constantly writing complaints about everything and everybody to the relevant authorities; Irina Valentinovna Selezneva, the young, beautiful but naive teacher from the local school, who feels she has buried her "treasures" out here in the back of beyond. It is characteristic of these people that their existence lacks meaning; they have widely different dreams, but they have one thing in common: they end with the appearance of the good man. Gradually they become united in love and solicitude for the barrels, and their dreams start to resemble each other under the influence of their common love for the barrels. The characters do not develop or change, but they unite in their common quest. Like marionettes they act mechanically according to their given characters, as in the reactions to events along the way, as for example when they meet the old man with a swollen finger: Volodya suggests vodka as a cure, Stepanida a wise man's prescription, Mochënkin wants to exploit the event to get an invalid's pension, Irina proposes some pork fat, Gleb amputation, and Vadim to go to the doctor.

In both Belyy and Aksënov the development of plot and characters does not lead to any solution. The expectations are not fulfilled, the time-bomb explodes but it does not kill the senator; Teleskopov brings the barrels to the town, but nobody wants them. In fact, most of Aksënov's experimental works have this feature in common, nothing really happens and on the last page the characters start all over again or continue their eternal waiting.

2c. The development of a lyrical theme

In *Petersburg* Nikolay has feverish hallucinations of having swallowed a sardine tin that in fact is a bomb. Here Belyy uses a technique taken from Gogol' (for example, the devil jumping out of the portrait in "The Portrait") and turns it into hyperbole: the fiction about the bomb becomes reality, the thoughts of the father and his son about the bomb make it a real bomb, threatening not only Ableukhov but the whole Empire; even the author is struck by fear: "Budet, budet prestarelyy senator gnat'sya i za toboyu, chitatel', v svoyey chërnoy karete" (yes, the aged senator will come chasing after you too, reader, in his black carriage; MG, 304). This way of transferring dream into reality is also found in Aksënov. In *The Burn* the sculptor Khvastishchev has made a marble sculpture of a dinosaurus, which is destroyed by the authorities, but in the heroes' last adventure it becomes alive and assumes hyperbolic dimensions, threatening the whole city of Moscow. Like the overcoat in Gogol's "Shinel'" (The Overcoat) and the red Domino (Nikolay) in *Petersburg*, the sculpture is supposed to frighten the people, to take revenge; but in *The Burn* nothing of the sort happens, people react simply by saying that the state has the matter in hand. In *Our Golden Hardware* the feverish dream is animated in the demonic surrealist Memozov, who threatens not only the heroes, their life work, the *Zhelezka* 'Hardware' and the author, but also the novel itself: "Why has Memozov come to Pikhty, and is he not laying claim on the most important—the very novel, the Hardware?"[19]

S.D. Cioran convincingly explains *Petersburg* in terms of the Apocalypse, maintaining that both a metaphysical and a family apocalypse are projected in the extremely simple "fabula."[20] The main symbol is the bomb, representing destruction and chaos. The apocalypse of the Ableukhovs is played out against a general apocalyptic atmosphere in Russia during 1904-5. This atmosphere is associated with the threat of Asia and Mongolism. The novel takes place shortly after the Russo-Japanese War and on the eve of the 1905 revolution. In Dudkin's nightmare the object of the fear is identified with the Mongolian threat:

> All the peoples of the earth these days are rushing from their places, great strife there will be, such strife as the world has never seen, a yellow horde of Asians [. . .] (90)

Petersburg is the Babylon, the streets of which lead into nothingness and the realm of Antichrist. But in Dudkin's nightmare Peter the Great comes alive as the Bronze Horseman, forming the opposition to the Mongolian threat. Both Dudkin, the former Nietzschean, and Nikolay, the neo-Kantian, believe in the coming Apocalypse. Nikolay's desire to kill his father (the internal Apocalypse) is intermingled with cosmic ideas in his dreams, in which his father in different incarnations is the tyrannical ruler (Chronus, Saturn). The assassination plan results in Nikolay's nightmare in the destruction of the whole universe:

> Nikolay Apollonovich began to hallucinate; he [. . .] was transferred into blood in order to fulfill the original purpose [. . .] devour everything with a flame, the ancient East has strewn our Age with a shower of bombs. (196-99)

Apollon has a similar dream, in which Nikolay appears as a Mongolian agent of chaos and destruction. It becomes clear that both are unable to hide their Asiatic origins and both serve Mongolism—Nikolay "Mongolizes" Europe and Apollon "Europeanizes" Mongolism.[21]

If we look at the development of the lyrical theme in Aksënov's works we will find out that he uses not only the same techniques but often also the same motifs. Thus, in *The Steel Bird* (and in other works) we find the motif of the struggle between East and West in Russian culture, here shown in metaphorical hyperboles. The evil, satanic Mongol, Venyamin Fedeoseyevich Popenkov (the Steel Bird), fights against the West, jumping around in Peter the Great's boots:

> The fact is, the oriental ornament was in direct and irreconcilable conflict with the ancient Greek amphora hanging directly above it [. . .] naturally they were all devilishly interested in the luckless amphora, nobody knew what was inside it [. . .]. So one day he [the Steel Bird—P.D.] [. . .] jumped up, tore down the Greek amphora, smashed it to smithereens on the floor, and, back in his niche, proclaimed: 'There's your despicable filthy dream, there's nothing in it but dead flies [. . .]. Is it understood now, who's boss?'[22]

Aksënov uses cosmic dreams and hallucinations in all the major works. In *The Burn* we find the same dream-motif as in *Petersburg*, namely the motif of the child-eater Cronos. As a last attempt to live and work in the USSR, the saxophone player Samsik Sabler tries to stage a show called "The Battle Between the Gods and the Giants." At the last moment it is stopped by the censorship; but before this happens Samsik has a hallucionary vision of it, in which the Gods fight against the Giants, but when Cronos, the dictator, appears they join in the common battle against him: "In Pergamon, in the marble, the Gods and the Giants fought together against Cronos."[23]

In *The Burn* Mongolism is associated with Stalinism and the system of oppression, while the West is identified with Youth and Freedom:

> Like it or not, all you nomenclaturists and protocolists and Marxist clerics, but you won't be able to wipe out this "insignificant proportion of our otherwise mentally healthy youth," and you will never completely crush out the Europe in Russia. (O, 349)

As in *Petersburg*, the heroes of *The Burn* are not able to control time and space; the time and space elements are constantly in a state of flux, even the five main characters appear to be five aspects of one person. The last chapter, which is this person's unsuccessful symbolic escape from Stalinism leading to suicide, is a surrealistic masterpiece, where time and space merge and mix. In a cosmic premortal hallucination the escape ends on the moon, where (as in *Petersburg*) it becomes clear that thoughts are autonomous forces and exist outside the body. The hero finds a Stalinist, Cheptsov, on the moon, but he is no longer a human being but a "philosophical structure." The hero dies and is carried through Moscow, and, as always in Aksënov, the eternal expectation is stressed:

> An immediate and deafening silence descended on Moscow, and in this silence millions of souls were trembling, not with fear, but with the closeness of the encounter, with a nameless feeling. (O, 441)

The main theme in *The Burn* is the struggle against the materialistic and rationalistic way of thinking, and a search for another, spiritual reality; but the people never find it, they will always be searching.

In all Aksënov's works the theme of humanity's search for spiritual values in the modern world could be called *the* lyrical theme. It is always described in different aspects, from different points of view, through series of symbols, metaphors and dreams, like a theme with variations in a poem or a piece of music. While Belyy's "prose-poetry" without doubt has made its impact on the poetical-lyrical side of Aksënov's prose, the roots of Aksënov's musicality are to be found on the other side of the ocean, in American jazz and literature.

3. Aksënov and American literature

> This is one of those strange things which you could call invisible pollination of flowers, some kind of strange connection between what would seem to be totally different cultures, different worlds . . . and yet similar phenomena occur simultaneously without having had influence

on each other, but apparently this influence does exist in an astral, nonreal sphere.

Aksënov on Bob Dylan and Vladimir Vysotsky

The American Beat poet Allen Ginsberg in his early poem "Death to Van Gogh's Ear" compares the suicides of two poets, Hart Crane (1899-1932) and Vladimir Mayakovsky (1893-1930)—who at almost the same time expressed a visionary belief in a utopian future of America and Russia respectively:

> Just as Mayakovsky committed suicide to avoid Russia
> Hart Crane distinguished Platonist committed suicide to cave in the wrong America [. . .][24]

Describing the horrors of life in both America and Russia he continues:

> I see nothing but bombs
> I am not interested in preventing Asia from being Asia
> and governments of Russia and Asia will rise and fall but Asia and Russia will not fall
> the government of America also will fall but how can America fall
> [. . .]

In many ways this poem sums up the attitudes not only of the American Beat Generation, as expressed in the works of Ginsberg, Ferlinghetti, Snyder, Kerouac and Burroughs, but also of its Russian counterpart, the "New Wave" in Russian literature of the sixties.

As the Beats totally identified themselves with a whole generation of hipsters and beatniks, so the "New Wave" represented the Soviet youth, the *stilyagi*, born of the destalinization era, The Thaw and the renewed influence of Western thought and lifestyle. Together with E. Evtushenko, B. Akhmadulina, A. Voznesensky, A. Gladilin, Vysotsky and Neizvestnyy, Aksënov was the most prominent representative of this movement.

Basically the Beat Generation and the "New Wave" were non-political movements, but they both rejected the blind materialism of their respective systems, as expressed in Ginsberg's poem, which ends by expressing a belief in the good ones who do not yet exist; but:

> They exist in the death of the Russian and American Governments
> they exist in the death of Hart Crane and Mayakovsky.

A similar belief in the human spirit despite all monstrous governments is expressed in Aksënov's otherwise pessimistic novel *The Burn*. Here the American Patrick Thunderjet in a discussion calls the USA and USSR "two monstrous octopi, gigantic bags of semiliving protoplasm" (O, 107), but his Russian friend Panteley objects that protoplasm consists of individuals with intellect, soul and longing for God.

In many ways Aksënov was close to the Beats, but his first acquaintance with American literature came through "The Lost Generation."

3a. From Hemingway to Kerouac

Aksënov's literary career started at the very peak of the renewed opening toward Western literature in Russia. By 1955 Americans began to be translated into Russian—Hemingway, Fitzgerald, Faulkner—in an attempt to satisfy the Russian reader who was eager to swallow all that came from the West, be it Coca Cola, jazz, books or jeans.

Aksënov has several times described his first acquaintance with American literature in Leningrad, 1955, where he read Hemingway's story "Cat in the Rain" and later other stories:

> Faulkner I adore, and I am amazed by his wonders, although I feel a little confined in his prose. Hemingway I simply love and I always think of him as an older friend. In the universe of his prose there is room for your own movements.[25]

He not only loves Hemingway, he also borrows from him, for example the title "Out of Season" (*In Search of a Genre*). The title of the story "On the Square and Across the River" (Na ploshchadi i za rekoy), which is about the symbolic death of a Hitler figure, parodies Hemingway's war novel *Across the River and into the Trees* (Russian translation: *Za rekoy v teni derev'yev*). In *The Burn* Hemingway becomes a symbol of love and freedom, and I think that Hemingway's significance in Aksënov is that of a symbol rather than as a writer. It is, in my opinion, an exaggeration to speak of a Hemingwayan period in Aksënov's writing—a view held by Aksënov's friend E. Neizvestnyy and others. In spite of Aksënov's statement, I find the parallel for Faulkner much clearer. Thus, it is very likely that Aksënov has been inspired by Faulkner's experiments with "shifting points of view" in the "epistolary" novel, *As I Lay Dying*—a technique widely used by Aksënov in *Oranges from Morocco, A Ticket to the Stars, The Tare of Empty Barrels* and other works.

In his early writing the most striking parallel is not to Hemingway or Faulkner nor to the Beats, but to J.D. Salinger. Aksënov denies having read *Catcher in the Rye* before writing *A Ticket to the Stars* (1961), which sounds quite probable because it was not translated at that time. *A Ticket to the Stars* was part of an international phenomenon in literature, named "Jeans Prose" by the Yugoslavian scholar A. Flaker in his book *Modelle der Jeans Prosa* (1975). Apart from the Russian Aksënov and the American Salinger, such writers as the Danish K. Rifbjerg, the Polish M. Hłasko, and the German U. Plenzdorf should be mentioned in this connection. What some of the works of these writers have in common is a new, young narrator creating a new style based on the language of big city youth, and expressing doubt in the social and cultural values of the established (grown-up) world.

In 1964, Aksënov, being already a famous writer in the Soviet Union, met with John Steinbeck and Edward Albee in Moscow, and in the following years he was allowed to travel abroad (see Biography). Aksënov certainly was a propagandist of the West in Russia, not only as a novelist and short story writer but also as a translator (e.g., Doctorow's *Ragtime* and John Updike's *The Coup*). Furthermore, he wrote a work in 1975-6 about his stay in America as a visiting lecturer, called *'Round the Clock, Non-Stop*. This is a very important work which can be regarded as a key to Aksënov's writing. Apart from writing about Hemingway, Faulkner, Fitzgerald, Salinger, Steinbeck, H. Miller, Orson Welles and Vonnegut, Aksënov here expresses his great admiration for the Beat Generation, the Hippie movement and Bob Dylan.

Comparing the Hippies with the Beats, he writes that they did not create any literature as the Beats had done, but they assimilated Kerouac, Ginsberg, Ferlinghetti and Corso. Displaying his enthusiasm for the Hippie movement, Aksënov points out that it became a certain life-style, music, rhythm and movement: "the new youth got certain wealthy people to doubt the values of the dollar world [. . .] and they brought a certain carnivalism into everyday life."[26]

Aksënov was apparently deeply moved by his visit to The Six Gallery in San Francisco, where Ginsberg in 1956 had read his famous poem "Howl," announcing the existence of the Beat Generation to enthusiastic listeners, while Kerouac acted as a conductor:

> There were other of Allen's friends too, Ferlinghetti, Corso, Peter Orlovsky, but Jack was the craziest of them all [. . .] Poor Kerouac, I feel sorry for Kerouac. I will never forget the 'Jazz of the Beat Generation' [. . .] Apparently there is something fatal in these outbursts, these flights over the heads of people in wild, spontaneous prose, that is impossible to stop. I used to know kids like Kerouac at home [. . .] We felt strangely close to the American writers of our generation [. . .] we seemed to stare into each others' eyes in a special way, as though we were searching for some unknown common childhood.[27]

Thus, Aksënov was impressed by the Beats; they even occur several times in his works, e.g., Ginsberg and Ferlinghetti in *The Burn*. In the following I shall try to illustrate some features which are common to Aksënov and Kerouac. I would like to underline that I am here talking about parallels rather than influences. In spite of the great differences between the two writers, they have some important features in common which are rooted in their common interest in jazz music and in their involvement in the New Wave and the Beat Generation, respectively.

3b. Musicality of style

Kerouac's theory of "Spontaneous Prose" was written down in 1958 in the article "Essentials of Spontaneous Prose." Here he describes the language of "Spontaneous Prose" as being "an undisturbed flow from the mind of personal secret idea-words, blowing (as per jazz musician) on subject of image." The idea was to give the reader "telepathic shocks and meaning excitement" by following free association of mind into "limitless blow-on-subject seas of thought, swimming sea of English with no other discipline than rhythms of exhalation and expostulated statement."[28]

Indeed, the style of his famous novel *On the Road* is expressive in the sense that it is surprising and emphasizes sound and rhythm. One example:

> The behatted tenorman was blowing at the peak of a wonderfully satisfactory free idea, a rising and falling riff that went from 'EE-yah!' to a crazier 'EE-de-lee-yah!' and blasted along the rolling crash of butt-scarred drums hammered by a big brutal Negro with a bullneck who didn't give a damn about anything but punishing his busted tubs, crash, rattle-ti-boom, crash. (OTR, 196-7)

In this extract there is no full stop, the narrative is led forward by the growing ecstasy of the music, a rising flow of the sound and the frequent use of short sentences and short, often monosyllabic words, which is supposed to imitate the rhythm of the drums. Thus, Warren Tallman is right when he writes that "Jazz is a dominant influence" in Kerouac's fiction.[29] He maintains that the music and language of the Negroes and the outcasts of the big cities was taken by the Beats, as an expression of acceptance of the *Now* as the only promised land, because these people had already lost the battle of establishing their psyche within the social continuum. It reflects a desire to release into the moment through the spontaneity, improvisation and association of jazz. According to Tallman, the Beat-writers assumed the principle of spontaneous creative freedom from jazz and bop-music in order to describe the "increasing ambiguity of meanings and relations between people."

Aksënov's style in comparison to Kerouac's is more compact and perfected, it is written-down music, but not without a similar kind of spontaneity. It is the result of a similar interest in jazz and it mirrors a similar carnivalistic jazz atmosphere. The purpose of Aksënov's style is perhaps best expressed by his "anti-author," Memozov, who wants to "bore into the narrative like a foreign body" and by means of the iron hand of the psychedelic experiment, to "rouse these fossilized brains."[30]

Aksënov made friends with the famous Russian saxophone player A. Kozlov (Kostya Rogov in *The Burn*), with Vysotsky and Okudzhava, and with the underground jazzworld of Leningrad. One of the five main characters of *The Burn*, Samsik Sabler, who also appears in *Our Golden Hardware*, is a professional saxophone player. Samsik's debut in 1956 is described, as is the whole atmosphere of the time:

> It was in November 1956 at a party in the Mining Institute of Leningrad in the orchestra of the first Leningrad jazz-musician Kostya Rogov. Then birds and guys stood shoulder to shoulder in the dancehall, miserable, greedy youth, drunk on the wind of Europe which had suddenly blown into our corner. Poor, tight-panted hipsters, despised by everybody, how they tried to look like those Broadway kids. (O, 29)

In this crowd Samsik suddenly sees Marina Vlady (French movie star, Vysotsky's wife):

> We hardly knew Bee-bop then, we had only just about heard of Parker and Gillespie, and weren't doing any improvising yet, but there we were swinging a treat. Suddenly I noticed my Marina Vlady dancing with some guy [. . .] and I literally started shaking with jealousy and resentment, and my sax suddenly howled so bitterly, so hopelessly [. . .] and Kostya then understood that a new kind of jazz was being born, or maybe it wasn't even jazz, but some powerful spirit blowing my whistle across oceans [. . .]:
> I am poor,
> > poor,
> > > poor
> And let everybody know it—I'm not rich
> I am poor,
> > poor,
> > > poor
> And let everybody know it—I have no rights [. . .] (O, 30)

As in real life, these musicians were arrested and "beatened" by the *militsiya*, but nevertheless: "We were playing then. But was it only a question of jazz? We wanted to be one with all the world, with the so-called 'freedom-seeking humanity.'" (O, 32) Essentially Aksënov here expresses the same thing as Kerouac through jazz. It is done in a different way because Aksënov personifies the saxophone and lets it speak, whereas Kerouac, so to speak, lets the style imitate; but the atmosphere is the same and jazz is in both cases used as a tool for the heroes to escape the cold reality of postwar America and Russia, to escape into the ecstatic *IT*.

3c. In Search of *IT*

One of the important characteristics of Ginsberg's poetry and Kerouac's prose is that it is highly autobiographical; they wrote about themselves, about their friends and what happened to them. The same is true of Aksënov, although he to some extent tries to hide it (see Interview); but his prose cannot be labelled "confessional" as can Kerouac's. In this respect Kerouac follows Henry Miller and Anais Nin, constantly analyzing himself, always occupied with his inner thoughts and desires. This, and the influence of W. Reich's *The Function of the Orgasm*, are the main reasons why love and sex are very vital parts of his writings (most clearly in the novel *The Subterraneans*). Kerouac and the other Beats shocked the American public by depicting sex in detail in all its aspects—from polygamy to homosexuality—and by the heroes' constant use of drugs and alcohol. Similar motifs occur in Aksënov, but most of his works containing political allusions and sex and drug addiction were not published in the USSR (e.g., *The Steel Bird, Our Golden Hardware, The Burn* and *The Island of Crimea*), not to mention the works he has written since he was forced to leave his country in 1980. And the ones that were published were censored; thus the parts describing sex, drugs or the use of "vulgar language" in *In Search of a Genre* were removed.

Sex, drugs, alcohol, speed, travels, jazz, etc. are all tools for the Beats and for the "New Waves" to achieve what Kerouac called "IT" or what in Aksënov has several names but is always connected to the notion of the "moment." In both cases it is a reflection of the writer's orientation towards the present—to experience and enjoy the present as a means to escape reality.

In *On the Road* the hipster hero, Dean, is living with several women at the same time and having babies with them; but this does not prevent him from visiting a public house in Mexico with the narrator, Sal. Smoking marijuana and drinking, they join in a gigantic orgy with drunk, underaged prostitutes. The purpose of this as well as of the two's rapid and uninterrupted journey around the United States is to reach the indefinable *IT*. Says Dean: "the point being that we know what IT is and we know TIME and we know that everything is really FINE." (OTR, 208) TIME is associated with *IT*, the highest level of which is ECSTASY:

> And for just a moment I had reached the point of ecstasy that I always wanted to reach, which was the complete step across chronological time into timeless shadows [. . .] I realized that I had died and been reborn numberless times. (OTR, 173)

Spiritual experience lasts only for a few minutes, and it seems as if it forces you to search for new ITs: "Wishing I were a Negro, feeling that the best the white world had offered was not enough ecstasy for me, not enough life, joy, kicks, darkness, music, not enough night. (OTR, 180)

Sal's search for ITs finally leads to his symbolical rebirth in the tropical jungle night of Mexico. The rebirth is based on his attempt to escape the banalities of reality. Both he and Dean want to become another person, not caring about materialistic values:

> I wished I were a Denver Mexican, or even a poor overworked Jap, anything but what I was so drearily, a 'white man' disillusioned. All my life I'd had white ambitions [...] but now [...] wishing I could exchange worlds with the happy, true-hearted, ecstatic Negroes of America. (OTR, 180)

During short periods of time, the ITs, a symbol of the eternal change is created. Such an ecstatic moment happens when you see the world in a new light. The permanent state of ECSTASY is madness. When you become "the holy saint" (as does Dean), you have IT permanently, you have entered a "new and unknown phase of things" with peace in the soul.

Aksënov does not seek any solutions for mankind in the basic primitive of Indian and Asiatic religions, as did many of the Beats, but he does turn to religion (see the short story "The Village of Sviyazhsk" and *The Burn*), and in many of his works people join in an almost religious and mystical love for, e.g., a whore (Nina in *The Four Temperaments*), a tare of empty barrels, or a metallic complex of scientific institutes (*Our Golden Hardware*). In Aksënov we find many similarities to the Beats—a jazzy carnivalistic atmosphere, use of drugs and alcohol. The scientist Gromson (*Our Golden Hardware*) makes experiments with narcotics, Tolik (*The Burn*) has his first sexual experience while drugged, and the son of Andrey Luchnikov (*The Crimean Island*) is constantly smoking marijuana.

The sexual descriptions, images and metaphors in Aksënov are frequent and detailed to a degree unseen before in Russian literature. From time to time, especially in *The Burn*, the naturalness of these depictions moves from the joy and beauty of love (as in Kerouac) to sexual harassment and abnormality (as in W. Burroughs), as for instance in the scene where the perverted Stalinist Cheptsov is raping his stepdaughter.

In general, the action of *The Burn* takes place in the underworld of Moscow and Magadan among drug addicts, alcoholics, prostitutes, perverts and miserable artists.

In both the Beats and the New Waves the heroes are constantly moving around in one way or the other, searching for something. The journey motif has its roots in both American literature (*The Adventures of Huckleberry Finn, Catcher in the Rye*, etc.) and in Russian literature (*A Journey from Petersburg to Moscow, Dead Souls*, etc.), but it is extraordinarily intensified in Kerouac and Aksënov. Most of Aksënov's early stories are based on journeys—in trains (*A Ticket to the Stars,* "Victory," "Lunches of 1943"), in airplanes ("Halfway to the Moon"), or on a truck (*The Tare of Empty Barrels*). In *In Search of a Genre,* more than in any other work, the journey motif is made the center of attention. The hero, Pavel Durov, is an artist in a dying genre. He is driving around in his *Lada,* searching for the meaning of his genre, "genre" being a metaphor of both "art" and "life." As in Kerouac, a great deal of attention is paid to the car, and from time to time Durov asks himself: "What is a car?" Among other things, he concludes that it is an armchair that moves forward in space at great speed, and that it is "a little house on wheels, part of your own protective sphere."[31] Thus, the car can be seen as a symbol of man's isolation and the road as a symbol of life as a search. But what are they searching for?—Sal and Dean used all sorts of means ("kicks") to achieve IT, the short glimpses of enlightened spiritual insight. Indeed, Aksënov's heroes have similar moments of enlightenment, for instance when Durov is dreaming of a happy time, when he has an aim in his life:

> At last this was the unceasing moment in firm space, part of which I had become. All three sorrows of ours, past, present and future, came together in this wonderful time of life.[32]

The concept of the moment in which time and space merge is very characteristic for Aksënov as a means to escape the cold, objective world into another spiritual, utopian world.

In *Our Golden Hardware* a group of scientists led by Velikiy-Salazkin builds a scientific complex of institutes in Siberia, searching for the mystical "Dabl'-f'yu" by "realistic means." But Salazkin's rival, Gromson, the "leader of the thinking youth," comes closer to it, using narcotic, surrealistic experiments. It is not made clear what "Dabl'-f'yu" is (as you cannot define IT), but it is what they all are searching for, the dreams, ideals and longings of man in the materialistic society depicted as a scientific complex of steel, bricks and glass.

Sal and Dean were reborn into a mystical, oriental religious belief (a development similar to Kerouac's own as described in the novel *The Dharma Bums*). Others of the Beats tended to develop into political radicals (Ginsberg, Ferlinghetti), or into total pessimists with no faith in the future of mankind (Burroughs). Only in *The Burn* (and "The Village of Sviyazhsk") does Aksënov describe his and his heroes' conversion (rebirth) to a religious belief. In the beginning of the seventies the five heroes of *The Burn* were desperately seeking spiritual and professional resurrection, but they were time and again disillusioned by the growing neostalinism in the USSR; and the book ends with the symbolic Christ's death, the body of the hero being carried through Moscow in "deathly-sharp premonition, in deathly-joyful hope, in deathly-near expectation." (O, 441)

Much more could be said about the similarities between Aksënov and the Beats, e.g., about the use of science-fiction (Burroughs), the attitude towards society, education, marriage, etc., and about the characters themselves. The heroes of *On the Road* and the Beats in general were:

> The mad ones, the ones who were mad to live, mad to talk, mad to be saved, desirous of everything at the same time, the ones who never yawn or say a commonplace thing, but burn, burn, burn. (OTR, 8)

The heroes burned out, as did the movements; but the phenomenon is an outstanding example of "invisible pollination of flowers" in modern literature, and some of the Beats and the New Waves are still going strong, which is exactly what Aksënov has proved by his remarkable novel *The Burn*.

FOOTNOTES

1. "Beseda s pisatelem Vasiliyem Aksënovym," *Kontinent*, No. 27, 1981, p. 445. *Fiesta* is the Russian title of *The Sun Also Rises*; however, this novel was also published in London (England) in 1927 under the title *Fiesta*—eds.

2. The two following chapters are revised versions of papers presented to the AATSEEL Annual Meeting in Chicago, December 1982 and the CAS section of the Learned Societies meeting in Vancouver, June 1983.

3. P. Meyer, "Interview with Vasily Aksenov," *Russian Literature Triquarterly*, No. 6, 1973, pp. 570-71.

4. A. Belyy, *Arabeski*, Moskva, 1911, Reprod. USA, p. 93.

5. A. Belyy, *Masterstvo Gogolya*, Michigan, 1962, p. 309. References to this edition will hereafter be given in the text abbreviated as MG.

6. Another important element in Belyy and Aksënov is their use of "skaz"—much more attention is paid to 'how the story is told' than to the story itself (hence B. Èykhenbaum's *Kak sdelana Shinel' Gogolya*)—an element doubtlessly coming from Gogol'; furthermore, the style in both writers is distinctly metaphorical. In the case of Belyy this was first noticed by Roman Jakobson in his "Randbemerkungen zur Prosa des Dichters Pasternaks," *Selected Writings*, Vol. 5, The Hague, 1979, pp. 424-25, and I have described this side of Aksënov's style in my book *The Function of the Grotesque in Vasilij Aksenov*, Aarhus, 1982.

7. These four examples are taken from: V.P. Aksënov, "Stal'naya ptitsa," *Glagol*, No. 1, 1977, p. 35, and *Zolotaya nasha Zhelezka*, Michigan, 1980, p. 30, and "Zatovarennaya bochkotara," *Yunost'*, No. 5, 1968, p. 42. Here and in the following examples I shall give no translation when analyzing the style of Belyy and Aksënov; wherever translations appear, they will be taken from my book, translated by Robert Porter, or Inger Lauridsen, to whom I am sincerely grateful.

8. A. Belyy, *Moskva*, München, 1968, pp. 15, 17.

9. V.P. Aksënov, "Stal'naya ptitsa," pp. 73-74, "Poiski zhanra," *Novyy mir*, No. 1, Moskva, 1978, p. 132, "Zatovarennaya bochkotara," p. 48.

10. A. Belyy, *Maski*, München, 1969, p. 84.

11. "Poiski zhanra," p. 120.

12. "Zatovarennaya bochkotara," pp. 37-38, 40, 50, 62, 63.

13. "Poiski zhanra," pp. 144, 146, "Zatovarennaya bochkotara," p. 57.

14. *Maski*, p. 11.

15. About this phenomenon see M. Bakhtin, *Problemy poètiki Dostoyevskogo*, Moskva, 1979.

16. A. Belyy, *Peterburg*, Moskva, 1978, pp. 63-66; references to this edition will hereafter be given in the text abbreviated as P.

17. S.C. Cioran, *The Apocalyptic Symbolism of Andrej Belyj*, The Hague, 1973, p. 155.

18. *Ibid*, p. 137. About Aksënov's 'beautiful ladies' see I. Lauridsen's article in this volume.

19. *Zolotaya nasha zhelezka*, p. 120.

20. *The Apocalyptic Symbolism of Andrej Belyj*, p. 137.

21. *Ibid.*, p. 149.

22. Here taken from *The Steel Bird* (transl. by Rae Slonek), in Vasily Aksenov, *The Steel Bird*, Michigan, 1979, pp. 17-18.

23. V.P. Aksënov, *Ozhog*, Michigan, 1980, p. 355. References to this edition will hereafter be given in the text abbreviated as O.

24. Allen Ginsberg, "Death to Van Gogh's Ear," in *Kaddish and Other Poems*, California, 1969.

25. V.P. Aksënov, "Kruglyye sutki non-stop," *Novyy mir*, no. 8, 1976, p. 118. About the influence of Western literature in Russia during these years, see M. Friedberg, *A Decade of Euphoria*, Bloomington, 1977.

26. *Ibid.*, pp. 92-93.

27. *Ibid.*, p. 117. After finishing this article I learned that Mr. Thimothy Pogacar had found similar "Beat" elements in Aksënov. Cf. "Vasily Aksyonov and the American Counterculture" (paper presented at the 1981 ATSEEL meeting), to be published.

28. Jack Kerouac, "Essentials of Spontaneous Prose," in *On the Road: Text and Criticism*, New York, 1975, p. 531; references to *On the Road* are given from this edition, abbreviated as OTR.

29. Warren Tallman, "Kerouac's Sound," in *On the Road, op. cit.*, p. 524.

30. *Zolotaya nasha zhelezka*, pp. 47-48, 102-3.

31. "Poiski zhanra," p. 121; about the journey motif in Aksënov see M.L. Gyldengren, "Mellan statik og dynamik," *Slavica Othiniensia*, no. 2, Odense, 1979.

32. "Poiski zhanra," p. 119.

NOTES ON AKSËNOV'S DRAMA

Konstantin Kustanovich

1. INTRODUCTION

From many possible approaches to the study of a body of literary works, I have chosen one which seems to me most interesting and expedient apropos of Aksënov's drama. Instead of giving a general thematic analysis of each play in its chronological order (the most traditional approach to works which have previously been very little dealt with by critics) or concentrating on a narrow specific topic, I intend to analyze several most important and distinctive features of Aksënov's drama. This approach, however, entails a certain arbitrariness in the selection of the features to be discussed and requires on the part of the reader familiarity with the plays' texts. But for a serious and dedicated student of Aksënov, this article might, I hope, prove a helpful tool in studying his work.

Aksënov has written five plays which were published in one volume issued by Hermitage in 1981.[1] Although four of them were written in the mid-60s, none was published in Russian until 1979, when *The Four Temperaments* (1967) appeared in the almanac *Metropol*. In 1980 Aksënov's last play, *The Heron*, appeared in *Kontinent*. His second play, originally titled *Your Murderer* (1964) and later renamed *PORK* (Potseluy, Orkestr, Ryba, Kolbasa), was translated into English and included in the Spring 1977 issue of *Performing Arts Journal*. His first play, *Always for Sale* (1963), and the fourth, *Aristophaniana and the Frogs* (1967-68), became available for the first time in the Hermitage volume. Only one play has been produced— *Always for Sale*, staged in the Moscow theater *Sovremennik* by Director Oleg Efremov in 1965*. There were plans for the production of *PORK* by A. Èfros in the Lenin Komsomol Theater, of *The Four Temperaments* by O. Efremov in the Sovremennik, and of *Aristophaniana and the Frogs* by V. Pluchek in the Moscow Satire Theater; but these plans have never materialized.

As a writer, Aksënov has always demonstrated a keen perception of the most subtle changes in the social and cultural life of his generation. He began his literary career as a spokesman for the young, for high school and university graduates. But as times changed, Aksënov matured and his writing changed too, reflecting not only the ideological and psychological

---

* *The Heron* was staged in Paris in 1984—eds.

transformations in his characters but new tendencies in politics and art as well. One of the most important and powerful trends in the literature of the 1960s was the reaction against the stiff style of socialist realism and consequently against realistic writing in general. As early as 1959 Andrey Sinyavsky wrote:

> I put my hope in a phantasmagoric art, with hypotheses instead of a Purpose, an art in which the grotesque will replace realistic description of ordinary life. Such an art would correspond best to the spirit of our time. May the fantastic imagery of Hoffmann and Dostoevsky, of Goya, Chagall [. . .] teach us how to be truthful with the aid of the absurd and the fantastic.[2]

A similar anti-realist reaction in literature took place in the first third of the twentieth century. A shift from the notion of art as a mere reflection of life to the romantic conception of art as creation manifested itself first in works of the symbolists. Later, literary groups and movements like the futurists, the Serapions, or the *Oberiuty* and authors like Babel', Olesha, or Bulgakov upheld the anti-realist trend. It is not a coincidence that Aksënov feels a special kinship with precisely the writers of this period and an affinity for their artistic methods. In an interview with Priscilla Meyer, he said the following:

> I'd like to write about the intelligentsia of the turn of the century as if they were my acquaintances: Gumilëv, Akhmatova, Mandelstam, Blok, the girls in their circle, how they sat around in the "Stray Dog" café.[3]

It is interesting to note that Aksënov's characters (and Aksënov himself as well) move from hope to disappointment and despair in a sequence that evokes the spiritual path of the younger symbolists: Blok, Belyy, and Solov'yëv. Hope and exuberance, the "gold and azure" of youth, music and worship of the Beautiful Lady were replaced in them by weariness, "blizzards," the hum of the coming revolution, and, finally, by emptiness, silence, death.

The similarity in general mood and sociopolitical atmosphere accounts for the similarity in artistic methods and means of expression in Aksënov's drama and that of the first third of the twentieth century.[4] Of course Russian modernist drama of that period was part of the general trend in European drama, away from the naturalist theater. It is hard to overestimate the influence of such Western playwrights as Ibsen, Strindberg, Maeterlinck or Hauptman on the Russian symbolists and neo-romantics. But while in the West the new theater could evolve from symbolism via the work of Brecht and Pirandello into an idiom marked by the experimentation of such contemporary playwrights as Frisch, Dürrenmatt, Sartre, Camus, Ionesco, and Beckett, in Russia the evolution of modern drama was brought to a halt and did not proceed beyond Mayakovsky, Bulgakov, Èrdman, and Olesha.

Only in the 1960s when modernist art was "legalized" (within very narrow limits) did the revival of anti-realist tendencies begin.

Thus Aksënov's drama, which manifests these tendencies more vividly than the work of any other contemporary Soviet playwright, has its roots in both the Russian theater of the first third of the twentieth century and contemporary Western drama. Though Aksënov's plays exhibit both influences, they also depart from the works of his predecessors and employ modernist devices to new purposes. I will therefore not only discuss the most important of these devices but also address the question of their artistic functions.

2. LITERARY TECHNIQUE

2.1 Theatricalism

One typical modernist technique, which can be called theatricalism, consists in "laying bare" the theatrical nature of the play. Blok's *The Fairground Booth* may serve as a classic example of this device. In Aksënov's *PORK*, the protagonist Alekhandro is also the author of the play, the creator of the other characters. There is, however, a very important structural difference between the roles of the two Authors. Blok's Author does not participate in the action, he carries out the purely external function of underscoring the parodic nature of the play. Alekhandro, however, is not only the author but also a character on the same level as the other characters. These two roles are inseparable. Alekhandro cannot exist independently from his creation. He lives only while his characters live and dies when they die. The character of Alekhandro expresses Aksënov's notions of the absolute equality of fantasy and reality and of the right of an artistic creation to be treated as a living phenomenon. In his fictionalized dispute with an American student Aksënov argues:

> But really, the artist's fantasy is reality too. Fantasy is perhaps no less real than a rustle of leaves. [. . .] Sometimes it seems to me that real phenomena which surround us, such as sunsets, river currents, stones, birds, sand are no less mysterious than fantasy. [. . .] One talented poetess and a no less talented prosaist believe that our writings already exist in the world even without our participation. The artist only names the yet unnamed.[5]

Incidentally, such a notion of art and the artist again leads us to the symbolists and their conception of the artist as a connecting link between *realia* and *realiora*.

The introduction of the author into the action of a play is usually a constituent element of the "play-within-a-play" construction. In *The Fair-*

ground Booth or *PORK* the fact of staging a play is not actually mentioned. But in such plays as Chekhov's *The Seagull*, Mayakovsky's *The Bathhouse*, or Bulgakov's *The Crimson Island* the process of staging is an explicit part of the plot. In different plays the "play-within-a-play" construction has various functions: parodic in *The Seagull*, satirical in *The Bathhouse* and *The Crimson Island*. One could consider Aksënov's *The Four Temperaments* as also belonging to the "play-within-a-play" genre. Some elements of the plot support this interpretation. When a wall in the tower where Razrailov conducts his experiment collapses, it turns out to be a set on the stage. Even stronger evidence is provided by the conflation of the figure of Evgeniy Aleksandrovich, the actor who plays the Eagle in the "theater" part, with the Eagle fighting the Steel Bird in the "tower" part. At the end of the penultimate scene the identification of the tower with the stage and the Eagle with Evgeniy Aleksandrovich seems indubitable. In the stage directions, Aksënov refers to the same pile of debris now as scenery, now as remnants of the tower laboratory. And it is not the actor Evgeniy Aleksandrovich but the Eagle who finally admits to the stagehand Katyusha that he loves her.

There are, however, also signs which would negate the "play-within-a-play" interpretation. In the last scene, the "four temperaments" and shepherdesses retain the social roles which they had in the "tower" part. While the roles of Razrailov and Kiber are slightly changed, none of these characters is presented as an actor who, after the play is over, comes to a café to meet other members of the theater group. This suggests that the action in the tower is not a play but reality (resembling Kistochkin's "dimension" in the first epilogue of *Always for Sale*), parallel as it were to the reality of the theater. And in the last scene these two realities merge.

Thus, there is obviously conflicting information in the play, which renders its plot ambiguous. This ambiguity, however, should not disturb the reader because, as P. Dalgård has noted, ". . . it is not the plot which is the essential thing in the work."[6] In fact, Aksënov takes the device of oxymoron, usually limited to the level of a single phrase or sentence, and applies it to the level of the entire plot. As any oxymoron, the plot of this play contains two contradictory elements or statements: one supporting the "play-within-a-play" interpretation and the other denying it. And, as in any oxymoron, neither of these statements should be taken literally; they rather constitute a new entity without which the author could not have carried out his artistic task. Indeed, if there were a consistent plot explicitly indicating a "play-within-a-play" construction, as in *The Crimson Island*, for example, it would make the work a clear-cut allegory. On the other hand, the complete separation between the two sub-plots, a parallel development without any overlapping, would render incongruous their conjoining within one 0play and create a problem with the last, most important scene in the play. By sacrificing consistency of plot, Aksënov gains in terms of expressiveness.

2.2 Features of the old theater

Like his modernist predecessors, Aksënov often turns to the techniques of earlier drama. He uses the structural elements of ancient drama (prologues and epilogues) in *Always for Sale*, and *Aristophaniana and the Frogs* is rendered completely in the manner of the ancient Greek comedy. His use of masks is a feature of the *commedia dell'arte*, which was very popular among the symbolist dramatists. In *The Heron*, Aksënov finds an interesting use for a structural element of the seventeenth century "school drama: "the "interludes." In the "school drama," a serious religious performance alternated with short comic skits or "interludes," which usually had nothing in common with the main action and served to entertain the tired audience. A kind of "interlude" also appears between the acts of Aksënov's play, but here the skits are inseparably connected with the main plot line and play a very important role. In the first "interlude," three sisters go to meet a bus full of Polish tourists returning home from a trip to the Soviet Union. The episode is a symbolic portrayal of the Russian people who, attracted to the values (more material than spiritual, perhaps) of European culture, simultaneously feel intimidated and inferior before it. ("The main thing now is to show them that we are not savages," says one of the sisters.) In the second "interlude," the fusion of Russia with Europe is achieved through the symbolic copulation of Monogamov and *Tsaplya* 'The Heron'. But Monogamov represents only an insignificant part of the Russian people, the intelligentsia, and not even the whole intelligentsia but those few who, in exchange for being able to pursue European humanitarian ideals, took the risk of breaking up with Stepanida Vlasovna[7] and refused all the privileges which loyalty to her could have secured. These "interludes" underscore the symbolic nature of the whole play. The fact that they are differentiated by being moved into the intermissions, combined with their transparent symbolism, endows them with great generalizing power which might be lost were they just ordinary scenes within an act.

2.3 Other literary borrowings

As was previously mentioned, Aksënov closely follows the structure of the ancient Greek comedy in his *Aristophaniana and the Frogs*. In fact, he goes even further. He directly borrows the plots of Aristophanes' two comedies *The Frogs* and *Lysistrata*[8] and uses them as the framework for his own play. Moreover, he often quotes whole lines from these comedies. This is nothing less than literary allusion in the broadest sense of this word: it includes not only individual passages but also motifs, episodes, and entire plot components. The subtitle of *Aristophaniana* is "A Burlesque in Ancient Traditions." It is a burlesque indeed. The characters who reside in ancient Athens and Pluto's kingdom of the dead, Hades, speak at times in stilted Sovietese or the contemporary colloquial language of Aksënov's generation, abundantly using slang and quoting from Russian poetry and prose, including Aksënov's own works. However, Aksënov has chosen the burlesque form not for its parodic and comic potential (although this too is important) but as still another means of *ostraneniye*, as an appropriate medium for conveying his views about the place and role of the artist in a totalitarian society.

In *The Heron*, Aksënov again uses the plot of well-known plays. He himself refers to it as a "paraphrase of Chekhov's *The Seagull*."[9] Another Chekhov play, *Three Sisters*, also serves as a source text for *The Heron*. These allusions, however, function differently from those in *Aristophaniana*. If in the latter Aksënov just borrows a "shell" for his comedy and the reader does not really have to know the original text to fully apprehend the play, in *The Heron* the role of the source texts is much more significant. Here Aksënov creates his characters in opposition to the equivalent characters in Chekhov. Instead of a seagull it is *The Heron* who is Monogamov's ideal. The symbolic load of this image is more complicated than that of the seagull in Chekhov and will be discussed later, but there are common aspects to both images: youth, femininity, love. What is important is the change in the nature of the ideal, the contrast between the ideals of Chekhov's and Aksënov's worlds. The ideal of Aksënov has not become less lofty, but in its transition from seagull to heron it has lost its romantic gloss, its beauty, become earthlier, more mundane, but also more tragic. The fate of *The Heron* is sealed not by the outcome of a "dachnyy roman" (a summer affair) but by the evil forces embodied in Kampaneyets and the Gannergeytses.

Aksënov also relies on contrast with a Chekhovian source in portraying his three sisters. The function of the contrast here is clearly to downgrade the sisters in Aksënov's play.[10] Like Chekhov's sisters, they seek a meaningful existence; only their ultimate dream is not Moscow but Europe. By association with Chekhov's sisters, one would assume that they are looking for spiritual meaning. And it seems that the author supports this assumption by telling us in the description of the sisters:

> The main thing for the sisters is the search for justification of their existence. Great discontent, yearning for something pure and bright brings them, perhaps, closer together than their questionable kinship.[11]

But a few lines later Aksënov concludes his description with the words, "The common feature of the sisters is the condition of being greatly undermilked" (sostoyaniye sil'noy nedodoyennosti),[12] indicating that their discontent is basically of a physical nature. And indeed, at the end of the play one of the sisters confesses to the Heron:

> I too fooled everyone, I fooled myself. Pretended to be a great aristocrat of spirit but actually dreamed only of a penis.[13]

In discussing any literary allusions, one inevitably has to consider the parodic function of their use. But in Aksënov this function plays no important role. To be sure, parody is one of Aksënov's favorite occupations. He parodies media clichés, political slogans, the speeches of Soviet leaders, popular songs, and popular literary characters including his own, but he rarely parodies specific literary texts.[14] The importance of distinguishing between parody and other uses of known literary texts has been underscored by V. Propp. He wrote:

> Parodies should be distinguished from the use of forms of well-known literary works for satirical purposes directed not against the authors of such works but against phenomena of a sociopolitical nature. [. . .] Such cases are not parodies. One can rather call them *travesties*,[15] meaning by the travesty a utilization of a ready-made literary form for purposes other than those intended by its author.[16]

But one should not conflate "The use of forms of well-known literary works" with satire alone. As previously stated, literary allusion has a variety of different functions. The dimensions of this article do not allow me to present an exhaustive discussion of these functions in Aksënov's drama, but they are by no means limited to satire.

2.4 The function of the fantastic

One of the most significant aspects of Aksënov's drama is the use of the fantastic.[17] All five plays employ it to a different extent and for different purposes. But, in general, the fantastic performs two functions in Aksënov's works: satirical, or allegorical, and generalizing, or symbolic.[18] Satire always has a specific target, not necessarily a concrete person or group of persons, but also perhaps a concrete social phenomenon, political event, literary movement, etc. When this target is hidden behind a more or less transparent fantastic mask (for purposes of *ostraneniye* or getting around the censorship or both), the function of the fantastic may be referred to as allegorical. The generalizing function is more complicated and more productive. Using this function, the writer does not imply a specific discernible person or phenomenon but combines, according to some generalizing principle, several phenomena or characters, thus creating a new reality more universal and complex than the existing one. If in the fantastic allegory the writer tries to preserve as many features of the phenomenon being allegorized as possible (without destroying the fantastic illusion), then in the fantastic generalization he tries to maximally disengage the resulting picture from concrete reality (without crossing the border separating the symbolic from the absurd[19]).

There are no purely allegorical or purely symbolic works among Aksënov's plays. All of his plays contain both allegorical and symbolic elements, so the character of a play depends on the balance between them. If we take the two plays most contrasting in this respect, *PORK* and *The Heron*, we can only say that the former is more allegorical than the latter but not that the former is allegorical while the latter, symbolic. Let us take a closer look at the two functions of the fantastic in these plays.

PORK was "written under the influence of the ideas expounded at the historical meeting of the party and government with representatives of the creative intelligentsia in March 1963 . . . ,"[20] as Aksënov sarcastically puts it. Thus the target of the play is the Soviet government's policy toward art and artists. But it is not an exclusively satirical work. Its main theme consists in an important ethical problem, that of the artist selling out his talent under some kind of social pressure. The combination of the two artistic tasks in the play, satirical and philosophical, results in a conglomeration of both allegorical and symbolic characters and images.

The action is transferred to an imaginary environment. But Aksënov preserves the *couleur locale* of Soviet reality, producing in the Soviet reader so-called "presence effect" (èffect prisutstviya)[21], i.e., immediate and continuous identification of the unfamiliar environment with Soviet life. Thus the allegorical connection is established and sustained. It is impossible to list here all the references to Soviet reality which create the "presence effect" in this play. To mention just a few, there is first the dialogue between the poet Alekhandro and the policemen who come to demolish his hut. This dialogue reproduces almost verbatim the shorthand record of Iosif Brodsky's trial in March, 1964. Then one of the Stockholders mispronounces certain words, an evident allusion to Khrushchëv's habit of mispronouncing the same words. The same Stockholder calls the U.S. a "paper tiger" and makes it clear that with the help of the national cavalry, that country should not be any threat whatsoever. This is doubtless a reference to the fact that the Soviet cavalry under Voroshilov was sent to the front to counter enemy tanks when the war broke out with Nazi Germany. Neither can there be any doubt about the prototypical institution for the Department of Public Harmony, where the rebellious artists are killed one by one. And finally, the very core of the plot, the idea of a whole country controlled by whiskey manufacturers, inevitably brings about an association with the major problem of alcoholism in Soviet society and the huge profits the government extracts from selling alcohol to the population.

Thus the majority of characters, places and images represented in the allegory are easily identifiable. But an allegorical reading proves ineffectual when applied to Pork Kabanos. What does he represent? Hack work that kills the artist's talent (as happened to Chartkov in Gogol's *The Portrait*), or a totalitarian power which destroys disobedient artists, or the tempting world of comforts and goods for the obedient? None of these interpretations is exclusively applicable to Pork, yet there is enough evidence in the play to support each of them. So Pork should be treated as a symbolic rather than allegoric figure.

Such polysemy is characteristic of many personages in *The Heron*, which renders it perhaps the most symbolic of Aksënov's plays. Monogamov is a Soviet diplomat working for UNESCO. At the same time he represents the Sovietized Russian people. His name, Ivan Vladlenovich,[22] suggests both Russian and Soviet aspects in Monogamov which are emphatically opposed in the play. (The surname may indicate his exceptional love for his motherland.) But Monogamov is also a typical idealistic Russian *intelligent*. He has had the rare opportunity of travelling abroad and yet has not been seized by the mercantilism so prominent in other characters of the play. As an *intelligent* he possesses the Dostoyevskian sense of personal responsibility for every suffering human being on earth. And finally there is evidence that Monogamov together with Lësha the Sewer and Lësha the Guard participated in the artistic revival of the early 60s.

The Heron is another example of a polysemous character. First of all she has two "phenomenal" hypostases, a bird and a girl who works at a sewing factory. I have already mentioned some symbolic aspects of the Heron: love, femininity, youth (specifically the youth of Monogamov's generation). She also represents European culture or possibly the link between Russian and European cultures. Still another symbolic meaning of the Heron is freedom. Stepanida says about her:

> No, she is not a heron! She is something beautiful. When I was little it seemed to me that she existed somewhere, but I've never seen her.[23]

If we remember that Stepanida Vlasovna is an alias for "Sovetskaya Vlast'" (Soviet Regime), then we deduce that she was a child during the years immediately following the revolution, when it indeed seemed that freedom was near. But Stepanida "has never seen her" after all.

Such characters as Stepanida and Kampaneyets are mostly satirical, although they too combine in themselves several different (but proximal) planes of meaning. Thus, owing to the polysemy of the characters, the whole play may elicit different interpretations. It may be a play about the Soviet intelligentsia whose hopes for liberalization have vanished into thin air; or a play about the great tide of Soviet literature which came ashore in the early 60s and completely ebbed by the late 70s; or, lastly, a play about the whole Russian people in the last 20 years of its thousand-year history.

Similarly, but in different proportions, the other plays combine the allegorical and symbolic functions of the fantastic. In *Always for Sale* the balance is upset in favor of allegory, in *The Four Temperaments*, in favor of symbolism. In *Aristophaniana and the Frogs* allegory and symbolism are divided between the upper world and Hades, respectively.

3. THE DRAMATIC WORKS AS AN ORGANIC PART OF AKSËNOV'S LITERARY PRODUCTION

When dealing with Aksënov's plays one cannot help remembering that he is also a prominent prose writer. There are two aspects that one should consider in order to establish a relation between the two genres: (1) prose elements within the plays and (2) thematic and/or ideological similarity between the plays and prose works. First of all I would like to turn to the structural confluence of prose and drama in Aksënov's last play, *The Heron*. The play, consisting of three acts, lacks the traditional subdivision into scenes. There are, however, ten prosaic inserts and a song in the play which both divide it into smaller units and carry out a very important structural function. They are written in rhymed prose and in most cases in an iambic meter. Three of the inserts provide additional information about the main character, Monogamov, but the rest have no direct connection with the action of the play. They are fictional narratives concerning various sociophilosophical issues, such as Russia's historical development, the evolution of her rulers in the new times (their "devilization"), the fate of her artists, the transience and immortality of art, the birth of fascism, and the complexity and diversity of the world. Since there are no direct semantic ties between the inserts and the dramatic action it would be more appropriate to call them "digressions," in the tradition of *Eugene Onegin* and *Dead Souls*. But as in these works, they are inseparable in *The Heron* from the main body of the text.

Similar digressions appear in *In Search of a Genre*, published just two years before *The Heron*. In both works they help to expand a concrete situation to the level of a social paradigm. In other words, a digression provides a general theme which is reproduced, as a variation, in specific episodes and characters. Thus, the digressions serve as yet another means (along with the use of the fantastic and the numerous allusions to and associations with Soviet life) to the symbolic elaboration of the strictly "dramatic" part of the play. For instance, there is a digression about a poet who used to be "a servant of extremely free muses" and who would write his creed every morning on the wall of his room. But one day, terrified by an official of some commission, he gave up his work and now plays cards with his stool-pigeon neighbor and has painted over his creed with brown paint. The same fate of a poet who gives up his work under political pressure is given by the author to Lësha the Guard. Such a parallel between the general (the poet in the digression) and the concrete (Lësha the Guard) suggests that Aksënov is interested in a more universal phenomenon than the case of an individual artist. In the same manner, the other digressions create an ideological background for the play.

Such intrusion of the prose into the drama is unique in Aksënov. In his other plays only the extensiveness of the stage directions and, in some cases, their belletristic character betray the fact that sometimes the framework of the drama is too narrow for the author.

The suggestion that a writer's works ought to be read as one text truly applies to Aksënov. His plays constitute a very significant chapter in this text. We find in both his prose and his drama the same or similar characters, motifs, ideas and images. A complete typological study of Aksënov's writings would probably make a book in its own right. It seems important, when discussing his drama, to demonstrate its contiguity with the prose works. However, in listing the main structural, ideological and "characterological" patterns common to Aksënov's drama and prose, his early novels (*The Colleagues, A Ticket to the Stars, Oranges from Morocco*, and *It's Time, My Friend, It's Time!*) as well as *The Island of Crimea* and "The Village of Sviyazhsk" should not be taken into consideration.[24] The first four belong to Aksënov's early, "happy" period and do not share many common features with his works of the mid 60s through the late 70s. The last two, although they contain some elements in common with the previous works, employ a different artistic method, slanting toward the realist tradition. Therefore an attempt at establishing general patterns within the whole body of Aksënov's *oeuvre* does not appear to be very productive.

Many of Aksënov's works depict a conflict between a totalitarian power and creativity or art, with each represented by one or several characters. In the following works this is the main conflict, the core around which the work is built.

— "Victory" (The antagonists are G.O. and the champion.)

— *PORK* (The Stockholders and Pork versus Alekhandro, Maria, Mikaelo, and Gregoro.)

— *The Four Temperaments* (Razrailov versus the "four temperaments" and Nina.)

— *The Rendezvous* (Smelldishchev and the Stinking Lady versus Leva Malakhitov.)

— *The Heron* (Stepanida and the devils versus Monogamov, the Heron and both Lëshas.)

— *The Burn* (Cheptsov and all his hypostases versus the Apollinariyeviches.)

In other works this conflict also appears either with a different antagonist (a non-artist) or as a secondary theme. In *Always for Sale* Kistochkin and *Bufetchitsa* 'the Waitress' perfectly fit the pattern of a totalitarian power, whereas their antagonist Treugol'nikov is not a creative individual but a survivor from Aksënov's earlier works (an affectionate parody of his "romantic" idealists). There is, though, a secondary character in this play, Serëzha, who is a journalist, that is, a writer of sorts who rebels against Kistochkin. The same pattern reappears in *The Steel Bird*. The residents of the house on Fonarnyy Lane, Popenkov's antagonists, are simple people of various professions like the residents of the house in *Always for Sale*. Here too, however, there is a detail which suggests the association with literature. The names of two residents are Vas'ka Aksiomov and Tolik Proglotilin, a clear allusion to Aksënov and Gladilin. In *Aristophaniana* the conflict between the dictator Alcibiades and the satirist Aristophanes is suggested but never realized.

In many works, the totalitarian power is associated with the image of a steel bird, a helicopter, or just metal. The characters which fit this pattern are Hitler ("On the Square and Across the River"), Kistochkin, Popenkov, Razrailov, and Smelldishchev. Quite often such characters appear as Evil Spirits, for instance, Kistochkin, Razrailov and the devils in *The Heron*. There is no direct indication that Popenkov (in *The Steel Bird*) or Smelldishchev and the Stinking Lady (in *The Rendezvous*) are also Evil Spirits; but the way they are depicted connects them with those characters who are. In "Victory," "On the Square and Across the River" and *The Heron*, such characters evoke, among others, associations with the Nazis.

The conflict between the totalitarian power and a character (or characters) representing creativity in general or art in particular proceeds usually in the following manner. The creative individual (I will further refer to him as the artist, implying by this term a general concept of creativity) is tempted by the power to use his talent in its services. In exchange, he will receive significant material rewards. The artist either refuses right away or yields to his greed (or fear), but his obedience does not last long. He rebels, is vanquished and is usually killed (in some cases the muse-figure, like Nina in *The Four Temperaments* or the Heron, perishes in his stead). But after death the artist rises and finds himself in a Utopian land, a land of freedom and harmony where he can now utilize his talent in full and where he, his beloved, and his friends live in complete accord with themselves and their art. This land and the dream of love and free creativity evoke Pushkin's "far sanctuary of work and chaste delights"[25] or the eternal refuge which Woland bestowed on the Master and Margarita. They reflect perhaps the greatest dream of any artist who has to live and work in a totalitarian society. Such a Utopia is realized in pure form in the short story "It's a Pity You Weren't With Us," in which bitter reality, as if by the wave of a magic wand, is transformed into a chain of happy meetings and events.

The above pattern of plot development applies, with insignificant deviations, to the following works: *PORK, The Four Temperaments* (the Utopian land is missing, but there is a moment of love and harmony before Nina is murdered, and when she reappears there is hope for her future liberation from Razrailov), *The Rendezvous*, the end of *In Search of a Genre* (the muse-figure is absent here), and *The Heron*. (In *The Heron*, Aksënov repeats the pattern of *The Four Temperaments*: like Nina, the Heron is killed, but before that she creates, in the thoroughly corrupt vacation home, an atmosphere of mutual love, understanding, and even repentance in the negative characters. And when she rises, there is also hope, although not for Monogamov's generation but for generations to come: the Heron, impregnated by Monogamov, has laid an egg.)

The ending of *The Tare of Empty Barrels* also agrees with this scheme. The *bochkotara*, rejected by the authorities, sails together in full harmony with all the other characters to the island where a Good Man is waiting. By analogy, this may suggest the interpretation of the *bochkotara* as art, which spreads love among people, unites them, yet remains extremely personal for each recipient.

I have outlined some motifs and patterns common to Aksënov's prose and drama. In my discussion, however, such titles as *Our Golden Hardware, In Search of a Genre*, and *The Burn* did not appear very often. The reason for this is that Aksënov employs in his longer works a different artistic method, one that accords with a different set of artistic tasks. When in a shorter work like *The Rendezvous, The Steel Bird*, or one of the plays he attempts to present a sociophilosophical problem within a limited space, the solution necessarily lies in greater generalization and hence greater schematization. His novels, on the other hand, tend toward a more epic depiction of life. Certainly there are common features in Kampaneyets (*The Heron*) and Cheptsov (*The Burn*), Stepanida Efimovna (*The Tare* . . .) and Mamanya (*In Search* . . .), Treugol'nikov (*Always for Sale*) and Kim Morzitser (*Our Golden Hardware*), Nina (*The Four Temperaments*) and Alisa (*The Burn*), the old man Mochënkin (*The Tare* . . .) and "Russian Homer" (the end of *The Burn*). But if the first members of these pairs are stereotypic characters lacking psychological completeness, the second, in spite of the fantastic circumstances surrounding them, are full-scale realistic figures.

This is not to say that one method is better or worse than the other. Each has its own merits and produces a different type of literature. Aksënov's plays are similar in type to the shorter prose, to such novellas as *The Steel Bird, The Tare of Empty Barrels*, and *The Rendezvous*. These works share one important feature: Aksënov is interested not in circumstantial or psychological conflict but rather in the conflict between two worlds. One is the world of free creativity by free man and the other the world of an inhumane, pragmatic force which tries to exploit the creative abilities of man and to suppress or destroy all that exceeds its narrow utilitarian purpose. Thus, the combination of the philosophical nature of these works with their satirical function gives rise to a fusion of symbolic generalization and allegory, a synthesis that defines Aksënov's major artistic method in his drama.

FOOTNOTES

1. V. Aksënov, *Aristofaniana s lyagushkami*, Ann Arbor, 1981.

2. Abram Tertz, *On Socialist Realism*, New York, 1960, pp. 94-95.

3. Priscilla Meyer, "Interview with Vasily Pavlovich Aksënov," *Russian Literature Triquarterly*, No. 6, V. II, Spring 1973, p. 571.

4. See detailed discussion of anti-realistic tendencies in Russian drama at the turn of the century in Harold B. Segel, *Twentieth-Century Russian Drama*, New York, 1979, Chs. 3 through 6.

5. V. Aksënov, "Kruglyye sutki non-stop," *Novyy mir*, No. 8, 1976, pp. 75-76. All translations quoted in this article, save the one on p. 99 (footnote 25), are mine—K.K.

6. Per Dalgård, *The Function of the Grotesque in Vasilij Aksenov*, Aarhus, 1982, p. 51.

7. Stepanida Vlasovna is the slang usage of a woman's name for the designation of the "Soviet regime" (Sovetskaya vlast'). Cf. a discussion of Stepanida Vlas'yevna in *Zolotaya nasha zhelezka*, Ann Arbor, 1980, p. 165.

8. Although Aksënov has changed the ending of the Lysistrata episode. Led away for two days by Alcibiades (not found among the dramatis personae in Aristophanes' play), she returns completely reformed and calls off the women's strike:

> O women of Athens, love a soldier
> Who smells of fire and fetid wild sweat!
> The more he is a bandit
> The better rider he is,
> And I, a little horse, have had a chance to learn this.

9. V. Aksënov, *Ozhog*, Ann Arbor, 1980, p. 269.
10. See a discussion of this function in Aksënov by Per Dalgård, pp. 10-11 and *passim*.
11. V. Aksënov, *Aristofaniana s lyagushkami*, p. 318.
12. *Ibid.*, p. 318.
13. *Ibid.*, p. 375.
14. One example of such parody is a poem by Lëva Malakhitov, "the idol" of Moscow of the 1960s as Aksënov introduces him in the cast of *Aristophaniana and the Frogs*. Malakhitov's poem, "Ya mozhzhevel'nik, mozhzhevel'nik malen'kiy . . ." (I am a little juniper bush) is a parody of one of the most powerful civic poems by Evtushenko. ("My karlikovyye berëzy"—We are dwarf birch trees). But even here the main purpose of this, no doubt, parodic poem is not to mock Evtushenko but rather to establish a solid connection between Lëva Malakhitov and the cultural milieu of the mid 60s.
15. Italics by V. Propp.
16. V. Ya. Propp. *Problemy komizma i smekha*, Moscow, 1976, p. 66.
17. In discussing this aspect I will intentionally avoid using the term grotesque since, as is, it has no concrete meaning. Different scholars attribute to it different functions, so anyone who attempts to use it should outline its semantic field (as has been done, for example, by Per Dalgård in his book on Aksënov, or S. Le. Fleming in his article on Mayakovsky and Bulgakov).
18. The term "symbolic" is used here in a broad sense with no reference to the symbolist movement at the turn of the century.
19. Unless the absurd is the writer's deliberate goal.
20. V. Aksënov, *Aristofaniana*, p. 7.
21. A term used by Soviet critics mostly for science fiction works.
22. Vladlen is an acronym for Vladimir Lenin.
23. V. Aksënov, *Aristofaniana*, p. 375.
24. Aksënov's last novel, *Paperscape*, was not available at the time this article was being written.
25. "'Tis time, my friend, 'tis time! . . ." Translation: Avril Pyman.

BEAUTIFUL LADIES
IN THE WORKS OF VASILIY AKSËNOV

Inger Lauridsen

Most of Aksënov's works are tales of a male quest. Men or groups of men fight or unite in quest of something: Pavel Durov is searching for his genre (*In Search of a Genre*); the scientists in *Our Golden Hardware* are digging for the mysterious particle W (*dabl'-f'yu*); the five main characters of *The Burn* are courting the elusive Alisa, etc. Thus, the object of the quest varies; but whether or not it is explicitly female, it is nearly always a "femininity" of sorts.

Male and female characters have fundamentally different functions in Aksënov's works, and they are seen as essentially different beings. This is underlined by the fact that many of the male characters, namely Pavel Durov, the scientists of *Our Golden Hardware*, and the five main characters of *The Burn* share the patronymic Apollinariyevich, which links them with the masculine sun-principle, whereas the female characters or femininities are often somehow linked with the moon as a feminine principle (notably Lunina in *The Island of Crimea* or the stewardess in "Halfway to the Moon"). In *Our Golden Hardware* the scientist Kitousov has the following to say on the nature of women:

> Kitousov: According to the Scriptures, Eve was created from Adam's rib, but before that there was Lilith, who was born of the moonlight. Some say that woman is the devil's vessel. Others sing that woman is love's shell. Is woman a human being, that is the question. A human being or a concomitant of humanity. No, I am not degrading women, not at all. Maybe this is a being more complicated than the human being? Woman is braver in love than man. Maybe this is a more important being? Maybe it is precisely the human being who is a concomitant of woman? Let's not compare. The important thing is that they are different beings.[1]

The category of gender, then, has a symbolic meaning in Aksënov's works. If, on the symbolic level, men are the subject, the "I" of Aksënov's world, then women are the Other, representing at the same time man's link with the world and the world itself. In this capacity woman can save man by making him whole and uniting him with the world, or she can destroy him by alienating him from the world and from himself.

The image of the world as a manifestation of the feminine in its destructive and saving aspects is deeply rooted in myth and literature; it is Eve who causes Adam's expulsion from Paradise, and it is the Virgin Mary who makes a return possible by reuniting man and God in Jesus. In literature, this world-view has at times been responsible for the replacement of real women characters by the twin images of angel and monster. In the early writings of Andrey Belyy the "Woman Clothed in the Sun" must confront the "Great Harlot," whereas the serene Lady of Aleksandr Blok's *Verses about the Beautiful Lady* gradually turns into the haunting prostitute of his famous, later poem "The Unknown Woman."

The early twentieth century non-realistic trends (including symbolism) in Russian literature have had a strong influence on Aksënov's development as a writer. Thus, the female type which this study aims to describe is in many ways comparable to the Ladies of the symbolists, and, as Aksënov has not yet provided a common term, I have chosen to call it the "Beautiful Lady." The Beautiful Ladies, who represent the saving aspect of the feminine, are discernible already in early works such as *A Ticket to the Stars*, but have become increasingly prominent as a type in Aksënov's later writing. Here, the type will be represented by the Unknown Woman (*'Round the Clock, Non-Stop*), Nina (*The Four Temperaments*), the Heron (*The Heron*), and Alisa (*The Burn*).

When the female character is made to serve as the agent of the male character's wholeness, she herself often becomes incomplete. This is the case with Belyy's Woman Clothed in the Sun and Blok's Beautiful Lady: Belyy's Woman becomes an increasingly complicated and abstract emblem of Belyy's philosophical and ideological aspirations, whereas Blok insists on the mystical, intuitive nature of his Lady. In this sense, Aksënov's ladies seem closest to Blok's and there are direct references to the Beautiful Lady, for instance, in *Our Golden Hardware* [see N. Kolesnikoff's article in this volume—eds.]. But the relationship between the female saviors and their admirers in Aksënov's works is more complicated than the one that obtains between the poet and the Beautiful Lady in Blok's verses. On the one hand, Aksënov's ladies have more independence: they may have some of Adam's rib in them, but they are also descendants of Lilith. They are not without their inner contradictions, and whoever wants to be saved by them must see and embrace them in their wholeness. On the other hand, they are not invulnerable, chaste and aloof like the Beautiful Lady. In other words, they retain a certain likeness to women, even when their appearance is fantastic or grotesque. It is interesting that Aksënov refers to Blok's Unknown Woman[2] in much the same way as he refers to the Beautiful Lady—they seem interchangeable to him.

One of the specific meanings with which Belyy invested the Woman

Clothed in the Sun seems to have been assimilated and transformed by Aksënov's female savior-figures. Under the impact of the Russo-Japanese War, Belyy comes to identify the Woman with Russia, whose mission it is to do battle with the Eastern "Beast," envisaged by Belyy not as an enemy army but as an alien, threatening force of apocalyptic dimensions. Similarly, Aksënov's ladies are sometimes symbolic of the original, free and innocent Russia. But to Aksënov the opposition is not so much between east and west as between Russia's real, Western, that is, European identity and her false, Soviet identity.

S.O. Cioran[3] has convincingly interpreted the Beautiful Lady and the Woman Clothed in the Sun as anima-images, and the same is possible with regard to the characters we are dealing with here. But when the partly unconscious anima-image is described, whether it is translated into a literary image or defined as a psychic entity in Jungian terms, it is necessarily transformed and individualized. Jungian theory, then, will be referred to here for comparison with, rather than interpretation of, literary characters. Aksënov's female characters are seen in the mirror of male consciousness—the author's and usually one of the male character's—and we shall compare them with the "archetypal Feminine" in Erich Neumann's interpretation as with a map of the mythologies surrounding man's perception of woman.

Neumann's model of the "archetypal Feminine" in *The Great Mother*[4] is so comprehensive that it can be said to represent an image of the world seen from the point of view of a son and lover. We shall summarize here some aspects which seem relevant to Aksënov's work and which will provide a framework for our investigations, while hopefully putting into perspective the mythic and the specifically Aksënovian content of the characters.

Neumann defines the Feminine in terms of four extremes: the Mother, the Virgin, the Old Witch (or the Terrible Mother) and the Young Witch. The Mother and the Old Witch represent the positive and negative poles of the "elementary character" of the Feminine. The "elementary character," according to Neumann, is determined by the material and maternal aspects of the Feminine; its significance is linked to such activities as bearing, releasing, growth, etc. on the positive scale, and holding fast, ensnaring, devouring, etc. on the negative scale. The Virgin and the Young Witch are the positive and negative poles of the "transformative character" of the Feminine. The "transformative character," which would seem to be identifiable with the anima-archetype, is the aspect of the Feminine which encourages male interaction leading to spiritual development. The functional spheres of the positive anima include sublimation, inspiration, wisdom, ecstasy, etc., whereas the negative anima is responsible for dissolution, madness, deliriousness, stupor, etc.

The four polar points in Neumann's model are not static, independent entities, they exist in a sort of dynamic equilibrium. A positive pole may easily turn into its negative counterpart and vice versa—madness may lead to inspiration, ecstasy may lead to madness, etc.

Aksënov's travel-memoir, *'Round the Clock, Non-Stop*,[5] includes a pure quest-tale, the TAA (Typical American Adventure). The TAA is set in a landscape of American mythology, including a trendy, possibly Mafia-infiltrated party at Topanga Canyon, a Western ghost town and a jazz festival. The plot and the constellation of characters are those of the fairy tale: in his quest for the beautiful princess, the naive hero is up against a devious adversary, but through the intervention of wise helpers his quest is finally successful.

Our hero, the Russian Moskvich, who has just arrived at UCLA as a visiting professor, is first reminded of his quest when he reads the following notice on a kiosk wall:

> Will the person who helped me up when I fell last Thursday on Westwood Boulevard at 11:35 p.m. please call 876-5432. (53)

Although he has never set foot on Westwood Boulevard, Moskvich immediately feels that the message is for him personally from Her, the object of his quest:

> the unknown Goal—something tall and sun-tanned with flashing eyes, something feminine in loose, white clothes. (53)

However, his adversary, the infamous "anti-author" Memozov, also sees the notice and takes down the telephone number while singing a frivolous song about an anti-adventure, a scheme to marry a girl rich and pretty enough to give you a good time (56).

The fallen woman, who is known alternately as "the Unknown Woman" (53), "She Herself" (82), "The Lady in Distress" (Zhenshchina-Zhertva) (95), "the Hazy Goal" (109), etc., is glimpsed a couple of times in the act of falling, while "helplessly, but beautifully waving a sleeve, or wing perhaps" (62). Apart from this, She makes three important appearances, again in accordance with the fairy tale pattern.

Moskvich's search first takes him to the Mafia party in Topanga (TAA II). On the way there, he passes the qualifying fairy tale trial by recognizing that his chauffeur, a "groovy" California beauty, is not the object of his quest:

> You who rose up from the city foam on the white crest of a Maserati! If you are a love goddess, then your hands are too grasping! If you are an angel, then you must be an angel of hell! (64)

At the party, he spots the Unknown Woman in the "Underground," that is, in the basement of the villa where she is engaged in a game of ping-pong with Memozov. She is losing, but "beautifully"—just as she fell beautifully—and there is an expression of "living human grief" (66) in her eyes. Moskvich seizes the ping-pong paddle in order to avenge his lady, but she is already fading away.

The second meeting takes place in the ghost town of Calico (TAA III). A full moon is hanging in the sky and Moskvich has been transformed into his childhood hero, the Ringo Kid (from the movie *Stagecoach*), fully equipped with guns, hat and menacing shadow, when She appears, this time out of the earth, her white clothes shining in the black of a mineshaft. In the conversation that takes place between them, the Unknown Woman confirms Moskvich as the true hero of this TAA:

> Was it you who fell on Westwood Boulevard?
> Yes it was me.
> Was it I who helped you up?
> Yes it was you.
> Was it you they kidnapped?
> Yes it was me.
> Was it you I was fighting for?
> Yes it was me.
> Can I come up to you?

But then the meeting is broken off by Memozov, who demands to see Moskvich's entrance ticket; in other words, he brings to attention the fact that the action is taking place in a museum and is therefore unreal. The Unknown Woman is saddened, but helpless, and she vanishes again.

By now Moskvich has found his helpers (TAA V). He joins forces with several John Waynes, Gregory Pecks, Gary Coopers, etc., the more experienced heroes of many a TAA. Together they go west, to Carmel-by-the-Sea, where the cowboys suddenly turn into American jazz stars of all times. With the moon shining down on them, the stage is set for the happy ending. While Memozov, now a music critic, succumbs to "natural forces" (109), She appears for the third time. She arises from the white sea foam like Aphrodite, steps onto the white sand of Carmel beach and starts singing like Ella Fitzgerald, Billie Holiday and Diana Ross. The fallen woman finally resurrected, Moskvich too breaks into song, revealing in himself the talents of several East European jazz musicians.

As the sweetheart of the western heroes, as the soul of jazz and as a typically Californian, long-legged, sun-tanned beauty, the Unknown Woman personifies the American essence which Moskvich came to look for. Yet she confirms his feeling that he knew her before he came to America and that he has been fighting for her (94). In this, I believe, there is a reference to the fight for renewal in Soviet arts during the years of thaw, a fight which was led by Aksënov and other young artists of the movement sometimes known as the "New Wave." The New Wave artists drew strength and optimism from the discovery of kinship with Western, particularly American, colleagues on the one hand, and from the rediscovery of a part of their own heritage, the Silver Age in Russian literature, on the other. This interpretation of the Unknown Woman as a symbol of the New Wave renaissance is reinforced by the references to silver which accompany her: before her appearance at the party, there is conversation about the Silver Age, later she is referred to as a "Silver Phantom," she comes out of a silver mine, in silvery moonlight, etc.

Although she shares her name with Blok's Unknown Woman, the heroine of TAA has more in common with his Beautiful Lady: we never quite know whether she is real or imagined; the vision of her is always ambiguous, hazy or dreamlike. Like Blok's Beautiful Lady, she is in many ways a typical positive anima-figure, a mystical known/unknown image of wholeness leading Moskvich through spiritual transformation. She fulfills the two tasks of making him whole as an individual—by bringing out his hidden singing talent—and uniting him with his fellow men, the Americans.

But unlike Blok's Beautiful Lady, Aksënov's Unknown Woman has human features: she is clumsy and sexy, she suffers and wants help. She is always accompanied by the moon, the favored feminine spiritual symbol, but she is not a purely spiritual, heavenly creature. She takes Moskvich on a journey through the domains of the underworld and the earth, finally uniting ocean and sky in her song: "How deep the ocean / How high the sky" (109). She is, then, the link between the three worlds of human existence: underworld, earth, heaven.

The Unknown Woman always wears white: she is not chaste, but innocent, as opposed to the groovy Mafia girl, the negative anima-image, who leads Moskvich into dangerous, delirious depravity. She represents a certain state of human innocence which is the basis of adventure, art and love, and as such she is eternal. She is powerless against Memozov, Moskvich's inner demon, who represents a rationalistic and essentially cynical approach; and yet Memozov cannot destroy her. To reach her, one must be like Moskvich: naive and totally committed.

In *The Four Temperaments*, Razrailov is attempting to create a new race of indestructible, programmable robot-people out of the raw material of dead human beings, including all the temperaments who have committed suicide on earth. However, the experiment, which is taking place in a tower outside time and space, is upset by the appearance of Nina.

Nina, a beautiful blonde in a mini-skirt, arrives in the tower with her eternal companion, the love-triangle, after being killed by her eleventh husband, who found her in bed with the tax collector. There is nothing virginal about her language; flirting seems to be her natural mode of communication:

> Hi there . . . But I thought . . . Now I recognize you, my dear. It seems you're a regular, ordinary man. Not bad, I might add. (gives him her hand) Well now, any suggestions?[6]

The reaction of the temperaments to Nina is like that of Moskvich when he first read the notice of the Unknown Woman: they did not know they knew her, but now they realize that they have been waiting for her all along. Razrailov's second-in-command, the computer Kiber, is the first to declare his love for Nina; he eventually grows first a head, then a penis, and becomes Nina's twelfth "de facto" husband. But Kiber is a new kind of husband: he seems to understand that Nina belongs rightfully to all who love her. On first meeting her he says: "But the triangle is not for you, Nina. It's too narrow a frame. End of transmission" (181). Later he willingly shares her with the temperaments: "Why confine yourself within the frame of one triangle when you can create a much more beautiful composition with lots of triangles?" (189)

Nina's promiscuity is of a symbolic nature. It is of course one of her all-too-human characteristics, reflected as such in her language and behavior; and yet, at the same time, the very fact that she has had twelve husbands, one of whom betrayed and killed her, points to her role as a Christ-like savior figure. This becomes evident in the grand apotheosis of picture nine. Here, Nina assures the temperaments and Kiber of her love for each of them, and they put her on a pedestal and start asking her questions. She reveals that she, like the Unknown Woman and Aphrodite, was born of the sea foam: "I can't quite remember. Some kind of bubbles, foam, blue sky . . . no, I don't remember" (195). When asked what she wants, she finally voices the innermost longings of the temperaments. Like her, they want to be living human beings: "Obviously I want to live, old man, I want to go down" (195). This idyllic scene is broken off by Razrailov, who first declares that he feels sexually attracted to Nina and then, seeing his experiment in extreme danger, tries to strangle her. He is prevented from doing so only through the intervention of the love-triangle, who has been strangely passive during the worshipping of Nina.

The love-triangle follows Nina everywhere and has done so since she was fourteen. Throughout most of the play, it makes a decidedly bad impression. When addressed, it goes into convulsions and repeats, in distorted form, the words of others mixed up with clichés of passion, creating a degrading caricature of Nina. Furthermore, Nina's death may be blamed on the triangle since it was a triangular intrigue that led to her murder. Thus, the triangle can be seen as a negative anima-figure, a symbol of Nina's sexuality in its destructive aspect as love that kills. But whereas the temperaments seem paralyzed by Razrailov's attack on Nina, the triangle comes to her aid, hurling itself at Razrailov: "I will not allow the hypotenuse to perish" (196). Here, then, the triangle represents the libido as a positive force, a necessary component of human love.

From Razrailov's point of view, human beings equal human material. When dealing with this material, the scientist (the intellect) must take its specific properties, such as sexuality and mortality, into consideration. Razrailov desires Nina as a body and then tries to strangle her. The temperaments, on the other hand, are worshipping Nina as an ideal, spiritual being, and insofar as they cannot save her from Razrailov, the latter is right about the "unity of opposites" (195). In the play, Razrailov's experiment is taking place high up in a tower; but in scene ten he talks about staging it deep down under the ground. The purely spiritual and the purely material are equally inhuman and can be equally evil. Nina is, as the love-triangle points out, the "hypotenuse" of human love linking the two catheti of spirit and body; she is what makes a triangle triangular and a human being human. None of the sides of the triangle is superfluous; says the love triangle: "The hypotenuse without both catheti is dead" (190).

Nina's gift of love belongs equally to each human being and it is the basis not only of individual love but of all noble aspirations including science (as represented by Kiber). As nothing human should be untouched by love, so nothing human is above or below Nina: she is a goddess and a tart. Like the Unknown Woman, Nina is independent of time: the temperaments will wait for her in the past, the present and the future; that is, they will always be human. As the divine aspect of the human, Nina is immortal; as Kiber explains to Razrailov: "You didn't understand me. I'm talking about eternal love" (185). Nina can be shot by her husband, but she cannot be strangled by Razrailov: "She is killed, but not dead" (186). Yet, she can be enslaved by Razrailov: "I always know that I am awaited, but I can't always come" (192).

In *The Heron*, a group of people staying at a boardinghouse in Lithuania are disturbed by the strange calls of a heron which flies in from Poland at night. Monogamov, a UNESCO worker on leave, arrives at the boardinghouse to see his wife and son. He immediately understands the language of the heron, falls in love with her and introduces her to the others, who also come to love her. However, according to the "iron laws of the drama,"[7] which are administered by Kampaneyets, the manager of the boardinghouse, the heron must now die. She is shot, but rises again and sits down to hatch out an egg which has been produced by her union with Monogamov.

By using the bird symbol, Aksënov inscribes his comedy in the particular tradition of bird plays such as Chekhov's *The Seagull*, Ibsen's *The Wild Duck* or Maeterlinck's *The Blue Bird*. Besides, the heron is likened to the firebird,[8] which sings so enchantingly in the gardens of Russian fairy tales that it eventually leads Ivan the Fool to the princess. In Aksënov's grotesque play, bird and princess have merged: it is the Heron herself who is the object of Ivan Monogamov's desire.

As a potential savior, the Heron has much in common with Blok's Beautiful Lady and also with the "Eternal Feminine" who appears in some of Blok's plays. Aksënov's play is, in fact, based on a scheme similar to that of Blok's: waiting for the ideal—appearance and disappearance of the ideal—renewed waiting. In Blok, however, the meeting with the ideal invariably leads to frustration, to the fear that the ideal is imaginary.

Although she is everything that the Beautiful Lady is, there is nothing immaterial about the Heron: the frogs she has eaten are dancing in her stomach, she is wearing a ragged old raincoat drenched in stinking mud, she works in a factory and has trouble making ends meet on her ninety roubles a month; her qualities as a sex partner are discussed, etc. By means of the grotesque principle of downgrading, Aksënov brings his miracle into the sphere of human experience and thereby overcomes the "iron laws," that is, the inherent determinism of Blok's and Chekhov's plays. The Heron is a metaphor, but a sexy one; she is equally at home in the swamp and in the sky, she is an animal and a goddess, she is as ambivalent and indefinable as life, she is simply the Heron. As Monogamov remarks:

> You're disgusting. You're sweet. You're sinful. You're holy. I ado-o-ore you! (penetrates) Are you the Heron? (361)

The levels of meaning united in the symbol of the Heron range from the most individual to the most universal, as suggested by the structure of the play: a relationship is established first between Monogamov and the Heron, then between the Heron and the other characters. The Heron touches Monogamov as a lover, the two Lëshas as artists, all the characters as individuals, Russians and inhabitants of the Earth.

When Monogamov first hears the hollow, longing cries of the Heron, he immediately knows that he is predestined to love her, that it is she whose existence he once guessed and whom he has unconsciously been waiting for. Like all true lovers he is unable to explain why he has chosen his beloved above all others, because explaining this would mean explaining the whole network of his personality into which her image is woven:

    Lësha textileworker. But why an animal?
    Monogamov. Because it's an animal!
    Lësha textileworker. But why a bird?
    Monogamov. Because it's a bird! (369)

The happy relationship with the Heron gives Monogamov new inspiration for his work, makes him appeal to the others—in high-strung rhetoric—for compassion and solidarity on a global scale.

Monogamov associates the Heron with youth, his own youth and youth as a state of mind. Thinking he has lost her he exclaims: "Farewell, farewell my youth!" (379). Similarly, two other characters, the Lëshas, recognize in the Heron the essence of a certain period in their youth, and it turns out that all three, Monogamov and the Lëshas, knew each other then. At that time Lësha-caretaker was an author and singer of songs about youth in opposition, while Lësha-textileworker wrote modernistic prose in the vein of Joyce. Both were part of a group that used to hang out in the café "Andromeda." However, when the authorities suddenly and brutally put an end to the period when such activities were permissible, both Lëshas were frightened and gave up their former identity. The period in question is obviously the "Thaw" of the early sixties, also dealt with in the novel *The Burn*. Incidentally, the heron as a symbol of the "Thaw" spirit also occurs in this novel. Like the main characters of *The Burn*, the Lëshas were part of the "New Wave" movement; like these, they got "burnt" and now they fear the calls of the Heron.

In the play, as well as in *The Burn* (and in *Our Golden Hardware*), the Heron is frequently associated with Europe: "You are Europe, youth, the dream!" (361). She flies in from Poland, paying no attention to state borders, and sometimes her appearance is accompanied by a vision of a gothic, European city. One of the things the internationalist Monogamov learns from the Heron is that Russia, like Poland, is essentially a European country: "You're the dream of all Russian men" (361), he tells her. Thus, the Heron, Europe, comes to signify the heart of Russia, her original identity. Part of this identity is the freedom of which Russia tasted a little during the "Thaw." The recent events in Poland have, as Aksënov points out,[9] given new, unexpected significance to the play.

The theme of freedom versus coercion is clearly articulated by the juxtaposition of the two climactic scenes of acts two and three. In act two, Kampaneyets walks about the stage, conducting his business over the telephone and gradually winding the cord around all the characters until they are all tied down and unable to move. In act three the Heron, now all splendor in a magnificent white dress, appears before the characters and they all move around the stage with her, confessing their sins and receiving forgiveness. Seeing the Heron in her splendid attire and recognizing her, the characters become themselves, shaking off the various personae they have been living. The oversized breasts and buttocks of Monogamov's wife, Stepanida Vlasovna (a common designation for *Sovetskaya vlast'* 'Soviet Power') suddenly explode, and she is now described as "wholly human" (375), perhaps with a reference to the concept of "socialism with a human face." At the same time as becoming themselves, the characters are reunited with each other:

> The Heron. And you, my Russian, you were the first to love me,
> and I loved you first, but now you are one of them.
> Monogamov. (radiant) Of course. I understand, my Heron.
> All. (with a sigh of complete happiness) Our Heron! (376)

Like the Unknown Woman and Nina, the Heron is at the same time a savior and someone who must be saved. Seeing Kampaneyets' gun pointed at her, she falls silent, clearly needing the help of the characters. But the characters feel powerless:

> Lësha-caretaker. (in despair) But what can we do against the laws of drama? We the unwashed?
> Lësha-textileworker. For that, you have to be born different. (378)

It takes a Monogamov to save the Heron, someone naive to the point of foolishness, but with enormous eyes and a great knack for learning foreign languages; that is, someone who is able and willing to cross the barrier of rationality.

The Heron, as a creature moving between heaven and earth, symbolizes the soul, that part of the human mind which is hardest to understand and which therefore comes closest to what we call divine. This, and her at the same time individuating and integrating effect on the characters, make the Heron a typical anima-image.

In her address to the characters (which she delivers in faultless Russian, as opposed to the half Russian, half Polish she used to speak), the Heron talks about salvation ("It has been said that all will be saved"; 377) as something not to be set apart from earthly life:

> I only know that around you is your world, my children. Sand and fir trees, my children. Swamp and sea, my children. (377)

She is giving the earth to the characters and this gesture is repeated in her giving Monogamov the egg. In her motherly aspect, the Heron is directly opposed to the Soviet bureaucrat and KGB informer Stepanida Vlasovna, who is an image of the "Terrible Mother." The same is true of the "woman with the cucumbers" (364) who once frightened Lësha-textileworker into his present state.

The Burn[10] has as its main characters five Russian artists and scientists. On the one hand, the five seem to be aspects of one individual—they all grow up as Tolya von Steinbock, they share the patronymic Apollinariyevich, and throughout the novel they are sometimes referred to as one ("the academic," *postradavshiy* 'the victim'). On the other hand, they can be seen as representing more than five individuals, namely, the Soviet intelligentsia of Aksënov's generation and persuasion.

The forces of good and evil are developed in the novel as two opposing metaphorical lines.[11] The main exponent of evil is Cheptsov, whom the child Tolya experiences as a sadistic *chekist*, who is "reanimated" at the beginning of the 70s and who appears in many different guises throughout the novel. When the victim, after his suicide, makes an excursion to the moon, that is, outside human consciousness, he finds that Cheptsov exists here too, as a "philosophical structure" (439). For the first time in Aksënov's work, God's voice is also heard clearly on the moon, sadly explaining that God never punishes, never uses force, but only reminds men of Himself. As each human being is endowed with a will to be near God or to move away from Him, God's power equals the power human beings give to Him. Among the reminders of God in the novel, we not surprisingly find a long row of "femininities" and women, who as mother-figures and lovers represent both characters of the Feminine according to Neumann and who are all epitomized in the figure of Alisa.

Alisa is part of what unites the five main characters, who will carry inside the image of her as Tolya von Steinbock saw her. The seventeen-year-old, half Polish, half English Alisa arrives in Magadan with a group of women on their way to the prison camp and Tolya, who is watching from a distance, immediately recognizes her as "His Girl" (201). She has the golden hair and the blue eyes of a fairy-tale princess:

and the whites of her eyes were enormous and pure and somehow
slightly bluish as if the blue, the color of the European sky, could not
be contained within the irises. (201)

Alisa asks Tolya for the name of the town and he senses the appeal for help in her voice. However, as a straight young Komsomol member he does not act, but only imagines himself vowing to save her, stripping her of her soiled clothes and warming her under his sweater:

> and her hair spread out on my chest, and her lips were whispering something incomprehensible in all 30 European languages right above my heart, and she was saved. (200)

This moment is determinant for the lives of the five: sometimes they are led astray, but they always come back to the search for the beautiful, helpless, European Alisa who needs to be saved. Four of the characters project her image onto other women (Masha Kulago, Nina, Marina Vlady, etc.), but the writer Panteley spends his time pursuing the adult Alisa around Moscow. His desperate efforts to win her love bear no little resemblance to the sufferings of the young Mayakovsky, one of the idols of the adolescent Tolya. Panteley is an outsider in the race for Alisa (as was Mayakovsky in relation to Lili Brik) and therefore has to rely on untraditional methods of getting her attention. He makes a total, if heroic, fool of himself by publicly declaring his love for her at a posh party which she is attending, as usual, in the company of her current lover and her imposing husband: "Mon amour, — said Panteley to Alisa. — God has sent you to me. You are my salvation." (53)

The adult Alisa is still recognizable by her golden hair and flashing blue eyes, but there seems to be nothing left of the innocence of the seventeen-year-old girl. The word *lisa* 'fox' is contained in her name; and it is with the cunning of a "golden-haired fox" (217) that she manages her life as an upperclass whore, spending her time having affairs—under the protection of her influential husband—with various prestigious men for whom she does not care. Time and again she is aware of a strange feeling that "something unique and concerning her personally" (218) is slipping away from her. This happens, for instance, when she hears a saxophone, sees a cardiogram, a sculpture, etc.—all things that identify the five. Rather than pursuing the "something," though, Alisa settles for the comforting "darkness" of sex: "This is good, — thought Alisa, — it's all dark and I am holding this hard, hot, pulsating little beast in my hand" (218). On one occasion when Alisa is with a lover in her car—a gift from a previous lover—she looks up at the star of Andromeda which, it would seem, holds a clue to her identity: the virgin Andromeda was chained to a rock to be sacrificed—for her mother's sins—to the sea monster.

Each of the five has a close friend who at one point betrays him. (The names of these friends, Argentov, Zil'berantsev, Sil'vestr, Serebro, Serebryannikov, all have to do with silver, as of the silver pieces of Judas.) Panteley confides his most sacred idea to his friend Serebryannikov, an idea for a play about a heron. He identifies the heron with their common youth during the "Thaw," with Europe, freedom, love; and to his great joy, Serebryannikov knows exactly what he is talking about:

> Almost a girl. She is ashamed of her legs—the knees stick out. A contemporary paraphrase of *The Seagull*. Right? An absurd, stupid-shy, lovely nymph of the swamps. Did I get it? At night our hero hears her hollow cries, the sound of wings. He sees the whole of Europe before him. The loveliness and moistness of life. True? (269)

However, Serebryannikov, who has by now joined the artistic establishment, soon loses interest and demands more drink. Panteley leaves him because he catches sight of Alisa, who is thereby identified with the heron. This is underlined by a dream Panteley has about taking his beloved on a trip to Lithuania—the place where the Heron appeared. Later, Panteley discovers that Alisa and Serebryannikov are having an affair. One night the two of them are having a rendezvous outside Alisa's home, significantly enough while the moon is hiding behind a tower, when suddenly Panteley, who has been following Alisa, steps out of the darkness and demands that she go with him. He is going to take her to the place where the moon sleeps, and she agrees. But then her husband appears, the three men have a fight, and eventually Alisa cannot bear to leave her husband. Panteley feels that he is acting out a familiar and extremely trivial plot and that "there could be no other, because we are on the ground of socialist realism" (382).

In book three Alisa rescues the Victim from the garbage pile and makes him see again the basic normality of life: "At last I caught sight of reality" (413). The long-suffering Victim sees the world with its trees and houses, he hears Mozart on the radio, has a bath, etc., and all this seems more fantastic, more magical to him than anything else he has seen. This is the significance of Alisa's first name, with its associations to *Alice in Wonderland*, and of her last name, Fokusova (which implies 'magic'). The Victim makes love to Alisa, first cynically, tearing at her hair, thinking of her as the whore—or fox—then tenderly, thinking of her as the girl—or heron,—opening her eyes and bringing her out of her darkness:

> but I understood then that I must open her eyes no matter what, and without words, without any commands and then I began to open them and I opened, opened, opened them, until she began to moan and mutter, until she opened her eyes, and in them I suddenly saw a wondering, amazed little girl, not a lioness at all. (416)

Still, the Victim is unable to trust Alisa for long, and in order to establish whether she is the real Alisa he puts her through a series of tests, all of which she fails. She doesn't speak Polish, doesn't remember what he remembers, etc., she simply loves him; but, convinced that she is taking him to a mental hospital, he escapes from her. She saves him once more, but he mistrusts her again and commits suicide. Still, on the Victim's "last journey," Alisa is with him.

The character of Alisa functions on many levels in the novel. Within the anima-sphere she is a woman, Woman, love, the Russian muse and the state of innocence (youth) necessary for love and creative activities. The basic innocence of Alisa is a result of her total defenselessness, her total lack of power in Cheptsov's sense. The situation where Panteley fails to understand Alisa's innocence has its parallels in the adventures of the other four main characters. During an attack by ruthless mercenaries on a hospital in Katanga where he is working, the doctor Mal'kol'mov and his patients are saved by his girlfriend, Masha, who goes to bed with the mercenaries. Mal'kol'mov's first reaction is concern, not for Masha, but for himself and the position which her action puts him in. The scientist Kunitser is seeing a girl, Nina, who is the stepdaughter of Cheptsov. When he learns that Nina has been raped by Cheptsov, he does not show Christian compassion but disgust, and he distances himself as a Christian from her who has been brought up in Marxism. The mutuality which is obviously a characteristic of an individual love relationship is preserved on the symbolic levels of the relationship between Alisa and the male characters. Alisa, love, the Russian muse can save the five if they let themselves be saved, and if they understand that she must also be saved.

In contrast to Alisa, such characters as Klarka and Tamarka appear to be totally untrustworthy (though not wholly unlikeable); they are prostitutes and KGB agents and when they decide to become nuns they constantly write letters from the convent asking not to be contacted. They are the negative anima-figures who distract the sculptor Khvastishchev from his purpose by locking him in an erotic triangle (the structure that was too "narrow" for Nina in *The Four Temperaments*). The woman who initiates Tolya into the mysteries of sex represents a similar danger. Tolya takes her for Artemis, the virgin goddess, but in reality she is a prostitute and the seduction takes place in the alcoholic and narcotic atmosphere of Krym, a strange underground camp for freed prisoners in Magadan.

Alisa has the power to make Panteley an outsider by rejecting him (as when she decides to stay with her husband) or to reconcile him with the world by bringing him into the Wonderland of reality. In this maternal aspect, Alisa is identified with Russia; that is, true, European Russia: "My love, my tenderness—Russia, Alisa, Moscow!" (413). Mother Russia has other representatives in the novel, such as the kind lady in the subway ticket office or Khvastishchev's dinosaur-like sculpture "Humility," which contains a cave where Khvastishchev loves to sit, or Masha Kulago's stomach, which is "the center of battle between Asia and Europe" (55).

But Russia can also be a Terrible Mother who in the shape of the hideous Sof'ya Stepanovna serves beer, not milk, to her children, the alcoholics of the "Men's club." The ticket-office lady is replaced by the "stepfather" Cheptsov, and "Humility" is subjected to an unflattering comparison when Mal'kol'mov reads from a Soviet textbook about a dinosaur that lives on after its head has been cut off.

Aksënov's Beautiful Ladies represent the divine as it can be experienced by human beings. Two questions need to be asked: firstly, why is the divine aspect of the human seen as feminine; and secondly, to what extent are Aksënov's female saviors like women?

The first question can be answered in a general way by pointing out firstly that, to a man, woman is at the same time the Other and a fellow human being, and secondly, that woman has traditionally been seen as a kind of "archetype of life." Since woman gives birth as well as experiencing death, she is seen as embodying the "mystery" of life, combining life's mortal and immortal dimensions. This is part of the reason why the moon, the light in the dark, is perceived as feminine.

Blok was attracted to a lady and frightened by a whore. Aksënov's female saviors are both ladies and whores. Saintly whores in literature have a tendency to become totally selfless. Aksënov's ladies, in contrast, thrive on mutuality. Tat'yana Lunina, the heroine of *The Island of Crimea*, is a realistically drawn character and yet it is obvious that she was created in the image of the 'Unknown Woman,' Nina, the Heron and Alisa. All these ladies, then, are probably created in the image of woman as Aksënov likes to see her. However, I prefer to see the type as the first not depressing image of the "good person" in Russian literature.

FOOTNOTES

1. V. Aksënov, *Zolotaya nasha zhelezka*, Michigan, 1980, p. 83; all translations of Aksënov in this paper are my own.

2. See V. Aksënov, *Ozhog*, Michigan, 1980, p. 88.

3. S.D. Cioran, *The Apocalyptic Symbolism of Andrej Belyj*, The Hague, 1973.

4. E. Neumann, *The Great Mother. An Analysis of the Archetype* (1955). Bollingen Series XLVII, New York, 1974.

5. "Kruglyye sutki non-stop," *Novyy mir*, No. 8, 1976; subsequent page references are to this edition.

6. V. Aksënov, "Chetyre temperamenta," *Aristofaniana s lyagushkami*, Michigan, 1981, p. 183; subsequent page references are to this edition.

7. The iron laws referred to in the play are an allusion to a famous dictum by Chekhov about the dramatic detail. According to Chekhov, any gun hanging on the wall of a stage set must be fired during the action of the play.

8. V. Aksënov, "Tsaplya," *Aristofaniana s lyagushkami*, Michigan, 1981, p. 315; subsequent page references are to this edition.

9. V. Aksënov, *Aristofaniana s lyagushkami*, Michigan, 1981, preface.

10. V. Aksënov, *Ozhog*, Michigan, 1980; subsequent page references are to this edition.

11. See P. Dalgård, *The Function of the Grotesque in Vasilij Aksenov*, Aarhus, 1982, pp. 115-16.

BASKETBALL, GOD, AND THE RINGO KID: PHILISTINISM AND THE IDEAL IN AKSËNOV'S SHORT STORIES

Priscilla Meyer

With the hindsight gained from Aksënov's recent work, particularly *The Burn* (1969-1975)[1] and "The Village of Sviyazhsk" (1981),[2] it becomes possible to identify a system of recurring emblems in his stories of the 60s.

Aksënov draws some of the most powerful scenes in *The Burn* from his life as a teenager in Magadan, as we may surmise from their detailed agreement with his mother's description of several of the same scenes in the second volume of her memoir, *Krutoy marshrut* (Within the Whirlwind).[3] After Evgeniya Ginzburg finished her 10-year term in prison camp in 1948, she obtained permission to have her son join her in Siberia, where she lived with her second husband, a Volga German and homeopathic physician whom Aksënov calls Martin in *The Burn*. Aksënov's autobiographical hero Tolya arrives in Magadan at the age of 16, ignorant about the Gulag and the underside of Stalin's world, but quickly realizes his status as the son of an enemy of the people, as an "apple that doesn't fall far from the tree," in an old Russian proverb which became the slogan of the times:

> Kak vsë-taki mne khotelos' ne otlichat'sya ot drugikh, zhit' v ètom stalinskom mire i obmanyvat' samogo sebya sochineniyami na "vol'- nuyu temu," basketbolom, molodetskimi drakami s synov'yami tyu- remshchikov i vlyublyënnost'yu v ikh docherey, ne schitat' sebya pariey v ètom stalinskom mire, prinimat' lozungi, i lozh', i vozhdya kak per- vozdannyye tsennosti, boyat'sya anket i ne obrashchat' vnimaniya na kolonny podnevol'noy rabochey sily.
>
> (But how I wanted not to be different from the others, to live in this Stalinist world and deceive myself with "free" compositions, basket- ball, heroic fights with the sons of the jailers and infatuation with their daughters, not to consider myself a pariah in this Stalinist world, to accept its slogans and its lies and its leader as absolute values, to fear filling out questionnaires and not to pay attention to the columns of the involuntary labor force. 195)

Initially, Tolya had been proud to be an "obychnyy sovetskiy shkol'nik" (ordinary Russian schoolboy; 192). He makes his mark among his class- mates through basketball, in which he is a "figura dovol'no avtoritetnaya" (a pretty authoritative figure; 195). He desperately wants to be the sports hero who wins the General's daughter. But this role of successful acceptability is the polar opposite of his home life, of which he is painfully ashamed. His mother's ten years in the camps and her Jewish background make him a pariah. Tolya tries to hide his name, Von Steynbock, by shortening it to the more Russian-sounding Bokov, but is unmasked when his mother is temporarily re-arrested. Furthermore, his stepfather, for whom he has great respect, is a devout practicing Catholic, a kind of unofficial priest. The ambivalence and confusion caused by the head-on collision of the unreconcilable realms of school and home create an unbearable tension:

> On znal uzhe davno, chto Martin veruyushchiy, chto on molitsya, chto u nego est' ètot skladnoy altarik i krokhotnaya bibliya i chëtki. Vsë èto bylo v takom nemyslimom dikom protivorechii s Tolinym sportivno-komsomol'skim idealom, s ego zhelaniyem stat' srednim "zdorovym chlenom obshchestva," vsë èto bylo tak stydno, chto Tolya staralsya ètogo kak by ne zamechat' i, uzh konechno, ne zadavat' nikakikh voprosov.
> (He had already known for a long time that Martin was a believer, that he prayed, that he had a folding altar and a tiny Bible and beads. All this was in such unthinkable contradiction to Tolya's sports-and-Komsomol ideal, with his desire to become an average "healthy member of society," all this was so shameful, that Tolya tried somehow not to notice it and, of course, not to ask any questions. 207)

To sacrifice either side of his existence for the other is impossible: Tolya has grown up as a normal Soviet school boy, but he has regained his beloved "enemy" mother after 12 years of separation. His unresolvable identity crisis leads him to fantasize suicide.

But Tolya finds some territory in Magadan that is untouched by the contradictions of his life: the world of the Ringo Kid, the hero of "Stagecoach" played by John Wayne:

> Nevidannyy geroy, smel'chak, kotoromu nichego ne stoit otdat' zhizn' za svobodu! Ringo Kid vselyal v Tolyu uverennost', [. . .] i, vykhodya iz kino, [. . .] chuvstvoval i sebya nemnogo Ringo Kidom.
> An unheard-of hero, brave, who'd have no trouble giving his life for freedom! The Ringo Kid gave Tolya self-assurance, [. . .] and, coming out of the movies, [. . .] he felt that he too was a little like the Ringo Kid. 304)

The world of foreign films provides an alternative to Tolya's choice both by its distance from Soviet reality and by the fantasy of actually combating its brutal tyranny; it can accommodate his ambivalence by allowing him to be brave, true to himself, and loyal to those he loves in imagination. Tolya imagines rescuing his friend Sanya from a brutal KGB interrogator in the style of a John Wayne scene, and his fantasy is recorded in English in the Russian text:

"Take it easy!" said Von Steynbock with a smile. "Stay where you are guys!"

He took off his overcoat and came into the interrogation room. The officers were both frightened. They found themselves without arms.

At the moment Tolya was throwing a chair at Cheptsov and right away hitting another officer in the stomach. (327)

Thus, three images in *The Burn* encapsulate Tolya's conflict and its potential resolution:
1. The basketball player as the pure boyish ideal of normalcy and acceptability, but an ideal tarnished by Tolya's knowledge of the truth of the official Stalinist world that sports belong to.
2. The religious mentor whose transcendent spiritual values inform his personal integrity, but in a manner Tolya knows is officially prohibited and feels to be shameful.
3. The Ringo Kid as an ideal of personal bravery which exists only in the fantasy world of a mythical "America," an imaginative space in which it is possible to challenge the authorities and thereby resolve the conflict between 1 and 2.

These are the images Aksënov used in his early stories to posit an Ideal in the Romantic tradition and to find ways to defend it against the forces preventing its realization. The Ideal may be represented by sport, but also by love, and by art in various manifestations (painting, architecture, chess, or simply an aesthetic sensitivity). The Ideal is caught between the polarities of hopeless philistinism, of which the pure form is the brutal oppression of spiritual freedom, and personal, aesthetically informed integrity, whose pure form is religion. Sport, love and art become places that test integrity. They exist in paired sets: the implied ideal and the betrayal of that ideal; the pure and the corrupt. Aggressive philistinism can only be combated by bravery; the alternative is cowardly retreat into fantasy. The opposed absolutes of oppression and of religious integrity have no duality; they are the principles at the basis of the opposition in *The Burn* between Tolya's public life at school and his private life at home, and the fiction generated by these opposing terms is the resolution provided in the imaginative universe stimulated by the Ringo Kid.

The stories are essentially variations of one model: the hero is limited, either by his naive unawareness of the philistinism of his world or by his fear of opposing it openly. He is capable of redemption through his thirst for an ideal, but his attempt to attain it is thwarted by the more brutal or unthinking people around him—they steal his girl; they "win" the game; or they have already contaminated the ideal. The pathos of the stories results from the hero's inability to combat the stronger forces that consistently thwart him. The true ideal is never attained but only implied—emblematically in the mentions of a church in the background or or by contrast with its corrupted form: competitive sport, cheap flirtation, or bad art. Here is a schematic representation of how these terms may be applied to eight of Aksënov's best stories of the early 60s:

Hero	Locus of the Hero's Ideal and What It Represents for Him	Opposing Forces	The Ideals Shown to Be Betrayed
"Halfway to the Moon" Kirpichenko	Tanya (ideal love)	the Banins father: Vokhrovets sister: cheap love brother: orgiast Manevich: a random philistine	Humaneness: Justice Love Memory Art Language
"The Local Hooligan Abramashvili" Gogi	Alina (Romantic Love)	Local druzhina Moscow youths	Love Art
"Parachuting" Narrator	Zina (Feminine delicacy) Skachkov	Air force parachutists	Physical bravery Artistic integrity
"Comrade Smart Cap" Uncle Mitya	Isabella (Romance) Smuggling (Adventure)	Ivan the policeman	The free play of fantasy Individuality
"Little Whale, Varnisher of Reality" Kolya (father)	"Whale" (son) (Freedom)	Wife Boss	The pure vision of child v. escapist fantasy
"Papa, What Does It Spell?" Sergey	Sport (Successful self-image)	Vyacha Sorokin Popular view of sport Art v. "Kultura"	Aesthetic vision (Olya) Sport v. competition
"Victory" Grandmaster	Chess (Memory) (Art)	G.O.	Aesthetic vision Personal integrity
"Breakfasts of '43" Narrator	Revenge (Justice) (Self-esteem)	He (the bully)	Bravery Integrity

BASKETBALL, GOD, AND THE RINGO KID

The first group of stories locates the ideal in a woman; the second in a child; the third in the realm of the imagination, often stimulated by a child's fresh vision.

"Halfway to the Moon" is the most clearly formulated version of the first type, in which the woman is more a muse-like abstraction in the romantic tradition than a realistic portrayal of an individual person.

The hero Kirpichenko is a worker who has grown up in orphanages and lived in barracks all his life. At thirty he has had no close personal relationships, and easily goes along with his acquaintance Banin's arrangements for a vacation: a few days of drinking and sex with Banin's sister and her friend. The orgy is characterized by its vulgarity and absence of feeling. It is important that the Banins' father had been a *Vokhrovets*, a prison camp guard; that is, the world of philistinism is directly linked to the *tyuremshchiki* 'jailers'. In opposition Aksënov places Tanya, the stewardess with whom Kirpichenko "falls in love" on a flight to Moscow after he escapes the Banins. He has never seen such a polished, sophisticated and, above all, respectfully polite woman in his years of orphanages and work barracks. That such well-manicured hands actually hold his sheepskin impresses him deeply, touching his humanity, it appears, for the first time in his deprived and brutalized life. This opens up a new world of memory, feeling, and even literature for him. His pursuit of her on the Moscow-Khabarovsk line is entirely metaphorical: he doesn't need actual Tanya, he needs his new-found Ideal, however false it may be, and in fact he comes to realize there are many such Tanyas to be found in Moscow. This of course is the pathos of the story—the poverty of Kirpichenko's Ideal, the modern day Tanya-moon-muse is easily 300,000 kilometers from Pushkin's romantic *baryshnya*. The everyday speech of Aksënov's characters is primitive, ignorant and degraded, as we realize as Kirpichenko's language develops in the course of the story from the vulgar pole toward the poetic. In the beginning, he thinks:

> Vchera bylo sil'no vypito. Ne to, chtoby uzh pryamo "v loskuty," no krepko. [. . .] Vsë—iz-za ètogo gada Banina i ego drazhayshey sestrukhi. Nu i raskololi oni tebya na tvoi trudovyye rubli!
> (Yesterday they'd really tied one on. Not exactly til they were "falling down drunk," but pretty far gone [. . .] All 'cause of that snake Banin and his precious sister. They sure took you for your paycheck. 150)[4]

After Kirpichenko has met Tanya, he imagines her in poetic terms:

> [. . .] eyë dlinnoye goloye telo—èto lunnaya plot', potomu chto vsë neponyatnoye, chto s nim bylo v detstve, kogda po vsemu telu prokhodyat murashki, i ego yunost', i sopki, otpechatannym rozovym

ognëm zari, i more v temnote, i talyy sneg, i ustalost' posle raboty [. . .] èto i est' ona.

([. . .] her long, naked body—it's the flesh of the moon because everything is incomprehensible, as in his childhood, when he would shiver all over, his youth, and the mounds, the dawn of vivid pink fire, and the sea in the darkness, and the melting snow and tiredness after work—that is she. 165)

The moon, the *sopki* 'mounds', the barracks, the sea all reappear in Tolya's landscape in *The Burn*. Aksënov distills an essence of his own childhood experience in Kirpichenko and demonstrates the power of the aesthetic vision to reconstruct the damaged self. The fantastic roundtrips between Moscow and Khabarovsk are less unreal than his own one-way flight on the same route to reclaim the poetic richness of the childhood he would have had with his lost mother. It is Kirpichenko's poetic language that shows his potential to transcend his debased surroundings, as is made explicit at the end of the story when he asks an acquaintance, "Ne znayesh' ty, skol'ko do Luny kilometrov?" (Do you know how many kilometers it is to the Moon?) and gets the rude and unimaginative reply:

"Perebral ty, vidno, v otpuske," serdito skazal Manevich i poshël.
("You sure had one too many on leave," Manevich said angrily and walked off. 169)[5]

Manevich speaks in the language Kirpichenko had used before he met Tanya to describe the Banin orgy, but Kirpichenko by the very positing of an ideal has transcended that sphere of sub-humanity, even though his world offers him only *ersatz* materials.

"The Local Hooligan Abramashvili" is also about the corruption of the ideal. Gogi Abramashvili is an 18-year-old noble savage from Georgia, himself an ideal of purity and natural physicality; "romanticheskoye voploshcheniye dney provedennykh na yuge" (the romantic embodiment of days spent in the south. 43). He is corrupted by his mistaken ideal, a sophisticated young woman from Moscow (Alina) who is attracted by his "Hellenic anatomy" (46), of which he is unconscious. She is an artist and sketches him as he plays badminton on the beach:

Igra èta Gogi kazalas' tupoy i vyaloy, ne to, chto ping-pong, i igral on v neyë s damami tol'ko iz chistoy lyubeznosti. A v ping-pong on igral, slovno shashkoy rubil—sprava, sleva i zashchishchalsya, kak voin.
(The game seemed dumb and limp to Gogi too, not like ping-pong, and he played it with the ladies out of pure graciousness. But he played ping-pong as if he were wielding a sabre—left, right, and defended himself like a warrior. 47)

The heroic game is contrasted to the trivial "sport" which his traditional peasant grandfather also disapproves of. Gogi visits his grandparents once a week up in the hills and brings their produce to market on his grandfather's "Staryy kon'" (old steed), i.e., his bicycle. Alina's sketch displeases Gogi:

> Tam on uvidel sebya, no tol'ko v strannom kakom-to vide—budto by on byl serdit, budto v gneve on podnyal nad golovoy ne raketu, a kamen' ili prashchu.
> "Nravitsya vam vash portret?" [. . .]
> "Pochemu u menya takiye dlinnyye nogi?" [. . .]
> "Èlementarnaya stilizatsiya." [. . .]
> (He saw himself, but in some strange form—as if he were angry, as if he had raised not a raquet but a stone or a sling over his head in rage.
> "Do you like your portrait?" [. . .]
> "Why do I have such long legs?" [. . .]
> "Elementary stylization." [. . .] 47)

Alina seduces Gogi out of lust, and is surprised to find him a virgin. Her *poshlost'* ("Nu i denëk—pervaya sigareta, pervaya zhenshchina." Quite a day—first cigarette, first woman. 55) is contrasted to Gogi's excitement and pride. But the belief that the Moscow beauty has become "his woman" is shattered when her husband appears. Gogi goes berserk and is branded a "hooligan" by the local druzhina. He quits his job as beach entertainer and joins the army. Walking on the beach he meets a soldier. Aksënov parodies the soldier's limited and pedestrian worldview:

> Mne v voyenno-stroitel'nom den'gi platyat. Verno? Ponyal? A ya ikh na sberknizhku kladu. Pravil'no? Vernus' s den'gami. Verno ili net? I togda my kupim motosikl s kolyaskoy [. . .]
> (They pay me in military construction. Right? Got it? And I put it in the bank. Right? Come home with money. Am I right or not? And then we'll buy a motorcycle with a side-car [. . .] 61)

In contrast, Gogi is suddenly seized with desire for something larger, something eternal: "Ya khochu stat' kosmonavtom!—yarostno zakrichal Georgiy" (I want to be a cosmonaut! Georgiy burst out furiously. 61). Gogi, an innocent and uneducated youth, a *tabula rasa*, hungers for some ideal; first he mistakenly thinks he has found it in Alina, and then tries to imagine something higher.[6] The ancient world either of the Grecian heroes or of the simple traditional Greek peasants like his grandfather no longer exists; the image of the cosmonaut is the closest Gogi can get to those lost values. The other forces in the story oppose his ideals: the druzhina that represses him for his "hooliganism" (which is in fact a thoroughly just and even heroic response to Alina's betrayal of love and art in her fashionable sketches).

The error of Kirpichenko's idealization of the stewardess in this story is made explicit: the noble savage finds no Nouvelle Heloïse.

"Parachuting" is based on the same premise: the hero imagines a waitress to be "like a chesspiece," accompanied by "chëtkiy stuk i tikhiy zvon" (a crisp tapping and quiet ring), but in fact she speaks in flippant clichés, and stands him up for a parachute jumper with whom the hero has narrowly escaped a flight. His friend Skachkov, an artist, has lied his way out of their encounter with the fliers. Parallel to the hero's relinquishing the girl, Skachkov exhibits his watercolors instead of his better graphics to avoid opposing his director. The scale of values within which we measure these two actions is marked at the one extreme by a church in the background at the opening of the story and at the other by a scrap of wrapping paper from an old exercise book on which is written "The stages of the development of capitalism in Europe [. . .]" (66). Like his art, Skachkov also betrays sport: he executes a perfect dive in front of the fliers, but realizing that he has misused his beautiful dive to impress them, later berates himself for showing off "like a 16-year-old" (68). The same principle is contained in Aksënov's own words when at 16 he was reunited with his mother, after 12 years, in front of an official's family: "Don't cry in front of them, Mama."[7]

The concept of sport as a manifestation of the ideal is central to "Papa, What Does It Spell?":

> [. . .] ikh komanda—èto byla komanda s bol'shoy bukvy, èto bylo to, chto po ikh mneniyu, bol'she vsego sootvetstvovalo vysokomu ponyatiyu "futbol'naya komanda." Na tribunakh oni ne topali nogami, ne svisteli i ne krichali pri neudachakh: "Men'she vodki nado pit'!"—potomu chto oni znali, [. . .] komanda—èto ne mekhanizm, a odinnadtsat' raznykh parney.
>
> (Their team was a Team with a capital T, it was what they thought most completely corresponded to the high ideal of a "soccer team." In the bleachers they didn't stamp, whistle, and yell "You shouldn't drink so much!" at missed shots because they knew [. . .] a team isn't a mechanism but 11 different guys. 119)

But this youthful ideal has become outmoded for Sergey, a place to avoid the important questions of his adulthood—the realization of a cliché. The story presents an array of verbal clichés: Sorokin's ironic comments on Leningrad's architecture ("Gorod-muzey"—A city-museum); a conversation overheard in a café ("Ne likvidatsiya a reorganizatsiya"—Not liquidation but reorganization); Sergey's own automatic language:

> "Konferentsii, konferentsii, [. . .] vechnyye èti konferentsii. I tëshcha segodnya uyekhala. Vesëloye voskresen'ye. Chego dobrogo, Alka stanet kandidatom nauk. Togda derzhis'. Ona i seychas tebya v grosh ne stavit."

("A conference, a conference, [. . .] these eternal conferences. And my mother-in-law's away today. Some Sunday. Terrific, Alka'll be a Ph. D. Then hang on! As it is she doesn't think I'm worth a damn." 122)

The forces that are capable of resurrecting Sergey's deadened spirit are represented by his six-year-old daughter, Olya, whose lively perception reawakens the imaginative potential he exhibits in the opening paragraph:

[. . .] po ovragam tekut ruch'i, pakhnet mokrymi sosnami, i belyye tserkvi stoyat na kholmakh. Emu vdrug zakhotelos' byt' gde-nibud' tam, zakutat' Ol'ku v pidzhak, vzyat' eyë na ruki i bezhat' pod dozhdëm k stantsii.

([. . .] streams run over the cliffs, it smells of wet pines, and white churches stand on the hills. He suddenly wanted to be somewhere there, to wrap Olya in his jacket, take her in his arms and run to the station in the rain. 115)

The freshness of nature, the love of his innocent daughter, and the churches on the hill (an emblem of the ideal potentially embodied in sport) form the moral and aesthetic basis for Sergey's growth, which together renovates his outmoded relation to the day's soccer match. Olya's learning to read suggests the possibility of vivid, meaningful language ("Do they really write nonsense in printed letters?"). As Olya writes "Olya—Papa" in the air over the stadium, she renovates the cliché of sport for Sergey by reuniting his ideal with its moral-aesthetic origins. This reading clarifies "Little Whale, Varnisher of Reality" as well; the title itself contains the juxtaposition of official dead sloganry to the child's virginal vision. Fantasy and imagination are means to overpower the moral and aesthetic oppressors of the word and spirit. The problem for the adult is to have the courage to act on the ideals attained through imaginative means.

This dilemma is addressed in "Victory" in almost abstract form, stripped of the analysis of *byt* and its representative clichés typical of the earlier stories. The grandmaster's aesthetic relation to the chess game involves the conflict of memories of beauty (Bach, nature) with those of brutality (the SS officers) as stimulated by his encounter with an aggressive competitor (G.O.). The Nazi association is motivated by G.O.'s remark that all chessplayers are Jews, but the grandmaster is not Jewish; he is a member of the Russian intelligentsia. His childhood memories merge with Aksënov's own experience of the KGB as described in Book Two of *The Burn*, the opening of which relates his personal experience to the larger plane of Russian history:

[. . .] kto vypustil dzhina iz butylki, kto otorvalsya ot naroda, kto zaiskival pered narodom, kto zhirel na sheye naroda, kto pustil tatar v goroda, priglasil na knyazhen'ye varyagov, presmykalsya pered Evropoy, otgorazhivalsya ot Evropy, bezumno protivoborstvoval vlasti, pokorno podchinyalsya tupym diktaturam? Vsë èto delali my—russkaya intelligentsia.

([. . .] who let the Genie out of the bottle, who cut themselves off from the people, who curried favor with the people, who got fat on the backs of the people, who let the Tatars into the cities, invited the Varangians to rule, grovelled before Europe, cut themselves off from Europe, madly struggled against the government, meekly submitted to thick-witted dictatorships? All this was done by us—the Russian intelligentsia. 189)

The grandmaster skillfully puts G.O. in checkmate, but what does it matter if G.O. doesn't even notice and goes on to win the game? The inner freedom the grandmaster maintains despite G.O.'s victory (represented ironically by the invisible "Dior" label on his tie) is a mockery. He is always prepared to lose to the G.O.'s and even to acknowledge their victory with gold medals.

It is only in "The Village of Sviyazhsk" that the hero finally openly opposes the deadening forces that surround him. This allows all the other components of Aksënov's system to fall into their proper alignment, resolving the opposition that caused Tolya such pain at the age of sixteen.

"The Village of Sviyazhsk" restates the ideas of "Papa, What Does It Spell?" (1962) in their essential form. In Oleg Shatunovsky at fifty, Aksënov resolves the contradictions that Sergey at thirty-two only dimly perceived and that Aksënov was obliged to disguise. At the beginning of both stories, the heroes are caught at a moment of transition. For Oleg, a basketball trainer, and Sergey, a soccer player, sport has lost its higher meaning: Oleg no longer "inspires" his players; Sergey is a forgotten "idol." The important difference is that while the force that renews Sergey is a fresh aesthetic appreciation of life, for Oleg it is religion. Sergey sees a tall schoolboy on the street who "promises to grow into an athlete, the center of the country's leading basketball team," whereas Oleg meets a young provincial who is a kind of Good Samaritan to him in a moment of pain. This young man's penetrating gaze recalls that of Sergey's daughter Olya, and there are other echoes that suggest a deliberate evocation of the earlier story.

Oleg is not as plebeian as Sergey. Aksënov gives him some autobiographical attributes—Oleg's parents, loyal party members, were arrested in 1937; his mother, whose name is "Dal'berg," returns to him after her term is up. The political dimension can finally be addressed directly as a destructive force pervading every aspect of existence. The obliteration of the old, architecturally and spiritually, is represented by the replacement of the Sviyazhsk church with an Intourist facility. On the secular side, Oleg imagines the architect who designed his Moscow "microregion" to have sneaked some "little bubble of live spirit" into his design which allows the hill, some forest, and the angle of the moon to make a composition of the "line of appalling living quarters" (130).[8] Analogously, the technical geniuses like Sikorsky become the sterile Soviet *tekhnar* 'technician', and sport is principally a political propaganda tool at the highest level where Oleg works. He is disgusted by the slogans bedecking the basketball court ("Tebe, Partiya, nashi uspekhi v sporte!"—Our Successes in Sport are for You, Party!); he refers to the opposing team (nicknamed "The Tanks") as a "military machine" run by a "great demagogue" (133). "The Tanks'" strength comes from assembling already accomplished individuals, rather than from the years of nurturing that Oleg gives his "children." In sum, spiritual life as potentially manifest in religion, art, sport, and technology is shown to be under assault by the political order in ways that were indicated only indirectly in the stories of the 1960s.

Oleg's mid-life crisis is resolved and the religious experiences of his childhood reclaimed when he learns that he was christened as an infant. The agent of his christening, his father's chauffeur Viktor Petrovich, is described as resembling an aviator in an old film, Russian but somehow strangely European. Viktor Petrovich carried a gun and drove an American car. By associating him with such fragments from the world of foreign films, Aksënov connects the agent of Oleg's religious self-realization to the fantasy realm of the "Ringo Kid." This is the source of the strength that ultimately leads Oleg to challenge the Soviet system in a spontaneous gesture: he makes the sign of the cross over his team at the beginning of a televised game against "the Tanks," which results in his being taken away by the men in white coats at the story's close.

The number sixteen recurs through Aksënov's works—Sergey sees an "amazing sixteen-year-old schoolboy," Skachkov shows off "like a sixteen-year-old kid," and Oleg lives on the fifteenth floor of a 16-story apartment building, clearly on the brink of something. Tolya's crisis was formulated by rejoining his mother when he was 16, and in "The Village of Sviyazhsk" that crisis is almost resolved. Oleg initially wonders, "Mozhno li pridumat' boleye dalëkuyu ot very professiyu, chem sovetskiy basketbol'nyy trener?" (Can you think of a profession any further removed from faith than a Soviet basketball trainer?). The opposition between sport and religion was caused by a repressive materialist society which in "The Village of Sviyazhsk" is finally explicitly shown to be antagonistic towards all spiritual values. This demonstrated, the shame associated with religion as well as the contamination of sport is eliminated. Religion means not the passive peasant orthodoxy of Oleg's nanny, nor the secular Jewishness of Tolya's mother nor the Catholicism of his stepfather. Oleg is inspired by Eastern religious ideas circulating in underground manuscripts. He understands these ideas in terms of the "inspiration" he imparts to his team before a game. This more generalized religious spirit entails memory, artistic sensitivity, and independence. It is nurtured by the fantasy characteristic of imaginative fiction in which total bravery is possible, in which an ideal can be realized. Without this (as represented by Viktor Petrovich), Oleg would not have made his challenge to the official world. From the age of 16, Tolya begins to reclaim the potential of poetry, spirituality and bravery that he had lost with the arrest of his mother; Oleg at 50 realizes that potential. The aesthetic ideal presented in Aksënov's early stories turns out to have disguised an important religious component which is present in all Aksënov's best work, and is carried by a fixed set of emblems.

FOOTNOTES

1. Vasiliy Pavlovich Aksënov, *Ozhog*, Ann Arbor, 1980; all page references to citations from *The Burn* refer to this edition.

2. Vasiliy Pavlovich Aksënov, "Sviyazhsk," *Kontinent*, No. 29, 1981, pp. 95-140.

3. Evgeniya Ginzburg, *Within the Whirlwind*, trans. Ian Boland, New York, 1981.

4. Vasiliy Pavlovich Aksënov, *Na polputi k lune*, Moscow, 1965. Page references to citations from all the stories refer to this collection.

5. I have provided my own translation, because the one by Ronald Hingley (in *Halfway to the Moon*, ed. Patricia Blake and Max Hayward, New York, 1965, pp. 82-103) obscures the distinctions between the two speaking styles.

6. *Cf.* Aksënov's statement about "Zatovarennaya bochkotara": "It turns out they love barrels, as if they were sublimating some religious feeling!" (P. Meyer, "Interview with Vasiliy Pavlovich Aksënov," *Russian Literature Triquarterly*, No. 6, 1973, p. 572).

7. Ginzburg, *op. cit.*, p. 265.

8. Compare the components of Oleg's landscape to Kirpichenko's and Tolya's quoted above, as well as Sergey's at the opening of "Papa, slozhi!"

THE FUNCTION OF CONVENTIONAL LANGUAGE PATTERN IN THE PROSE OF VASILIY AKSËNOV

A. Vishevsky and T. Pogacar

I. Introduction.

During the symposium on Russian emigrant literature held in Los Angeles in May 1980, a lady rose from the audience and asked the writers on the stage, including Vasiliy Aksënov, why they use vulgar language in their works. In her eyes, Aksënov and others were negligent in their choice of words. This reader's opinion may be indicative of a natural reaction to Aksënov and other contemporary Russian writers, who are widening the range of the literary language by breaking conventions as they apply to the use of street language. This paper is not intended as an argument in defense of Aksënov, who is generally recognized as one of the finest contemporary Russian stylists. Rather, we will consider one of Aksënov's techniques that demonstrates his scrupulous choice of words, even in passages that, superficially at least, are shocking for the reader of Russian literature. By examining the use of such conventional language patterns as popular songs, clichés, slogans and literary allusions in Aksënov's writings, we will attempt to show the increased value of the word in the structure of his works as a whole.

Aksënov's literary career has customarily been divided into three periods: "happy" (1958-1962), "angry" (1963-early 1970s), and "desperate" (early 1970s-1980).[1] This schematization is based on Aksënov's attitude toward the Soviet regime. However, we would like to propose an analysis of his prose based upon his stylistic evolution—his treatment of language as such. As a criterion of such an examination we would like to take the most apparent instances of Aksënov's adaptations of the above-mentioned conventional language patterns. Consequently, we propose to differentiate in his prose three successive periods of creative evolution: illustrative, ironic and analytical. The most apparent instances of this are his adaptations of conventional language patterns.

II. Illustrative and ironic periods.

The first period of Aksënov's writing is characterized by the illustrative application of these patterns. A song or poem is cited in order to reflect the sentiments of characters at a given moment, as when in the novel *Col-*

leagues Zelenin and his friend Dasha listen to the words of a waltz that promise lasting love: "Kak bereg krutoy / S burlivoy rekoy, / Tak my nerazluchny s toboy"[2] (Like the steep bank / And the turbulent river / We are inseparable). References to songs and literature are employed to help convey the mood of the characters and define their personalities. Instances of political clichés and slogans are rare; however, the theme of the use and misuse of political language arises in several key dialogues in *Colleagues*, where the characters refer to political rhetoric as "vysokiye slova" (high-sounding words).

We will name the second period the ironic period. In the work most characteristic of this tendency, *The Tare of Empty Barrels*, the narrator adopts a gently ironic stance vis-à-vis the characters. For example, when the barrelware has been rejected at the end of the story, we read:

> — S bochkami-to? A chego zh, sdam ikh po naryadu i kranty. — Volodya splyunul v storonu i . . . [. . .] i vot struna lopnula, i posledniy proshchal'nyy zvuk ushël v vysotu . . . i . . . i Volodya zaplakal.[3]
> ("And what about the barrels? What the heck, I'll turn them in according to the order and that's the end of it." . . . And the string snapped, and the final parting sound departed on high . . . and Volodya started to cry.)

Irony here derives from the narrator's interpolation, which is a clear allusion to a well-known stage direction in Chekhov's play *The Cherry Orchard*. Volodya's crying, which parallels Anya's tears in the play, underlines the melancholy irony of the situation. Irony is also common in the dream sequences, in which the narrator's voice merges with that of the character. One such example is Volodya Teleskopov's first dream ("Pervyy son Volodi Teleskopova"): He sees Simka and responds in the form of song containing a quote from Lermontov's poem, "Na smert' poèta" (The Poet's Death):

> Ponyatnoye delo, ne vynesla dusha poèta pozora melochnykh obid, ves' utop v pukhovykh podushkakh, zaputalsya v krasnom odeyale, rozha vsya v kil'kakh marinovannykh, lapy v ryapushke tomatnoy.[4]
> (Sure enough, "His spirit could not bear dishonor, infamy, and pain,"[5] he's gone completely under in down pillows, gotten tangled up in a red blanket, his mug covered with pickled sprats, paws in tomato sardines.)

The quote from Lermontov contrasts with the ordinary language and banal imagery surrounding it, resulting in an ironic and humorous effect. This example is similar to other citations of literature and song in *The Tare of Empty Barrels* which express characters' sentiments, usually with a slightly ironic coloring. This is Aksënov's first work with heavy irony directed at bureaucratic clichés, especially in the language of the old man, Mochënkin. Mochënkin suffers from an "Unter Prishibeyev's complex"; his style combines the language of bureaucratic reports with his own illiterate idiom.

Upon seeing Volodya and Simka together, Mochënkin remarks sentimentally: "Krasivaya lyubov' ukrashayet nashu zhis' peredovoy molodëzh'yu"[6] (Beautiful love pretties our life with politically aware youth). He uses the illiterate form *zhis'* in place of *zhizn'* and disrupts the cause and effect sequence of the sentence by combining two grammatically correct but logically incompatible noun phrases, thereby creating an ironic and humorous effect. Mochënkin's language is not satirized, however, as such clichés are in Aksënov's later works.

The illustrative and ironic use of conventional language patterns thus far discussed generally corresponds to the division of Aksënov's early career suggested by Meyer: 1959-1964; 1965- .[7] The process of identification inherent in the illustrative examples matches the first, largely autobiographical period, while the ironic examples properly belong to the following period, in which Aksënov turned his attention to stylistic innovation. In the third period, which we proposed to call analytical, Aksënov continues to employ conventional language patterns in an illustrative and ironic way. Whereas the first two methods are primarily forms of lexical borrowing, in the latter period Aksënov analyzes language patterns while simultaneously integrating them into a structure, thereby giving them new meaning, which is revealed in a broader context.

III. The analytical period.

The third period, from the early 1970s-1980, marks a return to autobiographical themes, but in a more critical and reflective manner. The analytic technique is indicative of this change.

The most succinct example of Aksënov's analytic technique as applied to conventional language patterns is seen in the reworking of an internationally recognized warning, which appears in the eyes of a character as:

> Nakonets zazhglos' tablo—chto-to naschët kureniya ili privyazyvaniya, naschët privyazyvaniya nedokurennykh okurkov ili vykurivaniya nezatyanutykh remney.[8]
> (At last a sign lit up—something about smoking or fastening, about fastening unfinished cigarette butts or smoking up unfastened seat belts.)

One of the most common language patterns found in Aksënov's later works are slogans. The physical predominance of slogans in the environment parallels their saturation of the language of officialdom and the media. In the novel *The Island of Crimea*, on the way from the airport, Tat'yana observes the Moscow skyline. The slogan, "Partiya—um, chest' i sovest' nashey èpokhi!" (The Party is the mind, honor and conscience of our epoch!) dominates the horizon and eclipses the sun. She would prefer to avoid looking at the dismal landscape, but is unable to: "[. . .] ona ne mogla otvernut'sya i smotrela na tuchi, na gryaz', [. . .] na blednyy pyatak i ognennyye bukvy"⁹ (She could not turn away, and looked at the clouds, the mud, [. . .] the pale five-kopeck piece and blazing letters). Colorless nature, as represented by the sun, is a poor rival for the bright fiery letters of the slogan. Elsewhere in the novel, the same road from the airport is described in more detail through the eyes of Andrey Luchnikov: upon leaving the airport, the fall day is bright and sunny, but natural description yields increasingly to the enumeration of urban features such as huge apartment buildings, bridges and especially slogans. The myriad official slogans along the highway and in the city clash with the associated images of freedom and nature, such as a small church, flowers and the sound of an imaginary bell. Each time some part of nature is mentioned, a slogan is juxtaposed to it in the next sentence:

> V nebe, kazalos', prisutstvoval neslyshnyy perezvon kolokola svobody. "Sovetskiye lyudi tvërdo znayut: tam, gde partiya, tam uspekh, tam pobeda," glasil ogromnyy shchit pri vyyezde na shosse. (OK, 110)
> (It seemed as if there was an inaudible ringing of a freedom bell in the sky. "The Soviet people know for certain that where the Party is, there is success, there is victory," announced a huge billboard at the highway entrance.)

Or: "Stoyal yasnyy osenniy den'. 'Slava nashey rodnoy kommunisticheskoy partii!'" (It was a clear fall day. "Glory to our dear Communist Party!" OK, 110). Just as in Tat'yana's view previously, the sun appears briefly and then Luchnikov sees the slogan, "Partiya—um, chest' i sovest' nashey èpokhi" (The Party is the mind, honor and conscience of our epoch), "s kryshi na nas shagali ognennyye bukvy" (spanning the rooftops in bright letters; OK, 111). This marks the end of the clash of imagery, and signals "the complete and final victory" of the slogans.¹⁰ Finally, upon entering the city, slogans dominate the landscape.

Upon arriving in the city, Luchnikov's attention is drawn to his "favorite" slogan: "'Gazeta—èto ne tol'ko kollektivnyy propagandist i kollektivnyy agitator, ona takzhe i kollektivnyy organizator'" ("The newspaper is not only a collective propagandist and collective agitator, it is also a collective organizer"; OK, 111). By musing ironically and at length upon the apparent cleverness of the slogan, which stems largely from its authoritative syntax (". . . ne tol'ko . . . i . . . takzhe i . . ."), Luchnikov reveals its meaninglessness. The basis of the irony lies in the playful supposition that there is actually a group of people who think that a newspaper is but a collective propagandist, while others recognize in it a collective agitator;

but only a genius could realize the newspaper's great organizational function. Luchnikov's analysis is a form of *ostraneniye* that shows seemingly deep wisdom to be a mere commonplace.

Panteley, one of the main characters in the novel *The Burn*, approaches the slogan, "'Kommunizm—èto sovetskaya vlast' plyus èlektrifikatsiya vsey strany'" ("Communism means Soviet power plus electrification of the entire country"), in the same way. The slogan stretches in lights ("nemerknushchiye lampochki Il'icha"—ever-burning bulbs of Il'ich) between two colossal buildings of the Stalinist epoch that screen the sky from the viewer. Thus the slogan obstructs the space between them as well and nature is excluded from the city, which is dominated by monstrous buildings and huge signs shining in the sky. Panteley wonders why communism has not been established if the prescriptions of the slogan have been fulfilled: "Neuzheli est' eshchë ugly, gde upornyye reaktsionery zhgut luchinu" (Is it possible that there still exist pockets where stubborn reactionaries burn splinters; O, 377). The breakdown of the slogan is based on pretended belief in the truth conveyed by its words, whereas the only enlightenment it offers is in fact in its own light bulbs.

The performance and fixity of the slogans in the cityscape is emphasized by the adjectives used to describe them: *vekovechnyy* 'age-old', *neizmennyy* 'unchanging', *neugasimyy* 'unextinguishable', *beskonechnyy* 'endless', *moguchiy* 'powerful', and *nezyblemyy* 'immovable'. In one instance, the roman numerals in the slogan, "Idei XXIV s"yezda—v zhizn'!" ("The Ideas of the XXIV Congress—Into Life!"), take on additional meaning in comparison with the roman numerals on an old building on which it sits (O, 345). The numerals in the foundation date suggest, by comparison, the unchanging nature of the interminable series of congresses, which could be numbered twenty-four or eighteen hundred and twenty-four. A comparison is also to be made between the eternal city of Rome (represented in the numerals of the building) and the stability of the Soviet system projected into perpetuity.[11]

Aksënov shows slogans in the absurdity of their parts in several works, but the most revealing example is found in the novel *The Island of Crimea*, when during the Soviet invasion one of the most ordinary and meaningless of them acquires significance and even originality in the mirror reality of the Crimea. The young Crimeans greet the Soviet invasion with banners:

"Privet, Moskva!", "Sovetskiy ostrov privetstvuyet sovetskiy materik!", "Krym + Kreml' = Lyubov'!", i samyy original'nyy: "Pust' vechno tsvetët nerushimaya druzhba narodov SSSR!" (OK, 301)

("Hi, Moscow!", "The Soviet Island Welcomes the Soviet Mainland!", "Crimea + Kremlin = Love!", and the most original one: "Let the Unbreakable Friendship of the Peoples of the USSR Flower Forever!")

The last greeting not only has ironic meaning in the given hostile situation, but its false pretentiousness is revealed in the context of the other unorthodox exclamations.

Soviet influence on the language of the Crimea is also apparent in the spread of acronyms such as ENOUMB ("Edinaya nedelimaya ubogaya i obil'naya moguchaya i bessil'naya"—One indivisible poor and abundant, powerful and powerless),[12] VSIuR ("Vooruzhënnyye sily yuga Rossii"—The Armed Forces of South Russia), VMPS ("Velikiy i moguchiy, pravdivyy i svobodnyy"—The great and powerful, true and free),[13] SOS ("Soyuz obshchey sud'by"—Union of Common Destiny), and IOS ("Ideya obshchey sud'by"—Idea of Common Destiny). A punning or ironic meaning is attached to all of them. The last one suggests Stalin's name Iosif, SOS is a distress call, and the greatness of the Russian language is squeezed into four letters that will remind the reader of many things from MTS to VTsSPS, but not of the language of Tolstoy and Turgenev.

Among the many examples of cliché language patterns found in Aksënov's recent works, there are some in the novel *The Island of Crimea* that also reflect various forms of "Soviet" literary style. One passage is a parody of the type of false and stereotyped dialogue which is often found in second-rate Soviet fiction. Here Aksënov uses it for a deadpan effect:

— Ya uveren, Flinch, chto my prinesëm bol'shuyu pol'zu velikomu Sovetskomu Soyuzu [. . .] Mne lyubopytno, chto vy, anglo-krymchane, dumayete o vossoyedinenii?
— Ya dumayu, chto my chorosho smozhem pomoch' sovetskim tovarishcham v organizatsii otel'nogo dela.
Bravo, Flinch, ya rad, chto rabotayu s takim progressivnym chelovekom, kak vy. (OK, 199)
("I am certain, Flinch, that we will be of great assistance to the great Soviet Union [. . .] I am curious about what you Anglo-Crimeans think of reunification?" "I think that we will be able to help our Soviet comrades well in the organization of the hotel business." "Bravo, Flinch! I am glad to work with such a progressive person as you.")

Another form of cliché found in recent works is the *doneseniye* 'report'. It was first used by Aksënov in Mochënkin's writings in *The Tare of Empty Barrels* and in the examples of technical reports in *The Steel Bird*. In both cases a blend of bureaucratic and illiterate styles is used. The same type of *doneseniye* is found in *The Burn* but the pattern is complicated by the mixing of various styles, instead of the simple juxtaposition of bureaucratic and illiterate elements. Secret agent Fruktozov's *doneseniye* begins with the friendly salutation, "Dorogiye tovarishchi!" (Dear comrades!), which immediately breaks the proper pattern of the style. The succession of events that he narrates is interrupted by stylistically alien expressions, characteristic of adventure or spy literature (*vnezapno* 'suddenly'), absurd elements ("Studentka filodendron-faka"—coed in the philodendron department), or folk-heroic elements ("Mikula nash Selyaninovich"—our Mikula Selyaninovich; O, 74-78). *Doneseniye* is not only used as a basis for humor, but is part of the central theme of the persistence of Stalinism. At one point in *The Island of Crimea* a comprehensive explanation is offered for the phenomenon of denunciations in the author's typically ironic way. The storekeeper Merkator, reflecting upon the Soviet practice of reporting on one's fellow citizen, concludes:

> [. . .] v osnove svoyey ona idët ot velikogo chuvstva obshchnosti, chuvstva edinoy sem'i, ot massovoy tyagi k sovershenstvu, ot chuvstva nekoy obshchey "materi," kotoroy mozhno i pozhalovat'sya na brata [. . .] (OK, 268)
> ([. . .] at the base of it [i.e., of denunciation—A.V. and T.P.] lies a great communal feeling, a feeling of common family, a mass attraction to perfection, a feeling of a common "mother," to whom you can complain about a brother [. . .])

When he uses the word *mat'* 'mother' (genitive case, *materi*), Merkator has in mind the abstract concept of motherland (common combinations are *Mat'-Rodina* 'Motherland' and *Mat'-Rossiya* 'Mother Russia'). In the same context with the word *brat* 'brother' it is the object of ironic treatment of the concept of nation-family, which becomes little more than a bickering group because of denunciation.

Another rich source of clichés in Aksënov are official speeches, such as a sergeant's attempted court testimony in *The Burn* which follows the "Unter-Prishibeyev" pattern found in *The Tare of Empty Barrels*. The fantastic in the sergeant's speech lends absurdity to it, alluding to the surreal atmosphere of Stalin's rule. Aksënov also uses a device wherein extended context rather than interior structure is the key to understanding the irony of the language pattern. For example, he represents a standard Soviet speech as it actually could be heard at a meeting of UNESCO, but it is viewed ironically because it is predicted word for word by the main character immediately before it is pronounced. The speech in its entirety constitutes a single cliché, which, despite the fact that it is composed of many words and otherwise recognizable clichés, functions as a single unit.

Speeches occur not only in official bodies and meetings, but also in the simplest of settings, which indicates that all parts of society have been infected by the same disease. One of the characters in *The Burn* is ineptly greeted by village officials who have mastered the form of the language but flout the content: "Dorogoy tov. Bokov, v vashem litse sel'skiy aktiv pri-vetstvuyet!" (Dear comrade Bokov, in your person the village cell greets! O, 424). The same absurd treatment of clichés characterizes the speech of the geometry teacher in *The Burn*. She concocts a collection of political clichés that are frightening in their implication but senseless in their arrangement:

> [. . .] geometrichka zakhlopnula klassnyy zhurnal i zavizzhala. — Est' psevdouchenik, kotoryy skryvayet svoyë podlinnoye litso, padaya, kak yabloko, nedaleko ot yabloni v vishnëvom sovetskom sadu, gde les rubyat, a shchepki letyat, i gde molotok za pilu ne otvetchik! Kosinusom stroim gigantskiye gipotenuzy, vyrashchivayem arbuz v kvadratno-peregnoynykh gnezdov'yakh, pod rukovodstvom velikogo vozhdya lesozashchitnymi polosami menyayem techeniye rek, a zmeinoye pogolov'ye vragov naroda, gnilostnym zlovoniyem smerdya, vpolzayet v druzhnuyu sem'yu narodov! (O, 240)
>
> ([. . .] The geometry teacher slammed her class roster shut and screamed, "We do have a pseudo-pupil who conceals his real face, falling as an apple, not far from the apple tree* in our Soviet cherry orchard, where woods are felled and the chips fly, where the hammer is not answerable for the saw! We build giant hypotheneuses by means of cosines, we raise watermelons in square fertilized settings, we alter the flow of rivers under the guidance of the great leader by means of forest belts, but the herd of serpentile enemies of the people, stinking of rotten putridness, crawls into the tightly knit family of nations.)

Some of her hysterical pronouncements are in themselves absurd ("kosinusom stroim gigantskiye gipotenuzy"), but they still retain a message that derives from their recognizable structure and key vocabulary (e.g., "stroim gigantskiye").

The type of language in the last example is capable of causing a physical response, because political rhetoric is often associated with violence and negative sexual imagery. In *The Burn*, the Stalinist officer Guliy beats his daughter on the inspiration of newspaper reports about capitalist oppression and the American occupation of Europe. While beating her he also repeats lines from a popular post-war song that expresses a strong isolationist feeling: "Ne nuzhen nam bereg turetskiy, i Afrika nam ne nuzhna" ('The Turkish shore we do not need, and we do not need Africa; O, 205-206). Later in the novel, Cheptsov, another face of Guliy, is incensed by his daughter's activities as a *samizdat* typist and rapes her. His action is calcu-

---

* "falling as an apple, not far from the apple tree"—a literal translation of the Russian proverb which means "like father, like son"—eds.

lated to punish rather than "instruct" her, as is the case in the previous example. Similarly, in a burlesque of the power of political clichés, Stepanov in *The Island of Crimea* is carried away by a profusion of fashionable political jargon:

> I tak, vot ona, russkaya triyada nashikh dney—kommunizm, sovetskaya vlast' i narodnost'! Nezyblemaya na vse veka narodnost', ibo narodnost'—èto nasha krov', nash dukh, nasha moshch' i tayna! (OK, 152)
> (And so that's the Russian triad of our time—communism, Soviet power and nationality. Eternally immovable nationality, for nationality is our blood, our spirit, our might and secret.)

His speech causes him to have an erection, which he becomes aware of only after the onlookers react.[14]

The power of words to produce a physical response is likewise shown by clichés used in the media. In a scene from *The Island of Crimea*, one of the characters watches television and comments ironically on the news: "Vakhta udarnogo goda. Svodka idioticheskoy tsifri. Chetyre milliona zernovykh—èto mnogo ili malo? (Watch on a banner year. A summary of idiotic figures. Four million of grain—is that a little or a lot?; OK, 53). His ironic pose belies a deeper attraction to television, and media propaganda in general, as a form of relaxation and sedation. This physical reaction is related to the theme of submission to outside forces, which extends to the main characters in *The Burn*, who are also aging resisters of the system.

One of the main characters in *The Burn* inadvertently comes upon a television screen on which the commentator is reading the evening news. Although there is no sound, he easily supplies the usual words for the program:

> Chto govoril nam ètot byurokrat? Chto-to vpolne privychnoye: ". . . opirayas' na resheniya. . . . rastit' bespredel'no predannykh . . . bezzavetnym trudom na blago . . . vyrazhayet edinodushnoye odobreniye . . ." (O, 280)
> (What did that bureaucrat tell us? Something quite ordinary: ". . . based on the decision . . . raise wholly devoted . . . by dedicated labor for the good of . . . expresses the unanimous approval . . .".)

After a digression about the announcer, the sound comes on and the expected clichés flow from him, just as the protagonist supposed. The commentator is yet another face of the omnipresent Stalinist Cheptsov, whose language is as insidious as the political danger that he represents. Language is a chief characteristic of Cheptsov and other Stalinist figures in Aksënov's works. It provides a sharp contrast with the language of their opposition. This antagonism can be seen in the reaction of some young musicians in *The Burn* to the authoritative order, "Prekratit' provokatsiyu" (End the provocation!), because of which the narrator is on the verge of fainting (O, 31). His friend answers the order with a barrage of swearing, which can be viewed as an anarchistic protest against the official-sounding threat.[15]

In *The Tare of Empty Barrels* and the play *The Heron*, newspaper writing is parodied in brief and absurd announcements, such as the epigraph to the first work and a report of raining frogs in the latter. In his later works, Aksënov injects absurd elements into otherwise genuine journalistic passages. In *The Burn*, for example, a Soviet newspaper, implausibly named *Russkiye vedomosti* (Russian Gazette), reports on an attack of Zionist-backed bandits on a UN hospital in Zaire. The report includes protests from workers in the *Sioux and Sons* factory in Moscow (!) alongside standard condemnations by workers' meetings in the Donbas.

The description of a crowd scene on the Black Sea in *The Burn* takes the form of a journalistic account of a parade. But by punctuating it with nomenclature not normally acceptable in the Soviet media, especially the word *blyad'* 'whore', the narrator gives a symbolic picture of the reality behind the cliché notion of "the Soviet people."

> [. . .] staleliteyshchiki i mastera vysokikh urozhayev, militsiya i voyennosluzhashchiye, blyadi, rybaki i inturisty, blyadi, fartsonniki i druzhinshchiki, tsirkoshniki i kinochi, byurokany i narkomraty, aptekanty i spekulyary, i blyadi. (O, 161)
>
> ([. . .] ironworkers and masters of large harvests, militiamen and servicemen, whores, fishermen and foreign tourists, whores, black marketmen and civil patrolateers, circusmakers and filmplayers, bureaucraties and junkacrats, druggators and speculatists, and whores.)

Allusions to songs and works of literature abound in all of Aksënov's works and therefore they best show the development of his use of conventional language patterns. They fall into the same categories as slogans, clichés and borrowings from the media. As mentioned before, in Aksënov's early writing, songs allude to a character's emotions or the mood of the story. For instance, in the story "Papa, What Does It Spell?", a love song based on S. Esenin's poem "Ty menya ne lyubish', ne zhaleyesh' [. . .]" (You don't love me, or pity me [. . .]) recurs in connection with the theme of unhappy marriage.[16] In *The Tare of Empty Barrels* and *The Steel Bird*, ironic meaning may be attached to a quotation from a song. In the former work, personified Romanticism entices a young character with an accordian:

— Pervyye svidaniya, pervyye lobzaniya, yunost' komsomol'skuyu nikak ne pozabyt' . . .
— Otstan'! — zakrichal Gleb. — Poymayu—kishki vypushchu!¹⁷
("First meetings, first kisses, I can't forget my Komsomol youth." "Lay off!", yelled Gleb. "If I catch you, I'll gut you!")

Gleb wards off Romanticism, who expresses herself in a song that is a shorthand equivalent for an era and Gleb's youth.

An interesting analytic technique is the insertion of interior monologue between several verses from the same or different songs. This device appears several times in *The Steel Bird*. For instance, "The March of the Aviators" provides the frame in the following passage:

Tema: My rozhdeny, chtob skazku sdelat' byl'yu, preodolet' prostranstvo i prostor . . .
Improvizatsiya: Dveri zakolocheny rzhavymi gvozdyami, chto zh teper' delat', zhitelyami s nim? Trudno probivat'sya gryaznym chërnym khodom, vse zhe, esli nado, budem tam khodit'. Lish' by byt' v soglas'i, v mire v blagolep'i, svod pozharnykh pravil lish' by soblyudat'.
Konets temy: . . . Nam razum dal stal'nyye ruki-kryl'ya, a vmesto serdtsa plamennyy motor.¹⁸
(Theme: We were born to make fantasy fact, overcome distance and space . . . Improvisation: The doors are nailed up with rusty nails, what are we tenants to do about him? It's hard to get through the dirty back way, but still if we must, we will go that way. As long as there's concord, peace and splendor, and the fire regulations are observed. End of theme: . . . Steel arm-wings give us reason, and in place of a heart, a combustion engine.)¹⁹

The intervening interior monologue of the house manager, subtitled "Improvisation," is the verbal representation of his musical variation on the theme of the song in the frame. The contrast between the frame and the improvisation expresses the struggle of the people with the dictatorial intruder. The same analytic technique is seen in this example from *The Burn*:

opustela bez tebya zemlya kak mne neskol'ko chasov prozhit'
smotrite akh noven'kaya desyatka nad gorodom letit vyporkhnula
noven'kaya rozoven'kaya so dvora i parit
kuda zh ty uletayesh'
nezhnost' (O, 148)
(The world has become empty without you how can I live even a few hours / Look, oh, a new ten-rouble note flies above the city / It fluttered out of the yard / a new and rose one, and soars / Where to are you flying / Tenderness.)

The first two and the last lines of the popular lyrical song of the sixties *Nezhnost'* 'Tenderness' bracket the narrator's description of a colorful bank-note flitting above the city. These whimsical lines are opposed to the illiterate language of the bigoted crowd that is attacking the protagonists. The stylistic clash is not only on the lexical level, but between totally nonsequential forms of communication, which correspond to the angry mob and the surrounded protagonists.

Songs often stand illustratively for particular cultural periods and ideologies in Aksënov's works. They may also be used in a given context to signify the struggle between conflicting points of view. This is what we have referred to as analytic use. Such is the case in *The Burn*, when the retired Stalinist general thinks,

> Ish', gady, napustili sopley—"pust' vsegda budet mama!"
> To li delo v nashi vremena gremeli pesni:
>> My otstavayem delo,
>> Sozdannoye Il'ichëm.
>> My, boytsy Narkomvnudela,
>> Vrazh'i golovy sechëm! (O, 153)
>
> (See, the slimes, they got soft—"Let there always be mother!" It's not like the songs that thundered in our times: "We defend the work / begun by Il'ich, / We the fighters of the Ministry of the Interior, / We cut off enemy heads!)

The contrast between the children's peace song and the general's bloody song about the secret police is clear. In another place the general drives his tank into a club and disrupts the protagonists' jazz jam. He then sits down at the piano and plays: "Ot Orla do Zamost'ya / Tleyut pol'skiye kosti, / Nad kostyami shumyat kovyli . . ." (From Orël to Zamost'e / rot the Polish bones, / Feather grass hushes above the bones . . . ; O, 162). The jazz music and the songs about brotherhood and love that are sung outside the club are countered by the general's Civil War song. The time in the novel corresponds to the invasion of Czechoslovakia in 1968, which lends special significance to the quotation (cf., "Polish bones").

On the same theme of intervention in Czechoslovakia, and the dire consequences it had for the protagonists of *The Burn*, Aksënov quotes the song "Marsh sovetskikh tankistov" (March of the Soviet Tank Drivers), which sounds bitterly ironic in the mouths of the heroes on the day of the invasion. They are standing in the rain before a line of people into the bathhouse. It has been raining hard for two days (paralleling the two-day-old invasion) and the queue for the bath is as ridiculous as the crowd's silent acceptance of events. The rains release a deluge of filth, which is a metaphor for the current political events, into "the pristine sea, on the second day of the invasion" (O, 25). The correspondence between natural phenomena and the protagonists' psychological state can be shown by the following scheme:

youth, ideals	"khrustal'noye more" /pristine sea/
invasion of Czechoslovakia	Two days of rain overflow of sewage
disillusionment, loss of faith	pollution

Literary references of different types appear throughout Aksënov's works. Besides numerous allusions to a variety of Russian and foreign authors who denote cultural phenomena (e.g., "Silver Age"), literary types (e.g., "Chelovek s ruzh'yëm—Man with a Rifle) and foreign comparisons (e.g., Allen Ginsberg's poem "Howl"), Aksënov occasionally borrows a character type or plot and recasts a character from his own work in it. For instance, a KGB officer in *The Island of Crimea* paraphrases the well known lines of Pavel Korchagin from Nikolay Ostrovsky's *How the Steel Was Tempered*:

> Da gori vsë ognëm—zhizn' prokhodit i v itoge budet muchitel'no gor'ko i obidno za bestsel'no prozhityye gody, da vot kak zakachus' na tri dnya k blyadyam. (OK, 275)
> (To hell with it all—life passes and in the end there will be torturing regrets for years without purpose, so I'll just take off after the whores for three days.)[20]

The Stalinist Cheptsov in *The Burn* alludes to the same passage when reminiscing about his violent activities as a KGB agent in the terror of the 1930s. In both cases Korchagin's originally idealistic prescription for a full communist life becomes a justification for indulging in violent and amoral acts. In a very real sense Cheptsov and the KGB agent are Aksënov's updated versions of Pavel Korchagin—examples of the Stalinist perversion of political power for personal satisfaction.

Aksënov employs literary references as thematic keys in the novel *The Burn*. Mandel'shtam's poem "Bessonitsa. Gomer" (Sleeplessness. Homer) is used epigraphically in the chapter of the same name. At face value the poem is an allusion to the Mediterranean world and Aksënov's favored Black Sea setting. However, the theme of war conquered by love in Mandel'shtam's poem keynotes the action of the chapter.

At the climax of the novel Innokentiy Annensky's poem "Sentyabr'" (September) brings into focus the pivotal theme of reality versus illusion by serving as the nexus of a group of motifs that are scattered throughout the last chapter. The color motifs of black and gold, the themes of refuge, the illusion of physical beauty and the motif of lying are present throughout the novel and are arranged into a symbolic cluster in the final pages. The protagonist suffers the full weight of their meaning when he perceives them together in the context of the poem.

Vladimir Mayakovsky is important in the novel both as a man and a poet. The images of him as a young Futurist poet and as a broken middle-aged man are prototypes important for understanding the development of the novel's main character. The poem is emblematic for Mayakovsky's early period, which was typified by a non-conventional approach to life and artistic innovation. The Mayakovsky of this time is the protagonist's hero in the early 1950s. The protagonist's naive identification with his hero is a natural impulse for a boy living under the conditions of late Stalinism and searching for a voice of freedom, that is, at the same time not opposed to Soviet power. [See P. Meyer's article in this volume—eds.] This identification is analogous to the literary technique in Aksënov's early works of expressing characters' ideas in the form of literary allusions. Just such an illustrative technique, commonly found in his early prose, is used in *The Burn* in order to contrast the viewpoints of the young and old protagonists. The person of the young Mayakovsky is juxtaposed to the brooding image of the poet, seen in the monument on Mayakovsky Square, which the protagonist, who is now approaching middle age, perceives as a statement of the poet's decline and his own weariness. The protagonist recalls the poem "Stikhi o sovetskom passporte" (My Soviet Passport), singling out the line, "Ya / dostayu / iz shirokikh shtanin / dublikatom / bestsennogo gruza" (I pull out / of my trouser-pockets / a priceless cargo's / Bill of Lading; O, 369)[21] which refers to the poet's passport. The position of the statue, however, with hands in pockets, also has a vulgar sexual connotation and is another sign of decline. The figure of the statue is an ironic comment on the poet's and protagonist's values and beliefs at an earlier stage of their lives. The poem—a declaration of pride in the Soviet Union—also provides an ironic contrast to the action in this passage, in which the *druzhinniki* are only interested in the protagonist should he be a foreigner.

IV. Conclusion.

Reflection on the Soviet past and historical reassessment is the central theme of Aksënov's recent major works. This process is personal, although it has often been viewed as the struggle of the generation to which Aksënov belongs. The development of the process of reflection in his works can be related directly to his use of conventional language patterns. As illustrative references they help to "fix" a period, or at least a character's conception of one, in images that can be readily grasped, in the fashion of a simile. Assessment of their underlying historical value, however, only begins with their ironic and analytic use, when they can no longer be simply termed "references" (i.e., illustrative tools), but become integral parts of the text. It is by making them the object of interpretive point of view (ironic use) and connecting them thematically with larger parts of the text (analytic use), that Aksënov infuses them with greater significance. . . .

The central historical theme in Aksënov's works is Stalinism, which is the temporal face of intransient *poshlost'* 'vulgarity'. Stalinism is based on lies, forgetting, and willful ignorance. Aksënov's works present vital ethical questions in vivid cultural and historical terms. The choice between individual freedom and submission to the power of *poshlost'* is offered in the realm of language. Language can be used as a powerful tool against human beings, or as a means of free expression. It is therefore both vehicle and object in the struggle between *poshlost'* and freedom, or art.

FOOTNOTES

1. Per Dalgård, *The Function of the Grotesque in Vasilij Aksënov*, Arhus, 1982, p. 6.

2. Vasiliy Aksënov, "Kollegi," in *Yunost'*, vol. 6, no. 6, 1960, p. 39 (all translations are ours, except when otherwise noted).

3. Vasiliy Aksënov, "Zatovarennaya bochkotara," in *Yunost'*, vol. 14, no. 8, 1968, p. 62.

4. "Zatovarennaya bochkotara," p. 44.

5. Mikhail Lermontov, "The Poet's Death," in *The Demon and Other Poems*, Eugene M. Kayden, trans., Yellow Springs, Ohio, 1965, p. 31.

6. "Zatovarennaya bochkotara," p. 54.

7. Priscilla Meyer, "Aksënov, Vasilii Pav.," in *The Modern Encyclopedia of Russian and Soviet Literature*, Harry B. Weber, ed., vol. 1, p. 94.

8. Vasiliy Aksënov, *Ozhog*, Ann Arbor, Michigan, 1980, pp. 132-33 (all page references to citations from *Ozhog* (O) refer to this edition).

9. Vasiliy Aksënov, *Ostrov Krym*, Ann Arbor, Michigan, 1981, p. 49 (all page references to citations from *Ostrov Krym* (OK) refer to this edition.

10. The physical presence of the slogans in huge red or neon letters arrayed throughout the city attests to the totemistic belief in the power of the printed word, which Vera Dunham has labeled the "Iskra complex"—"an obsession which mistakes the word for reality and attempts to transform the word into action." See Vera Dunham, *In Stalin's Time*, Cambridge, 1976, p. 27.

11. Aksënov compares the Soviet Union with ancient Rome in other works, notably "Gibel' Pompei."

12. The first part of this acronym was a motto of the White Army ("Edinaya nedelimaya"); the second part is from the poet N.A. Nekrasov's poem *Komu na Rusi zhit' khorosho*.

13. The words of Ivan S. Turgenev.

14. In the novels *Ozhog* and *Ostrov Krym*, not all sexual response to verbal stimuli is viewed negatively. See Per Dalgård, p. 97.

15. Some critics have interpreted obscene language in the works of other contemporary Russian writers as a verbal protest against the established order. See Petr Vail' and Aleksandr Genis, *Sovremennaya russkaya proza*, Ann Arbor, Michigan, 1982, p. 105.

16. Vasiliy Aksënov, "Papa, slozhi!," in *Novyy mir*, vol. 38, no. 7, 1962, pp. 98-107.

17. "Zatovarennaya bochkotara," p. 47.

18. Vasiliy Aksënov, "Stal'naya ptitsa," in *Glagol*, Ann Arbor, 1977, vol. 1, p. 65.

19. Vasiliy Aksënov, "The Steel Bird," in *The Steel Bird and Other Stories*, Rae Slonek, trans., Ann Arbor, Michigan, 1979, p. 31.

20. N. Ostrovsky, *How the Steel Was Tempered*, R. Prokofieva, trans., Moscow, 1952, p. 105.

21. *Mayakovsky*, Herbert Marshall, trans., London, 1965, p. 389.

PART III

ARTICLES ON SPECIFIC TOPICS

IN SEARCH OF A GENRE
The Meaning of the Title and the Idea of a "Genre"

B. Briker

A boundary, similar to the kind drawn between sovereign states, divides the works of Aksënov published in the Soviet Union from those printed in the West. This boundary extends into the chronology of his work, where it arranges everything neatly in its proper place. For those of us who have made a habit of following his *oeuvre* as it has appeared in successive publications, it is now difficult to believe that *The Steel Bird* was written even before *The Tare of Empty Barrels* and that the "Soviet" work *In Search of a Genre* appeared on his writing table after *The Burn*.

In Search of a Genre, published in 1978 in *Novyy mir*, marked the end of the Soviet period in Aksënov's writing.[1] Indeed, its very publication at that time in *Novyy mir* can only be explained—to get somewhat ahead of ourselves—as something of a minor miracle. (The publication of *The Burn* would have been a major one.) Both with respect to its experimental form and to a number of its motifs, *In Search of a Genre* is quite close to those of Aksënov's major works which were written at approximately the same time, but which never appeared in the author's homeland. Only in the context they help to provide can one understand such a phenomenon as Durov's "genre" in Aksënov's *In Search of a Genre*.

Pavel Durov travels about the country in his car and as a result of his contacts with sundry people the reader is told stories whose action takes place in the most far-flung parts of the USSR—while there are various principal characters, Pavel Durov invariably figures in each of the stories, now as protagonist, now as observer, now again as narrator or, as is usually the case, as all three at the same time.

A second element uniting these stories, compositionally, is Durov's membership in a strange profession, his practice of a strange genre. The various manifestations of the genre, as well as the very quest for the genre, are the motive, the overall inner plot of the entire story, which leads to the ultimate disclosure of the "genre" and to the very miracle that represents the final goal and apotheosis of the genre.

The third and last, but far from least, element comprising the work is found in the "scenes." Once again these are motivated by Durov's genre, but they also represent a free expression of the literary genre of the author, Aksënov himself, or at least represent his search for an appropriate form for this genre. The goal of this search involves freeing oneself from the conventions of traditional prose ("the prose writer really does choke on his own Adam's apple—don't lose control, Adam")[2] and creating a form in which bits of rhymed and rhythmic prose and elements of drama are combined. Instead of a plot underlying the movement of the prose, one would then have a chain of associations or reminiscences, and excerpts from favorite classical works. Over all of this reigns irony, which figures in Aksënov's scenes not only as a literary device, but even as a literary image (see p. 131). To borrow analogues from Aksënov himself, we can compare these scenes or devices with jazz improvisations. In *The Burn* and *Our Golden Hardware*, the jazz musician Samsik Sabler improvises Aksënov's own rhythmic prose on his saxophone. Thus, Aksënov uses prose to reproduce a non-literary genre, or conversely, he weaves the formal elements of a non-literary genre into his prose.

In Search of a Genre manifestly contains two quests for a genre: the quest, or rather artistic experiment of the author, and Durov's quest for his genre. Hence, the title of the work and its generic subtitle, set in a different sized type, coincide. Durov's "genre" and that of other artists is a multidimensional phenomenon, and, in one of its dimensions, it also subsumes the genre of Aksënov the writer.[3]

First of all, Durov's "genre" is the artistic genre to which he belongs, i.e., his profession. Profession and genre constantly appear as synonyms of each other: "not a word about my profession," "my genre," "what is your profession? . . .", "excuse me, what is your genre?", etc.

Durov is a performer by profession. At least this is the literal, everyday understanding of his "profession." As a performer he coexists with the world of reality around him: he earns money (he has saved enough for a car), performs before audiences (the scenes), and introduces himself to strangers (Alla, Lësha Kharitonov's family, Ekaterina, etc.).

The artistic genre which Durov performs is that of a magician (note the comparison of the "scenes" with tricks, the detailed descriptions of the props, "I am a magician," etc.). This is what is otherwise called in Russian the "original genre" (*original'nyy zhanr*). The ambiguity of this expression emphasizes the uniqueness, rarity and originality of this art form, and yet it also gives a totally satisfactory answer to the official head of the search team, since the "original genre" is a very specific genre encountered in circuses and on the stage. Durov's "genre" has its point of departure in this "original genre," and this aspect binds it to the real world. However, the ultimate purpose of Durov's genre is different.

Aksënov's choice of artistic genre for Durov is no accident. The goal of the "genre of illusions" or "original genre" presupposes producing the illusion of a miracle as in any magic trick. However, the goal of Durov's genre is the creation of a genuine miracle, not an illusory one.

This difference in goals (false miracle—real miracle) creates the ambiguity and metaphorical nature of all the vocabulary associated with a magician's work. A miracle itself is often described precisely in terms of this genre. The iceberg, one of the miracles of Durov's "genre," appears as a "trick." (See the chapter "The sea and the tricks," 167.) "And maybe we're somebody's magic trick, too?", asked little Sveta when she saw the pink iceberg, the product of Durov's and his friends' genre. This question, a metaphor for the entire chapter, arises as a result of the ambiguity in the word *fokus* 'trick', which in Durov's artistic vocabulary can also be a miracle. ("You can get famous with tricks like that . . ." "Maybe so with ones like that, but mine are of a different kind . . ." 166.) And if a trick is a miracle, then Sveta's line is nothing more than the invariant in the reply by Durov himself: "At bottom we human beings are also miraculous . . ." (i.e., likewise the result of tricks; 167).

A similar interpretation of the same kind of profession can be found in Aksënov's 1967 story "Ginger from Next Door." Ginger has the same profession as Durov, the same genre. He is a juggler and a magician. His tricks, his juggling of dishes, his double and triple somersaults in a bohemian restaurant interrupt the action of the story—which until then had moved within the limits of reality—and give it wings, so that the redhead's and the narrator's childhood dreams are revised in the new, fantastic reality which arises. However, the fact that this character's profession is magic, which more easily motivates the narrative flights of fancy, is rather the exception than the rule for Aksënov. In general, Aksënov and his protagonists freely cross the border where the search for some art form or other kind of human activity ends and the miraculous begins. More accurately, the search for a genre is itself the search for a miracle, even if the latter is produced by earthly means.

Aksënov's protagonists study science, paint pictures, play basketball or the saxophone, cure sick people, etc. In one of the early stories, "The Odd-Ball," a nearly illiterate peasant spends his entire life building a perpetual motion machine. Finally, he completes his project: "the board clicks as if it were ticking off the years of our lives to their outer limits, even beyond their limits, forwards and backwards, and one can't tell any longer where those noiseless wheels have rolled."[4]

In *Our Golden Hardware*, a nostalgic novel about the generation of the 60s, the goal of such quests was the *Dabl'-fyu*, a formula that the great

Salazkin had worked on together with young scientists. Like the "genre," which is reminiscent of "something unexperienced [. . .], something unspeakably beautiful, unnamed [. . .]" (153), *Dabl'-fyu* is described in such words and expressions as "ineffable," "sought for, yet elusive as a mirage." And although the precise function of *Dabl'-fyu* always eludes us ("we'll make it [. . .], say, cure malaria, or maybe butcher beefsteaks, or perhaps inspire procreation among the elderly [. . .],"[5] yet its discovery, like the final formulation of the genre, must result in a miracle.

One of the Apollinariyeviches, Dr. Mal'kol'mov in the novel *The Burn*, conducts medical experiments to find his *lympha-D*, which is described in the same terms as *Dabl'-fyu* and "genre." "Sometimes I feel the closeness of the mystery." "The mysterious *lympha-D*—that's the goal of his experiments," "Sometimes through the microscope I can see the strange question marks of fate." "*Lympha-D* is cosmic, mysterious [. . .],"[6] etc. *Lympha-D*, which Mal'kol'mov seeks through his science, became the goal of other Apollinariyevich affiliates, each of whom considered it to lie within his own field of activity, rather than in that of medicine: jazz musicianship, physics, literature, sculpture. And although all of them except Mal'kol'mov ultimately forget about *lympha-D*, i.e., about the precise medical term (invented, of course, by Aksënov), each of them nevertheless seeks his own *lympha-D*, or, if you will, a "genre" that is accessible to him by means of his own profession and creativity.

Thus, Aksënov characteristically combines both concreteness and reality of means (profession, creativity) and a metaphysical, unreal essence of goal ("genre," *lympha-D, Dabl'-fyu*). These vary in different works, depending on the variety of means and the different specific manifestations of the goal. The nature of these combinations explains many formal peculiarities in Aksënov's works. For example, in the last chapter of *In Search of a Genre*, *Dolina* 'The Valley', this combination is presented in a description of the preparations for miracles by fifteen performers. The very names of the "instruments" inherently combine both means and ends. Generally, this is achieved by a conjoining of words, organized according to the principle of grammatical government, the governing word of which is a substantive designating something in the professional activity of the individual: an instrument, an object designating the means, while the governed word designates something taken from abstract terminology: "Tarelki Èkho" (Plates of Echo), "Bochka Olitsetvoreniya" (The Cask of Personification), "Shlangi Proshlogo" (Hoses of the Past), "Porokhovyye niti budushchego" (Explosive Threads of the Future). The concreteness of means is strengthened through a number of verbs relating quite specific human activities:

"katili vverkh" (they rolled uphill), "razveshival" (he hung up), "ustanavlival" (mounted), "raskatyval vniz" (rolled down), "perebrasyval" (threw over), "zakruchivali" (they twirled around), "razduval mekhami" (fanned with bellows). I will not dwell on the linguistic aspects of this phenomenon, but I would like to note that this kind of combination of the concrete and the abstract permeates *In Search of a Genre*. For example: "This is not the doing of my hands alone," with regard to the miraculous iceberg in the aforementioned chapter "The Sea and the Tricks." The interrelationship of these parts is especially marked in the title of the work. The search is a process, tangible means, a path towards attainment. The "genre" is abstract, an ideal category, a dream and a miracle. And if we distance ourselves from this story and consider that *Dabl'-fyu* and *lympha-D* are merely alphabetical or medical designations of the same "genre" phenomenon, then the underlying sense of the title could be applied equally well to other works by Aksënov as, e.g., *The Burn, Our Golden Hardware*, and numerous short stories of the 60s.

However, one must add that a person's profession and creativity exhaust neither the concept of "means" nor the concept of the "search." There is another entire series of variants of the "search," and among Aksënov's protagonists the most important of these, besides (1) creativity and one's profession, are (2) travels, (3) relations with women, (4) memories.

In the short story "Swanny Lake" (1976) the protagonist, Tolya, is preoccupied with all the same things as the Apollinariyeviches in *The Burn*. When Tolya appears in the role of narrator and analyzes everything he has done in the course of the last year, he says:

> Let us fashion a carcass of the past year. And so the joints and the ganglions will be my great *works* of the past year. Between them are stretched taut, silver wires—my *travels*. Let us cover the entire edifice with the fluid soap film of *memory* [. . .] and you are creating a model of the year just passed, inside of which . . . inside of which, of course, there are *women*.[7] [My emphasis—B.B.]

This metaphorical carcass, this model, as Aksënov himself called it, is of course nothing other than a model of the "search for a genre" of the majority of his protagonists from the 60s and 70s.

There has already been ample discussion of the significance of the "open road" in Aksënov's work. Per Dalgård touches on this problem in his book and in an article in this collection. There are even whole treatises dealing with the function of the open road in Aksënov.[8] Therefore, I am not going to deal with all the functions and characteristics of Aksënov's open road; instead, let us again look at the open road from the perspective of the search versus goal.

It is evident from *In Search of a Genre* that Durov is constantly on the road. Even in chapters where the action does not take place on the road, as for example in the chapter "Out of Season," we still sense that this is but a break, a short, temporary haven, and that the road has led up to that point and still awaits us. Within the work itself, nothing takes place in Durov's hometown, and even his home is viewed as a temporary haven:

> . . . returning home to Moscow for a change of filter and oil [. . .] as if going homeward, as though for a rest, but your rest will turn into business in all kinds of spherical cravings [. . .] with a single goal—to move about in new spaces [. . .]. (108)

Durov's itinerary is quite concrete. Aksënov is assiduously precise in marking the map of Durov's journeys, the arc of his wanderings, the points of his rest stops, so that one can delineate the route of his travels on a real map of the Soviet Union. Often the descriptions of the roads themselves are not at all contrived, crossroads are accurately indicated, the speed limit is given, even the locations of speed zones, etc., all the way to his final destination, i.e., the valley itself. Just as detailed and precise are the descriptions of the "means of conveyance": of his own car and all its parts (and of other cars, especially in the chapter entitled "The Penalty Zone"). Such scrupulousness and precision of description are reminiscent of the travelogue genre. In Durov's case there is no specific goal for his journey. Nearly all other characters who travel along the same roads do so with a definite, well-established goal in mind: the search group is after a counterfeiter, *Mamanya* travels to restore her daughter's family, Lësha Kharitonov is travelling on a vacation with his family, Alla is on her way to pick up her husband, even the travels of the hippie Arkadius are relatively goal specific. Only Durov has no apparent practical goal in his travels, he just "rolls along behind the wheel of his car from north to south, from west to east, as though fleeing from his doubts [. . .]" (141). People close to him also express doubts as to the necessity of his travels around the country: "Haven't you had enough of knocking around? You'll just wear your car out and you won't find anything you're looking for . . ." (108). It is through the lack of a specific goal in the real sense that one can explain the appearance of Durov's car in various unexpected places and his unexpected changes of direction. Thus, in the chapter "The Valley," just as he reaches the outskirts of Moscow, his home, he veers south.

The true goal of Durov's perigrinations lies beyond the map of his various routes, but he nevertheless finds it, albeit by driving along the same roads and even entering it in his car: this goal is represented by the valley, the spatial incarnation of the genre, the place of miracles. Other performers have reached this valley at the same time, and not at all by previous arrangement. One supposes that their paths to the valley along the world's roads was no less tortuous than Durov's.

Yet the valley is still not the final goal of the genre, but rather, since it figures in the novel in a real dimension, it is still one more point on the road to the genre, because the genuine fantastic valley appears later:

> It turned out that it bordered on our valley, but it was as huge as an entire country, and it flourished beneath a dance of unknown heavenly bodies. We were enraptured when we realized that this was the true valley. (191-192)

The contrast between the two valleys, one of them marked on a map, the other one the "true" valley from another dimension, is in effect the contrast between search and genre, and it is here that the boundary between the search and the genre itself runs. The first valley represents the culmination of all searchings in the sphere of reality, while the true valley, which appears after the thundering of "avalanches" and the "death" of the fifteen genre performers, is the work's fantastic goal *qua* Utopian reality.

From the standpoint of a fantastic, ideal goal, one finds a similar function of the road image in the short story "Halfway to the Moon," although unlike *In Search of a Genre* there are no fantastic turns of plot in the story. Kirpichenko crisscrosses the country repeatedly by plane, always in search of a miracle, his ideal, which in his case has merged in a very real sense with the image of a stewardess, while in the fantastic sense his goal is identified with the image of the moon. Here we are again dealing with travels that are senseless from a practical point of view (Kirpichenko's motivation—his desire to meet the stewardess—keeps this story out of the realm of the fantastic), but which acquire quite another meaning when viewed from the perspective of the ideal. This dual meaning makes it possible for Kirpichenko and Aksënov to compare the route Kirpichenko has taken on the airplane with half the distance to the moon, and the "fingers of every easy girl" with the fingers of the moon.

The difference in the treatment of the wanderings is primarily that in *In Search of a Genre* an abstract goal is transformed into a reality, while Kirpichenko remains, at story's end, only half-way to his goal.

But an asphalt road or an air route or a "rusty funicular railway" (hence the title of Aksënov's short story "Rzhavaya kanatnaya doroga"), even more concretized by contemporary transportation and contemporary problems, leads to the fantastic goal. This provides the symbolic sense of the journey and conditions the description of its fantastic goal.

If we turn to the tradition of the journey in Russian literature, then the author of *Deal Souls* comes to mind: Chichikov, riding about in his carriage in search of a goal whose ostensible motivation has yet to satisfy anyone. And while we can speak of Chichikov's and Durov's journey in one breath, there is a crucial distinction between them: the carriage transporting the devil in the form of Chichikov leads to hell, while Durov's journey, as well as that of other genre performers, leads toward a valley that is transformed into paradise.

With regard to yet another kind of quest among Aksënov's characters, i.e., relations to women, it is noteworthy that *In Search of a Genre* displays this aspect of the quest relatively little. There are a few random references to Durov's former amours, to "one, and the other one, and my third and my tenth love . . ."; and all the genre performers confess to having experienced happiness in love, etc. This kind of search is well represented in other works by Aksënov [see I. Lauridsen's article in this volume—eds.]. In *The Burn, The Heron* and *The Island of Crimea* the protagonist's earthbound relations with women are a search for the ideal, in which the hero's dreams of the ideal, or of the Beautiful Lady or the Eternal Feminine, are realized.

The ideal (e.g., the heron, Alisa), which Aksënov's protagonists in *The Burn* and other works seek by meeting and entering into relationships with an endless series of women, is very often not even the woman of their dreams, but instead one of a number of abstract categories such as a dream itself, freedom, Europe (in this instance as an abstract concept). In every case it is a matter of physical love with the "ideal," sometimes giving birth to absurd situations (Monogamov and the heron). But each time the relationships of the protagonists to women, which Aksënov depicts in very earthy terms, acquire meaning as paths to the abstract ideal.

In Search of a Genre contains an echo of this approach in the chapter "Our Dear Mamanya's Hitchhiking," in which Durov, "in the mood for miracles," tells Zinaida, a brazen and drunken woman, on the night before his discovery of the genre: "Your laughter, your wonder are not from these idiotic phials, but from other spheres, my dearest Zinaida . . ." (155).

"Other spheres," of course, refer to the ideal of which we have spoken; it represents one of the aspects of the "genre". Thus, here again we have the same interrelationships of concrete, earthbound searchings and the exalted, ideal, ineffable genre.

The search for a genre in memories slightly violates the interrelationship of the concrete and the abstract since the word 'search' *poisk* itself tends to appear in its second, figurative sense in this context. In the short stories of the 60s, and in *The Burn, The Heron, Our Golden Hardware, Sviyazhsk,* memories can be reduced to two basic types: memories of a wartime childhood and memories of youth at the end of the 50s and beginning of the 60s in Moscow or Leningrad. What is most important for us here is that Aksënov draws his dream or ideal from these memories. Here we are most of all concerned with pointing out that this dream is once again close to the genre. In *In Search of a Genre* Durov does not return to his childhood. There are not even any direct accounts of his youth; however, the genre itself keeps returning us with increasing frequency to the past. Often, just by knowing Aksënov's other works, including those published in the West, one can comprehend the various allusions to the past.

When appearing before people or when ironically musing about his genre (as he so often does), Durov applies to it various epithets, the majority of which are negative. Durov's genre is either "semi-disgraceful" or "a strange form of art," "a rare and peculiar profession," "fraudulent," "buffoonish," "a performer of a rare, almost extinct art form," "people of an archaic, dying genre," "my own genre, an insignificant fraud," etc. In all of these attributes there is a single basic characteristic: its lack of popularity and hence its rarity and inevitable doom.

> We are dying out. Practically nobody ever comes to the squares anymore [. . .] What is there good about that—about turning into a museum piece? And if we're no good to anybody, then we're no good at all. (161)

None of this lessens in any way whatsoever the significance of the genre for Durov; instead, it emphasizes the sense of the genre's unsuitability for the present time. This thought is further underscored by there being only fifteen performers of the genre left in the whole world.

However, in the characterization of the genre there are various indications that at one time in the recent past the genre was popular, i.e., during the forty-year-old Durov's youth:

> Oh, how sure I used to be of the power and potential of art, and I used to consider my own genre to be a gift of the gods, the resonator of subterranean upheavals, the collision of storm clouds, the germination of seeds, a virtual justification of all civilization. (141)

> . . . thus it was at the zenith of our fortunes, when the entire genre suddenly came to life and the ancient traditions of rough-hewn street-corner wizardry all at once seized the world like some kind of revelation. (119)

The difference in time between Durov's cross-country trip (the mid-70s) and the period he recollects is about ten to twelve years. He is therefore referring to the so-called thaw in Soviet literature and life. Durov's (and

Aksënov's) youth falls in the period of the thaw. "The search of a genre" is dominated by the nostalgic motifs of the illusions of that generation's youth. These same motifs are more evident in *The Burn, The Heron* and *Our Golden Hardware*.

The generation to which Aksënov's creative people generally belong dreamed of changing the world. "I was carried away then with my young hero," Aksënov said in an interview on the subject of that generation. "It seemed to me that by his very existence he was changing Soviet life."[9]

Durov's genre is precisely what has remained for fifteen representatives of that generation: the desire to reform the world. Its "lack of popularity and extinction" speak about the extinction of illusions among that generation.

If we consider the creative aspects of the genre and its role in art, then we notice that besides the art of the "original genre" there figure also other art forms: "buffoonery, magic, comedy, the plastic arts, color, musical fragments, even texts" (140):

... right away toss into the air five multicolored bottles, and with the right hand toss up five multicolored plates, and then catch all of them and turn some of them into type and the rest into musical notes. (119)

The notes, of course, are music, and the type is nothing other than literature. The connection of Durov's genre with literature is proven both by Durov's "scenes," and by Durov's being in large part Aksënov himself, as he occasionally removes Durov's mask to become his real self (as, for instance, in the scene of the Venetian romance).

The search by the artists of the New Wave of the 60s for a synthesis of various forms of art is embodied in the "genre" as a synthesis of various art forms. The artistic, creative aspect of the genre reflects various types of activity of the Apollinariyeviches in *The Burn*. That the patronymic "Apollinariyevich" is the same as that of the five protagonists in *The Burn* attests to Pavel Durov's close kinship with them. Likewise, although there is never any mention of it, Pavel Durov may well have had the same Gulag past as Tolya von Steynbock.

Durov's dinner-time ruminations on his age also attest to the disparity between the genre and its time. These considerations of his amount to basically one thought—that Durov does not look or act his age. "Perhaps the whole mess is because I, Pavel Durov, missed a turn somewhere, or couldn't keep pace, or stayed young too long, or just the opposite, lost heart at an early age, or banged my head against a wall." (114)

The age of Aksënov's protagonists is very important. In almost all his works their ages are more or less indicated—and they are mostly people born in the 30s (and often, precisely in 1932). This makes them members of

Aksënov's generation. The later a work's date, the older the characters, but generally they are of one and the same generation: Pavel Durov and the genre performers, all the Apollinariyeviches in *Our Golden Hardware* and *The Burn*, Monogamov and both Lëshas in *The Heron*, O. Shatkovskiy in "Sviyazhsk" and the younger characters of the early stories—"Ginger from Next Door," "The Lunches of '43," "Victory," "Papa, What Does It Spell?", etc. That the author and Kirpichenko in "Halfway to the Moon" happen to be precisely the same age (both born in 1932) serves as the author's pretext for writing that story.

Aksënov's contemporaries are much more than just contemporaries. Most often they share a common or similar past, common memories, a common nostalgia. The conflict of two worlds that Aksënov depicts in *The Burn* and the short story "Victory" is often presented precisely as the conflict of generations. Aksënov assumes that the older generation is the one that has passed through youth in the Komsomol of the thirties and service in the security organs during wartime, producing the coat-check clerks and subway attendants of the 1970s, while the younger generation, the one that finished college in the late 50s and yielded the principal participants in the New Wave of the 60s, produced the jazz musicians, the writers of modern prose and the builders of *Zhelezka*.

The contemporaries in Aksënov's works, the participants in the New Wave or simply "our kind" (*nashi*) as in *The Burn*, often recognize each other by their shared experiences of the past, by various "convergences" in their wartime childhood or in their youth during the 1960s. An example is Lësha the Guard's and Lësha the Seamster's instant recognition of one another in the play *The Heron*: "I spotted you right away, old man." Having abandoned the ideals of their youth (in contrast to the genre performers) and having disguised themselves as a mushroom picker and a seamster, they recognize each other by signs visible to them alone. There is a similar, though more ironic, scene in *Our Golden Hardware*. Kim Morzitser thinks he recognizes one of the heroes of his generation in an alcoholic who tries to "hit him up" eleven kopecks:

> Old boy, you used to be an idol. You were the ideal of Mar'ina Roshcha in our distant, dusty past, back when nature was sidetracked in a continental digression. You were a famous soccer player, old boy, or a saxophonist at the Shestigrannik, . . . or simply one of those guys who put their arms around girls in reparation oilskin coats . . . Old boy, I can see you're not one of the gray pack of coyotes, you can shine in sports, and you have good breeding, too.[9]

In Search of a Genre's common denominator for all the representatives of the New Wave is contained in the "genre." What is important for the fifteen genre performers, fifteen representatives of different countries, is a common set of values, a common ideal. It is such a system of values that is outlined in the symbolic symposium of the genre performers. Thanks to it the path of the genre performers, in their search for a genre, is in many respects the same.

> "Who of us has experienced happiness in love these last years?"
> It so happened that all of them had.
> "Who of us has sunk, perished, swum out and crawled up unto the bank?"
> It so happened they all had.
> "Who of us has betrayed his youth for any sum of money?"
> There were no such men among them.
> "Who has been depressed and has raged in despair?"
> Each of them had.
> "Who has acquired brazenness, cruelty and swinishness in his wanderings?"
> None of us had acquired any of these treasures. (188)

Friendship is part membership in the "genre," as in loyalty to the ideals of one's youth and an immovable set of values. That is why it is important for a person, despite his "drowning, perishing, raging from despair" not to "sell his youth for any sum of money" in order to preserve friendship. In *The Burn*, for instance, each of the Apollinariyeviches has its counterpart, one with the same past, the same concepts, the same sense of nostalgia, but who has betrayed his ideal (Serebro, Serebryannikov, Sil'vester, Zil'berbrantsev). Lësha the Guard and Lësha the Seamster in *The Heron* wear stereotypical Soviet masks so that no one will suspect their close connection with the "genre."

It is worthwhile to examine the most nostalgic chapter of *In Search of a Genre*, "Out of Season," from the perspective of memories of a youth in the 60s and adherence to common ideals.

The action takes place in winter at a Crimean resort in the 70s. Three characters are representatives of the New Wave generation, "our kind": Pavel Durov, Ekaterina, and Sergey the musician. It goes without saying that Pavel Durov is the bearer of the genre and the ideals of the 60s. It is stressed that Ekaterina is a woman of Durov's circle, and that "their paths had crossed somewhere in Moscow." Ekaterina understands Durov and, moreover, she also shows a surprising understanding of the genre. By the end of the story it becomes clear that her profession as a parallel to the genre was fundamental in the working of the miracle. She is a woman with the power "to revive downed birds."

The third representative of that generation is Sergey the musician. At some time in the past he had been one of the jazz idols of that generation. It is worth remembering that Aksënov's jazz musicians are his most vivid exponents of the ideas and moods of the New Wave. Samsik in *The Burn* and *Our Golden Hardware* was a jazz musician. Like Samsik Sabler, Sergey plays "Solitude." In connection with Sergey, Durov recalls the names of a whole series of musicians who actually lived in the 60s. They are the same ones associated with Sabler.

Sergey participates in an official Soviet performing ensemble with a group of obedient youths who, while singing, show the audience with theatrical gestures that all of life is yet before them. This is precisely what the balladeer Vysotsky—independently of Aksënov—called the "crisis of the genre."

Durov's memories of the music of those years run parallel to the story's depiction of the band called *Spolokhi* and Sergey, the connecting link between the past and the present. The story line culminates in the incident with the duck which the musicians kill from sheer boredom. After the concert Pëtr Sigal brings the dead bird to the musicians as proof of their guilt. Later the bird revives in Ekaterina's arms to sing in a human voice the song that the musicians had just performed in their concert:

> Ne nado pechalit'sya
> Vsya zhizn' vperedi,
> Vsya zhizn' vperedi,
> Tol'ko khvost pozadi.
> (No need to worry
> Life is before you,
> Life is before you,
> Only the tail's behind.)

The last line of the song, instead of the anticipated "Hope and wait" (*Nadeysya i zhdi*), not only parodies the optimism of the Soviet youth song, but also sets the course of the entire story, in which the account of the duck's killing, although it occupies comparatively much of the narration, is only an author's trick aimed at drawing the reader into a moralistic tale of human cruelty to animals. The last two lines form a contrast:

1) life—ahead
2) tail—behind

where the word "tail" emanates from the real sphere (birds really do have them behind) and interacts with the word "life." Hence the irony and spuriousness of the first version of "life is before you," as well as the more abstract sense and greater irony of the second.

The story of the death and resurrection of the duck and its song-parody are connected with Sergey. In this respect the killing of the duck is reminiscent of the killing of the Heron and its resurrection, although the meaning of the Heron's death is stronger and is equated with the death of one's youthful ideals. Sergey himself, whose trumpet has accommodated the optimistic tempos of the band, recalls both Lëshas who turned into a seamster and a guard to avoid having anything remind them of their youth.

The persistent motif of the loss of one's youthful ideals is encountered in, for example, the "climatic booth" (artificially created climatic conditions for vacationing "out of season"), and in the very title of that chapter, taken as it is from Hemingway.

Thus, in memories, as in the "search for a genre," the nostalgia for the "illusions" of the "New Wave" and disillusionment over the possibility of changing reality are expressed. Such disillusionment in no way contradicts the optimistic conclusion of *In Search of a Genre*—the beautiful resurrection of the genre performers in their new valley and the advent of the miracle. Aksënov resorts to a supernatural miracle precisely because reality gives no cause to hope for one. Aksënov himself says in an interview given for this collection, "All that's left is our hope for a miracle."

The Genre as a Varnishing of Reality

In one of the short stories of the 60s, "Little Whale, Varnisher of Reality," three-year-old Kit, who does not know about or believe in the ironclad rules of the fairy tale, where good struggles with evil and always wins out, refuses to accept the existence of evil. (Kit evidently has not read Propp's classic study *The Morphology of the Fairy Tale*, with its painstaking analysis of these rules.) Therefore, he emends the fairy tales according to his own perceptions: the goat-kids are children, and the wolf is a father. Kit's own father meets with little success in the real world and he is especially annoyed by a certain phone call which he is either expecting or supposed to make himself. On the other end of the telephone line there lurks some unknown evil force, personified by his unjust boss. But apparently Kit's miniature imaginary world has expanded and subsumed the cruel world of adults. The threatening boss not only forgives the protagonist, but also pledges to be his spear carrier and protector.

Using the expression in the same ironic sense as Aksënov, we can conventionally term the device he applies in this story "varnishing reality." It consists of introducing a fantastic, utopian element into a realist narrative—a miracle that decorates or varnishes reality and brings it close to a dream. *In Search of a Genre* manifests this device via the genre itself, whose basic function is to change reality for the better through miracles.

In Search of a Genre's "varnishing of reality" may be supernatural, i.e., fantastic, or it may be real, or a combination of the two. The latter is the most characteristic. In the chapter "The Sea and Tricks" this combination occurs in the linking of the sea and the magic trick. The sea is a miracle of nature, not of the "genre," but the children's perception of it is as that of a supernatural miracle. The pink iceberg is a product of the genre. Such is also the supernatural union of a fantastic miracle and a natural one in the two valleys. An example of a purely terrestrial "miracle," also a product of the genre, is the "miracle" of mass faith at the wedding. All the wedding guests are convinced that Durov is a counterfeiter, even though there is no basis for their suspicions. Here the connection with a miracle ("the biggest miracle would be to convince them that I'm an honest man [. . .]" (179) "how unexpectedly came the night on which the miracle occurred. There was no need for thunder, or lightning, or sound or even light effects" (181)) is a bit ironic, because that which is (or which should be) normal and natural is presented as supernatural. The various "resuscitations," or revivals, can serve as examples of a purely fantastic miracle, e.g., the resurrection of the bird, the revival of "Mona Lisa" upon her meeting with Arkadius, and the resurrection of all fifteen genre performers after the avalanche.

Significantly, the avalanche is represented as the primary "anti-miracle," as opposed to the miracle of the heavenly valley.[11] The avalanche is the essence of the anti-genre, just as the valley is the essence of the genre, and it symbolizes the anti-genre's destructive force. Through the course of the whole work there is, aside from the search for a genre, a search for an anti-genre. Genre and anti-genre come into conflict, just as in the fairy tale, where good defeats evil. The "genre" defeats the anti-genre, the valley re-emerges in the wake of the avalanche, a good example of "varnishing reality."

In the chapter "A Portrait with Whiskers," the search party undertakes a search for the anti-genre. On the basis of the "portrait," which contains no distinguishing traits, the search party sets out after a counterfeiter. This group "in search of an anti-genre" is an obstacle to Durov: the soldier frisks him, then the officer detains him, and a crew of militiamen chases after him, and everyone else is sure that Durov is the counterfeiter. Not by chance does Durov require a miracle to persuade the mob of his innocence. Even the expression "slovesnyy portret" (literally, a verbal portrait, in fact, a police sketch) can be applied to literature. Aksënov has this in mind, for his "sketch" is a parody of banal Soviet art and of a stereotyped way of thinking. In this sense the story of the anti-genre resembles other phenomena of the anti-genre: the festive "Day sing out" (*Den' zveni*), the song "No need to worry," and other Soviet songs, the wedding at the garment factory, Alla Filipuk's thoughts on love, etc. From another standpoint, this banality becomes dangerous, since it makes it possible to see a criminal in every person. In this respect, the function of the anti-genre is destructive. Mamanya also participates in the same "search for an anti-genre," using the same methods as the search party when she insists that her daughter's unfaithful husband be arrested. The same holds for the drunk driver of the first chapter who almost took Durov's life.

Thus, the search for a genre is a constructive search and a preparation for miracles, while the search for an anti-genre is a destructive search (cf. the avalanche and the examples cited above). The search for a genre is a search for everything genuine: genuine love, genuine art (Don Juan, Mona Lisa)—the search for the anti-genre is the search for a substitute, a stereotype, a lie. The most important difference is that the search for a genre is the search for the spiritual, the exalted, while the search for an anti-genre is the search for the spiritless. This decisive contrast in *In Search of a Genre* is presented in such ironic formulae as:

"I want a miracle," Pavel confessed.
"There you go! I wouldn't mind getting a bit more to drink myself."
(152)

The story of the fifteen genre performers who dissolve in a crowd of people, bringing the world the "genre" and ultimately creating the miracle of the valley, has distant overtones in the Gospels. One can consider here the genre performers' breakfast in relation to the Last Supper of the Apostles. However, this affinity with the Gospels is one that meets the needs of Aksënov's literary world.

And should we recall other works of Aksënov, for example "The Village of Sviyazhsk" and *The Burn*, then the search for a genre among Aksënov's seekers, whether they realize it or not, is a search for a spiritual essence in a spiritless world. The miraculous valley, the sum of these quests, is the paradise that people have lost sight of, but which Durov and his genre performers have once again attained.

FOOTNOTES

1. There were some minor publications afterwards.

2. V. Aksënov, "Poiski zhanra," *Novyy mir*, No. 1, 1978, pp. 105-192; here and in the following, references to this work will be given in the text.

3. Concerning the relation of Durov's and Aksënov's genres see P. Dalgård's *The Function of the Grotesque in Vasilij Aksenov*, Aarhus 1982, pp. 121-135.

4. V. Aksënov, "Dikoy," *Na polputi k lune*, Moscow, 1965.
5. V. Aksënov, *Zolotaya nasha zhelezka*, Ann Arbor, 1980, p. 34.
6. V. Aksënov, *Ozhog*, Ann Arbor, 1980, pp. 279-280.
7. V. Aksënov, "Lebyazh'ye ozero," *Literaturnaya Rossiya*, June 4, 1976.
8. See V. Filip, "Tema begstva u Aksënova," *Novyy zhurnal*, No. 151, 1983, pp. 68-75, and M.L. Guldengren, "Mellan statik og dynamik," *Slavica Othiniensis*, No. 27, 1979, Odense.
9. Beseda s pisatelem Vasiliyem Aksënovym, *Kontinent*, No. 27, 1981, p. 435.
10. *Zolotaya nasha zhelezka, op. cit.*, p. 25.
11. See E. Evtushenko, "S raznykh tochek zreniya," *Literaturnoye obozreniye*, No. 7, 1978.

MYSTIANIC PROSE[1]

È. Etkind

Literary classifiers distinguish between several modes of prose: factual and rhetorical, ornamental and linear, single-voiced and polyphonic. How can one define the prose of Vasiliy Aksënov? It differs from work to work, but it does have one dominant characteristic. This we will define on the basis of a few episodes from *Our Golden Hardware*,[2] written in 1972.

One of the opening chapters tells of how the hero made the acquaintance of Rita, the beauty, "CO_2-girl" (*devchonkoy-saturatorshchitsey*). This event is preceded by a description of the *Zhelezka* (i.e., an iron-ore deposit in the Far East) as seen from an airplane:

1. Esli vy nichego o Ney ne znayete, vy mozhete Eyë ne zametit' s
2. vysoty poleta transsibirskogo aèro. Mozhet byt', vash bezuchastnyy
3. vzglyad i otmetit nebol'shuyu rozovatuyu propleshinu sredi "zeleno-
4. go morya taygi," no uzh vo vsyakom sluchaye vy ne pril'nëte k illyumi-
5. natoru i ne ispytayete nikakikh chuvstv, esli tol'ko vy vdrug ne po-
6. chuvstvuyete nichego osobennogo, chto ne isklyucheno. Esli zhe vy ne tol'-
7. ko znayete Eyë, no i sluzhite Ey uzhe mnogie gody, to est' esli vy Eyë
8. lyubite, to vy konechno zhe vlepites' v illyuminator zadolgo do pri-
9. blizheniya k Ney chtoby kak-nibud' ne proglyadet', i budete volno-
10. vat'sya, kak pered vstrechey s blizkim chelovekom ili lyubimym zhi-
11. votnym i razglyadite vse Eyë sostavnyye pyatnyshki, kameshki, prozhil-
12. ki, blestki i mozhet byt' vam ona dazhe pokazhetsya ne prosto bliz-
13. koy, volnuyushchey, no i krasivoy, mozhet byt', dazhe s desyatikilomet-
14. rovoy vysoty Ona napomnit vam nechto nezhnoye i bezzashchitnoye, s kry-
15. lyshkami i tonkim sterzhnem—tel'tsem, nechto vrode babochki, èdakiy
16. terrakotovyy batterflyay, izyashchnyy i neprochnyy kak inostrannoye
17. proizvedeniye iskusstva. Vot ona kakova s vysoty, nasha Zhelezka!

(If you do not know anything about Her, you may not notice Her from the altitude a trans-Siberian a-p. flies at. Perhaps your indifferent eye will notice a small pinkish bald-spot in the midst of the "green sea of the taiga," but in any case you won't lean towards the window, and you will experience no sensation, unless you suddenly feel nothing in particular, which eventuality is not excluded. If you not only know Her, but have already served Her for many years, that is, if you love Her, then, of course, you will glue yourself to the window long before you draw near to her so that you cannot possibly miss Her, and you will be as excited as before a meeting with someone dear to you or with a beloved animal, and you will try to make out all the specks, pebbles, streaks and sparkles of which she is made, and perhaps she will seem to you not only close and moving, but also beautiful, and perhaps she will (even from a height of 10 kilometers) remind you of something tender and defenseless, with delicate little wings and a small slender corpus similar to a butterfly, a kind of terracotta-colored lepidopterous, elegant and fragile like a piece of foreign art. That's what she looks like, our *Zhelezka*, from on high!)

What is peculiar to this description is the variety of quotations, of which the sources are sometimes obvious and sometimes unknown. The *Zhelezka* appears like a goddess—she is not named; the capitalized pronoun is deemed sufficiently solemn: "o Ney, Eyë, . . . vy ne tol'ko znayete Eyë, no i sluzhite Ey uzhe mnogie gody, to est' esli vy Eyë lyubite . . . , zadolgo do priblizheniya k Ney" (About Her, Her . . . you not only know Her, but have already served Her many years, that is, if you love Her . . . , long before drawing near to Her), etc. These "religious" phrases remind us, above all, of how, at the beginning of the century, Andrey Belyy and Alexander Blok wrote each other solemn and mystical letters about the "Eternal Feminine" whom Blok—following Vl. Solov'yëv—called "Maiden, Dawn, Cupidess" and about whom he wrote:

I vot—Ona i k Ney—moya Osanna—
Venets trudov—prevyshe vsekh nagrad.

Ya skryl litso, i prokhodili gody.
Ya prebyval v Sluzhen'i mnogo let . . .

(And here She is, and to Her my Hosannah
The crown of labors—higher than all rewards.

I hid my face, and the years passed.
I spent in Service many years . . .)[3]

The symbolist Blok "prebyval v Sluzhen'i mnogo let" (he spent in Service many years). Aksënov writes, as though repeating after Blok, "vy sluzhite Ey uzhe mnogie gody" (you have already served Her many years). Blok speaks about his real fiancée, Lyuba Mendeleyeva, in the mystical language of Solov'yëv's metaphysics; Aksënov speaks about an iron-ore deposit in the pseudo-mystical language of Blokian symbolism, which goes back to the Provençal troubadours—for them the theme of "service" was central.

Through this whole paragraph runs the theme of the Beautiful Lady, to which a parodic interpretation is given. The ironic attitude to industrial objects as to the newest, neo-symbolist "Devam Raduzhnykh Vorot" (Maidens of the Rainbow Gates) is characteristic of Aksënov's generation; it was expressed not so much in the poems of Evg. Evtushenko, who called his collection (also from 1972) *Poyushchaya damba* (The Singing Dam) as in the pun in the title: "Stikhi o prekrasnoy dambe" (Poems about the Beautiful Dam).[4] In Aksënov we find a description that comes close to "Poems about the Beautiful *Zhelezka*." It should be noted that two pages later "symbolism" appears openly; at this point, however, the mystical phraseology refers to the CO_2-girl, in the following context:

> Intelligentnaya devushka s voprositel'noy usmeshkoy posmotrela na menya. Mne polagalos' poshutit'. Ya znal, chto mne seychas polagayetsya poshutit', a mne khotelos' skhodu zanyt': "Lyubimaya, zhelannaya, schast'e moyë, na vsyu zhizn' Prekrasnaya Dama" . . .
> (An intelligent girl with a questioning smile looked at me. I was supposed to make a joke. I knew that right now I was supposed to make a joke, but I simply felt like whining: "My love, my desire, my happiness, for my whole life Beautiful Lady" . . .).

In the French edition of *Zhelezka* one finds the following footnote: "a line from a poem by Alexander Blok." This is a mistake. Such a line does not exist; however, the general atmosphere of the early Blok is present in this phrase just as it is in the preceding, stylistically related description of the *Zhelezka*.

This central, neo-symbolist motif combines with words and phrases from other stylistic layers:

2   *aèro* 'a.-p.'—a playful abbreviation of the word *aèroplan* 'airplane', which is not common usage but is characteristic of the speech of high-tech types;

3-4   "zelënogo morya taigi" (the green sea of the taiga)—a quotation from a banal-picturesque newspaper sketch which is also the source of the adjoining phrase (although it is here in negative form: *vy ne* (you will not));

4-5   "pril'nëte k illyuminatoru" (lean toward the window);[5]

5-6   "esli tol'ko vy vdrug ne pochuvstvuyete nichego osobennogo, chto ne isklyucheno" (unless you suddenly feel nothing in particular, which eventuality is not excluded). The expressions *Èto isklyucheno* (This is excluded/can be ruled out) and especially . . . *chto ne isklyucheno* ([here] which eventuality cannot be excluded) reflect a colloquial-bureaucratic style. The second example (the one found in the text) combines two elements of

	bureaucratese; the substitution of *èto* 'that' by *chto* 'which' was often parodied by Zoshchenko. The medic says to the patient: "Esli vy popravites' *chto vryad li*, togda i . . ." (If you get better, *what's hardly likely*,[6] then . . .), in "Istoriya bolezni" (1936; The History of an Illness).
3-8	*propleshina* 'bald spot', and *vlepites'* 'glue yourself to'—are from everyday vocabulary. The stylistic "prosaicalness" of *propleshina* is stressed by the fact that it is placed next to the religious-mystical *sluzhite Ey* (you have already served her), i.e., whom, the bald spot? The informality of the phrase "vlepites' v illyuminator" (you will glue yourself to the window) stands out clearly against the preceding parody-like journalese "ne pril'nete k illyuminatoru" (you will not lean towards the window).
11-12	"razglyadite vse eyë sostavnyye pyatnyshki, kameshki, prozhilki, blestki" (you will try to make out all the specks, pebbles, streaks, sparkles of which she is made)—here mineralogical terms gradually appear and then blend into a combined description of a woman and a landscape:
12-14	"i mozhet byt' vam ona dazhe pokazhetsya ne prosto blizkoy, volnuyushchey, no i krasivoy, mozhet byt' dazhe s desyatikilometrovoy vysoty" (and perhaps she will seem to you not only close and moving, but also beautiful, perhaps, even from a height of ten kilometers).
14-16	Following this is the poetic expression—"nechto nezhnoye i, bezzashchitnoye" (something tender and defenseless), which leads into an almost scientific, entomological description: "s krylyshkami i tonkim sterzhnem-tel'tsem, nechto vrode babochki, èdakiy terrakotovyy batterflyay . . ." (with delicate little wings and a small slender corpus, similar to a butterfly, a kind of terracotta-colored lepidopterous . . .). *Batterflyay* in Russian denotes a stroke in swimming, not an insect, the English word having been chosen in order to intensify the "scientific" entomological flavor of the passage. The other foreign word, *terrakotovyy*, plays a similar role, adding to the playfulness of the text.

In the concluding sentence, the word *Zhelezka* finally replaces all the preceding paraphrases and metaphors.

In seventeen lines we were able to point out at least "seven" different stylistic levels, united only by the voice of the narrator: high-tech vernacular, newspaper sketch style, colloquial-bureaucratese style, standard colloquialism, scientific (mineralogical and entomological) terminology, and poetic style.

The descriptive passage we chose for analysis is not the one most characteristic of Aksënov; yet even it proved to be a contradictory, multi-level construct. But now consider the continuation:

1. V desyati kilometrakh ot Zhelezki, to est' za uzen'koy peremych-
2. koy "zelënogo morya taygi" nachinalas' belosnezhnaya geometriya nashe-
3. go gorodka, no na neyë-to kak raz nikto ne obratil vnimaniya. Vse na-
4. shi provozhali vzglyadom uplyvavshuyu na zapad Zhelezky. Odna tol'ko
5. moya zhena Rita ne smotrela v okno. Vot uzhe bityy chas ona byla zanya-
6. ta besedoy s novym samolëtnym znakomym Memozovym. Voobrazite,
7. buka Rita vmesto obychnogo svoyego sigaretnogo prezritel'nogo i "ti-
8. anstvennogo," imenno "tianstvennogo," a ne tainstvennogo molchaniya
9. ozhivlenno beseduyet s chuzhim muzhchinoy, kivayet emu golovoy, poni-
10. mayushche ulybayetsya rtom, vyrabatyvayet tselyye periody ustnoy rechi, da
11. eshchë podbrasyvayet miloy ruchkoy—poyasnyayet skazannoye plenitel'nym
12. zhestom i dazhe eyë neizmennaya sigaretka veselo uchastvuyet v dialoge.
13. Chem zhe eyë tak rasshevelil Memozov?
14. Poznakomilis' na svoyu golovu. Ty, Rita, ne vidish' ryadom
15. ser'yëznoy dramaticheskoy natury, a verkhoglyady, okazyvayetsya, tebe po
16. dushe. Ty, Rita, dazhe ne povernula svoyu nefertitskuyu golovku, dazhe
17. ne skosila prodolgovatyy svoy "tianstvennyy" glaz, ty ravnodushno
18. proletela nad nashey Zhelezkoy, v nedrakh kotoroy desyatiletiye nazad
19. ty, glupaya Rita, pomnish' li, zvëzdochka moya vechernyaya . . .

(Ten kilometers from the *Zhelezka*, that is, behind the narrow rim of the "green sea of the taiga," the snow-white geometry of our town begins to appear, but, as it happened, nobody paid any attention to it. We all followed the *Zhelezka* with our eyes, as she receded to the west. Only my wife Rita did not look out the window. For a solid hour now she had been engaged in conversation with her new in-flight acquaintance, Memozov. Imagine, my unsociable Rita, instead of her usual, cigarette-smoking, contemptuous and "mystianic," namely "mystianic," not mysterious silence, engaged in a lively conversation with a strange man: she nods her head at him, smiles understandingly, produces whole periods of oral discourse, as well as flinging her sweet little hand about, explaining what she says with a captivating gesture, and even her eternal little cigarette gaily participates in the dialogue. How did Memozov manage to get her so worked up?

It was their own fault that they began their fateful acquaintance. Rita, you do not see the serious, dramatic soul next to you, but, it turns out, these mediocre types are to your taste. You, Rita, did not even turn your little Nefertiti head, you did not even squint your longish "mystianic" eye, you flew indifferently over our *Zhelezka*, in whose inner depths, a decade ago, you, silly Rita, remember, my little evening star . . .)

The passage opens matter-of-factly with a precise indication:

1	"V desyati kilometrakh" (Ten kilometers)—combined with the conventionally-colloquial predication *ot Zhelezki* (from the Zhelezka); subsequently we have a geographic term
1-2	"to est' za uzen'koy peremychkoy" (that is, behind the narrow rim), which connects with the quotation repeated from the banal-newspaper sketch "zelënogo morya taygi" (of the green sea of the taiga) and the author's own, striking (metonymic) image:
2	"belosnezhnaya geometriya nashego gorodka" (the snow-white geometry of our town). Further, the informative
5	"moya zhena Rita" (my wife Rita), is followed by the emphasized colloquial locution "uzhe bityy chas" (for a solid hour now), expressing the jealous irritation of the husband-narrator.
4-5	"Vse nashi provozhali vzglyadom . . . *Zhelezku*. Odna . . . Rita ne smotrela v okno." (All of us followed the *Zhelezka* with our eyes . . . Only . . . Rita did not look out the window.) The wife is further characterized by the childish phrase
7	"buka Rita" (*buka*, 'unsociable person', 'bogeyman'); apparently this infantile expression serves to render her particular brand of coquetry which is expressed below through the diminutives "miloy ruchkoy" (sweet little hand) and *sigaretka* 'little cigarette'. The narrator's wife, Rita, is characterized by means of a combination of not very compatible elements: the author's own expression "sigaretnoye . . . molchaniye" (cigarette-smoking . . . silence), the naively infantile
9	"s chuzhim muzhchinoy" (with a strange man),
10	the scientific linguistic "vyrabatyvayet tselyye periody ustnoy rechi" (produces whole periods of oral discourse),
11-12	epithets expressing at the same time Rita's image of herself and the narrator's jealous irritation: "podbrasyvayet miloy ruch-

koy—poyasnyayet skazannoye plenitel'nym zhestom" (flinging her sweet little hand about, explaining what she says with a captivating gesture); next we have one more colloquial-idiomatic expression in line 14 which represents a continuation of line 5:

14   "Poznakomilis' na svoyu golovu" (It was their own fault that they began their fateful acquaintance). This expression is superseded by rhetorical repetitions, which transfer the descriptive, narrative prose into the realm of poetry:

14   "Ty, Rita, ne vidish' . . . Ty, Rita, dazhe ne povernula . . . ty ravnodushno proletela . . . ty, glupaya Rita, pomnish' . . ." (. . . Rita, you do not see . . . Rita, you did not even turn . . . you flew indifferently . . . you, silly Rita, remember . . .) and the whole passage is broken off by a lyrical and, it would seem, wholly serious address:

19   "zvëzdochka moya vechernyaya" (my little evening star). The following chapter is called "A Decade Ago" and will be the story of that which in this phrase remains unsaid.

In addition to this hodgepodge of styles, there are two more details which characterize Rita. One of them,

16   "ne povernula svoyu nefertitskuyu golovku" (you did not turn your little Nefertiti head)—relates to the head of the Egyptian empress Nefertiti, which was extremely popular among the Soviet intelligentsia (following an exhibition in 1962); a plaster copy of it stood in the apartment of just about every writer. The second detail is the persistently repeated epithet in the phrase

7-8   "vmesto obychnogo svoyego sigaretnogo prezritel'nogo i "tianstvennogo," imenno "tianstvennogo," a ne tainstvennogo molchaniya . . ." (instead of her usual cigarette-smoking, contemptuous and "mystianic," namely "mystianic," not mysterious silence . . .).

Where does this word come from?

In one of the episodes of the next chapter the narrator, having learned that the one whom he had thought was the watchman is actually the great scholar-physicist Salazkin, says to the young girl Margarita, whose acquaintance he has just made, and who, full of admiration, has informed him that Salazkin "contemplates the question of the universe":

1.   — Khe, — skazal ya, — pfe, kha-kha, podumayesh', mezhdu prochim ne
2. on odin po nocham myslit i, zadykhayas' v metelyakh poludennoy pyli,
3. vryvayetsya k Bogu, boitsya, chto opozdal, plachet, tseluyet emu zhilistuyu
4. ruku, prosit . . .
5.   Vypaliv vsë èto odnim dukhom, ya ustavilsya na tselyye desyatiletiye
6. v palestinskiye margaritskiye tianstvennyye, imenno tianstvennyye, a
7. ne tainstvennyye, glaza.
8.   — . . . chtob obyazatel'no byla khotya by odna zvezda, — skazal chey-
9. to golos to li ryadom, to li v glubine tonnelya, i tam, v proyëme, za
10. dalëkimi sosnami, za vekovym debelym snegom deystvitel'no siyala
11. odna—edinstvennaya zvezda—pokrovitel'nitsa, vozmozhnaya rodina na-
12. shey Zhelezki.
13.   O veter, polynnyy zapakh kosmosa, gazirovannaya nochnaya mysl'
14. moyego kumira, kotorogo ya segodnya vpervyye uvidel, o devushka za sa-
15. turatorom, o tayny nochnoy smeny . . .
16.   — Davayte uydëm otsyuda?
17.   — No kto zhe budet poit' lyudey?
18.   — Zhazhdushchiy nap'yëtsya sam . . .

("Ha," I said, "bah, ha-ha, when you think about it, he's not the only one who contemplates at night, and choking in the storms of afternoon dust projects himself towards God, is afraid that he is too late, weeps, kisses his veiny hand, pleads . . ."

Having blurted this all out in one breath, I stared at the whole decade, at Margarita's Palestinian mystianic, namely mystianic, and not mysterious, eyes.

". . . that there absolutely be at least one star," said someone's voice seemingly at the same time nearby, and deep within the tunnel, and there, in the entrance, beyond the distant pines, beyond the ancient thick snow, a single solitary star really was shining—the patroness, possibly the homeland, of our *Zhelezka*.

O wind, o absinth scent of the cosmos, carbonated night thought of my idol, whom I saw today for the first time, o maiden behind the CO_2 tank, o secrets of the night shift . . .

"Come on, let's get out of here!"

"But who will help the people quench their thirst?"

"He who is thirsting will get his own drink . . .")

Here the narrator introduces into his speech quotations not only from other stylistic domains, but also from actual works: "ne on odin po nocham myslit" (he's not the only one who contemplates at night) grows into a quotation from Mayakovsky's poem *Poslushayte* (1914; Listen), where we read:

> And, striving forth,
> in the storms of afternoon dust
> projects himself towards God,
> is afraid that he is too late,
> weeps,
> kisses his veiny hand,
> requests—
> that there absolutely be a star![7]

The quotation is perfectly accurate (with a variant in the first and last line); Mayakovsky often functions as the backdrop for Aksënov's language. In the case of the epithet *tianstvennyy* 'mystianic' we should also turn to him; in the poem *Oblako v shtanakh* (1915; A Cloud in Trousers) we read:

> Mariya!
> Poèt sonety poyët Tiane,
> a ya—
> ves' iz myasa,
> chelovek ves'—
> telo tvoye prosto proshu
> kak prosyat khristiane—
> "khleb nash nasushchnyy
> dazhd' nam dnes'."
>
> (Maria!
> The poet sings sonnets to Tiana,
> but I
> am all flesh,
> a man every bit—
> I simply ask for your body
> as Christians pray:
> "Give us this day
> our daily bread!")[8]

Here Tiana is a distant, inaccessible woman, to whom it is possible 'to sing sonnets,' but not to love with the earthly passion with which Mayakovsky calls out to her "[. . .] telo tvoyë prosto proshu [. . .]" (I simply ask for your body . . .). Does not, therefore, mystianic mean inaccessible? Obviously, in Aksënov we find such a nuance—with irony; the more so considering that Mayakovsky's source was the elegantly refined and affected Igor Severyanin, who published, a year prior to *A Cloud in Trousers*, his poem (which was anything but a sonnet) "Tiana" (Nov. 1913). It begins as follows:

> Tiana, kak stranno! kak stranno, Tiana!
> Byloe uplylo, byloe ushlo . . .
> Ya plaval moryami, sadilsya v sedlo,
> Brodil piligrimom v opalakh tumana . . .
>
> Tiana, kak skuchno! kak skuchno, Tiana!
> Madlèna—Kak èkho . . . Madlèna—kak son . . .
> Ya bol'she uzhe ni v kogo ne vlyublën:
> Vlyublyayutsya serdtsem, no—kak, esli—rana? . . .
>
> Tiana, kak zhutko! kak zhutko, Tiana! . . . i t.d.
>
>
> (Tiana, how strange! how strange, Tiana!
> The past has floated away, the past is gone . . .
> I have sailed seas, sat in the saddle,
> Wandered as a pilgrim in confused disgrace . . .
>
> Tiana, how boring! how boring, Tiana!
> Madeleine—like an echo . . . Madeleine—like a dream . . .
> I'm no longer in love with anyone:
> One falls in love with the heart, but—how, if it is wounded? . . .
>
> Tiana, how horrible! how horrible, Tiana! . . . etc.)[9]

Here, probably, is why in the last-quoted passage from Aksënov side-by-side we find lines from Mayakovsky, which are cited first by the author, and then by the Great Salazkin, and the repeated characteristic ". . . palestinskiye margaritskiye tianstvennyye, imenno tianstvennyye, a ne tainstvennyye, glaza." (Margarita's Palestinian mystianic, namely mystianic, and not mysterious, eyes.)

These quotations from Mayakovsky and Severyanin are then supplanted by "stylistic" quotations, seemingly taken from an ode: "O veter . . . o devushka . . . o tayny . . ." (O wind . . . , o maiden . . . , o secrets . . .). Here, each "odish" exclamation is joined with a stylistically contradictory word or phrase: the solemn *o veter* with the prosaic plus solemn "gazirovannaya nochnaya mysl' moego kumira" (carbonated night thought of my idol), where the epithet "carbonated" is motivated by the fact that the girl works pouring soda water in the Institute's cafeteria—She has the scientific-sounding name *saturatorshchitsa* 'CO_2-girl' (*saturator* is an instrument which injects carbon dioxide into water, whereby producing soda water, *gazirovka*).[10] The second "odish" exclamation, *o devushka* . . . 'o maiden . . .', is linked to this same term—*za saturatorom* 'behind the CO_2 tank'. The third, *o tayny* . . . 'o mysteries . . .', paradoxically draws after itself the prosaic phrase "nochnoy smeny" (of the night shift). All three of the second parts of these "odish" phrases refer to different styles, so that even this small fragment of the text is many-layered.

The passage ends with a short dialogue between him and her in which the final remark, which is his, reads like a quotation from the Gospels: "Zhazhdushchiy nap'ëtsya sam" (He who is thirsting will get his own drink) (compare: "Vrachu, istselisya sam" (Physician heal yourself—Luke IV 23).

The number of stylistic and direct quotations used by Aksënov is great, and not only in the authorial text, but also in the conversations of his characters; the young physicist Kim, towards whom "a certain untypical young man . . . in a little cap-bouclé" has turned with a request to give him eleven kopecks, replies:

1. — Beri, starik, zabiray vsyu valyutu. Beri, ne tseremon'sya, my
2. lyudi svoi. Ya i sam ne raz perevorachivalsya kverkhu kilem, — zachastil
3. Kim, i tut ego poneslo. — Da chto tam, starik, mne li tebya ne ponyat',
4. ved' my odnoy krovi, ty da ya. Ved' ty, starik, rodom iz plemeni ku-
5. mirov. Ty byl kumirom Mar'inoy Roshchi, starik, v nashey dalëkoy
6. pyl'noy yunosti, kogda torzhestvoval kontinental'nyy uklon v pri-
7. rode. Ty byl znamenitym futbolistom, starik, soznaysya, ili sakso-
8. fonistom v "Shestigrannike" . . . Bessa me, bessa me mucho . . . ili pros-
9. to odnim iz tekh parney, chto tak lovko obnimali za spiny tekh devcho-
10. nok v kleyënchatykh reparatsionnykh plashchakh. A chto, starik, pochemu by
11. tebe ne rvanut' so mnoy v Pikhty? Khochesh', ya seychas tranzistor tolknu
12. i voz'mu tebe bilet? Sibir', starik, zolotaya strana El'dorado . . . molo-
13. dyye uchënyye, nashi, nashi parni, ne khanzhi, i nikogda ne pozdno vzyat'
14. zhizn' za kholku, starik, a ved' my s toboy muzhchiny, molodyye muzhchi-
15. ny,—chto, starik? Ty khochesh' skazat', chto korni tvoi gluboko v as-
16. fal'te, chto Zapad est' Zapad, Vostok est' Vostok? A ya tebe na èto ot-
17. vechu Alikom Gorodnitskim: i mne ne razu ne prividitsya vo snakh tu-
18. mannyy Zapad, nevernyy lzhivyy Zapad . . . izvini, starik, ya poyu . . .
19. Starik, ved' ya zhe vizhu, ty ne iz seroy staiy koyotov, ty i po sportu
20. mozhesh' i po chasti kul'tury . . . a khochesh', ya ustroyu tebya barmenom?
21. Vyshe golovu, starik . . . drug moy, brat moy, ustalyy stradayushchiy
22. brat . . .

("Take it, old man, take all the cash. Take it, don't worry, we're the same kind. Why, I've gone belly up more than once," said Kim, and here he really got carried away. "How could I not understand you, old man. I mean, we're of the same blood, you and I. I mean you're born of the tribe of gods, old man. You were the god of Mary's Grove, old man, in our distant dusty youth, when a continental slant was the rage in nature. You were a famous soccer player, old man, admit it, or a sax player in 'Hexagram,' . . . besame, besame mucho . . . or just one of those guys who so smoothly put their arms around those sweethearts in oil-cloth, reparation mackintoshes. What do you say, old man, what's stopping you from tearing off to Pikhty with me? If you want I can go right now and fence the transistor and get you a ticket? Siberia, old man, it's a golden land, an Eldorado . . . young scholars, like us, our kind of guys, not two-faced; and it's never too late to grab life by the pants, old man, and after all, you and I are men, young men, right, old man? Do you mean to tell me your roots run too deep in the asphalt, that East is East, and West is West? Well, I can answer that with the words of Alik Gorodnitsky: neither have I dreamt even once of the hazy West, the faithless lying West . . . Sorry, old man, I'm singing . . . Hey, look, old man, I can see that you don't come from a grey herd of coyotes, you're good at sports and you know a bit about cultural stuff too . . . want me to set you up as a bartender? Hold your head up high, old man . . . my friend, my brother, my tired, suff'ring brother . . .")

This is the same sort of "mosaic": the frequent repetition of *starik* 'old man', a form of mutual address among the intelligentsia in the 1960s;

1-2   *valyuta* 'cash' as money, this coming from the realm of underworld slang; "my lyudi svoi" (we're the same kind), a common colloquial leading phrasing used by the intelligentsia (cf. in Mayakovsky "Vo ves' golos"—At the Top of My Voice: "Sochtëmsya slavoyu—ved' my svoi zhe lyudi"—We'll come to terms with glory, after all, we're the same kind; it is a line based on the proverb that became the title of A. Ostrovsky's play, *Svoi lyudi, sochtëmsya*—Among One's Own Kind One Always Comes to Terms);

2   "[. . .] perevorachivalsya kverkhu kilem" (went belly up), i.e., was unsuccessful, this coming from sailors' jargon . . . Other echoes resound intermittently—now from Jack London, now from political journalism, now from post-war everyday colloquial usage

10   "devchonki v kleenchatykh reparatsionnykh plashchakh" (sweethearts in oil-cloth, reparation mackintoshes),

11	now from the periphery of the underworld slang "ya seychas tranzistor tolknu" (I'll go right now and fence [i.e., sell] the transistor). The number of stylistic citations is incalculable, but one can refer to the following as especially expressive:
16	"Zapad est' Zapad, Vostok est' Vostok" (East is East and West is West), Kipling's verse in E. Polonskaya's translation;
17-18	"[. . .] tumannyy Zapad, nevernyy lzhivyy Zapad" (the hazy West, the faithless, lying West) from the song by Alexandr Gorodnitsky;
21-22	"[. . .] drug moy, brat moy ustalyy stradayushciy brat" (my friend, my brother, my tired, suff'ring brother) from a poem by Nadson.

* * *

What can we call this prose? It is like a complex "mosaic," establishes many levels of associations, and is intended for an initiated, comprehending reader. It is contemporary by its very essence. It can only be thoroughly understood by a reader who shares the author's education and native culture, a reader who ideally comes from Aksënov's generation. But what about the others? A Frenchman can read the just cited phrases from *Zhelezka* in a very good, exceedingly resourceful translation by L. Denis. But what can the translator do with Rita's "mystianic eyes"? Denis invents: "Ton oeil tysmérieux" for mystérieux. That's good, but Tiana, together with Mayakovsky and Severyanin, goes out the window. Kipling's line was unwittingly rendered meaningless: l'ouest, c'est l'oeust, et l'est, l'est. Aksënov, his friends and fellow-sufferers alike remember the context for this line:

> Da, Zapad est' Zapad, Vostok est' Vostok, i s mesta oni ne soydut
> Poka ne predstanut Nebo s Zemlëy na strashnyy Gospodniy sud.
> No net Vostoka i Zapada net. Chto plemya, rodina, rod,
> Esli sil'nyy s sil'nym litsom k litsu u kraya zemli vstayët . . .
> (Oh, East is East, and West is West, and never the twain shall meet,
> Till Earth and Sky stand presently at God's great Judgement Seat;
> But there is neither East nor West. Border, nor Breed,
> nor Birth,
> When two strong men stand face to face, tho' they come
> from the ends of the earth! [See R. Kipling, "The Ballad of East and West"]

The French reader has to make do with the two words he is twice proffered: Ouest—Est. And so it must be, for such is the law of Aksënov's prose. It reveals itself fully to the initiate; it is, however, quite accessible to the outsider too; although in a rather bare, even impoverished form, it is nevertheless accessible. Here it is not so much a question of translation as of commentary: The initiated reader is the one who intuitively provides his own textual explanations. The outsider needs commentaries, although he can do without them, the bare text being quite enough to intrigue him. Such semantic multiplicity in a text, which is variously accessible to readers of various levels, is characteristic, for example, of Saltykov-Shchedrin. Here from the *Story of a Certain Town* is a passage about the French emigré Du-Chariot. It can be read profoundly or superficially, i.e., with or without an understanding of historical reality:

> [. . .] odnazhdy on nachal ob"yasnyat' glupovtsam prava cheloveka;[11] no k schast'yu, konchil tem, chto ob"yasnil prava Burbonov. V drugoy raz on nachal s togo, chto ubezhdal obyvateley uverovat' v boginyu Razuma, i konchil tem, chto prosil priznat' nepogreshimost' papy. Vsë èto byli, odnako zh, odni *façons de parler*; i v sushchnosti vikont gotov byl stat' na storonu kakogo ugodno ubezhdeniya ili dogmata, esli imel v vidu, chto za èto emu perepadët lishniy chetvertak.

> (On one occasion he began explaining the rights of man to the Foolishers; fortunately, however, he ended up by explaining the rights of the Bourbons. Another time he began by trying to persuade the citizenry to believe in the goddess of Reason and ended up by asking them to acknowledge the Pope's infallibility. Still, these were just so many "façons de parler." In actuality, the vicomte was ready to side with any conviction or dogmatic principle just so long as he could see that some extra kopecks would fall into his lap.)

Shchedrin's stylistic system is a forerunner of Aksënov's: both through its combining the comprehensible with material that requires commentary "prava cheloveka/Burbonov" (the rights of man or of the Bourbons), "boginya Razuma" (the goddess of Reason), "nepogreshimost' papy" (the infallibility of the Pope), *dogmat* 'a dogmatic principle', and through its combining incompatible styles—the judicial "prava cheloveka" (the rights of man), the lofty-biblical *uverovat'* 'believe in', the administrative *obyvateli* 'the citizenry', French phrases, the vulgar colloquial "perepadët lishniy chetvertak" (some extra kopecks would fall into his lap). Saltykov-Shchedrin, with his many-layered parodico-satirical prose, which is rife with citations and which is directed at an omniscient reader, was a worthy predecessor to Aksënov, who has enriched contemporary literature with a style deserving of the name "mystianic."

Translated by Allan Reid

FOOTNOTES

1. 'Mystianic' *tianstvennyy*, as will become evident, is the key word in this article. I have chosen to render it in this way, since it contains phonetic and semantic elements of both words from which it originates, i.e., 'mysterious' (*Tainstvennyy*) and 'Tiana'. Of course, to find a word which captures all the nuances of the original is impossible, but since this comes very close, it seemed preferable to a trans literation. The translator would like to express his thanks to Inger Lauridsen, Dr. R. Busch and Dr. E. Możejko, without whose assistance and perceptive suggestions this translation might never have been completed. Of course, responsibility for errors belongs entirely to the translator.

2. "Hardware" has apparently become the normative translation for *Zhelezka*. This is unfortunate as the two words have precious little in common. However, since I could find no better one-word equivalent and to remain in line with the translation of the title throughout this volume, I decided to follow standard practice here, but to resort to a transliteration in all subsequent references.

3. Here I have attempted no more than to capture some of the literal meaning.

4. If we translated 'Dama' as 'Dame' instead of 'Lady', the pun would be equally effective in English.

5. The Russian 'illyuminator' refers to portholes on a ship or boat and to airplane windows, but English has no special term for the latter. For this reason the ambiguous 'window' must be used here.

6. The interchange of relative pronouns which Ètkind is discussing here is not possible in English, so I have opted for a more colloquial and less bureaucratese form which at least indicates that there is a stylistic shift.

7. Translation mine—A.R. Other, even less satisfactory, translations of "Listen" do exist. E.g., in C.M. Bowra, ed., *A Second Book of Russian Verse* (London: Macmillan and Co. Ltd., 1948), p. 130, and Vl. Maiakovskii, *Electric Iron*, tr. J. Hirschman and V. Erlich (Berkeley: Maya, 1971), n.p.

8. Taken from Vl. Mayakovsky, *The Bedbug and Selected Poetry*, ed. P. Blake, tr. M. Hayward and G. Reavey (London: Weidenfeld and Nicolson, 1960), p. 103. Other, much weaker, versions can be found in, e.g., Hirschman and Erlich (n.p.), *Russian Poetry: The Modern Period*, eds. and tr. J. Glad, and D. Weissbort (Iowa City: University of Iowa Press, 1981), pp. 8-30, and *Mayakovsky*, ed. and tr. H. Marshall (London: Dennis Dobson, 1965), pp. 99-121.

9. Here, again, I have simply aimed to approach the literal meaning of the excerpt. To my knowledge no other English translation of this poem is available.

10. A popular beverage in the Soviet Union and other parts of Eastern Europe, not limited, as in North America, to use as a dilutant for alcohol.

11. It is interesting to note that in the Soviet edition of *Istoriya odnogo goroda*, published in 1947 (M.E. Saltykov-Shchedrin, *Izbrannyye sochineniya*, Moskva-Leningrad), this sentence was censored and its initial part, "[. . .]] odnazhdy on nachal ob"yasnyat' glupovtsam prava

cheloveka," is missing. See p. 65 of the above edition. Consequently, the comic effect of the following subordinate clause, "no k schast'yu, konchil tem, chto ob"yasnil prava Burbonov," is completely lost. For page references to quotations in this translation see the original Russian text in *Appendix*. Eds.

AKSËNOV AS TRAVEL WRITER: *'ROUND THE CLOCK, NON-STOP*

D. Barton Johnson

Vasiliy Aksënov is a prolific writer who has worked in many genres: the novel, the story, plays, film scripts, biography, literary essays, verse, and the travel memoir. A much-travelled man even prior to his emigration in 1980, Aksënov has published three travel memoirs: "Japanese Jottings," based on a 1962 visit; "Under the Skies of Sultry Argentina" in 1963; and *'Round the Clock, Non-Stop*, an account of his 1975 sojourn as Regents, Professor of the University of California at Los Angeles.[1] Our essay will examine Aksënov's travel writing with particular reference to the American account and will assess the role of these writing in his *oeuvre*.

Aksënov's travel memoirs are heir to a well-established tradition in Russian letters. The primogenitor of secular Russian travel literature is Tver merchant Afanasiy Nikitin, whose *Khozhdeniye za tri morya Afanasiya Nikitina* (Journey Beyond the Three Seas) recounts his journey to India in the late fifteenth century. The modern tradition may be said to start with Nikolay Karamzin's *Pis'ma russkogo puteshestvennika* (1791-92; Letters of a Russian Traveller), a work credited with initiating Sentimentalism in Russian literature. Among major literary figures of the nineteenth century, Pushkin contributes his *Puteshestviye v Arzrum* (1836; Journey to Arzrum), and Ivan Goncharov *Fregat Pallada* (1858; The Journey of the Frigate Pallas), an account of a trip around the world which is considered by some his best work after *Oblomov*.

The present century has yielded a number of Russian travel accounts of the United States. Maksim Gor'kiy, already at the height of his fame in 1906, paid a disastrous visit and took revenge in his book *On America*. (He avenged himself on literature at large by composing *Mat'* 'Mother', that bellwether of Socialist Realism, during a stay in the Adirondacks after being ejected from his New York hotel when his travelling companion proved to be his common law wife.) One of the earliest Soviet accounts was Mayakovsky's 1925 *My Discovery of America*. Boris Pil'nyak spent several months in the U.S. in 1931 and two years later published his *O'key* 'Okay', which he calls a novel but is in fact an often entertaining and ill-informed assessment of American life. His fame preceded him and he was briefly employed by a Hollywood studio, although nothing came of the venture since he reportedly refused to cooperate in making an anti-Soviet film. His travel account, although idiosyncratic, displays relatively little of the stylistic innovation that marked his writings of the twenties. Perhaps the most famous account is that of the Soviet humorists Il'f and Petrov, whose epic three-month, ten-thousand-mile car journey across the U.S. in the company of Mr. and Mrs. Adams is still excellent and informative reading after nearly fifty years. Their *Odnoètazhnaya Amerika* (One Storied America) was published in 1939 and appeared in translation the same year under the title *Little Golden America*.

Writing about the United States has always been a chancy business for Soviet writers—even Stalin Prize winners. Looking back from the vantage point of twenty years, the furor surrounding Victor Nekrasov's *On Both Sides of the Ocean* (1962) is hard to understand. Nekrasov's account of his carefully shepherded two-week visit is extremely superficial, heavily padded and shot through with dark suspicions about what he saw and didn't see. Why didn't the Russian students at Columbia flock to see him? Nonetheless, the attack on Nekrasov that appeared in *Izvestiya* (Jan. 20, 1963) and was later taken up by Khrushchëv played a cardinal role in the crackdown on the arts and on Evtushenko, Voznesensky and Aksënov in particular. The wisdom of letting certain writers go abroad was seriously questioned.[2]

Vasiliy Aksënov, whose officially endorsed and publicly acclaimed first novel *Colleagues* (1960), which put him at the forefront of new Soviet writing, was among the most favored in regard to foreign travel in the early sixties. Beginning with visits to Poland, Italy, Japan and India in 1962, and Argentina in 1963, Aksënov travelled to Rome and Yugoslavia in 1965; Japan, Austria, Switzerland and München in 1966; and to Bulgaria and London in 1967. This flurry of travel ended in 1967 and Aksënov was not to go abroad again until his U.S. visit in 1975, some five years before his expulsion from Russia.

Aksënov's first venture into travel literature was his "Japanese Jottings," written in 1963, soon after a three-week visit. It is a collection of "accidental observations" (259) in which the author records his impressions in a series of unrelated vignettes: Fujiyama, the temples and their idols, the human density of the cities and the countryside, the ancient tradition of the geishas, pinball arcades, fortune-telling machines, and, of course, reminders of Hiroshima. The writing is personal, often humorous, and vividly impressionistic. Apart from the fact that it is reportage, its style is much like that of Aksënov's fictional prose style of his early period.

Aksënov made his Argentinean visit in March of 1963 as a member of the Soviet delegation to an international film festival held in Buenos Aires and Mar-del-Plata. The Soviet entry was a film based on Aksënov's novel

Colleagues. The resulting travel memoir "Under the Skies of Sultry Argentina" (the name of a tango) is a much more complex and sophisticated work than his Japanese piece. Composed partly in 1963 and partly in 1966, "Under the Skies of Sultry Argentina" is a blend of the style used in the earlier Japanese essay and the surreal or grotesque manner that became an important element of Aksënov's post-1964 writing. Many of the seventeen numbered sections are firsthand reportage of various events connected with the festival—all handled with a deft and often comic touch. The opening departure from Moscow and the closing departure from Buenos Aires are of this sort, as is the satiric account of the reception of the Soviet delegates by suspicious Argentine customs officials. The customs official going through Aksënov's belongings peruses a copy of *Oranges from Morocco*, which he subjects to exactly the same sort of criticism that it received in the Soviet press:

> The problem of typicality is the most important problem of literature. Typical characters in typical circumstances with concretization of specific historic and social premises, and also taking into account the moral and aesthetic principles of the time—that's what the reader needs . . . ! (265)

Other segments are devoted to a touristic night visit to a lover's lane from which the voyeurs escape with a bullet hole in their car, the cavalcade of the film festival caravan through the pampas, commentary on the films themselves, and chance meetings with the locals. Some of the scenes mix comic fantasy with reportage. At the opening-night cocktail party Aksënov feels ill at ease and contemptuous of the tasteless bourgeois luxury of his surroundings and the elegant film stars. As he surveys the crowd his eye lights on three exotic and obviously mythic caricatures closely resembling the stereotype cartoons of capitalists found in the pages of *Krokodil* or in Soviet films of the thirties: the industrialist Sirakuzers, a meatpacking baron with alternate gold and platinum teeth and a ruby in his ear; a retired General Pistoleto-Naganero (cf. the Russian *nagan* 'revolver') wearing a helmet, armor and rusty sword, with three yards of braiding and seven rings; and Professor Bombardini, the bourgeois intellectual film critic and philosopher with the restless rear end. These cartoon figures appear fleetingly in most of the reportage sections but figure largely in a series of wholly fantastic episodes as, bedecked with starlets, they accompany the festival delegates as hangers-on. The Unholy Trinity engage in a series of increasingly bizarre antics which are intermingled among the reportage sections. These segments recount the saga of how the villains, badly hung over after an opening night orgy, pursue the festive caravan across the pampas from Buenos Aires to Mar-del-Plata. During a quarrel about the relative merits of wealth, power, and intellect, Sirakuzers nearly crashes into one of his own trucks hauling steers to market. One of the freed beasts gores the meat baron, who instantly restores himself with a band-aid and a mechanical valve that releases his internal gases. In a later episode, after the General recounts his leadership of a comic opera coup and the barracuda-like Bombardini devours an attacking shark, the three lose their collective fortune in a casino and are thrown out. In the final scene the departing Russians encounter them at the airport as beggar street musicians singing (of course) "Under the Skies of Sultry Argentina."

Aksënov's Argentinean travel memoir is a hybrid work combining a more or less factual, albeit humorously distorted and impressionistic account of his sojourn with an inset surreal episodic adventure story that is a mythic incarnation of the spirit of the country. By 1966 Aksënov has found the format that he will use for his much longer American travel memoir written after his 1975 sojourn.

Travel writing by its very nature tends to be a hybrid genre: the outer journey and the inner journey; reality and imagination. As such it affords an admirable playground for the subtle blend of reality and fantasy that has characterized Aksënov's work in recent years. The relationship between reality and imagination is a major theme of Aksënov's American travel memoir and is closely akin to a second theme—the artist's creative process, the topic of the writer's lectures at UCLA. Both are essential ingredients of the master theme—Aksënov's discovery of America.

Aksënov's travel memoir consists of sixteen diverse sections totalling about seventy pages in its *Novyy mir* publication. The sections fall into two categories: the first contains nine sections of more or less straightforward reportage accompanied by the author's reflections; the second consists of a set of episodes relating a wholly fantastic "Typical American Adventure" ("Tipichnoye Amerikanskoye Priklyucheniye") or "TAP." The sections are in approximate chronological order and are intermingled with "reportage" segments framing the first and last of the seven "TAP" episodes. The language of Aksënov's memoir, like that of his fiction, is racy, full of colloquialisms, slang and English expressions. The mode of narrative progression is what the author terms "associative reflections . . . those not determined by a room, a desk, or by the tape recorder of thought, i.e., *"reflections* or *meditations"* (71). As Aksënov humorously points out, his "nondetermined reflections" are one of the fruits of jogging, his favorite form of exercise.

"Imagination and Reality" is both the title and the theme of a section that in its content and structure embodies that relationship in small, as does the travel memoir itself on a larger, scale. Imagination and reality are likened to two chimneys between which a battered cat (appropriately named *Sermyaga* 'The Homespun Truth') roams along the ridge of the literary rooftop (56). The distance between the concepts is perhaps not so great as it might seem, says Aksënov, for of what use is our imagination without the beings and objects that populate the world of reality and, on the other hand, its denizens would remain nameless were it not for imagination. The argument is illustrated in the inevitable gap between our imaginary version of a city and the reality we find on our first visit. An impression then becomes a blend of the earlier imaginary version and the later reality, each enriching the other. With this preface, Aksënov launches into his account of the megapolis of Los Angeles. At first the description is straightforward, even mundane; the sights of Westwood Village, the gas stations, the restaurants, the people, the signs and billboards. Gradually the perspective widens. The surreal (in its etymological sense) edges into the real. The spectator is troubled by the absence of people on the night streets —only vehicles including a 1934 Cadillac with the inscription "Sodom & Gomorrah," driven by a figure of indeterminate gender, one cheek red, the other green. The sensation of alienation becomes yet more pronounced during a visit to the "Queen Mary," a tourist attraction permanently docked in Long Beach. On the return trip, Aksënov's companion, "the nicest Californian," misses a freeway interchange and the two are suspended in limbo, cruising the freeway above an endless, unpopulated, industrial wasteland that Aksënov likens to a barren lunar landscape. Eventually Westwood is regained where the writer is submerged in the equally unreal Saturday-night sidewalk Saturnalia of chanting Hari Krishnas, Jews for Jesus, Gay Pride demonstrators, and sidewalk swamis—all observed with bemused indifference by two policemen. The entranced author returns to the scene the next night to discover it deserted, but just as a clock shows 11:35, a tall woman in white falls as she crosses Westwood Boulevard. As Aksënov starts to her aid, a Rolls-Royce appears and whisks off what he knows to be a creature of his imagination (62). Starting from the real, mundane Los Angeles, the writer's perceptions have evolved first into the surreal (the industrial lunar desert, the bizarre fringe groups), and finally, with the mysterious abduction, into the world of myth and imagination. It is this thematic juxtaposition and interblending of Reality and Imagination, each feeding off the other, that provides the conceptual structure of Aksënov's travel memoir.

The "Reality" component of Aksënov's travel memoir consists of "reportage" sections which include such topics as the Los Angeles scene ("Imagination and Reality,"), students, the liberal intelligentsia, and politics ("Humanity, I Love You, Humanity . . ."), Aksënov's UCLA lectures ("The Pergamon Frieze"), the 'hippie' movement of the sixties and its evolution (commercialization) into the hippie style of the seventies ("The Movement and the Style"). A visit to the Renaissance Pleasure Fair leads to a long discourse on the reaction of American intellectuals to a technological supercivilization and cultural totalitarianism ("Crisis, Prosperity, Renaissance, Totalitarianism, Standard, the Establishment, and Various Other Fashionable Words"). Another section treats the theme of Russians in America ("The Sanitary City of Francisco"). One of the most interesting sections, "The Recollection of Prose," traces the influence of twentieth-century American literature on Russian writers of Aksënov's generation. There is much that is interesting and refreshing in Aksënov's off-center and occasionally off-base appraisals of various aspects of American life. Perhaps most striking, however, is the absence of the ill-informed tendentiousness characteristic of earlier Soviet cultural commentaries on the American scene. These sections, albeit not without a tinge of fantasy, recreate the "Reality" of Aksënov's America.

Counterposed to these 'Reality' sections are those in which Aksënov recreates the mythological America of his imagination: the Typical American Adventure which takes the form of a serial-myth. The author's humorous pledge to himself to adhere to 'reality' and avoid the use of an imaginary author-surrogate in his travel memoir is soon violated. The following section, the first installment of the "TAP," opens with Moskvich, a retiring Russian author suffering from jet-lag, standing on the edge of the UCLA campus looking at an odd notice attached to a kiosk wall: "Will the person who helped me up when I fell last Thursday on Westwood Boulevard at 11:35 PM please call 876-5432 . . ." Although Moskvich was in a plane over the Atlantic at the time in question, he feels strangely compelled to call the number of the Unknown Woman, the *Neznakomka*. He senses himself on the edge of a "TAP" which will include "secrets, abysses, horizons, and even a mysterious 'Goal' *Tsel'*—something tall, suntanned with flashing eyes, something feminine with loose white clothing" (53). He then begins to reflect on his youthful dreams of Western America and his imagination seizes control of his pen. Aksënov now grudgingly concedes the appearance of the imaginary Moskvich and the onset of the "TAP," but resolves that there is one particular character who will not be granted admission:

> the tiresome anti-author, the stupid avant-gardist Memozov with his pseudo-modern theories of black humor, telekinesis and occultism whose place is on page sixteen of the *Literaturnaya gazeta* and not in these notes. (54)

Just as the imaginary Moskvich arose in spite of his author's injunction, Memozov now appears and promptly inserts a Canadian quarter into a hot-drink machine in petty defiance of a sign to the contrary. An argument ensues in which Memozov recounts his latest escapade and Moskvich appeals to his nemesis to depart since he feels responsible for his actions. The author-persona Moskvich knows full well that Memozov the anti-author is, like the lady-in-white [see I. Lauridsen's analysis of women characters in Aksënov's writing—eds.], a creature of his imagination, but he is unable to banish him. Memozov notes the phone number on the notice and rides off towards Beverly Hills on his ostrich-camel amid the Porsches, Mercedes, and Alfa-Romeos. Moskvich feels his anticipated *TAP* may now be tainted and vulgarized by Memozov's presence, which may even further endanger the lady in distres. He must call and warn her.

The second episode begins with the phone call, which is answered by a Sinatra-like voice that ignores queries about the *Neznakomka* and sings a chorus of "Love and Marriage," which takes Moskvich back to the flooded Leningrad night in 1955 when he and a wet girlfriend danced to the song. The voice instructs Moskvich to get into a white Maseratti driven by a "groovy" girl who immediately gives him a joint. Mysteriously joined by a Mafia motorcycle escort, Moskvich arrives at a party in Topanga Canyon which is hosted by a man with shoulder-length grey hair. The guests, who seem to be simultaneously specialists in Russian literature of the Silver Age and Mafia gangsters, enter into conversation with Moskvich, but when he asks about the mysterious woman on Westwood Boulevard, an ominous hush falls. His host escorts him into an underground cavern where Memozov is annihilating the woman-in-white at ping-pong. After the defeated *Neznakomka* slowly fades into air, the enraged Moskvich challenges Memozov to a ping-pong duel. The scene changes and Moskvich finds himself on an outdoor deck with the party still in progress. The host, now in World War I flying attire, seats Moskvich in his Sopwith Camel and takes off over Topanga Canyon while singing the Sinatra hit "Come Fly with Me" and then, in response to his passenger's question, "From Here to Eternity."

The next episode of the "TAP," "Twenty-Four Hours Non-Stop," takes place at the fliers' destination, Caesar's Palace in Las Vegas. Moskvich is still in the clutches of the Mafia and is aghast at the kitsch vulgarity of his surroundings. It is all Memozov's invention, he thinks. His pilot abandons him to the temptations of the casino where, however, Moskvich soon falls in with one Steve Hedgehog, a UCLA mathematician, who enlists the writer's aid in a gambling scheme intended to defeat the industry of deceit and to shatter the pernicious myth of the American Dream.[3] Initially successful, the scheme goes awry and the two barely escape with their lives. In the course of his adventures, Moskvich again catches sight of the woman-in-white being forcibly whisked away by car. Our hero buys a Porsche with the remnants of the winnings and on his way out of town again acquires his Mafia escort, led by his former host and pilot. In the fourth installment, "Silver Phantoms," Moskvich drives into the ghost town of Calico, where he finds a pair of six-shooters on his gunbelt. He awaits the approaching shoot-out but instead the *Neznakomka*-in-white appears from the blackness of a mineshaft. He approaches. Suddenly Memozov, dressed as a mining company official, appears and demands Moskvich's admission ticket. The woman again fades away and Moskvich enters the saloon, where he finds his former host as bartender. Along the bar are John Wayne, Gary Cooper, Gregory Peck, and Clark Gable, who affirm that they have all sought the woman who fell on Westwood Boulevard. Just then, Memozov bursts in and shoots the piano player. The customers await the inevitable showdown, but Moskvich succeeds in willing Memozov to vanish (thus avoiding bloodshed) and resurrecting the piano player. At length Moskvich and his new friends ride out of Calico accompanied by the bartender, who tells Moskvich that the latter has saved him from corruption and cynicism. In the final segment of the "TAP," "She Who Was Born of the Sea Foam and Who Has Appeared on the Beach," the cavalcade wends its way west, eventually arriving at Carmel-by-the-Sea. Here the hero finds assembled the greats of American jazz, from King Oliver to Ornette Coleman, gathered for an inspired concert. As they play, Memozov, now a music critic, sits at a table on the sand writing a devastating review. The concert is saved when Memozov is buried under a sand dune and the circling gulls devour his fluttering papers. The apotheosis of Moskvich's "TAP" comes when the woman-in-white, Aphrodite-like, is cast up on the sands and begins to sing with the combined talents of Ella Fitzgerald, Billie Holiday and Diana Ross. He is joined by a Neptune-like figure with shoulder-length grey hair and Sinatra's voice. The duo becomes a trio when Moskvich, suddenly endowed with the gift of song, joins them in the obligatory "happy ending" of the "TAP." The journey of mythic discovery is at an end but there remains a double coda. The first is a curious blend of four lines of prose interlacing three couplets. It relates Moskvich's emerging from a phone booth and starting to cross Westwood Boulevard. He slips but is supported by an unknown passerby. The final coda, "In Parting," also very brief, is set on the return flight over the Atlantic. The wakeful Moskvich encounters his author, Aksënov, who inquires after his visit. Moskvich affirms its success, but is troubled that he failed to learn the name of the person who kept him from falling on Westwood. Aksënov promises to have notices posted at all of the places Moskvich visited.

Each episode of Moskvich's Typical American Adventure is an enactment of some aspect of Aksënov's mythic America: the Mafia; Las Vegas, the American Dream corrupted; the ghost town of Calico, the movie-inspired myth of the Wild West; and the Carmel Jazz Festival, the quintessential American music. All these serial episodes are set in a silvery twilight zone and are drawn together by the hero's search for the maiden-in-distress, variously known as "the Goal," 'the Unknown Woman' *Neznakomka*, 'the Woman-Sacrifice' *Zhenshchina-Zhertva*, 'She Herself' *Ta Samaya*, and "the Aphrodite-born-of-the-Sea-Foam." The hero, the author Moskvich, surmounts the temptations and dangers of his quest, repeatedly confronting the villainous kidnapper Memozov, the anti-author, until the villain is vanquished and the *Neznakomka*, presumably the incarnation of the author's America, stands safe by his side. Thwarted by the Mafia, he is aided by his friends and allies, the Western American film folk heroes and the jazz musicians. He even succeeds in saving the soul of one of Memozov's minions, the man with the shoulder-length grey hair. There is the obligatory "happy ending."

The nine reportage sections embody the "Reality" component of the creative process and the seven "TAP" installments enact the "Imaginative" component. The two realms, for the most part, are kept separate. The reportage sections are written by Aksënov in the first person; the "Imagination" sequences are in the third person with Moskvich as the protagonist. He and all of his fellow characters are explicitly the imaginary creatures of Aksënov, although they escape his control at times.[4] The two categories are not, however, entirely exclusive in their content. The imaginary figures flit at the fringes of reality and vice versa. The fantasy episodes are based on Aksënov's American experiences no less than the reportage scenes. The party in Topanga Canyon happened, as did the visit to Las Vegas and to the touristic ghost town of Calico. The Jazz Festival was real. Similarly, bits of Aksënov's mythic America infiltrate the reportage sections. The figure of Moskvich is first introduced at the end of an early reportage section, as is the abduction of the woman-in-white. Aksënov himself appears in a "TAP" segment in a final scene in the plane where he encounters Moskvich. The crucial notice which triggers the "TAP" also recurs in both categories. The arch villain Memozov of the dream sequence is referred to by Professor Aksënov as the subject of some pieces in the *Literaturnaya gazeta*.

It is no secret that Moskvich is the author's persona, for they share the same past. In the second installment of the "TAP" Moskvich hears Sinatra's

"Love and Marriage" and thinks back to a fall night in 1955 when he forded the flooded streets of Leningrad to take a girl to a party where the guests, all wet to the knees, danced to the song (63). The event is recounted in almost the same words in a first person account in the reportage section "Recollection of Prose," since it was this same girl, the "Cat in the Rain," who introduced Aksënov to Hemingway's story of that name and to the work of the American writer who was to exert a major influence on Aksënov and other budding writers of the Young Prose Movement (117-118). The scene resembles that in which Aksënov met his first wife, Kira.[5] Nor is it by chance that the presiding eminences of the two flashbacks are Frank Sinatra, the avatar of American pop music, and Ernest Hemingway. The two figures symbolize major aspects of the young Aksënov's vision of America—its music and its literature.

Which America is more real, Aksënov's reportage or the imaginary Moskvich's "TAP"? The answer is in the memoir's structure, which recapitulates its theme of interblended Imagination and Reality. Both are requisite for artistic truth. America consists of both the real and the mythic, and no absolute line can be drawn between them. The two realms resonate and enhance each other and collectively constitute the author's America. Aksënov's discovery of America is the dominant subject matter of his memoir, but the question of how the discovery is made is of scarcely less concern. The Reality (Reportage) / Imagination (Mythic Adventure) dichotomy plays the major role in both the form and content of Aksënov's travel memoir. This same opposition is equally central to an understanding of Aksënov's twenty-year literary career, and can be applied as a way of viewing his *oeuvre*.

The early novels, *Colleagues* (1960), A Ticket to the Stars (1961), *Oranges from Morocco* (1963), and *It's Time, My Friend, It's Time* (1964), although of increasing technical proficiency, are all heavily weighted toward the Reality end of the spectrum. Even here, however, a tentative move along the spectrum in the direction of Imagination may be seen in the last novel in the posthumous presence of Kyanukuk, a seemingly minor figure whom Aksënov has said to be the most important character in the book. The years 1964-1965 display an increasing proportion of the Imaginative component. Aksënov himself has described this reorientation as the dislocation of simple existence into unreality, with the result that the dislocation creates the meaning of the work.[6] This period is represented largely by the short stories which were eventually collected into the 1969 anthology *Zhal', chto vas ne bylo s nami* (It's a Pity You Weren't with Us) and culminates in the 1968 novella *The Tare of Empty Barrels*. The chilling *The Steel Bird* also belongs to this period. The seventies intensify the interblending of Reality and Imagination that characterized the previous period, but focus with increasing pessimism on the theme of twentieth century Russian history and its meaning for the intelligentsia, especially that of Aksënov's generation. This is the theme of the major novels of the seventies, all of which were published only after the author's 1980 emigration in the wake of the *Metropol'* scandal (for the sake of exactness, it should be mentioned that *Our Golden Hardware* appeared in the West a few months before Aksënov's emigration).

Our Golden Hardware, written in 1972, treats the scientific intelligentsia and is both technically adventurous and contains a fair measure of the fantastic. It also has a direct link with *'Round the Clock, Non-Stop* in that the arch villain, whose banal if fantastic activities first disrupt and then ultimately destroy the research institute, is none other than the mocking anti-author, Memozov. *The Burn*, written between 1969 and 1975, is an enormously complex work which is Aksënov's most explicit statement of his major theme of the seventies. It too contains many elements of the fantastic, especially in its use of parallel heroes and episodes. *The Island of Crimea*, written 1977-1978, which completes the thematic trilogy of the seventies, deals with the fate of a Russian technological supercivilization, a bourgeois democracy, established by White exiles in the Crimea after the revolution. In spite of the novel's fantastic geographic and historical premise, it represents a stylistic return toward more realistically oriented writing. Its depiction of a wealthy supercivilization obviously owes much to Aksënov's stay in Los Angeles. As a political summing-up of the nature of revolutionary Russia, it is a devastating conclusion to Aksënov's theme of Russia's political destiny.

Aksënov's 1975 American travel memoir has a clear place in his *oeuvre* both thematically and stylistically. Thematically, it represents the author's thoughtful assessment of another society's working out of its destiny. In a sense, it is a thematic counterpart to the Russian trilogy of the seventies. It is also an aesthetic statement. Not only does *'Round the Clock, Non-Stop* contain that stylistic mixture of reality and imagination that raises it to the level of art, but in its hybrid form and content Aksënov addresses the nature of his own creative process.[7]

FOOTNOTES

1. "Yaponskiye zametki" and "Pod nebom znoynoy Argentiny" appeared in Vasiliy Aksënov, *Zhal', chto vas ne bylo s nami*, Moscow, 1969, pp. 237-259 and 260-293. *Kruglyye sutki non-stop* appeared in *Novyy mir*, 52, 8, 1976, pp. 51-122. Only the first item has been translated

into English: "Japanese Jottings," tr. Rae Slonek in Vasily Aksënov, *The Steel Bird and Other Stories*, Ann Arbor, 1979, pp. 97-113.

2. John J. Johnson, Jr., "Introduction: The Life and Works of Aksënov" in Vasily Aksënov, *The Steel Bird and Other Stories*, p. xv. Subsequent information on Aksënov's foreign travels are from this source, pp. xii, xvi and xxv.

3. Aksënov's surreal vision of Las Vegas as the American Dream corrupted has points of similarity with that of Hunter S. Thompson, *Fear and Loathing in Las Vegas: A Savage Journey into the Heart of the American Dream*, New York, 1971.

4. The reportage section "Humanity, I Love You, Humanity . . ." opens with "Meantime, while the invented Moskvich and the invented Memozov, having burst out from under my control, develop their *TAP* [. . .], I continue my subdued account of my atypical but completely real life in LA" (67).

5. Johnson, p. ix. (Name supplied by editors.)

6. Priscilla Meyer, "Interview with Vasily Pavlovich Aksenov," *Russian Literature Triquarterly*, 6, 1973, p. 569. For a detailed study of this shift in orientation, see Per Dalgård, *The Function of the Grotesque in Vasilij Aksënov*, Aarhus, 1982.

7. The interrelations of reality and imagination are also central to two other Aksënov endeavors: his fictionalized biography, *Lyubov' k èlektrichestvu: povest' o Leonide Krasine*, Moscow, 1971, and his Russian translation of E.L. Doctorow's novel *Ragtime*, which interweaves fictional and real characters and events.

OUR GOLDEN HARDWARE AS A PARODY

Nina Kolesnikoff

Written in 1972 in the U.S.S.R., but first published seven years later in the U.S., *Our Golden Hardware* displays a great deal of comic absurdity, exaggeration and incongruity. From the very beginning the reader is baffled by the discrepancy between serious topic and low style, and has to wonder about the possible presence of parody.[1] The parody is, indeed, the key mode of "this nostalgic thing," intended by Aksënov to sum up the 1960s, "the decade of Soviet Don Quixotery."[2] The novel actually contains three levels of parody, each complementing the other and adding to the complexity of the novel and the plurality of its style.[3]

On the most obvious level the novel introduces short parodies of works by specific Russian writers, among them Velemir Khlebnikov (47; 177), Igor Severyanin (48), Aleksandr Blok (64-65), Andrey Voznesensky (82), Bulat Okudzhava (72), Vladimir Vysotsky (30), and others.[4] These parodies are easy to detect since Aksënov usually gives the name of the parodied author and chooses works well known to the Soviet reader. Thus in the case of Khlebnikov, he parodies his famous "Zaklyatiye smekhom" (Incantation by Laughter), a poem composed entirely of neologisms from the root "laugh."[5] Aksënov quotes directly from the poem: 'o, zasmeytes', smekhachi" (o laugh, you laughniks), repeats the words: *smeytes* 'laugh', *usmekhaytes'* 'smile', and even creates his own neologisms from the related word *khokhotat'* 'to laugh loudly': "khokhochite khakhachi." The parody on Khlebnikov appears in the section introducing Memozov, the strange figure of an anti-author, who interferes with the writing of the novel and pushes it toward destruction. Memozov is described in the novel as "avant-gardist," and as such he obviously has a lot in common with the most famous Russian *zaum'* poet. Throughout the entire novel, Memozov appears as a faithful follower of Khlebnikov, playing with neologisms (177), quoting from the famous Futurist manifesto "A Slap in the Public Face" (102), and generally believing that the time had arrived to reject the past and begin everything anew.

If the parody on Khlebnikov is based on analogy, the parody on Severyanin introduces incongruity between the pseudo-sophisticated style of the Russian Ego-Futurist and the colloquial speech of Aksënov's protagonist Velikiy-Salazkin (Great Salazkin). In the setting of an ordinary Soviet cafeteria, Salazkin suddenly orders "pineapples and champagne," clearly paraphrasing the title of Severyanin's famous poem "Ananasy v shampanskom" (Pineapples in Champagne).[6] Imitating Severyanin's fascination with elaborate forms and foreign words, Velikiy–Salazkin addresses the waitresses as: "metresses, patronesses, baronesses, s'il vous plait, mon plaisir, palais royale" (58). The comic effect of this passage is strengthened by the juxtaposition of these sophisticated forms with archaisms: *dlani* 'hands', *likovat'* 'to rejoice', and with Soviet cliches based on military terminology: *pritaranit'* 'to ram', "boyevyye podrugi pishchevogo fronta" (combatant friends of the front food-line).

Another obvious parody introduced in *Our Golden Hardware* is that of Aleksandr Blok's cycle "Stikhi o Prekrasnoy Dame" (Verses about the Beautiful Lady). A mysterious and enigmatic Lady not unlike Blok's heroine appears to three of Aksënov's heroes, wandering through the twilight of Leningrad. They stop in front of a building which in many ways resembles a mysterious house in Blok's "Tam v ulitse stoyal kakoy-to dom" (There on the Street Stood a House),[7] but it lacks the mysterious dimensions. Aksënov de-poetizes the house by introducing such prosaic details as "reliable window glass," and "the door made of fumed oak," and by replacing the poetic metaphor of "the cornice as the frown disfiguring the face of the wall," with a ridiculous image of "a moustache above the mouth, formed by naiads and grapes" (64). He also denies the special quality of Blok's twilight by qualifying it as "the smoky twilight of an industrial night." As in Blok's poem, the men at first do not see the Lady, they simply have a presentiment of her presence as they watch the flickering lights and listen to music and dance. When the Lady does appear, she possesses many of the attributes of her predecessor: pale shoulders, a scarf, pearls, except that they are described by absurd epithets: "a blissful scarf," "cursed pearls." The reaction of the men is bewildering; instead of being excited or overwhelmed, they are worried about mockery and beg the Lady not to laugh at them. As if taking pity on his characters, Aksënov forbids the Lady to laugh and forces Her to disappear.

The image of the Beautiful Lady reappears in *Our Golden Hardware* several times, and it is always associated with the search for a mysterious particle "W" (see below, p. 200), which haunts the imagination of the scientists of the second half of the XX century; in a similar way the Beautiful Lady fascinated the poets of the turn of the century. [See I. Lauridsen's article in this collection—eds.] Both Russian and Western scientists pursue the enigmatic particle by using different methods: the idealistically inclined professor Gromson relies on alchemy and black magic, while his Soviet counterpart Velikiy–Salazkin hopes to catch Her in a nuclear accelerator, built in the middle of the Siberian swamp and ironically named *Zhelezka* 'a piece of iron'.⁷

The construction of *Zhelezka* and the scientific experiments conducted there constitute the major theme of Aksënov's novel, thus bringing it close to the genre of the so-called "industrial novel," which in a literary form offers accounts of work at construction projects, factories or research institutes.⁹ Indeed, *Our Golden Hardware* has all the major features of that literary model, except that they are present in a distorted form and become the object of ridicule. Using the terminology of Henryk Markiewicz, this novel could be called a parody 'sensu stricto'; that is, it comically exaggerates and condenses the features of the literary model.¹⁰

First of all, Aksënov parodies three conflicts of the industrial novel: a struggle against nature, a struggle against political enemies, and a nonantagonistic conflict, the re-education of people through labor. The first of these conflicts—the struggle against nature—features most prominently in part II of the novel, depicting the construction of *Zhelezka*. As in a typical industrial novel, Aksënov speaks of difficulties, but he ridicules the idea by supplementing them with ordinary activities:

> the same difficulties, the same enthusiasm, the same cement [. . .], the same high floods and vodka, rush work and grub food, the tariff scales and wild volleyball among the rooted-out stumps. (69)

He also diminishes the efforts of the builders by suggesting the existence of a supernatural power which helps cement to set faster, motors to run faster and trucks to be driven without gasoline (69). He subtracts the indispensable components of the industrial novel, bulldozers and excavators, and replaces them with ordinary shovels (66). A primitive shovel becomes the most important working tool as well as a symbol of the times, somewhat similar to a rifle, a necessary attribute of the participants in the Civil War (here Aksënov alludes to the tendency to portray industrial work in terms of a military battle). Later in the novel the shovel, along with axes and perforators, becomes a sign of identification, so that the workers might enter the construction grounds. The paradox of the situation is that they enter a gate which stands in the middle of nowhere, and there is no fence around it (17). Moreover, the gate is built in the tradition of a monumental piece of Stalinist architecture, and clashes with the modern style of *Zhelezka*. The contrast between the elaborate gate and the simple design of other buildings is as striking as the discrepancy between the solemn opening of the construction and the finding of a simple piece of metal, which *post factum* justifies the designation of *Zhelezka*.

In the depiction of nature's hostility to men, Aksënov continues to scoff at the established patterns of the industrial novel. In part II he brings out the disparity between the harsh conditions described in the local song as "the storms breaking against the cliffs of our cheeks" and the actual mild weather (66). Later, he introduces the motif of men as victims of severe weather, but substitutes the idea of bravery and self-sacrifice with sheer stupidity: the leading Soviet mathematician Morkovnikov is almost frozen to death because he arrives in *Zhelezka* dressed in leather shorts and a summer shirt (73). The only true image of nature's hostility to men appears in part III, where a severe snow storm is depicted as lasting seven days and covering the streets of Pikhty with deep drifts. The storm is presented with the help of exaggeration and absurd animation, first by drawing an analogy with a volcanic eruption in Pompeii, which "grunted, echoed, clapped itself on the back, sat down, ran away and came back from behind the mountain again with an ironic compliment: 'what a freshness'" (137), and later with "the nomadic hordes" who attack the city (150). Despite its severity and long duration, the storm does not seem to interfere with the life of the people who go to work, gather for socializing, and even go for leisurely walks. There is only one victim—a local taxi driver, who is buried in a snow drift; but this is the result of his excessive drinking, and, furthermore, he is eventually rescued. The storm has, however, a devastating effect on the scientific experiments conducted in *Zhelezka*. The mesons, driven into an accelerator and until now in constant motion, suddenly freeze up, thus bringing to a halt the years-long pursuit of the particle "W." Such an unhappy ending is quite contrary to the rules of the industrial novel, which require the successful dissolution of all conflicts. There is also a departure from the usual solution to the antagonistic conflict: neither the Soviet nor Western scientists succeed in discovering the mysterious "W".[11]

In addition to introducing the motif of political rivalry, *Our Golden Hardware* also presents in parodied form a typical industrial conflict with an internal enemy, personified in the novel by Memozov. Interestingly, this arch-enemy of *Zhelezka* is not an agent of a foreign intelligence service, nor a saboteur who obstructs the work at the center, but an eccentric "avant-gardist, conquistador and surrealist" (46). Unlike all the other characters who "fall in love with *Zhelezka* at first sight" (29) and "serve Her with dedication and devotion," Memozov despises it, calling it "rubbish" (50), "a rusty piece of metal" (135), or simply an "object" (108). Moreover, from the very beginning he is determined to destroy *Zhelezka*. At first he resorts to the old-fashioned method of spreading gossip which is supposed to antagonize the scientists against each other; then he invites them all to a séance in which they watch the disappearance of their beloved *Zhelezka*. Significantly the guests refuse to fall asleep, but are forced to watch and participate in Memozov's dream, in which *Zhelezka* leaves the ground, hangs in mid-air for a while, and then floats upwards, finally disappearing altogether. The disappearance of *Zhelezka* has a devastating effect on the scientists, but even in Memozov's dream they manage to overcome the shock and begin to build a new project. The compromised Memozov has to leave; but nevertheless he succeeds in sowing seeds of doubt in the hearts of the scientists and they now question the validity of their work and their attitude towards it. As an enemy, Memozov scores at least a partial victory by destroying the happy ending of an industrial novel.

The portrayal of Memozov is based entirely on caricature, which brings out the discrepancy between the traditional accessories of a demonic figure, such as "a pale face," "long black hair," "a diabolic eye," "a cane," "a pair of kid boots" (7, 46), and modern attributes which include "a bright vest," "a tie," and "a bicycle" (95, 101, 122, 134). The bicycle seems to be an inseparable part of Memozov, much more so than an old-fashioned eagle with a downcast appearance somewhat resembling a plaster cast. As a magician, Memozov relies on such old-fashioned accessories as "centipedes preserved in alcohol, birds' claws, tables and signs of cabbalism" (176); but even they do not guarantee him success. In his final séance he fails to hypnotize his subjects, and can only present them with his own telekinetic dream.

Caricature is used in *Our Golden Hardware* to portray not only such an ambiguous character as Memozov, but also positive characters in the novel, including the director of *Zhelezka*, Velikiy–Salazkin. Such a name immediately conveys the suggestion of parody by combining the attribute "great" with an ordinary object, "toboggan." The hyphenated spelling of his name is also ironic for it suggests an aristocratic background, when in reality he comes from a poor family. Velikiy–Salazkin is introduced in the novel with the help of exaggeration and parodied Soviet cliches as the one:

> WHO wrote thirty volumes thirty thunders WHOSE echo does not run short in the Himalayas WHOSE brain joins with the sky with the science WHO brought to the taiga the first youth WHO erected on the swamp our beautiful Zhelezka. (10-11)

That image of a great scientist is immediately contrasted with his slovenly appearance and his dialectic speech: he wears "a dirty nylon quilted jacket," "shoes with worn heels" (9), and uses such dialect forms as *motri* 'smotri', *use* 'vse', *yetot* 'ètot', *tapericha* 'teper'. Throughout the entire novel V-S continues to keep up his simple looks and language, causing people to mistake him for a guard (9), a mushroom-picker, a worker in a steam bath (58), or a local peasant (79). He speaks basically in dialect intermixed with slang expressions, "chiya khokhma" (whose gag is it?, 67), "alle, rebya [. . .] valites' v kolymagu . . ." (hey boys, pile in the wagon, 48), and words with an 'aristocratic' stress, "kilómetr," "dótsent," "prótsent," "pórtfel'" (61).

Velikiy-Salazkin is portrayed in the novel as a man totally absorbed in his work and completely dedicated to it. He has no family, no personal life, spending nights and days in *Zhelezka* and attending conferences during his holidays. As a typical hero of the industrial novel, he believes that he is working for the betterment of society and that his scientific discoveries will bring benefit to humanity: "perhaps to cure malaria, perhaps to cut beefsteaks, or perhaps to improve the creative impulses in elderly people" (34). But unlike the majority of the positive heroes, V-S sometimes has doubts about his work and the meaning of his life (133-134). He also possesses some personal weaknesses, chief among them being his amorous disposition. This serious elderly man not only constantly falls in love but regards it as a means of rejuvenation and scientific inspiration. One of the objects of his platonic love is Rita, a young girl from Odessa who comes to *Zhelezka* with a rock group. Enchanted by her "galactic beauty," V-S suggests that she stay in *Zhelezka* in order to gain work experience. Rita agrees; and thus begins a non-antagonistic conflict: the re-education of people through labor.

As with the other two conflicts, Aksënov parodies the idea by assigning to Rita a meaningless job—the operation of a vending machine, and then by putting an end to her career through marriage to a young scientist, Vadim Kitousov. After the marriage Rita spends her time sitting on a couch, smoking, reading cheap romances and looking at foreign fashion magazines. She turns into an idle and empty woman, greatly resembling Severyanin's heroines of fifty years earlier. Like her predecessors, she is fascinated with anything mysterious or erotic; she dreams about love and is ready to pursue it. Characteristically Rita does not appreciate her husband's great dedication to *Zhelezka* and does not understand the importance of the project. She refuses to see anything special in *Zhelezka*, arguing that "it is simply scientific territory" (83). Her words echo the opinion of Memozov, making her an indirect accomplice of this arch-enemy of *Zhelezka*.

The parody is strengthened in the novel by linguistic means, which introduce absurd changes in the meaning of words, changes in literal and metaphorical functions of words, and changes in sociolect, idiolect, and other elements of lexicon. The most obvious linguistic parody involves the usage of proper names and designations. Among the major characters, many bear strange names suggesting parody by analogy, cf., Kitousov (Whalemustache), Slon (Elephant), Morkovnikov (Carrot). The names of minor characters are even more absurd: the new manager of the cafeteria is comically named Buryak Fasolevich Borshchëv (Beet Bean Beet-Soup), while the local taxi driver has a strange patronymic and last name: Vladimir Bat'kovich Teleskopov (Vladimir Son-of-a-Father Telescope). As suggested earlier, the designation "Zhelezka," attached to an important scientific center, is ironic in its understatement, and so is the name of the plant, *Burolyap* (an absurd abbreviation that resembles a compound of two words, *buryy* 'brown-grey' and *lyapat'* 'to spoil by clumsy work'), and of the accelerator, *Vykhukhol'* 'desman'. Even the particle "W" is intentionally misspelled in the novel as *Dabl'f'yu*, suggesting the feeling of disgust and impatience. Irony by analogy is conveyed in such designations as "Mërtvyy yakor'" (Dead Anchor) for a bar, "Ledovityy okean" (The Arctic Ocean) for a department store, and "Ugrium-reka" (The Gloom-River) for the fashion house.

Changes in the individual sociolect were mentioned earlier in the discussion of the strange mixture of dialecticisms with slang expressions in the speech of V-S, and in the unusual use of neologisms and foreign words by Memozov; but it must be stressed that the entire language of the novel is saturated with crude colloquialisms and taboo expressions. The shocking effect of slang expressions is intensified when the reader realizes that they are used by well-educated Soviet scientists who would be expected to speak a highly sophisticated language like their numerous counterparts in the industrial novel. In fact Aksënov parodies the scientific language of his heroes by intermixing highly technical phrases with colloquial expressions, exact scientific formulae with quotations from popular songs, foreign words with augmentatives (cf. the discussion of young scientists in the sawtimber storage on p. 72).

But it is not the language of science that becomes the object of Aksënov's sharpest parody. It is the language of the official Soviet propaganda as used in the media and in many industrial novels. Throughout the entire novel, Aksënov ridicules the well-known Soviet cliches by displaying their internal contradictions, fallacious reasoning, or absurd overstatement [see the article by A. Vishevsky and T. Pogocar—eds.]. Irony by analogy is conveyed in such typical cliches as "the taiga fortress" (135), "the fortpost Pikhty" (9), "the scientific avalanche" (60), equating the research center with a fortress or with a mighty natural phenomenon. In a similar way an internal contradiction is pointed out in such phrases as "the green sea of taiga" (8) or "the scientific thought has not been falling asleep" (71), while an overstatement is made apparent in the cliches, glorifying the progress of science in terms of "broadening the horizons" (50), "marching with seven-mile steps" (59) or "radiating for thousands of kilometers the beaming lights of futurism" (9).

A great many cliches parodied in the novel refer to the overstated praise of individual achievements or achievements of the whole country. Thus V-S is characterized as one "whose brain joins with the sky with science" (10), while the mathematician Morkovnikov is depicted as "a favorite of the world's science, *enfant terrible* of the Great Soviet Encyclopedia, and a promoter of the world's progress" (73). The new director of the local cafeteria, Buryak Borshchëv, is introduced in typical Soviet phraseology as "the laureat of the state prize UPRKhSTFROU" (a parody of the Soviet predilection for abbreviations), "a three-time bearer of the order of Bogdan Khmel'nitsky" (no logical connection between the Ukrainian national hero and a cafeteria manager), and "a recipient of the badge 'The Great Food-worker'" (148).

Aksënov is not even afraid to parody the official cliches describing the might of the Soviet Union, when he makes one of his heroes draw an absurd analogy between a middle-aged woman and Russia:

> "But no, my dear, we compare you not with that backward tsarist Russia, but with the today of our cosmic countryland. One could not think otherwise, seeing how slowly and majestically these atomic submarines are rising, with what powerful energy breathe these mines, with what feeling passes through these groves the aroma of a forty-rouble French perfume 'Klima.' We are together on the highest orbit . . ." (150)

The shocking effect of this passage is intensified by the fact that it in an "estranged" way depicts a sexual act involving two scientists and a rude woman. The contradictory image of the rising submarines, the animated mines that breathe energy and perfume, the analogy with reaching the highest orbit, all refer to an intercourse which is sarcastically described as "a return to the soil, to Russia."

The above-quoted passage is one of many instances of *ostraneniye* employed by Aksënov in the novel.[12] *Ostraneniye* is used throughout the entire novel in the depiction of the experiments with mesons, the search for the particle "W," and the attitude of the scientists toward *Zhelezka*. In all three cases, Aksënov relies on personification and endows the inanimate objects with qualities of living creatures. Thus, the mesons driven into an accelerator are depicted as "Prussian soldiers, practicing for a parade" (109), or as "African dancers, dancing to the rhythm of tom-tom" (142). The mysterious particle "W" is identified with the Beautiful Lady, who holds a magical power over the scientists, making them long for Her as for a beloved woman. The same feeling distinguishes the attitude of the scientists toward *Zhelezka*, depicted in the novel as "beautiful" (8, 29, 69), "bewitching" (70, 74), and "beloved" (29, 49, 86). The scientists get excited at the sight of Her, fall in love with Her at first sight, and are ready to serve Her with total devotion.

Personification, exaggeration, partial caricature, discrepancy—all these typical parodistic devices help Aksënov to mock the model of the industrial novel. The function of his parody *sensu stricto* is clearly satirical: the novel scoffs at the ideological and literary norms mandatory to Soviet literature, and calls for a total artistic freedom. That call is nowhere as apparent as in the parody of the mechanical theory of reflection which presupposes a truthful reflection of facts "in chronological order and by degree of importance." "No," says the author,

> I: does not want to reflect, wheels here and there, wiggles like an eel in the rapids of native speech, throws bright flags, forms a detachment, who knows for what, dives into the holds as if on an urgent matter, or fires fireworks from both sides of the ship in order to fool the reader, but not to reflect. (77)

The contradictory juxtapositions, the ambiguity, the ungrammatical usage of the pronoun "I" combined with the third person of the verbal form—all these devices stress the author's total freedom and his breaking away from all the rules.

The above parody on the theory of reflection is the most clear example of the third type of parody employed in *Our Golden Hardware*, namely the meta-fictional parody which demonstrates the processes involved in the production and reception of fiction from within a literary text.[13]

From the very beginning Aksënov breaks the illusion of fiction by introducing the figure of an author who appears simultaneously as one of the characters and as a creator of the novel who comments on his writing and the problems encountered. As one of the characters, the author goes out of his way to justify his presence in the novel. In the introduction he appears at the airport to send all the characters on the same flight, and buys a ticket for himself. In Pikhty he meets the protagonists and helps them to receive their luggage. He seems to remain in *Zhelezka*, and the reader catches glimpses of him in the streets of the city (63), at the construction (72), in the hotel (174), and finally at the Zimoyarsk airport (187). All these realistic details are combined in the novel with statements that disclose the fictional character of the author's world. Thus the author can easily forestall the plane (46), or come to *Zhelezka* in the middle of the storm when no planes or trucks can get there (174). He also knows the inner thoughts and feelings of his characters, something that is characteristic of an omniscient author. The author, however, does not like to act as an omniscient narrator and relinquishes his authority to his characters, allowing them to speak in their own voices, reminiscing about the past and confessing their most intimate thoughts and feelings.

While identifying himself with different characters, the author still preserves his control over them. He seems, however, totally powerless in relation to Memozov, who appears in the novel at his own free will contrary to the wishes of the author, and from the very beginning is determined to destroy the novel:

> I will enter this novel as a foreign body, like a hostile flying saucer, I will walk through its idyllic plot like a mean rodent; with the influence of my powerful magnetic field I will muddle up the orbits of the characters; then we shall see, and laugh at the luckless author. (48)

Throughout the entire novel Memozov interferes with the plot, changing the course of events and forcing the narrative into the wrong direction. In part IV he almost succeeds in taking over the narrative, and it is simply sheer luck that the "real author" arrives in Pikhty and rescues his novel from destruction. Interestingly, the real author treats his arch-enemy magnanimously: he lets him go and even gives him three roubles for a drink (187).

The introduction of the anti-author clearly demonstrates the clash between the world of fiction and the world of reality, casting doubts on the veracity of the fictional world. The same effect is achieved by numerous comments on the process of writing, stressing a more self-conscious use of art. Aksënov mocks in *Our Golden Hardware* the traditional elements of fiction, such as "an elegant introduction" (7), "the quiet narrative in the third person" (7), or "the authorial digressions" (71). He also makes fun of an ideal Soviet reader who is supposed to be "thoughtful, perceptive, tolerant, cheerful and congenial, who, as we know, is the best in the world because he reads so much in the subway" (12). Such fallacious reasoning enhances the ironic connotations of this statement, in the same way as the hidden polemic with the reader, elsewhere in the novel, brings into relief the parody of the naive reader who takes the fictional world to be "true" in the sense of being an accurate reflection of the external world. The mockery of such a reader is evident in the episode describing the meeting of the three heroes in a Leningrad cafeteria. At first the author goes out of his way to justify chance occurrences and then to convince the reader that the event described by him could have happened in reality. Finally, he succumbs to the native reader and admits that "coincidence" or "chance" cannot explain everything, and that the author has to provide a convincing, realistic motivation (56).

The references to the reader, and to the fictional nature of the world of characters, the introduction of the anti-author—all these devices "lay bare" the illusion of mimetic art and criticize naive concepts of art as a mirror to the world. The meta-fictional parody, therefore, tarnishes the essentials of the theory of Socialist Realism, which postulates "a truthful, historically concrete representation of reality in its revolutionary development." Now it becomes clear why *Our Golden Hardware* could not have been published in the Soviet Union: it impairs the literary, political and ideological canons established by the theory of Socialist Realism. And if the parody *sensu stricto* satirized the literary norms of the industrial novel, the meta-fictional parody brought into question the basic ideological premise of Socialist Realism: art as a reflection of reality. That was a "sacrilegious" act, and as a result the novel had to be banned to the Soviet reader.

FOOTNOTES

1. Like many other literary terms, "parody" has had a long history of usage, distinguished by considerable changes in meaning and connotations. In this paper I accepted the semiotic definition of parody as a complex structure that confuses the normal process of communication by offering two models of communication: that between the parodist and the author of a parodied text, and that between the parodist and the reader. The parodist acts both as decoder of a parodied text (TW2), and as an encoder who transforms the text into a different code (TW1). The transformation presupposes a comic discrepancy between the original work and its "imitation," by offering a parodied text in a distorted form, or by changing the style in the work of the parodist. The reader of parody is faced with the difficult task of recognizing the presence of two texts (TW1 and TW2), and understanding the relation between them, as well as the intentions of the author. See, for example, W. Karrer, *Parodie, Travestie, Pastiche*, München, 1977; M.A. Rose, *Parody Meta-Fiction: An Analysis of Parody as a Critical Mirror to the Writing and Reception of Fiction*, London, 1979; T. Shlonsky, "Literary Parody: Remarks on Its Method and Function," *Proceedings of the 4th Congress of the International Comparative Literature Association*, F. Jost, ed., The Hague, 1966, vol. 2, pp. 902-11.

2. Vasiliy Aksënov, *Zolotaya nasha Zhelezka*, Ann Arbor, 1980, p. 3. This edition will be used hereafter (all translations are mine—N.K.).

3. The complex structure of *Our Golden Hardware* is thoroughly analyzed in Per Dalgård, *The Function of the Grotesque in Vasilij Aksenov*, Aarhus, 1982, pp. 77-93, but primarily from the point of view of the use of grotesque. The existence of parody is simply acknowledged, but no attempt is made to study it. Per Dalgård's book is virtually the only study of his novel, since the other critical articles on Aksënov in English were written before the publication of the book, cf. P. Meyer, "Aksenov and Soviet Literature of the 1960's," *Russian Literature Triquarterly*, 6, 1973, pp. 447-60; J.J. Johnson, "Introduction," to Vasiliy Aksënov, *The Steel Bird*, Ann Arbor, 1973, pp. IX-XXVII.

4. Following Henryk Markiewicz, we could call this type of parody "sensus largo," comical recast or imitation of literary model. See Henryk Markiewicz, "On the Definition of Literary Parody," *To Honour Roman Jakobson*, The Hague, 1966, pp. 1264-72.

5. Velimir Khlebnikov, "Zaklyatiye smekhom," rpt. in *Sobraniye sochineniy*, München, 1968, 2, p. 35.

6. Igor' Severyanin, "Ananasy v shampanskom," *Ananasy v shampanskom*, Moskva, 1915.

7. Aleksandr Blok, "Tam v ulitse stoyal kakoy-to dom," in *Sobraniye sochineniy*, Moskva, 1960, 1, p. 192.

8. In his depiction of the search for the mysterious "W," Aksënov relied to a large extent on actual scientific experiments on isolated large transverse energy conducted both in the West and the Soviet Union; see C. Rubbia, "Intermediate Vector Boson," *Scientific American*, vol. 246, no. 3, 1982, pp. 48-59.

9. For a detailed account of the poetics of the industrial novel see: H. Borland, *Soviet Literary Theory and Practice during the First Five-Year Plan 1928-1932*, New York, 1950; S. Shput, *Tema sotsialisticheskogo stroitel'stva v proze 30-ykh godov*, Moskva, 1963; Ershov, *Russkiy sovetskiy roman: Natsional'nyye traditsii i novatorstvo*, Moskva, 1967.

10. H. Markiewicz, "On the Definition of Parody," p. 1268.

11. In reality particle "W" was discovered by Western scientists working at the CERN Collider in Switzerland, but this took place ten years after Aksënov had written his book: see "Experimental Observation of Isolated Large Transverse Energy Electrons with Associated Missing Energy at s=540 GeV," *Physics Letters*, vol. 122B, no. 1, 24 February, 1983, p. 103.

12. V. Shklovsky, "Iskusstvo kak priyëm," *Poètika: Sborniki po teorii poèticheskogo yazyka*, Petrograd, 1919, pp. 101-14.

13. See Margaret Rose, "Parody Meta-Fiction" and Tuvia Shlonsky, "Literary Parody: Remarks on Its Method and Function," *Proceedings of the 4th Congress of the International Comparative Literature Association*, F. Jost, ed., The Hague, 1966, vol. 2, pp. 797-801.

THE STEEL BIRD AND AKSËNOV'S PROSE OF THE SEVENTIES*

Edward Możejko

Whoever is familiar with Aksënov's evolution as a writer will note that one of the most striking characteristics of his literary output published in the last fifteen years or so remains experimentation. Through the creative endeavor of his maturing years as an artist, the author of *The Burn* seems to have almost programmatically committed himself to a constant search for new forms of artistic expression, to the revision and renewal of textual constituents of his early realistic prose. It is, perhaps, not a fortuity that one of his works, published as late as 1978, was entitled *In Search of a Genre*. Indeed, one is tempted to surmise that in this particular case, the title reflects not so much on the nature of the literary work in question as it reveals a general aesthetic attitude of the author. It can be considered to be a symbol or a commentary on the effort made by the writer throughout an extended period of time.

To be sure, it is difficult to say with all certainty when this process of transition from one mode of writing to another began. Even in some early stories, such as "The Odd-Ball" or "Little Whale, Varnisher of Reality," one can discern Aksënov's predilection for "symbolic detail"[1] which unsettles the basically realistic advance of discourse, evokes ambiguity and, above all, tends to blur the boundaries between the principle of verisimilitude and fantasy—features undoubtedly predominant in the modern mode of writing.

If approached from this vantage point, Aksënov's prose poses a number of interesting questions to both the reader and the critic. The former, although aware of the *strangeness* or *otherness* of such works as *Our Golden Hardware*, "Destruction of Pompeii," or *The Burn*, and at times perhaps even able to intuitively grasp their meaning, remains desperately at a loss when it comes to explaining some components of these texts, their semantic value and the essence of Aksënov's evolution as a writer. It is at this point that a critic should appear to be helpful; however, facing a structure of texts such as those mentioned above, he must also experience serious doubts, if not frustrations, about interpreting their "meaning." The Barthesian dis-

---

* I would like to express my sincere appreciation to Professor L. Doležel from the University of Toronto for his extremely valuable comments made with regard to the final version of this paper.

tinction between what is *lisible* or *illisible* applies with full force to him as well. Therefore, all he can offer are *variations on a theme* rather than an "objective" or "final" explanation of the texts.

Or, to make it more explicit, a claim to the contrary would be particularly unjustifiable in relation to literary texts which can be qualified as modernistic (or "avantgardist," depending on the chosen terminology) because of their transgressive nature (transgressive, of course, in relation to the convention of realism), which raises the possibility of deriving from them more than one meaning. The difficulty of their interpretation increases exactly at the very moment when a critic, in choosing his analytic strategy, decides to go beyond a sheer technical description of so-called artistic devices (a relatively easy task to accomplish) and wants to decipher obscure turnings of the narrative; that is, when he poses himself a more ambitious task of explaining, so to speak, the "meaning" or rather polysemic content of a given text or group of texts. Perhaps R. Barthes[2] was right, after all, in his reluctance to interpret modern works of literature ("unreadable" texts) and in his advice not to analyze their structure to "make sense" of them.

In the case of Aksënov, however, such an approach seems to be unwarranted,[3] and the semantic aspect of his writing cannot be ignored because it is conditioned by a different cultural tradition[4] which is reluctant to accept "pure" experimentation. The above difficulties notwithstanding, it is my intention to examine in this paper some major characteristics which, in my opinion, constitute the most important and distinct components of Aksënov's prose published in the seventies, in conjunction with their semantic function. Before doing so, I would like to give a short account of his creative attitude as reflected in the early period of his literary career, a period he describes as "happy."[5]

By and large, Aksënov's early novellas and short stories tell us about young people who are disappointed with the established way of life, but who refrain from criticizing the essential principles on which the system relies. They rebel against sterile, ossified social norms and moral mendacity; they question parental authority and want to exercise greater control over their own destiny; but first of all, they want to be honest to themselves and in human relationships. An air of optimism surrounds the actions of protagonists, who hope for change and a better future. This message finds its semantic manifestation in a basically "realistic" type of narrative.[6]

The case in point is the novella *Colleagues*. Here, the point of view of the narrator is strictly fixed; and although at the outset of the novella his presence is *revealed* in a short and direct comment about the main protagonists, the narration as a whole is conducted in the third person. The story starts with a characterization of three young men, Vladislav Karpov, Aleksandr Zelenin and Aleksey Maksimov, who graduated from the faculty of medicine in Leningrad and now are faced with their first serious test: they have to enter their profession as physicians. Their choice is limited because of the Soviet law which assigns graduates to the kind of job (and site) as authorities see fit (the so-called *raspredeleniye*). The most rebellious of the three is Maksimov, who calls *raspredeleniye* a "prinuditel'nyy akt" (a compulsory act); Zelenin, on the other hand, remains quite content with it. All three of them are in some respect lucky: Maksimov and Karpov, in accordance with their wishes, practice in Leningrad's port, allowing them to prepare for sailing on commercial ships as crew doctors, and Zelenin becomes a country doctor. From this point on, the action of the novel concentrates on two extremes: Maksimov and Zelenin; consequently, the setting of the events alternates between Leningrad and Kruglogor'ye, located somewhere north of Leningrad.

The characters, too, are presented in quite a traditional, realistic manner although different from the one required by the normative rules of socialist realism: Maksimov represents the generation of "angry young men" who are longing for an adventurous life, but he is morally chaste and therefore not condemned for his feelings; Karpov is interested in the enjoyment of life, sport, and dating girls. His behavior can be described as a middle-of-the-road attitude. The most socially motivated, a sort of "positive" hero who has a great sense of responsibility, yet devoid of ideological rigidity, is Zelenin. His approach to life can be described as commonsensical. When Egorov, the chairman of the council, tells a story about a man who was called a "scoundrel" because during the war he renounced his party membership to escape a German firing squad, Zelenin has this to say:

> I do not know [. . .], it's a terrible choice. Maybe he is a scoundrel, but not a communist. Simply a human being.[7] (82)

There is only one *bête noire*, a negative character in the novel: the bandit Fëdor Bugrov, who knifes Zelenin.

In *Colleagues*, the narrative line preserves its linear continuity; it follows—with only two exceptions—the chronological sequence of happenings or actions which, in turn, are linked by the principles of causality. In short, the world presented in this novel does not contradict our sense of perception of the outer reality, and the poetics of verisimilitude remain unchallenged.

The above-described narrative pattern of Aksënov's first novel generated similar structural variants of his early prose in general. In *A Ticket to the Stars*, for example, the story of Victor Denisov is told by the character himself (first person narrator), and that of his brother Dima in both the third person (Chapters IV, V, VI, VII and VIII), and then in the first person narrator in the last two chapters of the novella. Basically, however, in spite of these shifts (first person V. Denisov—third person about Dimka—first person D. Denisov; incidentally, testing the shifts in narrative perspective seems to belong to Aksënov's favorite devices at the early stage of his literary activity), the narration interchanges between two points of view of the two brothers. In spite of this split, the theme differs little from the one the reader encounters in *Colleagues*. Victor is more mature and determined to pursue his career as a scientist, but not " at all costs," which such a career may require; he definitely does not want to compromise on some essential moral issues. He does not see it appropriate to write phony papers to please his superiors or *protégés* of the party. He wants to pursue his career in honest competition with others. However, throughout the whole novel he reappears as the voice of moderation. The first sentence uttered by Victor: "Ya chelovek loyal'nyy" (I am a law-abiding citizen) sets the framework for all of his thoughts, confessions, observations and deeds as a first person narrator.

At the opposite pole stands Dimka. He is rebellious, impatient and dislikes those who are prompt to give "reasonable" advice with regard to what to do with his life. He wants to escape both the totalitarian pressure of the social system and the authoritarian rule of parents. Therefore, he rejects the usual and most popular pattern of advancement: high school—university—professional career. Together with his friends, he leaves for Estonia to become a working member of a fishing *kolkhoz*. Consequently, as in *Colleagues*, the setting of events alternates between two places: Moscow and the Baltic seashore.

In the above-discussed paradigms of Aksënov's early prose, the modus of presentation follows the rules of what Chatman calls "natural logic":[8] these and other works do not offend our sense of normalcy, if the everyday reality is to be taken as a criterion of comparison, or referential measure.

The stereotyped realistic externalization of human conditions and relationships is called into question for the first time in the long story *The Steel Bird*. Let us then take a closer look at this example as a point of departure for the description of a poetic world which Aksënov has since constructed with ever increasing eagerness in his subsequent works and especially those published in the seventies.

The story starts with the arrival of a stranger, Veniamin Fedoseyevich Popenkov, nicknamed "*Stal'naya ptitsa*" (The Steel Bird), at the house on Fonarnyy Lane, no. 14. His appearance is unusual as he carries with him two bags, one filled with raw meat and the other with fish. Something black, reminiscent of blood, is dripping from the bags, and evokes curiosity on the part of the dismayed onlookers—the inhabitants of the house. Intending to stay in the house, Popenkov has to overcome two obstacles: to see the caretaker, Nikolay Nikolayevich Nikolayev, who has already retired and *locked his apartment door*, hoping to play undisturbed on his cornet-à-piston; secondly, a place has to be found in the old house which is already overcrowded, with families sharing one apartment. From this point on, some strange things happen: Popenkov appears "suddenly" behind Nikolay Nikolayevich's back, he listens for a moment to his music, and understands that it includes a distinct motif about Stalin. Neither the reader nor Nikolay Nikolayevich will ever learn how the mysterious penetration of a locked apartment occurrred. Nikolay suspects that his wife must have forgotten to lock the door and he scolds her for that. However, when she tells the truth, the only explanation he has is that Popenkov must be from the "organs," that is, from the omnipotent secret police. Nikolayev feels ill at ease when Popenkov asks him the favor of having "a roof over his head," yet he finally succumbs to the request by accommodating the protagonist in the elevator. The inhabitants of the apartment building accept his absurd solution without any reservation whatsoever. The story continues as Popenkov slowly gains power. From the elevator, he moves to the entrance-hall, which he rebuilds according to his needs and comfort; he wins the beautiful Zina away from her husband, the deputy minister Z.; he forces the majority of the tenants to get involved in the illegal production of forged tapestries; and *de facto* becomes the undisputed master of the apartment building.

The story ends with the tenants rebelling against Popenkov, and Nikolay Nikolayevich arriving on a white horse to announce that all inhabitants of the house at Fonarnyy Lane no. 14 have been granted new apartments in an *experimental* district because the old building is to be torn down. While all rush to gather their belongings and move, Popenkov takes the elevator and rides to the top level. The building falls apart in minutes and the only remaining part of it is the elevator with Popenkov sitting in it. He sits there for months and when bulldozers arrive to demolish the remnants, Popenkov *flies away* into the blue.

The story is interrupted by lapses of time (e.g., at the end of *The Steel Bird* most of the tenants are "retired" people), flashbacks (*analepse*), flashforwards (*prolepse*), "recollections" of some tenants (e.g., the recollections of the doctor and the barber) or "reports" of the inspector, the narrator's comments, and so on. For example, just after the introduction of Popenkov (something that can be called *exposition*), the author inserts the "reminiscences" of a doctor. At this point the reader does not know who the doctor is (no causal links are indicated), nor of whom he speaks, as he merely uses the personal pronouns "he," "his," "him" in the first part of his reminiscences. To whom does it refer? Only subsequent sections of the text gradually reveal the identity of the doctor and clarify that he refers to Popenkov.

To summarize, what we definitely observe in *The Steel Bird* is the obvious breakdown of the linear temporal and causal continuity of the narrative, or in short: its fragmentation. Secondly, we can speak here of the introduction of the fantastic. Both characteristics constitute a major departure from Aksënov's early prose but the question of what the text means for the reader remains, at least in my view, ambiguous. What sense can be made of it? A few reviews and remarks that were written on this subject offer little consolation and differ considerably in their interpretation of the story.

A. Gladilin maintains that Aksënov's story "does not go beyond the limits of Soviet literature" and suggests that it can be explained as a satire against 'the petty bourgeoisie' *meshchanstvo*. In his final remarks, he admits the possibility of a different interpretation, yet he still insists that *The Steel Bird* should be considered a "prosoviet" work, and avoids drawing definite conclusions by simply saying that literary works of art escape "trivial political assessment."

V. Dukas, however, did not hesitate, and rightly so, to make a political judgment when in a passage devoted to *The Steel Bird* he wrote the following:

> The hero of the novel, Popenkov, although he is not Stalin, acts like him by opposing people and by establishing his own cult of personality [. . .] While Aksenov perhaps wished to expose the crooked road to communism, the Soviet censors (editors) saw something else and neglected the work. And indeed the novella is full of allusions not only to various literary and historical mileposts of Russian civilization but also to Stalin and KGB.[10]

V. Dukas clearly stresses the political meaning of the story. With some slight variations, other American critics expressed similar views. In his competent introduction to Aksënov's short stories translated into English,[11] J.J. Johnson gives quite a lengthy discussion of *The Steel Bird* and warns against a simplified interpretation of the story. What the work implies, according to him, is "that human beings must avoid accepting and getting used to their oppression. [. . .] Popenkov is not Stalin, as some would guess, but in the tradition of Stalin" (pp. xxi-xxii). In their introduction to *Contemporary Russian Prose* (Ardis, 1982, p. xii), Carl and Ellendia Proffer perceive *The Steel Bird* as a "warning story: Stalin may have died, but there are other men of steel ready to take his place, if an ignorant, fearful populace permits it."[12]

Finally, P. Dalgård, in his painstaking analysis of Aksënov's stories, comes to the following conclusion: "The grotesque structure of *The Steel Bird*, through the development of its metaphor, becomes a parable about power-lust and the struggle against spiritual emptiness."[13] Three different interpretations emerge from this inevitably abbreviated account: *The Steel Bird* is (a) an allegory or metaphor of Stalinism, (b) a "prosoviet" satire, (c) a representation of the theme of spiritual emptiness (what Dalgård calls "a parable about power-lust" can be included in (a)). Although each of them has its merits, I am inclined to favor the first one, albeit with some complements. First of all, one should try to answer the question of why the critics, in interpreting the story, refer it to Soviet reality by saying that it tells us about Stalinism or the danger of its revival. According to J.J. Johnson—and he is a reliable source of information—Aksënov dissociated himself (and so did Gladilin, for that matter) from such an interpretation; he wanted to see in it some transcendental values, a satire "on mankind as a whole and more specifically on the nature of man in a totalitarian society" (p. xx). Of course the author wished to see his work printed, and the only way to achieve it was through convincing the editors or censors that the story does not contain "hidden meanings," alluding by any means to the political and social fabric of the country. As for the reader (and a critic is, after all, a reader), he does not have to take into consideration any of the author's apprehensions. At the same time, his recollection of the Stalinist past remains very vivid and he confronts it with the given text. The parallel seems to be undeniable: a man of little renown, as was Stalin when taking power in 1924, settles down in an apartment building and gradually terrorizes its inhabitants. But there is additional material, "signals" or "hints" implicit in the text which provide even greater ammunition for treating it as a reference to Soviet society. This material opens, at least in my view, an avenue for yet another interpretation of the story and thus augments, so to speak, its semantic field. Apart from building up his own cult of personality—*Popenkov develops the production of handicrafts: counterfeit French tapestries*. To clarify the significance of Popenkov's "dual" existence at Fonarnyy Lane no. 14, let us turn again for a moment to the text. As we remember, Popenkov is treated many times by the doctor, Zel'dovich, who admits in his reminiscences that each time he met him "the diagnosis was completely unclear" and he suspects the treatment he prescribes his patient does not help him. It is the protagonist's own will that really cures him; the doctor feels very uncomfortable whenever summoned by him. Finally, the doctor's Consilium is convened to establish the essence of Popenkov's personality. But neither the expertise of the famous airplane constructor Tupolev nor that of the ornithologist "academician Bukhvostov" helps to resolve the puzzle and pose a diagnosis. The Consilium comes to the conclusion that Popenkov is neither an airplane nor a bird but "a completely new species with a unique combination of organic and inorganic features." The members of the Consilium decide, however, to keep their findings "absolutely confidential."

If we are to look for Aksënov's literary antecedents, the name of Franz Kafka inevitably comes to mind. It was in the famous story "The Metamorphosis" that he described the strange transformation of Gregor Samsa into a repulsive creature that combines both human and animalistic features. A few years later, he would return to this theme in "Eine Kreuzung" (A Crossbreed), a short story about an animal—"half kitten," "half lamb." It is this type of prose, and "The Metamorphosis" in particular, that provoked innumerable interpretations and brought Kafka the fame of being the master of modernistic prose, distinct from mimetic tradition by its polyvalence and indeterminacy. There is, however, one fundamental, semantic difference to be noted between Kafka and Aksënov: while the former depicts a victim (or victims, if we take his other works into account) of oppression and alienation, the latter creates a monster who imposes his total domination over those who surround him. "Inhumanity" in Kafka is a consequence of external conditions (be it social, economic, religious or family related conflicts). With Aksënov, Popenkov's inhumanity is *the source* of terror and humiliation of others. Thus, the role of the hybrid created by the Russian author is reversed: his monstrosity, inhuman features generate conditions of human misery and oppression.

Popenkov's "split" is reflected, of course, in the title of the story and has further implications for the way it can be interpreted. If we read the text carefully, we shall realize that all happenings, deeds and actions concentrate along two essential lines of Popenkov's public activity: the one which allows him to gain a firm grip over the tenants of the apartment building, and the other which promotes his role as a sort of entrepreneur who organizes the home-weaving of counterfeit tapestries. One can even talk about a symmetric "alignment" of these events: those which enhance Popenkov's role as a dictator or builder of a totalitarian community relate to the adjective "steel" and bear the stamp of "supernatural" qualities: he arrives from nowhere, he miraculously penetrates Nikolay Nikolayevich's apartment, understands his cornet-à-piston playing; Marina Tsvetkova experiences his "superhuman" strength in the elevator (and so does, for instance, Fuchinian in an arm wrestling contest with Popenkov which leaves the ex-paratrooper filled with respect for his challenger), he possesses the ability to make people suddenly change their mind. Finally, he speaks an incomprehensible language—different from the one of ordinary humans.

His *earthly* side might be associated with the noun "bird": he drags Maria Samopalova into tapestry weaving and makes Zina buy his products (after she has practically turned her apartment into a second-hand shop, he calls her "a true Soviet Citizen"), likes comfort and is a womanizer. Support for such a claim could be found in the meaning of the word "bird" itself. In a metaphorical, mythological sense the word may signify a higher spiritual value; but in the colloquial Russian use, *bird* has an ironic meaning with a clearly negative tinge, as in "what a character!" (*vot ptitsa!*). All contemporary dictionaries of the Russian language[14] strongly emphasize this figurative current expression. It can be associated wiht the word "charlatan." In this connection, Gladilin's remark that Aksënov critized *meshchanstvo* should not be disregarded: indeed Popenkov represents such features. If they were exposed as a simple dominating trait of weakness of a protagonist throughout the whole story, Aksënov probably would have had no difficulty in publishing it, but they manifest themselves in combination with Popenkov's totalitarian aspirations, and thus it would be safe to suggest that they are meant to represent the two most negative aspects of Soviet society: the principle of authoritarian rule, and what is often stigmatized in the U.S.S.R. as the *petty bourgeois* longing for prosperity, especially if it involves the kind of business operations practiced by Popenkov. On the surface, there is no interdependence between the two. However, there exists an invisible, mutually conditioned linkage between these two spheres of Popenkov's activity: whereas a totalitarian system such as the Soviet calls for "austerity," "sacrifice," "devotion to a cause," at the same time it feeds human dreams about a "better life" or even enrichment through whatever means are available. In short, it feeds greed. In the ideological view of the party, these two characteristics are incompatible; yet in the story they coexist as a sort of a hybrid[15] (metaphorically speaking, "neither fish nor fowl") which incarnates the strange world at Fonarnyy Lane no. 14.

The Steel Bird is a marvelous story, written in a lively narrative, keeping the reader in suspense, providing him with many occasions for laughter but first of all containing collateral motifs which lend the story a universal or even metaphysical significance. One of them is the motif of warning against totalitarianism: both political and economic. The former breeds the latter. After all, as soon as Popenkov feels he is in the saddle, he threatens the inhabitants of Fonarnyy Lane no. 14 with making them all work for him. Yet we should not lose sight of the fact that the story's *Stoff*, that is, material through which the artistic intention has been implemented, points to a sharply increased criticism of Aksënov's own country; he does not only warn against the revival or existence of Stalinism, as the majority of critics seems to suggest, but he strikes at, or at least puts a question mark over, the validity of the whole political and socio-economic system, and even extends his criticism beyond the present by scoffing at its history. The grotesque struggle between the oriental ornament and the ancient Greek amphora in the vestibule, resulting in Popenkov smashing the latter (he knows it contains nothing "but a half a century of dust"), his effort to prevent samurais dashing "for the fair ladies" or knights mixing with geishas bears unmistakable allusion to Russia's centuries-old internal conflict between occidentalism and the asiatic element.

The "happy" period was over and the "angry" had arrived. Aksënov moves now from a simple description of the disillusioned characters of his "youth prose" to a more serious questioning of what his generation has inherited. To accomplish this, he turned, as I have mentioned before, to the fantastic and what J. Frank defined almost forty years ago as "spatial form" in literature.[16]

In the following I shall deal with only some of the artistic consequences of the above-mentioned transition, as limited space does not permit discussion at any greater length.

The use of the fantastic seems to be by far the most important innovation in Aksënov's later prose and constitutes its underlying structural principle. In an interview with B. Hellman, Aksënov himself stressed the significance of the "fantastic tradition." He said the following:

> I myself look upon the fantastic tradition as being primordial [*ursprungliga* in the original—E.M.]. In our country one considers it to be an imported vogue but it is a great mistake. In the folklore of all cultures, one can find a hyperbolic, allegorical tradition. In it lies also the meaning of art: to create one's own world, nothing that is a copy of reality. This holds for all cultures but most of all for the Russian culture. Russian people have always known a strong attraction to mysticism and a sort of anarchism.[17]

He made an almost identical statement in the aforementioned article in *Le Monde*, where he explained his artistic experimentation in terms of his close connection with the popular tradition of Russian folklore (see footnote 3). Evidence of Aksënov's fascination with the fantastic or the unusual and unexpected dates from the early period of his writing. He made a timid attempt to tackle this question in the novella *Colleagues*. In the subchapter

"Realism or abstraction," two episodic characters, Veselin and Foma, argue about the aesthetic merits of two opposed creative attitudes: realism vs. abstractionism. The former defends the principle of verisimilitude while the latter favors abstraction because it involves human imagination to a much greater extent than does realism. According to him, painting should bring itself nearer to music if it wants to exercise emotional ascendancy on man, it "should become the vibration of human spirit." Foma (an association with the evangelical "doubting Thomas" is obvious and self-explanatory, as are many symbolic names in the later works of Aksënov) calls realism "obsolete" and identifies new art with evolution, progress and contemporaneity. In fact, Foma, by virtue of his doubt, can be viewed as the prototype of the "young avantgardist" Memozov, who would appear in Aksënov's prose-sketches at the end of the sixties [published in the pages of *Literaturnaya gazeta*; see J.J. Johnson's "V.P. Aksënov: A Literary Biography," p. 22—eds.], and who would constantly disturb or interfere with the realistic intentions of the author or the realistic order of his narrative. There are two other *voices* reflecting on the subject. Maksimov is confused: on the one hand, he remains sympathetic to the traditional, realistic concept of art, yet on the other, he is prepared "to fight" for Picasso and Matisse. The fourth, an old professor, speaks out in support of Art— spelled with a capital letter because it implies the "most subtle psychologism" (*tonchayshiy psikhologizm*) and rejection of *isms* which express a vogue of time rather than true art. The point of view of the narrator does not commit itself to either side of the dispute (although the description of Foma's appearance is unfavorable) and no application of abstractionist technique is to be found in the novel itself. The episode simply reflects a genuine interest of Soviet intelligentsia in what's happening in the arts.

However, in the novella *The Tare of Empty Barrels* and the novel *Our Golden Hardware*, Aksënov confirms his determination to continue the line of experimentation which he initiated in *The Steel Bird*.[18] It seems to be especially true of *Our Golden Hardware*: thanks to the introduction of Memozov's figure, one can read it as a continuous interplay between fantasy and the real or as a short aesthetic justification for the change in Aksënov's style of writing. In the first page of the novel the narrator sets out (and he makes his intentions explicit) to conduct a "quiet narration" in the third person, yet all of a sudden he:

> zametil na trape figuru v kozhanoy krylatke, figuru svoyego nedavnego i nepriyatnogo znakomogo—molodogo "avangardista" Memozova, kotoryy za posledniye neskol'ko let umudrilsya probit' tri breshi v ego tvorcheskoy tsitadeli.
> (he noticed on the accommodation ladder the figure of his recent and

unpleasant acquaintance—the young "avantgardist" Memozov who in the past few years managed to make three breaches in his creative citadel.)[19]

The "three breaches" may refer exactly to the above-mentioned works: *The Steel Bird, The Tare of Empty Barrels* and *Always for Sale*. They signify, no doubt, the breach of realistic tradition. But who is Memozov and how does he make these breaches in the author's prose and plays? Of course, the author treats him ironically. He, that is the author, pretends to be the one who gladly would apply mimetic principles in his writing, yet Memozov thwarts his efforts. The narrator states that he intends to conduct the story of *Zhelezka* in the third person but as soon as he sees Memozov, he realizes the impossibility of doing so. Consequently, on the surface, Memozov is presented as an "evil spirit" who tries to lead the author astray, as it were, from his "healthy" "realistic" intentions, a kind of gnome (or goblin) known from folklore tales who lures one to mischief, while in fact he personifies fancy. He is the author's other "I," a benediction. No wonder then that at the end of the novel he does not speak of him as an enemy, but rather as a rival. Consequently, from now on Memozov will haunt the author throughout all his works. One of the most interesting recurrences of this figure can be found in *'Round the Clock, Non-Stop*. Aksënov writes an account of his own sojourn in the United States as a teacher of Russian literature. Traditionally, the genre of travel literature had to be contained within the limits of realistic convention and required a reasonable degree of veracity in description (of course J. Verne's novels precede the genre of science fiction); yet Aksënov violates these principles by introducing two fictitious stock-characters: Moskvich and the anti-author, Memozov. When the former (who seems to be "closer" to the author himself) expresses his surprise, if not displeasure, at Memozov's appearance, the latter's response is simple: "Imagination travels without visas . . .". Again the function of Memozov is to disrupt the mimetic "normalcy" of a literary work in question. Consequently, the author has to "tolerate," so to speak, his fictitious narrators and is constantly forced to deviate from "solid," "realistic" reporting of his own experiences as a teacher of Russian literature in Los Angeles. In fact, *'Round the Clock, Non-Stop* becomes both a testing ground for weighing the virtues of fantasy vs. reality and a kind of self-commentary on Aksënov's own prose. In the subchapter "Voobrazheniye i real'nost'" (Imagination and Reality), he notes that although imagination may not be a reliable source of presenting objects or events, it is by no means inferior to reality itself, and later in the text he reinforces this statement by saying that an artist's imagination is part of reality itself. It is within this context that the symbol of Hemingway may be explained. In the final part of *'Round the Clock, Non-Stop*, Aksënov bids farewell to the author of *For Whom the Bell Tolls*. It starts with the words "Proshchay, proshchay, Hemingway!" (Goodbye, goodbye, Hemingway!). Exactly the same passage appeared earlier in the ending of *Our Golden Hardware*.[20] However, in *'Round the Clock, Non-Stop* the passage is followed by some reflections about other writers such as Faulkner, Salinger and so on. Here, it seems to me that Hemingway does not appear as a symbol of freedom (a suggestion made by P. Dalgård) but as a symbol of a certain aesthetic attitude. Aksënov bids farewell to the idol of his youth prose whom he still adores but does not want to follow any longer as an artist.

It is important to realize that the creation of a hybrid world in which the boundaries between real and unreal phenomena are neutralized or entirely removed is applied by Aksënov on a global scale; that is, not only as curious isolated details[21] within the narrative, but as the basic structural principle of whole short stores, novels and plays. Let's again illustrate it with examples. The events of *Our Golden Hardware* take place in a fictitious place, *Zhelezka*, a place that does not exist in reality. The setting of "Destruction of Pompeii" is also non-existent. The ancient city of Pompeii was destroyed by natural disaster a long time ago. The fictitious nature of the place is emphasized by the fact that whatever happens in the story happens in modern times (actions, characters, institutions or all objects presented evoke association with contemporaneity). And when the writer moves his imagination over to a real place, Crimea (in *The Island of Crimea*), he changes its realities, too: Crimea does not constitute an integral part of the Soviet Union but is separated from it both geographically (the peninsula has become an island) and politically: it has been saved by the Whites in 1917 and developed into a Western-style democracy.

Of course, the use of the fantastic bore significant consequences for other strata of Aksënov's prose and included such stylistic characteristics as (1) a conspicuous uncertainty of the narrator, who now loses his omniscient power (or olympic perspective) and displays an extremely subjective view of events; (2) fragmented, incoherent and *illogical* narration; (3) the enhanced role of symbols and a clear tendency towards an allegorization of discourse; (4) the abandonment of traditional characters who are no longer regarded as analogies of a "real life" but treated as narrative devices.[22]

I shall confine myself to just a few sketchy observations on such questions as narrator-narration characters, and what I propose to describe as *modern pictorial representation*.

The uncertainty or even ignorance of a narrator about the identity of his protagonists becomes evident, for example, in the second chapter of *T. Steel Bird*. There, the narrator turns directly to the reader to tell him th he "knows absolutely nothing about Popenkov" and hopes to shape certain image of the "hero" in the course of the story. In the third chapte he promises to establish a strict chronological order of events, yet constantl deviates from this intention.

Further disintegration of the narrator's compact and stable position i discernible in *Our Golden Hardware*, where he has to face a sort of anti author, Memozov. As a result of Memozov's intervention, the narrator abandons the third person, "objective" point of view. He reveals limitations of his knowledge, for example, by saying that he does not feel competent to write about the scientific center in Pikhty. He fears that someone in the Academy of Sciences may accuse him of being a dilettante. The narrator pledges *not to be realistic* and, in fact, declares himself to be in favor of what Frenchmen call *invraisemblance*, in which the story is not constructed according to outer reality but governed by laws of its own artistic structure. He "cannot reflect" because he does not know (or at least he pretends not to know) reality in its depth. He "lays the device bare" and shows the motivation behind his narrative strategy. At times, the narration switches to the plural "we," and at others the reader has difficulties in identifying the narrator altogether. Aksënov takes full advantage of this "multi-narrative" perspective in *The Burn*, one of the most complex novels he has written so far.

Generally speaking, there are six major narrative voices in this novel. They intersect with each other at various points in time or space and create an amazing multiplicity of perspectives. The seventh narrator, the "real" author[23] as it were, gloats over all of them but his "authority" and frequency of appearance are severely restricted and kept in the background.

The above-described scheme of experimentation with the narrator leads to extreme fragmentation, relativization and subjectivization of the semantic components, which are further enhanced by an unusual variety of linguistic measures and tropes of poetic language.

A typical device of this prose is *glissement* 'sliding', a term invented by the leading author of the French *roman nouveau*, Robbe-Grillet, with whom Aksënov has many characteristics in common. It means a sudden break in the continuity of narration, a transition from one narrative unit to another without any motivation or logical linkage between them. There exist various types of *glissements*: temporal, spatial, narrative and so on. One possible example is the above-mentioned description of Aristarkh Apollinariyevich Kunitser's day by two different narrative voices. In the same opening episode of the novel, Kunitser feels a sudden urge to call out after the departing Nina: "Inna, he was on the verge of shouting after her, Nina, Marina please come back [. . .]".[24] But who are these females,[25] what are the connections between them? The above examples are chosen at random.

Among other procedures applied by Aksënov are repetitions. In all five episodes entitled "ABCDE," Mashka Kulago meets each of the Apollinariyeviches in quite unusual circumstances. Each time, she is dressed in a red shirt (tied under her breasts) and in "invariable" jeans; she is always tipsy or drunk. This image repeats itself like a refrain five times in succession and contributes to the dynamic flow of the narrative; yet its true function consists of building a sense of unity among these fragments, suggesting at the same time that nothing has changed: time is not progressing, but going in circles. It also reveals in an abbreviated manner that at one time or another Kulago was the lover of all Apollinariyeviches. *The Burn* abounds in such repetitions throughout its whole text and they are to be found in other short stories and novels of this period.

I have mentioned the above example for yet another reason: the five Apollinariyeviches constitute a new category of literary character which G.S. Smith aptly proposes to call *polypersona*—"one individual who appears in several different embodiments."[26] Their patronymicum seems to suggest that they are of the same origin—children of the Stalinist epoch. Their personal experiences are similar and tragic but their professions are different: Aristarkh Apollinariyevich Kunitser is a scientist, Samson Apollinariyevich Sabler—a jazz musician, Gennadiy Apollinariyevich Mal'kolmov represents the medical profession, Radiy Apollinariyevich Khvastishchev is a sculptor and Panteley Apollinariyevich Panteley—a writer. Their confrontation with political and social conditions delivers a collective knowledge about the system which reigns in the Soviet Union. They cannot, however, be analyzed in terms of traditional characters, as executors of action or as psychological types. Unlike the realistic novel, the essence of modern narrative consists of promoting character at the expense of the plot. Thus, the Apollinariyeviches symbolize various aspects of life of the Soviet intelligentsia under Stalin and shortly after his death. Or perhaps, at least in some instances, it would be more appropriate to speak of "eponymy,"[27] that is, the ability of literary texts to transform anonymity of a character into a signifying subject which becomes a nickname for a certain phenomena of life in general. A good example of such a transformation would be Goncharov's *Oblomov* and its derivative form *Oblomovshchina*—meaning idle and incapable of acting efficiently. Modern literature tries to avoid eponymy by promoting its opposite: anonymity (especially, for example, visible in the novels of A. Robbe-Grillet). In this respect, Aksënov seems to follow his own and very original path. His actants (in A.J. Greimas' sense of the word) do not remind one of the heroes, types, and psychological characters known in realistic prose. They are consistent with the peculiarity of discourse as a whole. Consequently, they often behave in an "illogical," eccentric, "strange" by normal standards, and extravagant way. Yet they are not entirely detached from reality and certainly not devoid of an allusive power. Sometimes, to achieve this effect, Aksënov employs the device of defamiliarization by contraction: two or more names are combined into one, which again brings to mind the principle of the hybrid. Thus we have Kukita Kuseyevich (reference to Nikita Khrushchëv and Kuusinen), Beriy Yagodovich (Beriya and Yagoda—both commissars of the Soviet security apparatus), Vadim Mokeyevich Kozhemyakin—a combination of Vadim Kozhevnikov and a Gor'ky hero's name. Metonymical substitutions such as *Glava* 'Head', "Glavnyy Zhrets" (The Chief Priest) are no exception. Aksënov makes familiar names sound unfamiliar. Paradoxically, through this *à rebours* device, he achieves both eponymy and anonymity. After all, what does it matter whether it is a Kukita Kuseyevich or a Beriy Yagodovich. They are all external signs of the upper echelon of the dreadful Soviet and party bureaucracy. They are not individuals but faceless executors of the will of a nameless group of people, and as such they do not deserve to be individualized by "normal" proper names. An element of irony becomes an essential attribute of these characters.

In my closing remarks I would like to emphasize that while discussing Aksënov's narrative technique, one should mention, at least in passing, a characteristic which has been overlooked so far by critics but which, in my view, will become a subject of serious attention in the future. I am speaking of what I suggested be called *modern pictorial representation*; its organizing principle rests on the opposition of unity vs. a dissected world. It has been said that Aksënov's poetic world in his later works is fragmented. However, one cannot deny it a certain unity. The same characters, symbols, places recur in the novels and plays he wrote during the seventies (the heron, Memozov, some of the Apollinariyeviches, and so on). They lend to this literary corps a sense of textual unity. One gets the impression that Aksënov writes one text—and one can hardly avoid a parallel with H. Balzac. Aksënov's *comèdie humaine*, however, is modern in that he creates cosmopolitan, fictitious or real protagonists who easily cross all borders (Marina Vlady, E. Hemingway, Patrick Thunderjet, Marian Kulago, Gromson, and so on) and remain in sporadic contact with each other. What is achieved through such a device is the sense of living in a small world, or to use

McLuhan's term—in a "global village." At the same time, such a world is devoid of personal safety and its protagonists live with a feeling of constant insecurity.[28] His way of describing such a world reminds us at times of modern paintings, a fresco like Picasso's *Guerenica* on which we see fragmented bodies of a bull, a horse and men, and yet we cannot compose a consistent whole out of it. The visual perception of events is also strongly evident on the level of presenting smaller units of text—images. When Tolya is to be taken from the school by secret police agents, he has to cross the huge yard in order to reach the police car. The yard is described with almost geometrical precision; and since Tolya knows that he has to cross it while others are looking on, he calls the yard "prostranstvo pozora" or "kartina pozora" (the space of disgrace, the picture of disgrace; see *The Burn*, pp. 252-253). The shame, despair and humiliation of a young boy are rendered through the medium of the described picture, or are identified with this picture. Images that have a clear association with some scenes from Italian films of the post-war neorealism are also to be found in *Our Golden Hardware*.

It is interesting to ask the question of what prompted Aksënov's deviation from the "promising" career of a realistic Soviet writer to one whose works (comparable to those of the European modernist or post-modernist period) are banned in his country. Apart from a rich literary tradition (Gogol, Saltykov-Shchedrin, Belyy, Bulgakov), a variety of reasons may have played a role. Perhaps he was forced by the need to take a more critical stand towards the Soviet social system and to smuggle these ideas to the reader by the use of Aesopian language. Judging from Aksënov's increased difficulties with the Soviet censors and publishers, such an explanation should not be excluded. Another reason was given by Aksënov himself: his fascination with Russian folklore—an inexhaustible source of the fantastic. E.S. Rabkin, in his excellent book *The Fantastic in Literature* (1977), maintains that the fantastic is used by writers as an escape route from reality. Perhaps the combination of all these factors contributed to Aksënov's remarkable rebirth as a writer. Yet I still would prefer to believe what the writer himself said in the aforementioned article from *Le Monde*:

> C'est seulement après qu'apparaissent des étrangetés, des ruptures, des bouleversements et une tentative d'absurdisation de la réalité qui represente à mes yeux l'intervention de l'art dans le réel.

I would suggest that this explanation be taken at its face value.

FOOTNOTES

1. An expression used by the editors of Aksënov's first collection of short stories, *Na polputi k lune*, Moskva, Sovetskaya Rossiya, 1965, p. 5; I have tried to analyze the symbol of "The Odd-Ball" in terms of the traditional Russian concept of *narodnost'* and in connection with Aksënov's interest in folklore; see "Folklore, *narodnost'* and Aksënov's Novelette 'Dikoy,'" *Scando Slavica*, vol. XVII, 1971, pp. 5-19. P. Meyer devotes a whole chapter to these questions in her Ph. D. dissertation, *Aksenov and Soviet Prose of 1950's and 1960's*, Princeton University, Ph. D., 1971. See "Escape into Fantasy," pp. 110-151. On p. 111 she notes: "The transition from realism to fantasy is gradual." In his interview with Priscilla Meyer, *Russian Literature Triquarterly*, 1973, no. 6 (Spring), p. 569, Aksënov made a remark to the effect that in such stories as "The Odd-Ball," "Little Whale, Varnisher of Reality," "Victory," "It Is a Pity You Weren't with Us," "Ginger from Next Door," "simple existence is dislocated into unreality and this dislocation creates the meaning of the work." The dislocation, however, at least in my view, is still very moderate in these stories.

2. R. Barthes, *Sollers ecrivain*, Paris, Seuil, 1979, p. 69, and his *S/Z*, Paris, Seuil, pp. 4-5.

3. Aksënov himself made an extremely important statement with regard to this question. In his article published in *Le Monde*, 14.IV, 1978, Aksënov emphasized that when the first period of his literary career was over, he intended 'to master' *maîtriser* the genre of the short story. However, he made it perfectly clear that he did not want to conform completely to the pressure of historical tradition and wished to make a turn towards Russian avant-garde, without severing his ties with realism. And he adds this important sentence: "La reserve que je formule n'est nécessaire: *en Russie l'avant-garde ne c'est jamais coupeé du réel*" (italics mine—E.M.; [. . .] in Russia, the avant-garde never cut itself off from the real).

4. P. Dalgård, in his article on the literary roots of Aksënov's prose [included in this volume—eds.], ties him rightly with the tradition of Russian Symbolism. Russian Symbolists were deeply involved in the search for new forms of literary expression, yet they were less self-centered than, e.g., their French counterparts, and they never abandoned social, national issues of their country, or universal questions of mankind. In their conversation [included in this volume—eds.], V. Maksimov, N. Gorbanevskaya and È. Kuznetsov rightly noted that Aksënov is a Western-oriented author (a modern Westernizer, one could say) and yet at the same time is deeply rooted in Russian-Soviet reality.

5. P. Dalgård, *The Function of the Grotesque in Vasilij Aksenov*, Aarhus, Arkona, 1982, p. 6.

6. An interesting discussion of Aksënov's early prose is to be found in P. Meyer's article "Aksenov and Soviet Literature of the 1960's," *Russian Literature Triquarterly*, 1973, no. 6 (Spring), pp. 447-460.

7. *Kollegi*, Moskva, Sovetskiy pisatel', 1969, p. 82; translation mine—E.M.

8. S. Chatman, *Story and Discourse, Narrative Structure in Fiction and Film*, Ithaca and London, Cornell University Press, 1980, pp. 48-53.

9. A. Gladilin, "Stal'naya ptitsa," *Kontinent*, 1977, no. 14, pp. 356-359.

10. V. Dukas, "Vasily Aksenov. *The Steel Bird and Other Stories*," a review published in *World Literature Today*, 1979 (Summer), no. 3 (Vol. 53), p. 520.

11. J.J. Johnson, "Introduction: The Life and Works of Aksenov," in *The Steel Bird and Other Stories*, Ann Arbor, Michigan, Ardis, 1979, pp. xix-xxii.

12. Carl and Ellendea Proffer, eds., *Contemporary Russian Prose*, Ardis, 1982. "Introduction: Russian Fiction into the Eighties," pp. xi-xii.

It is noteworthy that the reputable French monthly *Esprit* published a review of "L'oiseau d'acier" (The Steel Bird) in its April issue of 1981); but its author, Chr. Mouze, has only one thing to say: it's a satire about the social truth that "the king is naked."

13. P. Dalgård, *op. cit.*, p. 41.

14. I have consulted four available dictionaries of the contemporary Russian language and they all emphasize the ironic meaning of the word *ptitsa*.

15. I have borrowed this term from L. Doležel's excellent paper, "Kafka's Fictional World," presented by him at the University of Alberta. According to Doležel, the hybrid world signifies a semantic structure in which the "model opposition" between the natural and the fantastic is neutralized. They both coexist as integral parts of "one and the same world."

16. J. Frank, "Spatial Form in Modern Literature," in: *Twentieth Century Criticism. The Major Statements.*, eds. W.J. Handy, M. Westbrook, New York, The Free Press, pp. 85-94. I am using the term *spatial* to denote the disintegration of the *classic* novel, and the new modernistic technique of prose as developed by such writers as Joyce, Kafka, Borges, Robbe-Grillet. It discards causality on all structural levels of artistic prose, e.g., chronology, space, action, and so on.

17. B. Hellman, "At skapa en egen värld," in: *Vasabladet*, December 23, 1978, p. 2. My translation from the Swedish—E.M.

18. The same holds for Aksënov's first play, *Always for Sale*, completed in 1965.

19. V. Aksënov, *Zolotaya nasha Zhelezka*, Ann Arbor, Michigan, Ardis, 1980, p. 7; translation mine—E.M.

20. Compare *Zolotaya nasha Zhelezka*, p. 179, and "Kruglyye sutki, non-stop," *Novyy mir*, 1976, no. 8, p. 118.

21. As is the case with *Poiski zhanra*, where simple details seem to suggest the intervention of supernatural forces in the life of Pavel Apollinariyevich Durov.

22. U. Margolin, "Characterization in Narrative: Some Theoretical Prolegomena," *Neophilologus*, 67 (1983), pp. 1-14.

23. To be sure, a character's deeds and thoughts are sometimes described through the prism of a first and third person narration, even within a short span of time. Such is the case with, e.g., Aristrakh Apollinariyevich Kunitser, whose early morning is related by the "I" narrator, and whatever happens at work is told by a third person narrator (see *Ozhog*, Ann Arbor, Michigan, Ardis, 1980, pp. 11-19). Sometimes all five of the Apollinariyeviches appear through the voice of the plural personal pronoun "we."

24. *Ozhog*, p. 17; translation mine—E.M.

25. Of course, within the artistic structure of the novel, they may acquire certain meaning [see I. Lauridsen's article, "Beautiful Ladies in the Works of Aksënov"—eds.]; but from the viewpoint of *realism*, they constitute a violation of logic.

26. See G.S. Smith, "Vasiliĭ Aksënov's Novel *Ozhog*." *Radio Liberty Research Bulletin*, 1981 (November 11), no. 45, p. 2.

27. G. Genette, *Mimologiques*, Paris, Seuil, 1976, p. 76.

28. Polish philosopher L. Kolakowski makes an interesting remark to the effect that such a world is prone to generate fantasy, a desire to recover the lost innocence of the past when people lived in close personal relationships. See his *Czy diabeł może być zbawiony i 27 innych kazań* (Can the devil be redeemed and 27 other sermons), particularly the chapter "Wieś utracona" (The Village Lost), Londyn, "Aneks," 1982, pp. 25-45.

AKSËNOV'S "'VICTORY'": A POST-ANALYSIS

Alexander Zholkovsky[1]

> Nashe delo pravoye, pobeda budet za nami!
> (Our cause is righteous, the victory will be ours!)
> *A Soviet World War II slogan*
>
> Ya imi vsemi pobezhdën
> I tol'ko v tom moya pobeda.
> (I am defeated by them all
> And only therein lies my victory.)
> *Boris Pasternak*
>
> Ya tozhe delayu kar'yeru—
> Tem, chto ne delayu eyë.
> (I am also making a career—
> By not making it.)
> *Evg. Evtushenko*

"'Victory'—a story with hyperboles" (1965) is Aksënov's little masterpiece.[2] It has a striking conflict and is craftily written, without the unnecessary repetitions or *poliv* 'banter',[3] from which his work sometimes suffers. The parable-like terseness and ambiguity of "Victory" prompted me to offer a two-part commentary: a close and possibly objective reading of the story's "content" and "form" and its more subjective interpretation against the background of the Soviet '60s. The bi-partition, valid for general theoretical reasons, seems to be especially appropriate for this particular story, which is apt to be misread (with all respect to Harold Bloom) by readers unfamiliar with Soviet realities.

I. A Close Reading

1. *Plot and characters: Who won it? Who's who?*

Briefly here is what happens in six pages: A traveller on a train (referred to as G.O. by the narrator) recognizes a chess grandmaster (hereafter G-M) and is consumed by the idea of defeating him at chess. G-M agrees to a game and plays rather passively, letting G.O. gain some advantages, but then begins to take the game more seriously. While G.O.

starts an attack, his king is threatened with a checkmate (or is actually checkmated), but G.O. does not notice this and declares first check and then checkmate to G-M. The latter congratulates him and to certify G.O.'s victory gives him a gold medal, of which he has many.

If the finale produces the "hyperboles" announced in the title, the ambiguity of the plot's culmination can be said to reify the quotes around the word "victory" in the same title.[4] Whose and what kind of victory is it? It remains unclear whether G.O. is the victor, due to his checkmating G-M, or vice versa, or perhaps that G-M is the victor in the higher sense of "not arguing with the fool" (Pushkin) and even crowning him. In a sense, the answer cannot be separated from the nature of the characters and of their conflict. For instance, one reading of "Victory" is prompted by a detail in G-M's characterization. That G-M might have actually checkmated G.O. and just refrained from declaring so, is borne out not only by his title and his successes on the chessboard, but by the following as well: "No one but the grandmaster himself knew that his simple ties bore the label *House of Dior*." The text immediately following (about G-M's hiding his eyes behind glasses and his desire to hide his lips, something that, "alas, was not accepted in society as yet"[5]) stresses still further his obsession with "concealment," "privacy," to the point of providing the first mild hyperbole. As a result, the paragraph in its entirety functions as a foreshadowing. Even before the action proper starts, the reader is given a hint that G-M has an elitist penchant for something we can call "undisclosed triumph."

G.O., on the other hand, only cares for external success. For him, proofs of victory and the possibility to brag about it are more important than the process of playing the game or the victory itself. The opposition "the external/the internal" is also expressed, among other things, in the way G.O. is named in the story. His tattooed initials combine "symbolic anonymity" (see below) with "vulgar externalization."

The contrasts between the two are many. G.O. is physical (note his fists), vulgar (his singing the popular song "Khas-Bulat"; his vocabulary, see below), aggressive, noisy. He is focussed on the adversary, on the immediate course of the game, on success and fame. G-M is a *khilyak* 'runt' (weak lips, etc.), an intellectual (looks Jewish, likes philosophizing), an esthete (Dior, Bach). He is a striking individual who protects his privacy, is concentrated on his own personal life and on life in general, on universal harmony. He is interested in perceiving and retaining rather than in intruding, grabbing, conquering. It is G.O. who engages him in the game, wants to break him down, attacks, mentally accuses him of cheating, presses down his shoulders, and so on. G-M is, on the contrary, passive and defensive. He merely agrees to play, defends his position, wants to get out of it ("accept my refusal"), covers his face with a handkerchief. He just wants to save the position from cacophony and absurdity. He is proud of his omissions—non-commission of any really base acts. He 'cringes' *morshchitsya*, imagining blows from G.O.'s fists, and so on and so forth.

G.O. is a mass type; significantly, G-M needs lots of medals for people like him ("I ordered a lot of these medals and I shall replenish my stock continually"). G.O.'s vulgar banality is, predictably in Aksënov, reflected in the character's speech: "a little game of chess" *shakhmatishki*, "comrade," "ho-ho-ho," "baiting me?" *podlavlivayete*, "I missed it" *prokhlopal*, "I'll squash him anyway, let my nose bleed" (*zadavlyu, khot' krov' iz nosa*). Particularly prominent are the hackneyed clichés, which stand for G.O.'s thoughts: "We've got to kill time, right, [. . .] you can't beat a game of chess on a trip," "what a coincidence!", "sacrificing the rook for the attack?", "I beg of you" (*ochen' vas umolyayu*), "I am not in that league" (*Gde uzh mne?*), "it's not evening yet" (*eshchë ne vecher*), "Incredible, but a fact" (*Neroyatno, no fakt*), "You chickened out, right?" (*Nervishki ne vyderzhali?*), "No kidding?" (*Bez obmana?*)

G-M's speech, of course, contrasts with that of G.O., but not, as one might expect, by being complex and intellectually sophisticated. Rather it is very sparse, modest, defensive, aware of and sensitive to clichés. Mostly he simply responds to G.O. in monosyllables ("Yes," "Left," "Yes, of course, of course," "What's one to do?", "Excuse me," etc.), in accordance with his principle of "concealment and elitism" (Tyutchev's "Silentium": *Molchi, skryvaysya i tai*—"Be silent, hide and keep secret" comes to mind). As for his interior monologues and rare verbal sallies against G.O., they are short sentences, display hidden irony, sometimes they mock clichés and "others' words" in general. E.g.: "Fork [. . .] Fork in the behind [. . .] Property. Personal fork, spoon and knife [. . .] Also remember the 'lyre bird' coat [. . .] It's a shame to lose the old folks," "Oh, no, you are a strong player," "Well, take you, for example, you are not Jewish, are you?" (*Nu vot vy, naprimer, ved' vy ne evrey?*), "You are a strong player, with will power" (*Vy sil'nyy, volevoy igrok*), "Allow me [. . .] I will give you convincing proof [. . .]," "The bearer of this defeated me at chess . . . ," "It remains only to add the date" (*Ostayëtsya tol'ko prostavit' chislo*). The last examples, that involve the handing over of the gold certificate with an engraved bureaucratic cliché, crown the series.[6]

2. Counterpoints

The contrast between the heroes is underscored by the graphic symmetry of the structure: two adversaries, both anonymous, facing each other over a chessboard. The same principle of contrast in symmetry is reflected in the names by which the two characters go in the story: both begin with a "G," with the difference that one of them is a long, lexically foreign and prestigious title, while the other is a vulgar tattooed abbreviation quite transparently alluding to *govno* 'shit'. (Both the first letters of *govno* and the first and the last are "g," "o.") A similar pattern is used to highlight the opposition "individual/mass." The opponents quickly recognize each other—but how: "The man had recognized the grandmaster immediately," "The grandmaster [. . .] too, immediately recognized the man's type."

Incidentally, the two paragraphs about mutual recognition (paragraphs 2 and 3), following an introductory sentence, are also balanced with regard to the attention accorded to the two protagonists. This sets the compositional pattern of alternating points of view. The story is told by an omniscient narrator, including short dialogues, and presents in detail the thoughts of now one, now the other protagonist. In this way the two are given, as it were, equal compositional rights and their contrasting behavior is set in greater relief by the structural parallelism.

The contrapuntal principle is also evident in the characters' comportment. G-M is genuinely quiet, taciturn, introverted, low-keyed: "this small secret," "the grandmaster said quietly," "muttered the grandmaster," "filled him with adoration and quiet joy," etc. G.O. is also quiet, but his quietness is feigned, failing to disguise his cheeky aggressiveness: "stretched with an expression of naive cunning and asked indifferently," "grabbed it with an eagerness that belied indifference," "'I missed it,' said G.O. in a bass voice. Only the last words betrayed his irritation," "'Check,' said G.O. quietly and carefully [. . .] He could barely contain his inner bellow," "'Checkmate,' G.O. shrieked like a copper horn," "'Ugh, ugh, umph,'" "'I'm all sweated up' [. . .] G.O. broke out laughing [. . .] 'I'm quite a guy' [*Ay da ya,* goes the Russian—*A. Zh.*] [. . .] he buzzed."

Both partners play to music: G-M to Bach, G.O. to the song about Khas-Bulat, which at first sounds, to G-M, as a "weak inner drone of an irritating, plaintive note, like the buzz of a mosquito" (and the rest goes on: "'Khas-Bulat [. . .]' G.O. hummed tunelessly on the same note") and ends up resounding as a distant "orchestra [. . .] playing with bravura 'Khas-Bulat, the Bold' ('Checkmate,' G.O. shrieked like a copper horn)".[7] It is not only the tastes that differ but the style of performance as well: G-M plays his Bach to his mind's ear, while G.O. turns on the volume.

Especially striking are, of course, the differences between the protagonists' inner worlds as manifested in their reactions to the progress of the game. In G-M it evokes reminiscences of childhood (castor oil; diarrhea; sit it out squatting comfortably), images of nature (gliding along a pond; dragonflies over a field; waves splashing), art (Bach), scenes of social life (barracks; stench of chlorine; Hong Kong; execution), ethical and philosophical reflections (committing no base acts; the 64 squares of the chessboard, "accommodating not only his personal life, but an infinite number of other lives [. . .]"). These associations are not always pleasant, but in any case they open a window from the miniature world of chess positions onto the wide world of human life, a principle that is stated explicitly in the example cited last.

In G.O.'s mind, the chess positions trigger reactions characteristic of *his* personal world. But this time the associations are one-dimensional, pragmatic: G.O. is obsessed with the prospect of defeating and humiliating G-M. The motif of G.O.'s power play dominates all the episodes that involve him: thus the fork and then the checkmate to the "grandmaster himself"; his gloating/grieving over taking/losing pieces; the "Jewish question" in the world of chess; behind-the-scenes cheating and plotting at championships; primitive strategic calculations ("'If I do this, he'll do that [. . .]'"); bragging and even physical aggression (squeezing G-M's shoulders); demands for proofs of his victory.

3. *Point-of-view effects and ambiguities*

The narrator's sympathy, of course, rests with G-M. He secretly confers on G-M some of his own functions, all the while maintaining the appearance of "compositional equality" of the two parties. Quantitatively, the narrator resorts to G-M's perspective more often and for longer stretches than to that of G.O. Also, G-M's point-of-view is richer qualitatively.

In addition to G-M's greater originality as a human being, it is his point-of-view that gets all the instances of what can be called "double exposure." I mean the characteristic trope-like effect when the action seems to take place both on the chessboard and in the real world. E.g.: "The whole left flank stank of the bathroom and chlorine [. . .] with a whiff of the early childhood smells of castor oil and diarrhea," "A fork on grandma and grandpa. It's a shame to lose the old folks," "He got up for a moment, peeked from behind the terrace and noticed that G.O. had removed the rook," *Uvy, krup konya s otstavshey gryazno-lilovoy baykoy byl tak ubeditelen, chto grossmeyster pozhal plechami* ("Alas, the knight's rump with the loose dirty-lilac flannel was so convincing that the grandmaster shrugged his shoulders"),[8] "Dragging the bishop lightly across the board would substitute to a degree for a headlong glide in a skiff along the sunlit and slightly stagnant water of a Moscow pond, from light to shade, from shade to light."

Quite often the reader gets a first glimpse of a move on the chessboard or in the plot in general "through G-M's eyes" and only after that is he offered more direct information. It is in this way that the tune of "Khas-Bulat" is introduced. Still more veiled is the first hint of G-M's taking G.O.'s rook: "The grandmaster felt an overwhelming, passionate desire to conquer square [*pole*, lit. 'field'—*A. Zh.*] h-8, because it was a field of love, a mound of love, with transparent dragonflies hovering over it,"[9] "That was clever, the way you got my rook and I missed it [. . .] ."

Both types of effects—the "double exposure" and the "glimpsing through G-M's eyes"—are in harmony with the richness and subtlety of G-M's artistic nature and the related thematic complex of concealment, implicitness, ambiguity, ambivalence. Let us dwell on this complex in some detail.

The switches from G-M's perspective to that of the narrator or to dialogue obstruct the perception of the plot ("who made what move?") to some extent, but this can only fool some of the (less experienced) readers[10] some of the time. In other words, the function of these switches is to engage the readers' attention and involve them in the plot.[11] But ultimately this series of ambiguities, resulting from temporary misreadings, culminates in a really ambiguous outcome of the game. I have cited arguments in favor of seeing it as G-M's bona fide victory, won but not formally declared. In light of some other details, however, the checkmate can be seen as just a possibility that presented itself to G-M's mind, but was never realized—a reading shared by quite a few sophisticated readers who are contemporaries and compatriots of the writer. Let us take a closer look at the fragment in question: "Logically, like a Bach coda, came the checkmate to the black. A dim and beautiful light lit the opaque position, now complete like an egg (*Matovaya situatsiya tusklo i krasivo zasvetilas', zavershënnaya, kak yaytso*) [. . .] G.O. [. . .] did not notice the checkmate to his king."

In chessplayers' language the last sentence (*mata* [. . .] *ne zametil*) can mean "did not notice the threat of a checkmate." Linguistically this is in part due to a nominal (and not finite verbal) reference to the checkmate. Note that the preceding sentence also contains a nominal, and at that, a highly figurative, reference to it (*matovaya situatsiya*). Figurativeness also undermines the credibility of the one predicative statement about the checkmate (*nastupil mat*—came the checkmate, in the past tense, perfective aspect). After all, it could well have "come" in that same imaginary space in which "exist" Bach codas, affinities between music and splashing waves, or the magic power of harmonies that brings about victories.

The checkmate's cerebral status has several foreshadowings: G-M repeatedly refuses to checkmate G.O. ("[. . .] possible checkmate moves of the queen appeared like lightning before his eyes, but he extinguished these flashes," "[. . .] the phosphorescent lines and dots of the possible pre-checkmate sacrifices and raids flashed again before the grandmaster's eyes. Alas [. . .]"). To be sure, these foreshadowings can also be seen as evidence of G-M's gradual shift from a passive to an active strategy (cf. a little later on: "Ahead was struggle—complicated, intricate, entrancing and calculating. Ahead was life"). In that case the reluctance to attack could be just a manifestation of G-M's general pattern of "undisclosed triumph."

The motifs of "non-disclosure, implicitness" and "triumph, perfection" find their most accomplished expression in the metaphorical description of the checkmate (the middle sentence of the cited fragment), which is probably the most elaborate of the *chess/life* similes introduced "through G-M's eyes."[12] An "egg" is a natural symbol of both simplicity, completeness, well-roundedness, as well as of an inner, invisible plenitude, while the opaque light (as in devices for checking the freshness of eggs) stresses the element of "concealment," "semi-transparency." But how is the comparison of the checkmate with an opaque egg motivated in the first place? They are linked by the double-entendre on the word *matovaya*, which can mean both (i) 'related to checkmate'; (ii) 'opaque' (like in *matovaya lampochka*—opaque bulb).[13]

Thus, in one of the high points of the plot, once again, this time by clearly poetic means, the themes of "concealment, ambiguity" and "artistry, richness" are expressed. The devices of both narrative and linguistic ambiguity join hands in order to split the readers into two groups: the "mass," who, like G.O., fail to notice the actual checkmate, and the "initiated," who, like G-M, see the checkmate or, at least, the ambiguity of the situation. This episode is only one in a series of ambiguities. Equivocation is the structural principle of the story. Hence the "double exposure," the "information through G-M's eyes" and the manifold ambiguity of the *matovaya situatsiya*. The series culminates in the scene where the gold medal is awarded. It is here that ambiguity finally leaves the subjective consciousness of a character (G-M) and conquers "real" narrative space, turning it into a fantastic one. Thus the motifs of quotes and hyperboles are simultaneously realized. "Victory" belongs to G-M's point of view.

4. Simplicity and structural density

Thematic concerns determine also the story's symbolic transparence and laconicity, combined with a wealth of internal compositional interlockings. The story has two characters, representing symbolically the two sides of the conflict. Both remain practically nameless, in accordance with the parable-like symbolism of the genre. The story line too is in the spirit of a parable: the action centers around a chess game seen as a metaphor of life. The plot easily observes the three unities—of place, time and action. External action is almost absent, except for the movement of the train, of which nothing is made in the story (in keeping with the hero's "spirituality and reticence").

How then does this brief and transparent story produce the impression of internal density fraught with elusive meanings, not unlike that of an opaque egg? In part this is inherent in the symbolic, i.e., dual content of any parable, and is further reinforced by the ambiguity of the plot. Last but not least, this impression of density is due to the abundance of structural links per text unit: laconicity notwithstanding, each and every relevant motif recurs in the story at least twice. We have noted some foreshadowings and plot "rhymes." Here are several more examples. G.O.'s "pink steep forehead" is mentioned in the very beginning and in the very end, both times through G-M's eyes. The "blows from his [G.O.'s—*A. Zh.*] fists, either the left, or the right," imagined by G-M, partly materialize in the end, when G.O. "put his hands on the grandmaster's shoulders and squeezed them familiarly." A series of recurrences underpins the associations evoked in G-M by G.O.'s disgusting style of chess-playing. In the order of appearance: "a bundle of cabbalistic charlatan symbols," "the smell of the john and chlorine," "the sour smell of barracks," "of castor oil and diarrhea," "heartburn and a sudden attack of migraine," "the accumulation of externally logical but internally absurd forces in the center," "cacophony and the smell of chlorine," "senseless and terrible actions [. . .] chills of flu [. . .] postwar discomfort, the itching all over the body," and so on and so forth.

G.O.'s aggressive fixation on his partner produces the following chain of repetitions: "So what, he's just a runt," "Big deal, grandmaster-cheatmaster, your muscle still can't match mine," "Oh, you grandmaster, my dear grandmaster [read "cheatmaster"—*A. Zh.*]," "[. . .] you chickened out, right?". On the other hand, G-M's successes on the chessboard are consistently presented as results of his absolutely disinterested, purely esthetic drives: "[. . .] Ahead was life. The grandmaster took a pawn [. . .]," "The grandmaster felt an overwhelming, passionate desire to conquer square h8 [. . .] the field of love, [. . .]. 'That was clever, the way you got my rook [. . .],' "He began to analyze the position, to harmonize it [. . .] Logically [. . .] came the checkmate." We are, in fact, already familiar with this last group of compositional rhymes—in their capacity of point-of-view effects. As we will see, their structural prominence is not accidental—they are of paramount importance for the story's message.

II. An Interpretation

1. *The social equation. What is victory?*

The action takes place on the chessboard, but is obviously related to Soviet reality. To begin with, the story abounds in realistic detail: a train compartment, a conductor, a chess set of the type provided on trains, with traces of tea-glasses, the Chess Club on the Gogol Boulevard, the tattoo, the Dior necktie, the knight with loose flannel, etc. More important still is the transparent social subtext. G.O. is, as we recall, a mass type, banal, aggressive, physical. He is, of course, the clichéd "rank-and-file Soviet man," "simple working guy." After all, he is the one who uses the word "comrade"—its single occurrence in the text. He refuses to accept subtlety, individuality, harmony. He sticks to proverbialized wisdom and popular myths ("All chess players are Jewish") and is probably an antisemite: it is not by chance that his "victory" is associated with a Nazi execution.[14] As for G-M, he is the archetypal image of a liberal-Westernized-refined Soviet intellectual, an artist, an individualist, i.e., an admirer of privacy and private property (grandpa's fork and "lyre-bird" coat; his own "gold reserves"),[15] a cosmopolitan (French tie, Hong Kong), an exponent of dissident, anti-collaborationist ethics ("committed no base acts"),[16] punished by the regime.

The word chosen as the title of the story is one of the most important and value-laden in the Soviet ideology. Cf.: "Victory over Fascist Germany," "Everything for the front, everything for the victory," "Victory Day," *Pobeda* 'Victory car', "the victory (victorious march) of Communism," "a great victory of the forces of peace and socialism," and other similar Soviet clichés. The liberal-dissident morality is opposed to this aggressive official set toward victory. It renounces the use of force, abstains from the struggle for power and a place in the establishment, and tries to escape into pure spirituality, into the world of truth and not that of power, and, in extreme cases, into Christianity with its acceptance of the cross. Consider, for instance, Pasternak's lines in the epigraph and also *No porazhen'ya ot pobedy / Ty sam ne dolzhen otlichat'* ("But you yourself should not distinguish / A defeat from a victory") in another poem.

And yet, in spite of obvious references to Soviet cultural clichés, the conflict in the story remains somewhat enigmatic: it is not clear how to project it onto the familiar alignments of contemporary Soviet literature and ideology, whether liberal or orthodox. What, then, is the original twist given to the conflict, and who wins out after all? Where exactly do Aksënov and his hero stand on the matter of power and victory, or rather, between what stands do they balance in their peculiar ambiguous way?

2. The balancing act

Indeed, the position they occupy is somewhere in-between, and it is skillfully balanced and veiled by the structure's elaborate ambiguities. Belonging to an archetype, this position is familiar from the Christian, Romantic and, in the Russian context, Pushkinian tradition. The conflict of the spirit, truth and art with material reality appears to be resolved here according to the principle "Render unto Caesar that which is Caesar's": for the romantic master, triumph in the realm of chess truth and beauty; for G.O., spoils of victory in the world of material values and incentives. G-M seems to follow the classical precepts as formulated, for instance, in Pushkin's "Monument" and "To the Poet." We witness a conscientious (*vzyskatel'nyy*) artist, who sets his own standards for himself, does not argue with a fool representing the crowd, indifferently accepts praise, slander, spitting and offense, and who, finally, does not demand a crown or awards and even ironically gives them away to the crowd.[17]

There are, however, interesting differences in the balance of power, to begin with, in which, theoretically, a wide range of options is possible. Jesus Christ can perform miracles and command "thousands of winged legions" (*t'my krylatykh legionov*—Pasternak), but prefers to be crucified by the crowd and the powers that be. Pushkin's poet usually sets his hopes on posthumous fame, divine judgment, etc. Babel's intellectuals strive to transform the power of the word into carnal power over life.[18] Bulgakov has his Preobrazhenskiy perform a successful surgical counter-revolution against the Soviet crowd, represented by Sharikov.[19] Olesha's intellectuals Kavalerov and Ivan Babichev can only fantasize and perorate; they sustain a total defeat in real life and another one in the realm of spirit.

Incidentally, the situations in Bulgakov and Olesha are an instance of an interesting inversion. In Bulgakov's *Heart of a Dog*, an omnipotent scientist, a representative of the old regime and old intelligentsia, picks up out of the gutter a proletarian underdog. The professor retains, throughout the peripeties of the plot, a more or less clear physical, legal and numerical superiority (his team outnumbers Sharikov 5 or 6 to 1), and finally reduces Sharikov to the subordinate position that befits him. In *Envy*, on the contrary, a powerful representative of the Soviet regime picks up out of the gutter a helpless intellectual, feeds, sleeps and employs him, dominates and oppresses him socially, morally, physically and numerically (the ratio is this time something like 3:1 or 3:2), and, finally, throws him out. In each case the writer loads the deck in accordance with his theme.

Let us see how Aksënov deals the deck with regard to his *intelligent* and what chances he gives him for victory. To be sure, G-M is not of this world and is weak in it. He is a runt, he has pitiable lips, he is shy, modest, defensive. His strength is purely spiritual, belonging in the world of chess. But, since the action takes place precisely in that world, the spiritual strength becomes "real." He is a grandmaster, he has every chance to really win. Moreover, he wants to win, and, to all appearances, does win. Numerically they are made equal: although G.O. represents the "mass," in the compartment he is alone face to face with G-M, there is no crowd cheering for G.O. and hissing at G-M, no party organization to pressure G-M, etc. The narrator, as we recall, gives the two adversaries equal compositional rights and even secretly tips the scales in G-M's favor. As a result, the author's favorite, the "rotten individualist intellectual," wins in a sense and the story becomes a case of wish fulfillment, almost as classical as in *Heart of a Dog*.

Come to think of it, G-M is not completely oblivious to the temptations of this world. After all, the symbols of his elitist spirituality are quite secular: a tie from Dior, a Soviet-style trip (*zagranpoezdka*) to Hong Kong (i.e., to Ostap Bender's Rio-de-Janeiro), a tape-recorder reel (of Bach), gold medals and engraving tools (albeit fantastic). In other words, we are faced with an Aksënov superman, a connoisseur of good life, only of a more spiritual and quiet kind than usual,[20] as befits the theme. The creation of a peculiar blend of Christian recluse with Nietzschean superman was an interesting literary problem that preoccupied many a Soviet writer of the '60s.

3. *The good with fists and in bluejeans*

Dobro dolzhno byt' s kulakami ("The good must have fists—Evtushenko") was a famous line of the times. In another poem Evtushenko debated and answered in the affirmative the question whether Hemingway-type guys in bluejeans could be loyal fighters for the cause of peace and socialism. In a sense, Aksënov's own message in his early works, *Colleagues, A Ticket to the Stars* and others, was similar. In a novel by the Strugatsky brothers (*An Inhabited Island*) there is just this combination of spiritual values with tough-guy body culture. The hero is a Christ-like figure who, coming from a perfect future civilization, lands in a dismal feudal-industrial-totalitarian reality, not unlike the Soviet. He preaches peace and love, and is perfect spiritually, intellectually and physically. His body is impervious to radiation, and he walks around in his tanned nudity save for his trunks (cf. Christ's loin-cloth). And lo!—when he is forced to take on single-handedly a dozen local hoodlums, he just switches his inner sense of time, yoga-style, and easily cripples his foes one by one as if in a slow-motion picture. (In the end he stages a successful revolution against the totalitarian Unknown Fathers.) The episode and the hero's character effectively combine a typical saloon fight from a Western with elements of yoga and the gospels.²¹

In the times of the Khrushchëvian peaceful revolution, the young liberal intelligentsia sincerely hoped to achieve victory over Stalinism in this and not the other world, "during the lifetime of this generation." This credo has been ironically formulated by Okudzhava in a recent song, *Kabinety* 'Offices', where a transfer of power (in the literary establishment) to Bella Akhmadulina, Fazil' Iskander, and the poet's other close friends and comrades-in-arms seems imminent. What is more, the expected victory was to come about easily, by itself, a career was to be made by not-making it (cf. the epigraph from Evtushenko), by mere reliance on the omnipotence of true values, which just could not help but triumph. Such was the optimistic atmosphere of The Thaw in the late '50s–early '60s. It even continued into the post-Khrushchëv era *podpisanstvo* 'the letter-signing campaign', when a handful of dissident intellectuals believed that a hundred signatures of "the best people" was all it would take to stop political reaction. In our story this belief is represented by the recurrent motif of "disinterested esthetic values resulting in successes actually scored on the chessboard." If G-M does wage war, he does so by purely esthetic, peaceful, clean means. The checkmate comes about of its own accord, "logically, like a Bach coda."

4. The "American" dream

To be sure, this easy victory for the liberals is only one side of the coin. The story is full of irony. G-M does not declare his checkmate, and the gold medals are of purely fantastic nature, so that the denouement remains enigmatic and ambivalent. For that matter, an ironically ambiguous plurality of readings is quite typical of Aksënov. In fact, at one point in the story he cites with obvious irony several romantic clichés that go back to his early work and to the teenage culture of his generation. "It is all true, there are jolly fools wandering in the world—Sailor Billy, Cowboy Harry, the beautiful Mary and Nelly, and the brigantine raises its sails; but [. . .]"²²

Ironic variations on his own themes abound in Aksënov's other texts as well. In *The Tare of Empty Barrels* (1968) we meet the "refined intellectual" Drozhzhinin, with his total ignorance of life yet complete knowledge of Hullygalia, with his immaculate *anglichanstvo* 'Englishery' (involving a pipe, a mustache, two tweed suits, and so on), "an undercurrent of hopes for noble origin" (*podspudnyye nadezhdy na dvoryanskoye proiskhozhdeniye*),²³ and unassuming yet aristocratic manners ("few could guess, practically no one guessed that the slim gentleman in a strict gray (brown) three-piece suit [. . .]," recall G-M's tie). All this looks like a deliberate parody of G-M. As for G-M's opponent, *The Tare of Empty Barrels* offers three variations on the G.O. type. There is the "Navy man" (*voyennyy moryak*) Shustikov Gleb, a Mucius Scaevola fan, who envisages service to Science as a violent struggle against Pseudoscience that involves thrusting, together with Scaevola, his burning hand into the "aggressive mugs" of the imperialists (recall G.O.'s tattooed hand). Then there is the irresistible Volod'ka Teleskopov who, unlike Drozhzhinin, did visit Hullygalia and even had some "platonic" relationships with its beauties. And, finally, there is the "old man Mochënkin," a stereotypical self-appointed Soviet informer (cf. the SS motif in "Victory"). Thus *The Tare of Empty Barrels* essentially replicates the situation in "Victory" in an ironically fairytale-like, undramatic manner.

The very short and little-known story "A Taxidriver's Dream" (*Literaturnaya Gazeta*, Aug. 26, 1970.) offers another instructive parallel. Its hero dreams of one day giving a ride, maybe all the way from Moscow to Sochi (on the Black Sea), to the hero of his fantasies, the fabulously rich Vanya-of-the-Gold-Nuggets ("Vanya-Zolotishnik"), a smuggling worker from the Siberian gold mines (cf. G-M's gold medals). But when the driver actually meets him, Vanya is absolutely penniless, bedraggled and helpless. The driver pays Vanya's fare, buys him food and drinks, "puts him on the master bunk" (*ukladyvayet na glavnuyu koyku*), and finally states his dream: "You see, I [. . .] don't want his big money [. . .] What I really need is that he be there, my Vanya-of-the-Gold-Nuggets, that he exist in nature" (*Ved' mne [. . .] ot nego nikakikh beshenykh deneg ne nuzhno [. . .] Mne vazhno, chtob on byl, Vanya-moy-Zolotishnik, chtob sushchestvoval v prirode*).

One cannot help recalling such Benderisms as "I see, you disinterestedly love money," "Those little gold circles which I love so much," "I am an idealistic fighter for money-bills" (*Ya ideynyy borets za denezhnyye znaki*). This parallel is not fortuitous, especially if we take into consideration the reference to Hong Kong, alias Rio-de-Janeiro, Aksënov's play with Soviet and other clichés, reflecting his indebtedness to Il'f and Petrov, and, last but not least, Ostap's subversive impact on the ideological formation of several generations of the Soviet intelligentsia. The witty loner-millionaire oppressed by the hegemonic class represented, in a brilliant blow-up, the interests of a normal human being living under the Soviet regime. Of course, in accordance with the times, the image was represented in a deliberately detached fashion, almost to the point of cynicism: the synthesis of the protagonist's positive characteristics, calling for the reader's identification, with negative, alienating ones, was purely literary in nature. Aksënov's heir to Bender is much more human and accessible to the reader (to say nothing of his being a more authentic grandmaster). The taxidriver's dream about Vanya-of-the-Gold-Nuggets rings touchingly, if ironically, serious. Incidentally, the taxidriver finds himself somewhere in between G.O. and G-M: like the former, he is a simple, 'folksy' type who wants gold but, like the latter, he in fact gives money away and has the impossible dream of Aksënov and his generation: a longing for an "ideal materialism," "clean capitalism," so to speak, a "spiritual love for imported threads." This "American" dream reflects the hopes the Khrushchëv generation placed in the magical powers of economic incentive to somehow bring about universal good and justice.

In "Victory" this dream is expressed with particular subtlety. The equilibrium of the possible opposite readings of the paradox is accomplished with utmost precision. Who is this G-M: a sensitive and creative esthete or a consumer of *dolce vita*? An ascetic bent on introspection and spirituality or an arrogant elitist? A weak victim or a triumphant superman? The latter terms of these alternatives point to his affinity with his opponent, G.O., suggesting that perhaps ultimately Aksënov is preoccupied with a singular archeprotagonist, who is simultaneously an idealist and a tough guy, a refined intellectual and a Navy man. The characteristics of this type are variously distributed among the real characters of Aksënov's real texts. A successful treatment of this recurrent archetheme in one of its variations turns the story into a genuine victory for the author—without quotation marks or hyperboles.

Postscript

After this essay was completed, "Victory's" intertextual links with Nabokov's *The Defense* and *Invitation to a Beheading* and Stefan Zweig's "The Royal Game" were brought to my attention. To put it in a nutshell, Aksënov seems to have borrowed the figure of the grandmaster defending his private artistic world from the banal surroundings, as well as the equation "chess = life" and the "double exposure" technique, from *The Defense* and to have superimposed this on the figure of the protagonist of *Invitation*, imprisoned and executed by the regime and forced to play games, in particular chess, with the future executioner, the tattooed M-sieur Pierre, whom he defeats at chess and fantastically eludes on the scaffold as everything crumbles after the hero's disappearance into another world. The motif of the false checkmate can be traced, although in a different form, to the Zweig story (where, in turn, it may go back to the culmination episode of "The Queen of Spades"), while the pun on the word *matovyy* parallels/replicates the wordplay hidden in *Zashchita Luzhina* (1930) and spelled out by Nabokov himself in his *Foreword* to the second Russian edition (Paris, 1967; written in 1963).

Aksënov, however, uses his intertexts in an original way. He presses Nabokov's modernist techniques into the service of a "traditional," this-worldly struggle to succeed. The final shift into surreality demonstrates not the hero's incompatibility with the world, but rather a wished-for (albeit illusory) happy end. Hence the reversal of the "chess = life" equation: whereas for Luzhin all life is reduced to chess, for G-M chess is part and symbol of real life's harmony.[24]

FOOTNOTES

1. For very helpful discussion I am grateful to Pat Carden, Caryl Emerson, George Gibian and Olga Matich. The *Postscript* was prompted by the stimulating suggestions of Katya Kompaneyets, Vladimir Papernyy and Boris Gasparov.

2. It is, in fact, one of his favorites. See P. Meyer, "Interview with Vasiliy Aksënov," *Russian Literature Triquarterly*, 16, 1973, p. 572.

3. Vayl and Genis have recently turned this Russian colloquialism into a literary-critical term. See P. Vayl and A. Genis, *Sovremennaya Russkaya Proza*, Ann Arbor, 1982, pp. 146-148.

4. This important detail is missing in the English version (V. Aksënov, *The Steel Bird and Other Stories*, Ann Arbor, 1979). The translation (by Greta Slobin) is on the whole accurate and I am using it in my text, amending it where necessary without further notice. (For some comments, see Notes 8, 9, 13.) The original story first appeared in *Yunost'*, 6, 1965, and was later reprinted in V. P. Aksënov, *Zhal', chto vas ne bylo s nami*, Moscow, 1969.

5. Cf. also later on in the story: "the few moments of complete solitude, when both lips and nose are hidden by the handkerchief," and the possibility to "sit it out squatting comfortably" behind the terrace, where the "ego does not suffer."

6. This interplay of G-M's portrait with the denouement of the plot was first discussed in A. Zholkovsky and Y. Shcheglov, "K opisaniyu priyëma vyrazitel'nosti 'Var'irovaniye'," *Semiotika i Informatika* (Moscow), 9, 1977, p. 147.

7. The crescendo of the "Khas-Bulat" tune reminds one of the famous crescendo of the "fascist" theme in the first movement of Shostakovich's *Seventh Symphony*, which can be related, intertextually or at least typologically, to the SS motif in the same paragraph.

8. This is one of the untranslatable passages, partly because the "double-exposure" has to be preserved. The Russian word for the chess knight is *kon'*, lit. 'horse', and Aksënov brings in the horse's very physical *krup* 'rump'. The translator tried to keep the effect by introducing the knight's 'neck' instead, which, however, loses sight of the location of the flannel: she has the flannel "sticking out on the knight's neck," while in chess it lines the bottom of the piece. The effect of "double-exposure" as used in the story in general and with the *kon'* 'horse/knight' in particular, probably, goes back to similar devices in John Updike's *The Centaur*, which was popular in Russian translation just at the time. Note that the *kon'* is double-exposed on two more occasions: "the intrusion of the black knight into the senseless crowd on the left flank [. . .] demands further thought"—"[. . .] one feels the dangerous and real proximity of the black knight in square b-4 [. . .] Ahead was life."

9. This again is hard to translate, because Aksënov plays on the two meanings of *pole*: (i) 'field' (ii) 'square' (in chess). The translator omitted the effect and also replaced dragonflies with grasshoppers (which as a result find themselves hanging above the mound of love) for some reason, probably because Krylov's fable "Strekoza i muravey" has as its English counterpart "The Ant and the Grasshopper."

10. American students invariably stumble in these places.

11. See T. Todorov, "Poètique," in: O. Ducrot et al., *Qu'est ce que le structuralisme?*, Paris, 1968, p. 127.

12. The sentence might have been influenced by the one that opens the episode of the re-operation in *Heart of a Dog*: *Prestupleniye sozrelo i upalo kak kamen', kak èto obychno i byvayet* "The crime ripened and fell like a stone, the way it usually happens".

13. This word-play could hardly be preserved in translation (cf. Notes 4, 8, 9).

14. The primary function of this mention of the SS is, of course, a thinly disguised reference to Soviet reality according to the principle "when it says Gestapo, read KGB" (cf. Iskander's "On a Summer Day"). Incidentally, this sentence about the SS is the only change made in the original text due to censorship, or more precisely, to the pressure of the editor of *Yunost'* (oral communication by Aksënov).

15. An artist whose conflict with the powers that be and conventional morality manifests itself, among other things, in his love of private property, sounds, to a post-industrial Western audience, as a paradox. Not so in Soviet Russia, where privacy, property, etc. are symbols of human rights and liberties threatened by the totalitarian state and communist ideology.

16. The ethics of "passive resistance," non-collaboration with the regime, and balancing on the brink between complete submission and an open challenge is an important theme of the liberal literature of the time: cf., for instance, Aksënov's "Lunches of '43" and "Little Whale, Varnisher of Reality" and Iskander's "On a Summer Day." This brinkmanship is so precarious a game that it is really hard to say where the difference between *sokhraneniye nravstvennykh muskulov natsii* (the preservation of the moral muscles of the nation—Iskander) and the so-called *kukish v karmane* (approximately: giving them the finger in the pocket) really lies (on *kukish v karmane*, see A. Zholkovsky, "19 oktyabrya 1982 g., or The semiotics of a Soviet cookie wrapper," *Wiener Slawistischer Almanach*, 11 (special *Mel'chuk Festschrift* issue), pp. 341-354.

17. On the posture of "superior calm" in Pushkin, see A. Zholkovsky, "Prevoskhoditel'nyy pokoy: ob odnom invariantnom motive Pushkina," in: A. Zholkovsky i Yu. Shcheglov, *Poètika Vyrazitel'nosti. Sbornik Statey, Wiener Slawistischer Almanach*, Sonderband II, 1980.

18. For instance, both "My First Fee" and "Guy de Maupassant" are about a socially deprived narrator whose literary talents win him the love of a woman. Incidentally, in the second story, there is a detail which might have been at the source of a plot line in *The Tare of Empty Barrels* (Aksënov disagrees; his oral communication). Cf. Babel: "Kazantsev had never so much as passed through Spain, but his love for that country filled his whole being. He knew every castle, every garden and every river in Spain." Aksënov: "He knew all the dialects of that country [. . .], its entire folklore, entire history, entire economy, all the streets [. . .] all the stores and shops on these streets, the names of their owners and of the members of their families, the names and the character of their pets and animals, although never had he been in that country." Note that Kazantsev is a typical bookworm and dreamer (all his castles are in Spain), which by contrast sets in relief the erotic prowess of the narrator, and that Drozhzhinin is in a similar relation to Teleskopov.

19. Cf. also the numerous acts of revenge inflicted on Soviet people in *The Master and Margarita* with the permission of the gloating author.

20. There is practically no external physical action in the story, no carnival (on carnival in Aksënov, see P. Dalgård, *The Function of the Grotesque in V. Aksenov*, Aarhus, 1982), no "journey" (except the motion of the train, which is forgotten soon after the first sentence; on "journey" in Aksënov, see V. Filipp, "Tema begstva u Aksënova," *Novyy zhurnal*, no. 151, 1983, pp. 68-75), no drinking and no sex (except for the highly sublimated desire to conquer h8, the mound of love).

21. The scene might have been influenced by Kurosawa's *Red Beard*, whose hero, a humane doctor and karate master, first breaks and then sets the bones of thugs who attacked him. (Note that one of the Strugatsky brothers, Arkadiy, is a Japanist.)

22. The references are to Anglo-American songs popular in the Soviet subculture of the 40s-50s and to the poem-song *Brigantina* 'Brigantine' (text by the Komsomol poet of the late 30s, Pavel Kogan), an unofficial anthem of Moscow University students in the 50s-60s.

23. Even in Okudzhava, the most genuinely Christian writer of the generation (see A. Zholkovsky, "Ray, zamaskirovannyy pod dvor: zametki o poèticheskom mire Bulata Okudzhavy," *Neue Russische Literatur*, 1, 1979, pp. 281-306 (German version), pp. 101-120 (Russian version)), love for "worn suits" and "little old shoes" goes hand in hand with dreams of "laces, golden boots" and the elegance of "young princes."

24. For more detail see the chapter on "Pobeda" in Yu. Shcheglov and A. Zholkovsky, *Mir Autora i Struktura Teksta. Stat'i o Russkoy Literature*. Hermitage Press (forthcoming in 1986).

APPENDIX

ТИАНСТВЕННАЯ ПРОЗА

Е. Эткинд

Классификаторы различают немало видов прозы: деловую и риторическую, орнаментальную и линейную, одноголосую и полифоническую. Как определить прозу Василия Аксенова? В разных его вещах она различна, однако ей свойственна доминанта. Определим таковую по нескольким эпизодам из повести *Золотая наша железка* (1972).

В одной из начальных главок рассказывается о том, как герой познакомился с красоткой Ритой, «девчонкой-сатураторщицей». Этому событию предшествует описание «Железки» (т.е. дальневосточного железорудного бассейна), увиденной из самолета:

1. Если вы ничего о Ней не знаете, вы можете Ее и не заметить с
2. высоты полета транссибирского аэро. Может быть, ваш безучастный
3. взгляд и отметит небольшую розоватую проплешину среди «зелено-
4. го моря тайги», но уж во всяком случае вы не прильнете к иллюми-
5. натору и не испытаете никаких чувств, если только вы вдруг не по-
6. чувствуете ничего особенного, что не исключено. Если же вы не толь-
7. ко знаете Ее, но и служите Ей многие годы, то есть вы Ее
8. любите, то вы конечно же влепитесь в иллюминатор задолго до при-
9. ближения к Ней, чтобы как-нибудь не проглядеть, и будете волно-
10. ваться, как перед встречей с близким человеком или любимым жи-
11. вотным и разглядите все ее составные пятнышки, камешки, прожил-
12. ки, блестки и может быть вам она даже покажется не просто близ-
13. кой, волнующей, но и красивой, может быть, даже с десятикиломет-
14. ровой высоты Она напомнит вам нечто нежное и беззащитное, с кры-
15. лышками и тонким стержнем-тельцем, нечто вроде бабочки, эдакий
16. терракотовый баттерфляй, изящный и непрочный как иностранное
17. произведение искусства. Вот она какова с высоты, наша Железка![1]

(стр. 8)

Особенность этого описания—в *цитатах* разного рода, причем их источники иногда ясны, иногда же неизвестны. «Железка» появляется как некая богиня—она не названа, достаточно торжественного местоимения с заглавной буквы: *о Ней, Ее, . . . вы не только знаете Ее, но и служите Ей уже многие годы, то есть если вы Ее любите . . . , задолго до приближения к Ней*[2] *и т.д.* Эти «религиозные» обороты напоминают более всего, как Андрей Белый и Александр Блок писали друг другу в начале века торжественно-мистические письма о Вечной Женственности, которую Блок—следом за Вл. Соловьевым—называл «Дева, Заря, Купина» и о которой он писал:

> И вот—Она, и к Ней—моя Осанна—
> Венец трудов—превыше всех наград.
>
> Я скрыл лицо, и проходили годы.
> Я пребывал в Служеньи много лет . . .

Символист Блок «пребывал в Служеньи много лет»; Аксенов пишет, как бы повторяя Блока, *вы [. . .] служите Ей уже многие годы*. Блок говорит о своей реальной невесте, Любе Менделеевой, мистическим языком соловьевской метафизики; Аксенов говорит о железорудном бассейне псевдомистическим языком блоковского символизма, восходящего к провансальским трубадурам—тема «служения» была для них центральной.

Через весь этот абзац проходит тема Прекрасной Дамы, осмысленная пародийно. Ироническое отношение к промышленным объектам как к новейшим, новосимволическим «Девам Радужных Ворот» характерно для аксеновского поколения; оно проявилось не столько в стихах Евг. Евтушенко, назвавшего свой сборник (того же 1972 года) «Поющая дамба», сколько в шутке по поводу этого названия: «Стихи о прекрасной Дамбе». У Аксенова—описание, приближающееся к «Стихам о Прекрасной Железке». Замечу, что двумя страницами ниже «символизм» появляется открыто; теперь, впрочем, его мистическая фразеология отнесена к девушке сатураторщице—вот в каком контексте: «Интеллигентная девушка с вопросительной усмешкой посмотрела на меня. Мне полагалось пошутить. Я знал, что мне сейчас полагается пошутить, а мне хотелось сходу заныть: "Любимая, желанная, счастье мое, на всю жизнь Прекрасная Дама". Во французском издании—сноска: «Стих поэта Александра Блока»; это ошибка, такого стиха нет, но общая атмосфера раннего Блока присутствует как в этой фразе, так и в предшествующем ей и стилистически с ней связанным описанием Железки.

С этим центральным, неосимволистским мотивом сопрягаются слова и обороты из иных стилистических сфер:

Строка 2	*аэро*—неупотребительное в обиходе, но характерное для речи «технарей» игривое сокращение слова «аэроплан»;
Строки 3-4	среди "*зеленого моря тайги*" цитата из пошло-живописного газетного очерка, из него же и примыкающий оборот, правда в отрицательной форме: (вы не)
Строки 4-5	*прильнете к иллюминатору,*
Строки 5-6	*если только вы вдруг не почувствуете ничего особенного, что не исключено.* Обороты *Это исключено* и, в особенности ... *чтó не исключено*—из разговорно-бюрократического слога. Во втором примере (имеющемся в тексте) совмещены два бюрократических элемента; выражение с *что*, замещающем *это*, многократно пародировалось Зощенко (Фельдшер говорит больному: «Если вы поправитесь, *что вряд ли*, тогда и ...» «История болезни», 1936).
Строки 3-8	*проплешина* и *влепитесь*—слова из фамильярного лексикона. Стилистическая прозаичность *проплешины* подчеркнута тем, что она стоит рядом с религиозно-мистическим *служите Ей* (проплешине?). Фамильярность сочетания *влепитесь в иллюминатор* отчетливо выявляется после предшествующего пародийно-очеркового—*не прильнете к иллюминатору.*
Строки 11-12	*разглядите все ее составные пятнышки, камешки, прожилки, блестки*—здесь постепенно появляются терминологические элементы из области минералогии, которые переходят в смешанное описание женщины и ландшафта:
Строки 12-14	*и может быть вам она даже покажется не просто близкой, волнующей, но и красивой, может быть, даже с десятикилометровой высоты.*
Строки 14-16	Вслед за этим—поэтическое сочетание *нечто нежное и беззащитное*, переходящее в описание почти профессионально-энтомологическое: *с крылышками и тонким стержнем-тельцем, нечто вроде бабочки, этакий терракотовый баттер-*

фляй ... *Баттерфляй* по-русски означает стиль плавания, а не бабочку; английское слово взято для усиления энтомологической «научности» (другое иностранное слово *терракотовый* играет ту же роль), чтобы придать тексту дополнительную игривость.

В заключительной фразе слово *Железка* наконец-то заменяет все предшествующие перифразы и метафоры.

Семнадцать строк позволили выделить по меньшей мере *семь* стилистических пластов, соединенных только голосом повествователя: разговорная речь «технарей», стиль газетного очерка, разговорно-бюрократический слог, фамильярное просторечье, научно-минералогическая и энтомологическая терминология, поэтический слог.

Нами взят не самый характерный для Аксенова пассаж, содержащий описание; как видим, и он представляет собой многопластовое, противоречивое соединение. Но вот продолжение:

1. В десяти километрах от Железки, то есть за узенькой перемыч-
2. кой «зеленого моря тайги» начиналась белоснежная геометрия наше-
3. го городка, но на нее-то как раз никто не обратил внимания. Все на-
4. ши провожали взглядом уплывавшую на запад Железку. Одна только
5. моя жена Рита не смотрела в окно. Вот уже битый час она была заня-
6. та беседой с новым самолетным знакомым Мемозовым. Вообразите,
7. бука Рита вместо обычного своего сигаретного презрительного и «ти-
8. анственного», именно «тианственного», а не таинственного молчания
9. оживленно беседует с чужим мужчиной, кивает ему головой, пони-
10. мающе улыбается ртом, вырабатывает целые периоды устной речи, да
11. еще подбрасывает милой ручкой—поясняет сказанное пленительным
12. жестом и даже ее неизменная сигаретка весело участвует в диалоге.
13. Чем же ее так расшевелил Мемозов?
14. Познакомились на свою голову. Ты, Рита, не видишь рядом
15. серьезной драматической натуры, а верхогляды, оказывается, тебе по
16. душе. Ты, Рита, даже не повернула свою нефертитскую головку, даже
17. не скосила продолговатый свой «тианственный» глаз, ты равнодушно
18. пролетела над нашей Железкой, в недрах которой десятилетие назад.
19. ты, глупая Рита, помнишь ли, звездочка моя вечерняя ...

(стр. 8)

Пассаж открывается деловито точным указанием—

Строка 1	*В десяти километрах*—соединенным с условно-разговорным обозначением *от Железки*, вслед за этим географически- терминологическое
Строки 1-2	*то есть за узенькой перемычкой*, к которому примыкает повторенная цитата из пошлого газетного очерка *зеленого моря тайги* и авторски-индивидуальный яркий (метонимический) образ
Строка 2	*белоснежная геометрия нашего городка*. Далее, после информирующего
Строка 5	*моя жена Рита*, идет подчеркнутый разговорный оборот *вот уже битый час*, выражающий ревнивую досаду мужа- рассказчика.
Строки 4-5	(*Все наши провожали взглядом . . . Железку. Одна . . . Рита не смотрела в окно.*) Жена далее охарактеризована детским словечком
Строка 7	*бука Рита*—видимо такое инфантильное сочетание призвано передать своеобразие ее кокетства, которое ниже выражено уменьшительными *милой ручкой* и *сигаретка*. Жена Рита охарактеризована соединением не слишком-то сочетающихся элементов: индивидуально-авторское *сигаретное . . . молчание*,
Строка 9	наивно-инфантильное *с чужим мужчиной*,
Строка 10	научно-лингвистическое *вырабатывает целые периоды устной речи*,
Строки 11-12	передающие ее собственное представление о себе эпитеты *подбрасывает милой ручкой—поясняет* сказанное *пленительным жестом*—причем оба эпитета тоже выражают ревнивую досаду автора; далее следует еще один фамильярно-идиоматический оборот, продолжающий строку 5:
Строка 14	*Познакомились на свою голову*. Его сменяют риторические повторы, которые переключают описательно-повествовательную прозу в поэтический ряд:
Строка 14	*Ты, Рита, не видишь . . . Ты, Рита, даже не повернула . . . ты равнодушно пролетела . . . ты, глупая Рита, помнишь ли . . .* И весь пассаж обрывается на лирическом и, кажется, вполне серьезном обращении:

Строка 19	*звездочка моя вечерняя.* Следующая глава, названная «Десятилетие назад», и будет рассказом о том, что в этой фразе недоговорено.
	Ко всей этой мешанине стилей добавим еще две детали, характеризующие Риту. Одна из них—
Строка 16	*не повернула свою нефертитскую головку*—связана с необыкновенно популярной среди советской интеллигенции (после выставки 1962 года) головой египетской царевны Нефертити (ее гипсовый слепок стоял чуть ли не во всех писательских квартирах). Другая деталь—это настойчиво повторенный эпитет во фразе:
Строки 7-8	*вместо обычного своего сигаретного презрительного и «тианственного», именно «тианственного», а не таинственного молчания* ...
	Откуда берется это слово?

В одном из эпизодов следующей главы рассказчик, узнав, что тот, кого он принял за сторожа—великий ученый-физик Салазкин, произносит девушке Маргарите, с которой он только что познакомился и которая ему с восхищением сообщила, что Салазкин «мыслит по вопросам мироздания»:

1. — Хе, — сказал я, — пфе, ха-ха, подумаешь, между прочим не
2. он один по ночам мыслит и, задыхаясь в метелях полуденной пыли,
3. врывается к Богу, боится, что опоздал, плачет, целует ему жилистую
4. руку, просит ...
5. Выпалив все это одним духом, я уставился на целое десятилетие
6. в палестинские маргаритские тианственные, именно тианственные, а
7. не таинственные глаза.
8. — ... чтоб обязательно была хотя бы одна звезда, — сказал чей-
9. то голос то ли рядом, то ли в глубине тоннеля, и там, в проеме, за
10. далекими соснами, за вековым дебелым снегом действительно сияла
11. одна-единственная звезда-покровительница, возможная родина на-
12. шей Железки.
13. О ветер, полынный запах космоса, газированная ночная мысль
14. моего кумира, которого я сегодня впервые увидел, о девушка за са-
15. туратором, о тайны ночной смены ...
16. — Давайте уйдем отсюда?
17. — Но кто же будет поить людей?
18. — Жаждущий напьется сам ... (стр. 11)

Здесь рассказчик вводит в свою речь цитаты не только из иных стилистических областей, но и из реальных произведений: *не он один по ночам мыслит* переходит в цитату из стих. Маяковского Послушайте» (1914):

И, надрываясь,
в метелях полуденной пыли,
врывается к Богу,
боится, что опоздал,
плачет,
целует ему жилистую руку,
просит —
чтоб обязательно была звезда!

Цитата вполне точна (с вариантом в первой и последней строках); Маяковский нередко оказывается фоном аксеновской речи. В случае с эпитетом *тианственный* следует обратиться к нему же; в поэме «Облако в штанах» (1915) читаем:

Мария!
Поэт сонеты поет Тиане,
а я —
весь из мяса,
человек весь —
тело твое просто прошу,
как просят христиане —
«хлеб наш насущный
даждь нам днесь».

Здесь Тиана—далекая, недоступная женщина, ей можно «петь сонеты», но не любить с той земной страстью, с которой Маяковский взывает к Марии: «. . . тело твое просто прошу . . .» *Тианственная*—не значит ли, следовательно, недоступная? Разумеется, оттенок у Аксенова—иронический; тем более, что источником Маяковского был манерный, салонно изысканный Игорь Северянин, за год до «Облака в штанах» опубликовавший свое стихотворение (отнюдь не сонет!) «Тиана» (ноябрь 1913), которое начинается так:

Тиана, как странно! как странно, Тиана!
Былое уплыло, былое ушло . . .
Я плавал морями, садился в седло,
Бродил пилигримом в опалах тумана . . .

Тиана, как скучно! как скучно, Тиана!
Мадлэна—как эхо . . . Мадлэна—как сон . . .
Я больше уже ни в кого не влюблен:
Влюбляются сердцем, но—как, если—рана? . . .

Тиана, как жутко! как жутко, Тиана! . . . и т.д.

Вот, вероятно, почему в последнем пассаже стоят рядом строки из Маяковского, которого цитируют сначала автор, а потом Великий Салазкин, и повторенная характеристика: ... *палестинские маргаритские тианственные, именно тианственные, глаза.*

Эти цитаты из Маяковского и Северянина сменяются цитатой «стилистической», как бы взятой из оды: *О ветер... , о девушка..., о тайны...* При этом каждое одическое восклицание соединяется со стилистически противоречащим ему словом или оборотом: торжественное *о ветер*—с прозаическим плюс торжественным *газированная ночная мысль моего кумира*, где эпитет *газированная* мотивирован тем, что девушка наливает в институтском буфете газированную воду,— она называется по-научному звучащим словом *сатураторщица* (сатуратор—прибор, насыщающий воду углекислым газом и таким образом производящий «газировку»). Второе одическое восклицание *о девушка*—соединено с этим самым термином—*за сатуратором*. Третье— *о тайны...*—парадоксально влечет за собой прозаический оборот— *ночной смены*. Все три вторые половины одических фраз относятся к разным стилям,—даже этот малый отрезок текста многослоен.

Пассаж кончается кратким диалогом между ним и ею, причем последняя реплика его воспринимается цитатой из Евангелия: *Жаждущий напьется сам* (ср.: «Врачу, исцелися сам»—Лк, 4,23).

Число стилистических и текстовых цитат у Аксенова велико—и не только в авторском тексте, но и в разговорах его персонажей; молодой физик Ким, к которому «некий нетипичный человек... в кепчонке-буклé» обратился с просьбой дать ему одиннадцать копеек, отвечает:

1. — Бери, старик, забирай всю валюту. Бери, не церемонься,
2. люди свои. Я и сам не раз переворачивался кверху килем,—зачастил
3. Ким, и тут его понесло.—Да что там, старик, мне ли тебя не понять,
4. ведь мы одной крови, ты да я. Ведь ты, старик, родом из племени ку-
5. миров. Ты был кумиром Марьиной Рощи, старик, в нашей далекой
6. пыльной юности, когда торжествовал континентальный уклон в при-
7. роде. Ты был знаменитым футболистом, старик, сознайся, или саксо-
8. фонистом в «Шестиграннике»... Бесса ме, бесса ме мучо... или прос-
9. то одним из тех парней, что так ловко обнимали за спины тех девчо-
10. нок в клеенчатых репарационных плащах. А что, старик, почему бы
11. тебе не рвануть со мной в Пихты? Хочешь, я сейчас транзистор толкну
12. и возьму тебе билет? Сибирь, старик, золотая страна Эльдорадо... мо-
13. лодые ученые, наши парни, не ханжи, и никогда не поздно взять
14. жизнь за холку, старик, а ведь мы с тобой мужчины, молодые мужчи-
15. ны,—что, старик? Ты хочешь сказать, что корни твои глубоко в ас-

16. фальте, что Запад есть Запад, Восток есть Восток? А я тебе на это от-
17. вечу Аликом Городницким: и мне не разу не привидится во снах ту-
18. манный Запад, неверный лживый Запад...извини, старик, я пою...
19. Старик, ведь я же вижу, ты не из серой стаи койотов, ты и по спорту
20. можешь и по части культуры...а хочешь, я устрою тебя барменом?
21. Выше голову, старик ... друг мой, усталый страдающий
22. брат ... (стр. 25).

Картина «мозаики» та же. Многократно повторенное слово *старик*—обращение интеллигентов друг к другу (60е годы);

Строки 1-2	*валюта* (в смысле—деньги)—из блатного жаргона; *мы люди свои*—привычно-разговорная интеллигентская присказка (ср. у Маяковского в «Во весь голос»—«Сочтемся славою—ведь мы свои же люди», строка, опирающаяся на поговорку «Свои люди, сочтемся», ставшая заглавием пьесы А. Островского»);
Строка 2	... *переворачивался кверху килем* — т.е. терпел неудачу — из жаргона моряков... Дальше вспыхивают отзвуки то из Джека Лондона, то из газетной публицистики, то из популярных песен-шлягеров 60х годов, то из послевоенного разговорного обихода-девчонки
Строка 10	*в клеенчатых репарационных плащах*, то из околоблатных жаргонов—
Строка 11	*я сейчас транзистор толкну* (в смысле: продам). Стилистических цитат не сосчитать—их несметное множество. Но и таковые весьма выразительны:
Строка 16	*Запад есть Запад, Восток есть Восток*—это стихи Р. Киплинга в переводе Е. Полонской;
Строки 17-18	... *туманный Запад, неверный лживый Запад*—из песни Александра Городницкого;
Строки 21-22	... *друг мой, брат мой, усталый страдающий брат*—из стихотворения Надсона.

* * *

Как же можно назвать эту прозу? Она мозаична, многоэтажно-ассоциативна, рассчитана на понимающего ее, посвященного читателя,— по самой сути своей она современна. Она оказывается до конца понятной только читателю, который совпадает с автором по образованности, по национальной культуре, желательно по поколению. А все прочие? Француз читает только что цитированные фразы из «Железки»—в очень хорошем, полном блестящих находок переводе (Лили Дени); но что переводчице делать с «тианственными глазами» Риты? Она придумывает: Ton oeil "tysmérieux" (вместо mystérieux); это хорошо,—но Тиана вместе с Маяковским и Северяниным улетучилась. Строка Киплинга поневоле превратилась в ничего не значащее: l'ouest, c'est l'ouest, et l'est, l'est. Аксенов помнит контекст этих строк, а вместе с Аксеновым их помнят его друзья, его братья по судьбе:

> Да, Запад есть Запад, Восток есть Восток, и с места они не сойдут
> Пока не предстанут Небо с Землей на страшный Господний суд.
> Но нет Востока и Запада нет. Что племя, родина, род,
> Если сильный с сильным лицом к лицу у края земли встает . . .

Французский читатель останется в пределах, предложенных ему дважды двух слов: Ouest—Est. Так оно и должно быть, это закон аксеновской прозы: она до конца открывается посвященному, однако вполне доступна и постороннему; пусть в обедненном и даже оголенном виде, но все же доступна. Дело тут не столько в переводе, сколько в комментарии: посвященный читатель—это тот, который интуитивно привносит в текст объяснения; посторонний же нуждается в примечаниях, хотя может обойтись и без них, потому что обедненный вариант его вполне способен заинтересовать. Такая многозначность текста, доступного в разной мере читателям разного уровня, свойственна, например, Салтыкову-Щедрину. Вот пассаж из *Истории одного города*,—о французском эмигранте Дю-Шарио,—можно его читать и поверхностно и глубоко, то есть без понимания исторических реалий или с их учетом:

> . . . однажды он начал объяснять глуповцам права человека; но, к счастью, кончил тем, что объяснил права Бурбонов. В другой раз он начал с того, что убеждал обывателей уверовать в богиню Разума, и кончил тем, что просил признать непогрешимость папы. Все это были, однако ж, одни façons de parler; и в сущности, виконт готов был стать на сторону какого угодно убеждения или догмата, если имел в виду, что за это ему перепадет лишний четвертак.

Стилистическая система Щедрина—предшественница аксеновской: соединение понятного с требующим комментария (*права человека или*

Бурбонов, богиня Разума, непогрешимость папы, догмат), соединение несопрягаемых стилей,—юридического (*права человека*), торжественно-библейского (*уверовать*), административного (*обыватели*), французских оборотов, разговорно-вульгарного (*перепадет лишний четвертак*). Салтыков-Щедрин с его разнослойной, рассчитанной на всезнающего читателя пародийно-сатирической, кишащей цитатами прозой—достойный предок Аксенова, который обогатил современную литературу стилем, заслуживающим названия ТИАНСТВЕННОГО.

СНОСКИ

1. Все цитаты даются по изданию: В. Аксенов, *Золотая наша железка*, Ардис 1980, 189 с.

2. Все подчеркивания в цитатах принадлежат автору статьи.

A Bibliography of Works By and About V.P. Aksënov

*Compiled by B. Briker and P. Dalgård**

---

* We would like to express our sincere gratitude to Professor Priscilla Meyer, who kindly has given us permission to include the material from her *A Bibliography of works by and about Vasili Pavlovich Aksenov* (1973/1977).

ABBREVIATIONS USED IN THIS BIBLIOGRAPHY:

DN	—	*Druzhba Narodov*
Iu	—	*Iunost'*
KO	—	*Knizhnoye Obozreniye*
KP	—	*Komsomol'skaya Pravda*
KZ	—	*Krugozor*
L	—	Leningrad
LG	—	*Literaturnaya Gazeta*
LO	—	*Literaturnoye Obozreniye*
LR	—	*Literaturnaya Rossiya*
LZ	—	*Literatura i Zhizn'*
M	—	Moskva
MG	—	*Molodaya Gvardiya*
MK	—	*Moskovskiy Komsomolets*
NA	—	*Novyy Amerikanets*
Ne	—	*Nedelya*
NM	—	*Novyy Mir*
NY	—	New York
RLT	—	*Russian Literature Triquarterly*
RM	—	*Russkaya mysl'*
SEEJ	—	*Slavic and East European Journal*
SO	—	*Sibirskiye ogni*
TLS	—	*The Times Literary Supplement*
VL	—	*Voprosy Literatury*
Vlen	—	*Vecherniy Leningrad*
WLT	—	*World Literature Today*

I. Original works in Russian by Aksënov

1. "Apel'siny iz Marokko," *Iu*, No. 1, 1963.
2. *Aristofoniana s lyagushkami*, Ann Arbor, 1981. Contains: "Aristofoniana s lyagushkami," "Vsegda v prodazhe," "Tsaplya," "Chetyre temperamenta," "Potseluy, Orkestr, Ryba, Kolbasa" (original title: "Vash ubiytsa").
3. *Bumazhnyy peyzazh*, Ann Arbor, 1983.
4. "Chetyre temperamenta," *Metropol'*, Ann Arbor, 1979.
5. "Derzkiy gost'," *Tret'ya volna*, No. 10, Jersey City, 1980.
6. "Dikoy," *Yunost'—Isbrannoye*, M. 1965, pp. 10-36.
7. "Duèt—rasskaz byvalogo cheloveka," *LR*, Oct. 9, 1970, pp. 12-13.
8. *Dzhin Grin Neprikasayemyy*, pseudonym Grivadiy Gorpozhaks (with O. Gorchakov and G. Pozhenian), M. 1972.
9. "Dvor v Fonarnom pereulke," *LG*, July 31, 1966, p. 3 (excerpt from "Stal'naya ptitsa").
10. "Fenomen 'Puzyrya'," *LG*, Nov. 19, 1969, p. 16.
11. "Gerbariy," *LG*, Feb. 18, 1961, p. 2.
12. "Geografiya lyubvi," 1975.
13. "Gibel' Pompei," *Vremya i my*, No. 57, NY (1980).
14. "Golubyye morskiye pushki," *Trud*, Apr. 14, 1967, p. 4.
15. "Goryachiy sneg v rukakh," *LG*, 1960, p. 3.
16. "Kardiogramma pisatel'skogo serdtsa," *Sovetskaya Belorussiya*, Aug. 22, 1963.
17. "Katapul'ta," *Ne*, Jan. 28-Feb. 3, 1962.
18. *Katapul'ta*, M. 1964, Contains: "S utra do temnoty," "Samson i Samsonikha," "Poltory vrachebnykh edinitsy," "Syurprizy," "Katapul'ta," "Peremena obraza zhizni," "Zavtraki sorok tret'yego goda," "Papa, slozhi," "Apel'siny iz Marokko."
19. "Kollegi," *Iu*, June-July, 1960.
20. *Kollegi*, M. 1961.
21. "Kruglyye sutki non-stop," *NM*, No. 8, 1976.
22. "Kto ty, syn Gippokrata," *KO*, Nov. 25, 1967, pp. 10-11.
23. "Lebyazh'ye ozero," *LR*, June 4, 1976.
24. "Literatura i yazyk" (otvet na anketu), *VL*, No. 6, 1967, pp. 89-90.
25. "Literaturnaya zhizn'—pisateli za rabotoy," *VL*, No. 3, 1964, p. 240.
26. "Lyubitelyam basketbola," *LG*, March 29, 1967, p. 8.
27. "Lyubov' k èlektrichestvu, Roman—Khronika," *Iu*, Nos. 3-5, 1971.
28. *Lyubov' k èlektrichestvu*, M. 1971.
29. "Mechta taksista (ironicheskaya proza)," *LG*, Aug. 26, 1970, p. 16.
30. "Mne dorogi sud'by romana," *LG*, Aug. 27, 1963, p. 3.
31. "Mnogotochiye nadezhdy," *LG*, Apr. 10, 1962, p. 4.
32. "Moy dedushka—pamyatnik," *Kostër*, 1970, No. 7, pp. 38-50, No. 8, pp. 22-36, Nos. 9-10, pp. 44-56.
33. "More i fokusy," *Ne*, June 13, 1976, p. 20 (excerpt from "Poiski zhanra").
34. "Na ploshchadi i za rekoy," *Iu*, No. 5, 1966, pp. 40-44.
35. "Na polputi k lune," *NM*, No. 7, 1962.
36. "Na polputi k lune," *Modern Russian Short Stories* (sel. by G. Gibian and M. Samaylov), NY, 1965.
37. "Na polputi k lune," and "Pobeda," *Russisk Litteratur i det 20' Århunorede* (K. Björnager, ed.), Aarhus, 1976.
38. *Na polputi k lune*, M, 1965. Contains: "Dikoy," "Zavtraki sorok tret'yego goda," "Mestnyy Khuligan Abramashvili," "Katapul'ta," "Peremena obraza zhizni," "Yaponskiye zametki," "Papa, slozhi!", "Tovarishch Krasivyy Furazhkin," "Na polputi k lune," "Malen'kiy Kit, lakirovshchik deystvitel'nosti."
39. "Na polputi v redaktsiyu," *LG*, Sept. 1, 1962, p. 3.
40. "Nasha anketa (molodyye o sebe)," *VL*, No. 9, 1962, pp. 117-119.
41. "Nasha Vera Ivanovna" and "Asfal'tovyye dorogi," *Iu*, No. 7, 1959, pp. 50-63.

42. "Neobyknovennyy amerikanets," *Inostrannaya literatura*, No. 3, 1966.
43. "Ne otstavaya ot bystronogogo," *LG*, June 15, 1961, pp. 1, 3.
44. "Novyye rasskazy," *Iu*, No. 12, 1964.
45. "Odno sploshnoye Karuzo," *Russika—81* (A. Sumerkin, ed.), NY, 1982.
46. "Opyt zapisi letnego sna," *Kodry* (Kishinëv), No. 2, 1970.
47. *Ostrov Krym*, Ann Arbor, 1981.
48. "Ostrov Krym; otryvok iz romana," *Vremya i my*, No. 56, NY (1980).
49. "Otvetstvennost' pered narodom," *Iu*, No. 4, 1963; and in *Pravda*, Apr. 3, 1963, p. 4.
50. *Ozhog*, Ann Arbor, 1980.
51. "Ozhog (otryvok iz romana)," *NA*, Aug. 27, 1980.
52. "Pamyati Vysotskogo," *NA*, Sept. 27, 1980; and in *Tret'ya volna*, Jersey City, Sept. 1980.
53. "Papa, slozhi!", *NM*, No. 7, 1962.
54. "Perepiska iz Ameriki v Rossiyu i obratno cherez Italiyu," *NA*, May 17-23, 1981.
55. "Pobeda," *Iu*, No. 6, 1965.
56. 'Pobeda," *NA*, May 2-8, 1980.
57. "Pod nebom znoynoy Argentiny," *LR*, May 13, 1966, pp. 21-24.
58. "Poèma èkstaza," *LG*, Jan. 1, 1968, p. 5.
59. "Poèma èkstaza," *Anthology of Soviet Satire* (P. Henry, ed.), Vol. 2, London, 1974, pp. 49-59.
60. "Poiski zhanra," *NM*, No. 1, 1978.
61. "Poltory vrachebnykh edinitsy" and "Na ploshchadi i za rekoy," *Biblioteka sovremennoy molodëzhnoy prozy i poèzii*, M. 1967, Vol. 1, pp. 59-94.
62. "Pora, moy drug, pora!", *MG*, Nos. 4-5, 1964.
63. *Pora, moy drug, pora!*, M, 1965.
64. "Pravo na ostrov," *Glagol*, No. 3, 1981.
65. *Pravo na ostrov*, Ann Arbor, 1983. Contains: "predisloviye" (by P. Meyer), "Zavtraki sorok tret'yego goda," "Mestnyy khuligan Abramashvili," "Na polputi k lune," "Malen'kiy Kit, lakirovshchik deystvitel'nosti," "Pobeda," "Zhal' chto vas ne bylo s nami," "Papa, slozhi!", "Sviyazhsk," "Pravo na ostrov."
66. "Preds"yezdovskaya tribuna; Anketa," *VL*, No. 5, 1966, pp. 12-13.
67. "Printsy, nishchiye dukhom," *LG*, Sept. 17, 1960, p. 2.
68. "Promezhutochnaya posadka v Saygone," *Trud*, No. 111, May 14, 1969, p. 3.
69. "Prostak v mire dzhaza," *Iu*, No. 8, 1967, pp. 94-99.
70. "Punktir progressa," *LG*, Feb. 8, 1966, p. 1.
71. "Puteshestviye v Meskhetiyu," *Sel'skaya molodëzh'*, No. 1, 1965, pp. 26-28.
72. "Puteshestviya Lëvy Ermolayeva," *Pioner*, No. 10, 1968, pp. 31-32.
73. "Randevu," *Avrora*, No. 5, 1971, pp. 26-35.
74. "Ranimaya lichnost'," *LG*, Jan. 21, 1970, p. 16.
75. "Razgovory v sochel'nik," *NM*, No. 1, 1961, pp. 258-61.
76. "Ryadom s nami," *Leningradskaya pravda*, Oct. 22, 1970.
77. "Romantik Kitousov, Akademik Velikiy-Salazkin i Tainstvennaya Margarita," *LG*, July 11, 1973, p. 16 (excerpt from *Zolotaya nasha zhelezka*).
78. "Ryzhiy s togo dvora," *LR*, Aug. 20, 1966, pp. 12-14.
79. "Rzhavaya kanatnaya doroga," *NA*, Aug. 17-23, 1982.
80. "Rzhavaya kanatnaya doroga," *Russika—81* (A. Sumerkin, ed.), NY, 1982.
81. "Schast'ye na beregu zagryaznënnogo okeana," *LG*, Sept. 23, 1970, p. 16.
82. "Semisvetnaya raduga," *LG*, Nov. 21, 1964, p. 3.
83. "Shkola prozy (za kruglym stolom)," *VL*, No. 7, 1969, pp. 84-85.
84. "Smeyëtsya tot, kto smeyëtsya. Kollektivnyy roman (Glava 5)," *Ne*, May 24-30, 1964, pp. 6, 16.
85. "S pervym aprelya," *LG*, Feb. 1, 1967, p. 16.
86. "Stal'naya ptitsa," *Glagol*, No. 1, Ann Arbor, 1977, pp. 25-95.
87. *Sunduchok v kotorom chto-to stuchit*, M, 1976.

88. "Superlyuks," *LR*, Aug. 4, 1978, pp. 12-14.
89. "S utra do temnoty," *LG*, Sept. 24, 1960, pp. 3, 5.
90. "Sviyazhsk," *Kontinent*, No. 29, 1981, pp. 95-140.
91. "Tam, gde rastut rododendrony," *Ne*, No. 20, 1967.
92. "Tovarishch Krasivyy Furazhkin," *Iu*, No. 12, 1964.
93. "Tovarishch Krasivyy Furazhkin," *Sovetskaya Èstoniya*, Oct. 11, 1964.
94. "Tsaplya," *Kontinent*, No. 22, 1980, pp. 118-194.
95. "Tuchi nashego detstva," *LR*, Apr. 22, 1965, pp. 10-11.
96. "U pisateley Rossii," *LR*, Dec. 22, 1967, p. 4.
97. "Vne sezona," *LG*, Apr. 21, 1976, p. 7 (excerpt from "Poiski zhanra").
98. "V svete podgotovki k predstoyashchey vesne. Rasskaz bez edinogo svoyego slova," *Iu*, No. 4, 1969, p. 110.
99. "Vyvod nezhelatel'nogo gostya iz doma," *LG*, No. 41, Oct. 8, 1969, p. 16.
100. "Zayavleniye dlya pressy," *NA*, Oct. 29, 1980.
101. "Zayavleniye dlya pressy," *Kontinent*, No. 27, 1981.
102. "Zametka k povesti Vyacheslava Shugayeva 'Begu i vozvrashchayus'," *Iu*, No. 11, 1965.
103. "Zatovarennaya bochkotara," *Iu*, No. 3, 1968, pp. 37-63.
104. *Zatovarennaya bochkotara. Randevu*, NY, 1981.
105. "Zavtraki sorok tret'yego goda," *Antologiya sovetskoy prozy* (S. Andreyeva, eds.), M, n.d.
106. "Zavtraki sorok tret'yego goda," *Ne*, Sept. 16-22, 1962.
107. "Zavtraki sorok tret'yego goda," *Russkaya sovetskaya proza* (S.I. Timina, ed.), M, 1978.
108. "Zemnaya solnechnaya krov'," *LG*, Oct. 13, 1962, pp. 2, 3.
109. "Zhal, chto vas ne bylo s nami," *Moskva*, No. 6, 1965.
110. *Zhal', chto vas ne bylo s nami*, M, 1969. Contains: "Kollegi," "Malen'kiy Kit, lakirovshchik deystvitel'nosti," "Mestnyy khuligan Abramashvili," "Yaponskiye zametki," "Pod nebom zvyozdnoy Argentiny," "Pobeda," "Ryzhiy s togo dvora," "Na ploshchadi i za rekoy," "Zhal', chto vas ne bylo s nami."
111. *Zolotaya nasha zhelezka*, Ann Arbor, 1980.
112. "Zvëzdnyy bilet," *Iu*, Nos. 6-7, 1961.
113. *Zvëzdnyy bilet* (Reprint), Aarhus, 1970.

II. Aksënov's Translations into Russian

114. T. Aktanov, *Buran*, Alma-Ata, 1971.
115. M. Baydzhiyev, "Duel'," *Teatr*, No. 3, 1968.
116. E.L. Doctorow, "Ragtime," *Innostrannaya literatura*, Nos. 9, 10, 1978.
117. J. Updike, "The Coup" (excerpt from the novel), *Metropol'*, Ann Arbor, 1979.

III. Interviews given by Aksënov

118. "Beseda s pisatelem Vasiliyem Aksënovym," *Kontinent*, No. 27, 1981, 433-445.
119. "Havde kun den udvej at rejse" (P. Dalgård), *Aarhus Stiftstidende*, Aug. 17, 1980.
120. "Interview with V.P. Aksënov" (P. Meyer), *RLT*, No. 6, 1973.
121. "Interv'yu s pisatelem Vasiliyem Aksënovym," *RM*, Aug. 3, 1980.
122. "Literaturoy pokorën," *NA*, Nov. 5, 1980.
123. (in) *Otblizo. Intervyuta—portreti* (A. Svilenov), Sof'ia, 1969.
124. "Att skapa en egen värld" (B. Hellman), *Vasabladet*, Dec. 23, Helsinki, 1978.
125. (in) *Samtal med Sovjetiska Forfattare* (D. Håstad), Stockholm, 1979, pp. 24-31.

IV. Works by Aksënov
in other languages (translations)

Azerbaijan (titles in Russian)
126. *Kollegi* (G. Sharifov, tr.), Baku, 1970.

Bulgarian
127. *Na polovinata păt do lunata; Izbrani rasskazi* (V. Sarandeva, tr.), Danov, 1969.
128. (in) *Săvremenni Săvetski razkazi* (sost. D. Stankova and T. Cheshmedzhiyeva), Narodna Kultura, 1971.

Czech
129. *Jak jsem zachránil fotbalovou republiku* (L. Dušková, tr.), Olympia, 1975.
130. *Překvarka* (15 stories) (L. Dušková and J. Zábruna), Rudé právo, 1967.
131. *Sudy osudu* (L. Duškova, tr.), Odeon, 1971.

Danish
132. "Den lokale laederjakke Abramasjevili," *Noveller fra Sovjetunionen*, Köbenhavn, 1968.
133. "En slagets kunstner," *Samvirke*, No. 8, 1980.
134. "Halvvejs til månen," *Ny Russisk Prosa*, Köbenhavn, 1964.
135. *På Jagt efter en Genre* (P. Alberg, tr.), Kobenhavn, 1981.
136. *Stjernebilletten*, Köbenhavn, 1962.
137. "Svanet sö," "Lille Kit, virkelighedsforgylder" and "Sejren," *Ansigter i et tiår* (H. Dalgård and K. Björnager, eds.), Köbenhavn, 1977.

Dutch
138. *Geen markt voor holl vaten en andre verhalen* (T. Eekman, tr.), Amst., 1979.
139. *Kaartje naar de sterren* (F. Hubers, tr.), De Fontein, 1963.

English
140. "An unusual American" (C.R. Proffer, tr.), *Soviet Criticism of American Literature in the Sixties* (C.R. Proffer, ed.), Ann Arbor, 1972.
141. *The Burn*, Random House, NY, 1984.
142. *Colleagues* (A. Brown, tr.), London, 1962.
143. *Colleagues* (M. Wettlin, tr.), M, n.d.
144. "Colleagues" (M. Wettlin, tr.), *Soviet Literature Monthly*, No. 4, 1961.
145. *The Crimean Island*, Random House, NY, 1983.
146. "Daddy, what do they say?", *Modern Russian Short Stories*, I (C.G. Bearne, ed.), Lond., 1968.
147. "Destruction of Pompei," *The Partisan Review*, No. 1, 1983.
148. "Halfway to the Moon," *Halfway to the Moon* (M. Hayward and P. Blake, eds.), York, 1965.
149. "Halfway to the Moon" (R. Hingley, tr.), *Encounter*, Apr., 1963.
150. "Halfway to the Moon," *Four Soviet Masterpieces* (A. MacAndrew, tr.), NY, 1965.
151. "Halfway to the Moon," *The New Writing in Russia* (Th. Whitney, ed.), Mich., 1964.
152. "Halfway to the Moon" (A. Miller, tr.), *Anthology of Soviet Short Stories* (N. Atarov, ed.), Vol. 2, M, 1976.
153. *It's Time, My Friend, It's Time* (O. Stevens, tr.), NY, 1969.
154. *It's Time, My Love, It's Time* (O. Stevens, tr.), Lond., 1969.
155. "On the Square and Across the River," *Soviet Literature*, No. 4, M, 1967.
156. "Papa, What Does It Spell?", *The New Writing in Russia* (T. Whitney, ed.), Mich., 1964.
157. "A Poem of Ecstasy" (V. Dukas, tr.), *Twelve Contemporary Russian Stories*, Lond., 1973.
158. "Russia is losing a whole layer of culture to emigration," *United States World News & World Report*, Vol. 90, March 2, 1981, p. 51.
159. (Aksënov recalling his mother in article, title unknown), *Sunday Times*, Dec. 6, 1981.
160. *A Starry Ticket* (A. Brown, tr.), Lond., 1962.
161. "The Metropol Affair," *The Wilson Quarterly* (Spec. Edition), 1982, p. 158.

162. "The Steel Bird," *Contemporary Russian Prose* C.R. Proffer and E. Proffer, eds.), Mich., 1982.
163. *The Steel Bird*, Ann Arbor, 1979 (J.J. Johnson, Jr., ed.). Contains: "Introduction" (by J.J. Johnson, Jr.), "The Steel Bird," "Victory," "Halfway to the Moon," "Little Whale, Varnisher of Reality," "The Lunches of '43," "Japanese Jottings," "It's a Pity You Weren't with Us," "Changing a Way of Life," "Ginger from Next Door," "Oranges from Morocco."
164. "Surprises," *Russian Writing Today* (R.M. Gulland and M. Dewhirst, eds.), Lond., 1977. Also contains Aksënov's comments on his own writing.
165. "Thoughts of a Prose Writer," *Soviet Literature*, No. 5, 1966.
166. *A Ticket to the Stars* (A. MacAndrew, tr.), NY, 1963.
167. "Your Murderer; a play" (D.C. Gerould and J. Kosicha, tr.), *Performing Arts Journal*, Spring 1977, No. 2, pp. 111-144.
168. "Victory" (G. Slobin, tr.), *RLT*, No. 5, 1973, pp. 191-197.

Estonian (titles in Russian)

169. "Na polputi k redaktsii," *Lipovyye allei* (B. Ilus, tr.), Aug. 19, 1966.
170. "Poèma èkstaza" (T. Hujk, tr.), *Noorte Hjaèl*, Jan. 21, 1968.
171. "Zhal', chto vas ne bylo s nami" (V. Toors, tr.), *Edagi*, May 15, 1966.
172. "Zhal', chto vas ne bylo s nami" (T. Kallas, tr.), *Kultuur ja älu*, No. 10, 1968.

Finnish

173. *Matkalippu täktün* (E. Adrian, tr.), Helsinki, 1964.
174. *Vikaveljet* (A. Airola, tr.), Suomi Finland, 1963.

French

175. *L'Amour De L'électricité*, Temps Actuels, 1976.
176. *Billet pour les Étoiles* (J. Cathala, tr.), Julliard, 1963.
177. "Comment on devient un produit d'exportation en Union Sovietique," *Le Monde*, Apr. 14, 1978.
178. *Confrères* (J. Cathala, tr.), Editeurs Français Reunis, 1963.
179. *L'île De Crimée* (L. Denis, tr.), Paris, 1983.
180. *Notre ferraille en or* (L. Denis, tr.; Introduction by Victor Erofeyev), Paris, 1978.
181. *L'Oiseau d'acier*, Gallimard, 1980.
182. *Les Oranges Du Maroc* (I. Sokologorsky, tr.), Editeurs Français Reunis, 1966.
183. *Recherche d'un genre* (L. Denis, tr.), Paris, 1979.
184. *Surplus en Stock- Futille* (L. Denis, tr.), Paris, 1966.

Georgian (titles in Russian)

185. "Mestnyy khuligan Abramashvili" (N. Evralidze, tr.), *Nakadum*, Tblisi, 1966.

German

186. "Apfelsinen aus Marokko," *Kultur und Fortschritt*, Berlin, 1963.
187. *Auf Halben Weg Zur Mond. Erzählungen* (Ju. Elperin, tr.), Berl., 1977.
188. *Defizitposten Fasslergut* (Th. Resche, tr.), Münch., 1975.
189. *Drei trafen sich wieder*, Berlin, 1967.
190. *Drei trafen sich wieder* (Ju. Elperin, tr.), Berlin, 1976.
191. *Ein Denkmal für meinen Urgrossvater* (Th. Resche, tr.), Berl., 1978.
192. *Eine Million Trennungen: Erzählungen* (Th. Resche, tr.), Berl., 1978.
193. *Es ist Zeit, mein Freund, es ist Zeit* (I. Tinzmann, tr.), Stuttgart, 1967.
194. *Fahrkarte zu den Sternen*, Köln, 1963.
195. *Fahrkarte zu den Sternen*, Guterslok, 1965.
196. *Der Genosse mit den Schönen Uniform*, Münch., 1966.
197. "Genosse Prachtmütze," *Kultur und Fortschritt*, Nos. 43, 44, 1966.
198. "Der Jahr der Scheidung," *Kultur und Fortschritt*, 1966.
199. *Die Liebe zur Elektrizität* (G. Jänicke, tr.), Berl., 1973.
200. "Das Rendezvous," *Sinn und Form*, No. 1, 1973.
201. "Das Rendezvous," in *Rendezvous mit dem Schatten* (Ch. Kossuth, ed.), Berl., 1973.
202. *Der Rosa Eisberg oder auf der Suche nach der Gattung* (R. Tietze, tr.), Berl., Wienna, 1981.

Hungarian
203. *Ejjel- nappol non-stop* (Soproni András, tr.), Budapest, 1978.
204. *Emléku, lett a nagyapam* (Lénárt Éva, tr.), Budapest, 1978.
205. *Félúton a hold felé* (Domokus Géza, tr.), Bukarest, 1969.
206. *Örvényes ifjusag* (Por Judit, tr.), Budapest, 1976.

Italian
207. *Rottame d'oro* (C.L. Marinelli), Editori Riuniti, 1981.
208. *Ustione (L')* (G. Buttafava and S. Rapetti, trs.), Mondadori, 1980.

Lithuanian *(titles in Russian)*
209. "Lyubitelyam voleybola" (A. Barstitis, tr.), *Niamus*, No. 2, 1970, pp. 34-37.

Norwegian
210. *Kolleger* (N. Frederiksen, tr.), Asheboug, 1963.

Polish
211. *Gwiazdzisty bilet* (I. Piotrowska, tr.), War., 1962.
212. *Koledzy* (J. Dziarnowska), War., 1963.
213. "Szkoda, że was tam nie bylo" (Z. Fedecki, tr.), Państowy Institute Wydawniczy, 1971.
214. *W pól drogi do księżyca* (Z. Fedecki, tr.), War., 1967.
215. (in) *Dwadzieścia dziewięć* (A. Drawicz, ed.), War., 1967.

Slovak
216. *Katapuľta* (contains 8 stories) (I. Krolik, tr.), Bratislava, 1966.
217. *Kolegovia* (Ju. Stabovoj, tr.), Bratislava, 1975.

Swedish
218. *Stjärnbiljetten* (G. Hjelm, tr.), Stockholm/Helsinki, 1963.
219. *Tomma tunnor* (H. Björkegren, tr.), Stockholm, 1969.

Yugoslavia *(Serbo-Croatian, Macedonian, Slovenian)*
220. *Kolege* (D. Jakšić, tr.), Beogr., 1963.
221. "Na pola puta do mjeseca" (A. Flaker, tr.), *Suvremeni Sovjetski pisci, Četvrta knjiga: 1961-63* (A. Flaker, ed.), 1963.
222. *Pomorandže iz Maroko* (B. Kitanovič and B. Miloslavljevič, tr.), Novi Sad, 1963.
223. *Portokali od Maroko* (S. Drakul, tr.), Skopje, 1964.
224. *Prijatelji* (J. Moder, tr.), Ljubljana, 1962.
225. *Vremje e, prijatele* (E. Manea, tr.), Skopje, 1965.
226. *Zvezdana vozna karta* (D. Jakšić, tr.), Beogr., 1963.

V. Reviews of works by Aksënov
(in Russian, English and other languages)

227. Baturina, T., "Zrelost' romantikov," *MG*, No. 6, 1965, pp. 306-312.
228. Chaykovsky, B., "A dal'she chto?", *Uchiteľskaya gazeta*, March 21, 1963, p. 4.
229. Chalmayev, V., "K novym pobedam kommunisticheskoy ideologii," *DN*, No. 8, 1963.
230. Dymshits, A., "Rasskazy o rasskazakh," *Ogonëk*, No. 13, 1963, pp. 30-31.
231. El'yaskevich, A., "Nerushimoye edinstvo," *Zvezda*, No. 8, 1963, pp. 185-202.
232. Ermolayev, H., in *Books Abroad*, Vol. 38, No. 3, Summer 1964.
233. Fëderov, V., "Dorozhit' pravdoy," *LG*, Apr. 2, 1963, p. 1.
234. Fomenko, L., "Gde oni, zavtrashniye zaboty?", *Moskovskaya pravda*, Feb. 16, 1963.
235. Gagarin, Iu., "Slovo k pisatelyam," *LR*, No. 16, 1963, pp. 2-3.
236. Kedrina, Z., "Chelovek—sovremennik—grazhdanin," *VL*, No. 8, 1963, pp. 27-50.
237. Kozhemyako, V., "Imenem revolyutsii," *KP*, Mar. 27, 1963.
238. Kuznetsov, F., "Molodoy pisateľ i zhizn'," *Iu*, No. 5, 1963, pp. 73-80.
239. Lomidze, G., "Sila realizma," *VL*, No. 5, 1963, pp. 47-68.
240. Makarov, A., "Chitaya pis'ma," *LG*, Dec. 19, 1963, pp. 1, 3.
241. Markov, G., "Velikaya pravda nashikh dney," *LG*, Mar. 30, 1963, p. 3.
242. Novgorodov, A., "Tsena apel'sina," *MK*, No. 4, 1963, pp. 119-122.
243. Novikov, V., "Geroicheskomu vremeni—geroicheskoye iskusstvo." *Znamya*, No. 10, 1963, pp. 187-96.

244. Osetrov, E., "Darovaniye igry," *LG*, Feb. 9, 1963, p. 3.
245. Pankin, B., "Ni slovechka v prostote," *KP*, Feb. 17, 1963.
246. "Plenum TS.K.KPSS," *LG*, June 20, 1963, p. 2.
247. Raskin, A., "Moroka s bananami" (parody), *Krokodil*, No. 6, 1963.
248. Ryurikov, Yu., "Tri vlecheniya," *VL*, No. 8, 1965, pp. 25-47.
249. Shamota, N., "Chem bogat chelovek," *LG*, June 15, 1963.
250. Sinel'nikov, M., "Geroy truda—geroy literatury," *Trud*, No. 14, 1963.
251. Sinel'nikov, M., "Videt' strezhen'," *LR*, Apr., 1963, pp. 14-15.
252. Slobodian, D., "O spornom i besspornom," *LG*, Oct. 1, 1963, p. 3.
253. Titov, V., "Pust' kniga uchit zhit'," *VL*, Apr. 1963, p. 1, and *Pravda*, Apr. 11, 1963, p. 4.
254. Verchenko, Yu., "Gde zhe obeshchaniye Korchagina?", *Smena*, No. 8, 1963, pp. 10-11.

Bumazhnyy Peyzazh

255. Golovskoy, V., "Takaya istoriya . . . ," *Novoye Russkoye Slovo*, Oct. 16, 1983.

Dzhin-Grin Neprikasayemyy

256. Evtushenko, E., "Tresk razryvayemykh rubashek," *LG*, Jan. 31, 1973, p. 5.

Katapul'ta and *Pora, moy drug, pora*
(It's Time, My Friend, It's Time)

257. "The Hard Road to Peace" (n.a., *TLS*, Sept. 3, 1964.
258. "Review," *TLS*, Apr. 10, 1969.
259. R.V., "Recommended by our reviewer." *Books Abroad*, Autumn 1965, Vol. 39, No. 4, p. 475.

Kollegi (Colleagues)

260. Anninsky, L., "Ot prostoty do mudrosti," *LG*, May 27, 1961, pp. 2, 3.
261. Blinkova, M., "Sasha Zelenin i ego druz'ya," *NM*, No. 11, 1960, pp. 248-53.
262. Borisov, S., "Sverstniki," *LG*, June 11, 1960, p. 3.
263. Fomenko, L., "Vremya zovët," *Nash sovremennik*, No. 2, 1961, pp. 194-211.
264. Girvich, A., "Chelovek uchitsya zhit'," *Iu*, No. 2, 1961, pp. 69-74.
265. Kadran, V., "Vechnyye voprosy—novyye otvety," *VL*, No. 3, 1961, pp. 25-28.
266. Kuznetsov, F., "Chetvërtoye pokoleniye," *LG*, July 29, 1961, pp. 1, 2, 3.
267. Kuznetsov, F., "Geroy nashey zhizni," *Smena*, Apr. 2, 1963, p. 3.
268. Kuznetsov, F., "Kakim byt'," *LG*, July 14, 1960, p. 3.
269. Kuznetsov, F., "Ottsu Serafimu," *KP*, July 13, 1964.
270. Kuznetsov, F., "V mire boyets," *Iu*, No. 4, 1966, pp. 83-90.
271. Kuznetsov, F., "Vozmuzhaniye geroya," *VL*, Dec. 13, 1963, p. 3.
272. Kuznetsov, M., "Spor reshit zhizn'," *NM*, No. 9, 1960, pp. 236-50.
273. Makarov, A., "Ser'ëznaya zhizn'," *Znamya*, No. 1, 1961, pp. 188-211.
274. Maslin, N., "Krasivaya molodost'," *Moskva*, No. 2, 1961, pp. 200-201.
275. Mikhaylov, O., "Lyudi truda i mysli," *Znamya*, No. 4, 1961, pp. 195-208.
276. Mikhaylov, O., "Nashey molodosti spory," *Iu*, No. 10, 1964, pp. 52-57.
277. Ozerov, V., "Novyy chelovek v tsentre vnimaniya," *VL*, No. 12, 1960, pp. 3-26.
278. Podopulo, G., "Partiynost'—iskhodnaya pozitsiya molodogo khudozhnika," *MK*, No. 11, 1960, pp. 248-53.
279. Rassadin, S., "Shestidesyatniki," *Iu*, No. 12, 1960, pp. 58-62.
280. "Review," *TLS*, Oct. 26, 1962.
281. Savel'ëv, B., "Istoricheskoye i povsednevnoye," *Neva*, No. 3, 1961, pp. 187-201.
283. Trifonova, T., "S lyubov'yu k cheloveku," *KZ*, No. 1, 1961, pp. 20-22.

Lyubov' k èlektrichestvu

284. Pankov, V., "Brillianty dlya literatury," *Ogonëk*, No. 42, 1971, pp. 26-27.
285. Pankov, V., "Gody—desyatiletiya—èpokha," *Znamya*, No. 2, 1972, pp. 217-32.
286. Ryabikova, T., "Vo imya revolyutsii," *Tuvinskaya pravda*, July 28, 1971.
287. Roslyakov, V., "Dorogoy revolyutsii," *LG*, May 26, 1971, p. 6.
288. Tsurikova, G., "Chelovek i vremya," *Neva*, No. 3, 1972, pp. 162-70.
289. Veshnyakov, V., "Odna, no plamennaya strast'," *Krasnoye znamya*, Feb. 22, 1972.

Metropol' ("Chetyre temperamenta")

290. Lawton, A.M., (in) *Slavic and East European Journal*, New Series, Vol. 24, No. 3, Fall 1980, pp. 302-3.

291. Milivojević, D., "Review," *WLT*, Vol. 54, No. 4, Autumn 1980.
292. Mouze, C., (in) *Esprit*, No. 4, 1981, pp. 167-8.
293. "Ob al'manakhe 'Metropol'," *Grani*, No. 118, 1980, pp. 151-7.
294. "Review" (n.a.), *New York Times Book Review*, March 2, 1980, p. 3.
295. Zolkin, H., (in) *Slavic and East European Journal*, Vol. 24, 1980, p. 322.

Na polputi k lune (Halfway to the Moon)
296. Aleksandrova, T., "Skvoz' okno restorana," *Zvezda*, Feb. 12, 1963.
297. Antopol'skiy, L., "Korni cheloveka," *Iu*, No. 1, 1969, pp. 67-70.
298. Brovman, G., "Dialog o geroye," *LR*, No. 6, 1964, pp. 6-7.
299. Brovman, G., "Pravda istoricheskogo optimizma," *Moskva*, No. 1, 1964.
300. Brovman, G., "Sut'—v ideynoy pozitsii," *Oktyabr'*, No. 5, 1963, pp. 180-90.
301. Chalmayev, V., "Pervoye slagayemoye," *LG*, Aug. 24, 1963, pp. 1, 4.
302. Chudakov, A., "Iskusstvo tselogo," *NM*, No. 2, 1963, pp. 239-54.
303. Kryachko, L., "Puti, zabluzhdeniya i nakhodki," *Oktyabr'*, No. 3, 1963, pp. 200-209.
304. Kryachko, L., "V 'kadre' i 'za kadrom'," *LG*, June 27, 1964, p. 3.
305. Kuznetsov, M., "Chelovechnost'," *V mire knig*, No. 1, 1963, pp. 22-27.
306. Ianovsky, N., "V romanticheskom klyuche," *Oktyabr'*, No. 1, 1963, pp. 188-95.
307. Maksimov, N., "Snezhnyy chelovek," *Sovetskiy Sakhalin*, Oct. 14, 1962.
308. Rekemchuk, A., "Da ne oskudeyet," *VL*, No. 7, 1969, pp. 90-93.
309. Volynsky, K., "Zhivaya voda," *LG*, Jan. 11, 1964, p. 1.
310. Khovanskaya, A., "S kogo oni portrety pishut?", *Sovetskiy Sakhalin*, Oct. 21, 1962.

Ozhog and *Ostrov Krym*
311. Austin, A., (in) *New York Times Book Review*, No. 85, 1980, p. 3.
312. Brown, D., (Review of *Ostrov Krym*), *Slavic Review*, Vol. 42, No. 2, Summer 1983.
313. Dukas, V., "Review," *WLT*, Summer 1981.
314. Hosking, G., "The Ascent out of Inhumanity," *TLS*, Sept. 25, 1981.
315. Iur'yenen, S., (in) *Novoye Russkoye Slovo*, (n.d.), 1982.
316. Iverni, V., (in) *Kontinent*, No. 33, 1982.
317. Lowe, D., "E. Ginzburg's *Krutoĭ marshrut* and V. Aksënov's *Ožog*: The Magadan Connection," *SEEJ*, Summer 1983, pp. 200-210.
318. Mal'tsev, Yu., "*Ozhog* Vasiliya Aksënova," *RM*, Apr. 3, 1980.
319. Mal'tsev, Yu., "Ozhog," *Kontinent*, No. 29, 1981.
320. Milivojević, D., "Review" (*Ostrov Krym*), *WLT*, Winter 1982.
321. O.K., (in) *Nouvelles Litteraires*, (n.d.), 1983.
322. Sand, N., (in) *Le Monde*, (n.d.), 1983.
323. Schneman, S., (in) *New York Times Book Review*, No. 87, 1982, p. 3.
324. Smith, G.S., "Vasilii Aksenov's Novel *Ozhog*," *Radio Liberty Research Bulletin*, No. 45, Nov. 11, 1981.
325. Zhedilyagin, Yu., "Pryzhok v storonu," *Grani*, No. 124, 1982, pp. 269-78.

Papa, slozhi! (Papa, What Does It Spell?)
326. Gorlovskiy, A., "Chtoby byli schastlivy," *Smena*, No. 15, 1965, pp. 13-15.
327. Kryachko, L., "Zhit' dlya bor'by," *Moskva*, No. 10, 1966, pp. 194-203.
328. Solov'ëva, I., "Nachalo puti," *NM*, No. 9, 1967.

Poiski zhanra (In Search of a Genre)
329. Anninskiy, L., "Zhanr-to naydëtsya," *LO*, No. 7, 1978.
330. Bjelke, H., "Russisk digter rejse i sprogets verden," *Kristeligt Dagblad* (Copenhagen), Sept. 20, 1981.
331. Bredsdorf, Th., "Fantasiens magt og afmagt," *Politiken* (Copenhagen), Oct. 27, 1981.
332. Dalgård, P., "Sprogkunstnere," *Fyens Stiftstidende* (Odense), Nov. 20, 1981.
333. Elyashev, A., (in) *Soviet Studies in Literature*, No. 15, 1979, p. 26.
334. Evtushenko, E., "Neobkhodimost' chudes," *LO*, No. 7, 1978.
335. Flaker, A., "Nostaligična potraga Vasilija Aksjonova," *Književna Smotra*, XI, Zagreb, 1979.
336. Mailand Hansen, Chr., "Det lyseröde isbjerg i Sortehavet," *Information* (Copenhagen), Jan. 22, 1982.

337. Nielsen, F.C., "En trumf i baghånden," *Jyllands Posten*, Sept. 4, 1981 (Aarhus).
338. Ravn, P., "Vender op og ned på gaengse forestillinger," *Aarhus Stiftstidende* (Aarhus), Sept. 16, 1981.
339. Storm, J., "Livets gang i Sovjet," *Ekstra Bladet* (Copenhagen), Nov. 2, 1981.

Pora, moy drug, pora *(It's Time, My Friend, It's Time)*

340. Aneneva, A., "Preuvelicheniye chuvstv," *SO*, No. 2, 1966, pp. 169-76.
341. Bocharov, A., "Potok i pisatel'," *KP*, Nov. 21, 1964.
342. Bocharov, A., "Utverzhdaya tsel'nost' lichnosti," *VL*, No. 1, 1965, pp. 26-32.
343. Brovman, G., "Dykhaniye zhizni," *Izvestiya*, Feb. 26, 1965, p. 5.
344. Brovman, G., "Pora vozmuzhaniya," *Trud*, July 3, 1965, p. 5.
345. Geydeko, V., "Pered sleduyushchim shagom," *LG*, June 6, 1964, p. 3.
346. Glinkin, P., "Proza dlya molodëzhi," *SO*, No. 10, 1964, p. 180.
347. Glinkin, P., "Chemu pora?", *Smena*, July 2, 1964.
348. Golyshev, G., "Staromodnyye klassiki i urbanist Kovrigin," *Dal'niy Vostok*, No. 5, 1966.
349. Kireyeva, A., "Letyat za dnyami dni . . . ," *Smena*, No. 1, 1965, pp. 26-27.
350. Khvatov, A., "Dukhovnyy mir cheloveka i koordinaty vremeni," *Zvezda*, No. 4, 1968, pp. 192-208.
351. Kryachko, L., "Poistine—pora!", *Moskva*, No. 9, 1964, p. 213.
352. Kuznetsov, F., "Grazhdanin ili meshchanin?", *Iu*, No. 12, 1964, pp. 75-80.
353. Lugovskoy, V., "Vroven' s vekom," *Trud*, July 12, 1964.
354. Maksimov, N., "Ob istorizme podlinnom i mnimom," *Volga*, No. 9, 1966.
355. Mitin, G., "Ishchu sebya v knige," *MK*, No. 7, 1964, pp. 122-127.
356. Motyashov, I., "K bor'be zovushchaya," *Uchitel'skaya gazeta*, June 20, 1964.
357. Nechayeva, L., "Ten' geroya," *MK*, No. 4, 1965, pp. 118-23.
358. Ozerov, N., "Proza 1964-ogo goda," *VL*, No. 1, 1965, pp. 18-26.
359. Popov, N., "V poiskakh geroya," *Leninskiy put'*, Aug. 30, 1964.
360. Zhak, L., "Pokoya ne budet," *Znamya*, No. 1, 1965, pp. 229-31.

Potseluy, orkestr, ryba, kolbasa *(Your Murderer)*

361. Gerould, D., "Vasili Aksenov: Contemporary Russian Playwright," *Performing Arts Journal*, Spring 1977, No. 2, pp. 108-110.
362. (in) *Soviet Literature in the Sixties: An International Symposium* (M. Hayward and E.I. Crowley, eds.), NY 1964.

Randevu and Zatovarennaya bochkotara

363. Vayl', P., and Genis, A., "Randevu s bochkotaroy," *NA*, Aug. 27, 1980.

Stal'naya ptitsa *(The Steel Bird and other stories)*

364. Dukas, V., "Review," *WLT*, Vol. 53, No. 3, Summer 1979, p. 520.
365. Gladilin, A., "Stal'naya ptitsa," *Kontinent*, No. 14, 1977.
366. Mouze, C., (review of *Oiseau d'acier*), *Esprit*, No. 4, 1981, pp. 167-168.
367. "Review" (n.a.), *Library Journal*, Vol. 104, Feb. 1, 1979, p. 509.
368. "Review" (n.a.), *Publishers Weekly*, Vol. 215, Jan. 1, 1979, p. 46.

Vsegda v prodazhe *(staged 1965;*
***cf.* Aristofoniana s lyagushkami)**

369. Anninsky, L., "Idei i lyudi," *Iu*, No. 11, 1965, pp. 72-74.
370. Farbshteyn, A., (in) *VL*, June 28, 1966.
371. Georgiyevskiy, G., "Kak ya okazalsya na lestnitse," *Teatr*, No. 9, 1965, pp. 3-13.
372. Goldobin, V., "V luchshikh traditsiyakh," *Teatr*, No. 2, 1966, pp. 3-8.
373. Kagarlitskiy, Yu., "Simpatii u nas obshchiye," *Teatr*, No. 9, 1965, pp. 35-43.
374. Mitin, G., "Pomogi sebe sam!", *VL*, No. 4, 1966, pp. 12-17.
375. Shcherbanov, K., "V spore o zhizni," *KP*, June 19, 1965, p. 3.
376. Solodovnikov, A., "Puti obnovleniya," *Sovetskaya kul'tura*, March 24, 1966, pp. 3-4.
377. Velekhova, N., "Stol ne kruglyy," *Teatr*, No. 12, 1965, pp. 23-33.
378. "Vsegda v prodazhe" (n.a.), *Vechernyaya Moskva*, June 2, 1965, p. 3.
379. "'Sovremennik'," *Sovetskaya kul'tura*, June 5, 1965, p. 1.

Zatovarennaya bochkotara *(The Tare of Empty Barrels)*

380. Brovman, G., "Voploshcheniye zhizni, ili literaturnaya igra?", *LR*, May 24, 1965.

381. Elkin, A., "O 'khoroshem cheloveke' i 'Zatovarennoy bochkotare'," *Vechernyaya Moskva*, Aug. 1, 1968.
382. Elkin, A., "Pered kem snimet shlyapu Shekspir?", *Moskva*, No. 10, 1968, pp. 190-210.
383. Lokonov, V., "Poslesloviye k obsuzhdeniyu," *Uchitel'skaya gazeta*, Sept. 21, 1968.
384. Ognev, Gr., "Kuda spisat' bochkotaru?", *KP*, Apr. 30, 1968.
385. Rassadin, S., "Shestero v kuzove, ne schitaya bochkotary," *VL*, No. 10, 1968, pp. 93-115.
386. Solov'yëva, I., "S preuvelicheniyami i snovideniyami," *LG*, May 1, 1968, p. 6.
387. Vladin, V.L., "Zabochkotarennyy tovar" (Parody), *LG*, Oct. 2, 1968.

Zolotaya nasha zhelezka (Our Golden Hardware)
388. Kolonsky, W.F., "Review," *WLT*, Vol. 55, No. 2, Spring 1981.

Zvëzdnyy bilet (A Ticket to the Stars)
389. Bertse, V., "Karta i marshruty," *LG*, Aug. 24, 1961, p. 2.
390. Bondarev, Yu., "Poiski semnadtsatiletnikh," *LG*, July, 1961, pp. 1, 2, 3.
391. Brovman, G., "Pafos zhizneutverzhdeniya ili zhupel' lakirovki?", *VL*, No. 12, 1963.
392. Bryl', Ya., "Chto pishut o tebe, lyubov'," *LG*, Sept. 30, 1966, pp. 2, 3.
393. Charnyy, M., "O svobode lyubvi," *Zvezda*, No. 10, 1962, pp. 193-99.
394. Ivashchenko, V., "Zemskaya statistika," *VL*, No. 2, 1966, pp. 38-41.
395. Kholopov, G., "Liniya razvitiya—sovremennost'," *Vlen*, Sept. 26, 1961, p. 3.
396. Lavlinskiy, L., "Bilet, no kuda?", *KP*, Sept. 15, 1961.
397. Panova, V., "Prochtite, chto interesno!", *Ne*, Sept. 3-9, 1966, p. 18.
398. Rifbjerg, K., "Rend mig i traditionerne," *Politiken* (Copenhagen), Oct. 24, 1962.
399. Shaw, N.D., "Review," *SEEJ*, New Series, Vol. 8, 1964.
400. Shishkina, A., "Moral' i moralisty," *Neva*, No. 1, 1963.
401. "Too Many Beaks," (n.a.), *TLS*, June 1, 1962.
402. Zabrana, J., "Druhý román Vasilje Aksjonova," *Svetová Literatura*, No. 7, c. 3, Praha, 1962.

VI. General Studies in Russian, English and other languages

403. Anninskiy, L., "Poslednyaya kniga Makarova," *DN*, No. 10, 1968, pp. 268-70.
404. Anninskiy, L., "Real'nost' prozy," *Don*, No. 3, 1964, pp. 152-58.
405. Antol'skiy, P., "Ottsy i deti," *LG*, Dec. 11, 1962, p. 3.
406. Baygusev, "Schast'ye," *Vechernyaya Moskva*, Sept. 2, 1963.
407. Baranov, V., "V glub' okeana," *Ural*, No. 5, pp. 163-79.
408. Belash, Yu., "Na Sashu Zelenina oni ne pokhozhi," *MG*, No. 4, 1961.
409. Björnager, K., and Dalgård, H., *Portraet af et tiår*, Copenhagen, 1976, pp. 65-75.
410. Blair, K.H., *A Review of Soviet Literature*, Lond., 1966.
411. Blake, P., "Washington is Halfway to the Moon," *Time*, No. 8, 1982.
412. Blomquist, L.E., "Rysk Litteratur efter Stalin," Stockholm, 1968.
413. Borisov, S., and Sorin, S., "Malaya entsiklopediya Iunosti," *Iu*, No. 10, 1962, pp. 11-51.
414. Borshchagovskiy, A., "Krovnaya svyaz' pokoleniy," *LG*, Sept. 29, 1962, pp. 1, 2.
415. Borshchagovskiy, A., "Poiski molodoy prozy," *Moskva*, No. 12, 1962.
416. Brovman, G., "Grazhdanskoye chuvstvo i kharakter sovremennika," *Moskva*, No. 4, 1966, pp. 197-203.
417. Brovman, G., "Grazhdanstvennost' geroya," *Moskva*, No. 6, 1963, pp. 197-203.
418. Brovman, G., "Obraz sovremennika," *Nash Sovremennik*, No. 1, 1965, pp. 110-114.
419. Brown, D., "Vasily Aksenov at 33," *Triquarterly*, No. 3, 1965, pp. 78-83.
420. Brown, D., *Soviet Russian Literature since Stalin*, Lond., 1978.
421. Brown, E., *Russian Literature since the Revolution*, Harvard University Press, 1982, pp. 358-365.
422. Bukhanov, V., "Ne tol'ko pisatel'," *MK*, Aug. 27, 1964, p. 4.
423. Burg, D., "Molodoye pokoleniye," *Mosty*, No. 11, 1965, pp. 211-29.
424. Bursov, B., "Literatura nashego veka," *Pravda*, Nov. 27, 1967.
425. Bushin, V., "Shtampy byvayut raznyye," *LZ*, Aug. 19, 1959.

426. Bussewitz, W., "Tendenzen in der Entwicklung der Sovjetischen Roman der 60er Jahre," *Zeitschrift für Slawistik*, Bd. XV, No. 2, 1970, pp. 208-18.
427. Chernov, A., "Schast'ye mnimoye," *Znamya*, No. 1, 1964, p. 248.
428. Chukovskaya, L., "Zerkalo, kotoroye ne otrazhayet," *NM*, No. 2, 1965, pp. 241-49.
429. Chulkovskiy, K., "Nechto o labude," *LG*, Aug. 12, 1961, p. 4.
430. Dalada, N., "Pered novoy vstrechey," *LZ*, May 10, 1961.
431. Dalgård, P., "En Sovjetforfatters skaebne," *Aarhus Stiftstidende* (Aarhus), Aug. 14, 1980.
432. Dalgård, P., *The Function of the Grotesque in Vasilij Aksenov*, Aarhus, 1982.
433. Dovlatov, S., "Vstretilis', pogovorili," *NA*, Aug. 27, 1980.
434. Drawicz, A., *Literatura Radziecka, 1917-1967*, Warszawa, 1968.
435. Dymshits, A., "I vpryam'—pora!", *LR*, Aug. 20, 1965, pp. 10-11.
436. Elkin, A., "Sovremenniki," *MG*, No. 10, 1961, pp. 294-305.
437. Èrenburg, I., *Lyudi, gody, zhizn'*, Sobr. soch., t. 6, M, 1966, p. 767.
438. Erlich, V., "Post-Stalin Trends in Russian Literature," *Slavic Review*, Vol. XXIII, No. 3, 1964, pp. 405-19.
439. Ermachenko, V., "Tsvet lyubvi," *Yuzhnyy Kazakhstan*, March 26, 1964.
440. Esmein, I., "Polemique autour des oeuvres Axionov et de Tendriakov," *Table Ronde*, No. 215, 1965, pp. 175-79.
441. Evtushenko, E., "V lesu" (a poem), *Ottsovskiy slukh*, M, 1975, p. 34.
442. Favorin, V., "Grazhdane bol'shogo mira," *Ural*, No. 10, 1962.
443. Ferenczi László, "Akszjonov" (in) *Az új szovjet irodalom* (János Elberd and Kardos László, eds.), Budapest, 1966-67.
444. Filipp. V., "Tema begstva u Aksënova," *Novyy zhurnal*, No. 151, 1983, pp. 68-75.
445. Filippov, Yu., "Vot takim Makarom," *LG*, Apr. 8, 1970, p. 5.
446. Flaker, A., *Modelle der Jeans Proza*, Kronberg, 1975.
447. Flaker, A., *Proza u tropericama: prilog izgradnji modela prozne formacije na gradji suvremenih književnosti sredja i istočnoevropske regije*, Zagreb, 1976.
448. Fomenko, L., "Naslediya klassikov," *LG*, Dec. 5, 1963.
449. Fomenko, L., "Proza dlya yunoshestva," *Pravda*, Sept. 2, 1967, p. 3.
450. Foster, L.A., "A configuration of the non-absolute, the structure and the nature of the grotesque," *Zagadnienia Rodzajów Literackich*, Vol. IX, 1967, pp. 38-45.
451. Frolov, V., "Sovremennost'," *Oktyabr'*, No. 10, 1959.
452. Gasiorowska, X., *Women in Soviet Fiction, 1917-1964*, Lond., 1968.
453. "Gesprach zwischen Wassili Axjonow und Wassili Rosljakov," *Kunst und Literatur*, Vol. 22, Berlin, 1974, pp. 725-33.
454. Gibian, G., "The Urban Theme in Recent Soviet Russian Prose," *Slavic Review*, No. 37, 1978, pp. 40-50.
455. Ginzburg, E.S., *Journey into the Whirlwind*, (P. Stevenson and M. Hayward, trs.), NY, 1967.
456. Ginzburg, E.S., *Krutoy marshrut* (Part 2), Milano, 1979.
457. Ginzburg, E.S., *Within the Whirlwind*, (I. Boland, tr.), NY, 1981.
458. "Given permission to leave," *TLS*, May 13, 1980.
459. Gladilin, A., *The Making and Unmaking of a Soviet Writer*, Ann Arbor, 1979.
460. Golubev, P., "Svuchal li zvon 'bregeta'," *Smena*, No. 19, 1964, p. 24.
461. Gyldengren, M.L., "Aksjonov—en ny type sovjetforfatter," *Information* (Copenhagen), Nov. 28, 1978.
462. Gyldengren, M.L., "Genrediskussionen i sovjetisk litteraturkritik och V.P. Aksënovs 'Poiski Žanra'," *Svantevit* (Denmark), Vol. VI, No. 2, 1980.
463. Gyldengren, M.L., "Mellan statik og dynamik," *Slavica Othiniensia*, No. 2, Odense, 1979.
464. Hassanoff, O., "The Style of Molodaja Malaja Proza" (unpublished Ph.D. dissertation), University of Alberta, Canada, 1978.

465. Hassanoff Bakich, O., "A new type of character in the Soviet Literature of the 1960's: the early works of Andreĭ Bitov," *Canadian Slavonic Papers*, Vol. XXIII, No. 2, June 1981.
466. Hayward, M. (ed.), *Soviet Literature in the Sixties*, Lond., 1965.
467. Hayward, M., and Labedz, L. (eds.), *Literature and Revolution in Soviet Russia 1917-1962*, Lond., 1963.
468. Hingley, R., *Russian Writers and Soviet Society*, Lond., 1978.
469. Holthusen, J., "Vasilij Aksenov and Anatolij Gladilin," *Russische Gegenwartsliteratur*, Bk. II, 1941-1967, Munch., 1968.
470. Hosking, G., *Beyond Socialist Realism*, NY, 1980.
471. Idashkin, Yu., "Istoki podviga," *Oktyabr'*, No. 12, 1962, pp. 182-87.
472. Ireland, R., "A Note on Aksenov," *Meanjim Quarterly*, Vol. XXIII, No. 117, 1964.
473. Ivanova, L., "Nartsiss ne iz legendy," *MG*, No. 9, 1963.
474. Johnson, J.J., Jr., "Introduction" (Biography) (in) Vasily Aksenov: *The Steel Bird*, Mich., 1979.
475. Kahler, D., and Globy, K. (eds.), *Begegnung und Bundnis*, Berlin, 1973.
476. Kamyanov, V., "Ispytaniye krasotoy," *Literatura v shkole*, No. 4, 1966.
477. Kamyanov, V., "Tak nazyvayemyy zhanr . . . ," *LG*, June 23, 1964.
478. Karetnikova, M., "Ostanovleniye mgnoven'ya," *MG*, No. 5, 1964.
479. Karyakin, Yu., "An episode in the current battle of ideas" (translated from *NM*, No. 9, 1964), *The Soviet Review*, No. 3, 1965, pp. 21-31.
480. Kasach, W., *Die Russische Litteratur 1945-1976*, Münch., 1980.
481. Kassil', L., "Moy mladshiy brat," *Pravda*, Nov. 18, 1962.
482. Kedrina, Z., "Glavnoye—chelovek," *DN*, No. 3, 1963, pp. 246-62.
483. Klepikova, E., and Solov'yëv, V., "Traditsii i pisateli," *Neva*, No. 8, 1960, pp. 172-78.
484. Kogan, A., "Venets delu," *LR*, Oct. 2, 1964, p. 14.
485. Kogan, A., "Odin rasskaz," *SO*, No. 9, 1964, pp. 183-86.
486. Kovalëv, V.A., *Mnogoobraziye stiley v sovetskoy literature*, M"L, 1965.
487. Kovsky, V., "Zhizn' i stil'" (in) *Zhanrovo-stilevyye iskaniya sovremennoy sovetskoy prozy*, M, 1971.
488. Kozhevnikov, V., "Molodost' sovetskoy literatury," *Smena*, Oct. 20, 1962, pp. 1, 3.
489. Kozhevnikova, K., *Spontannaya ustnaya rech' v èpicheskoy proze*, Praha, 1970.
490. Kozlov, I., "Chutkaya dusha khudozhnika," *Ogonëk*, No. 20, 1966, p. 23.
491. Kryachko, L., "Geroy ne khochet vzroslet'," *LG*, March 19, 1963.
492. Kryachko, L., "Pogovorim o geroye," *MG*, No. 12, 1964, pp. 292-306.
493. Kustanovich, K., "Aksyonov, V.P.," *Encyclopedia of World Literature in the 20th Century* (L.S. Klein, ed.), Vol. 1, NY, 1981.
494. Kuz'lichev, I., "Puti i pereput'ya," *Oktyabr'*, No. 5, 1966, pp. 183-200.
495. Labedz, L., "Soviet Art Must Be Beautiful," *Partisan Review*, No. 30, Sept., 1963.
496. Lehrman, E.H., "Soviet Russian Prose Fiction in 1963, *Books Abroad*, Vol. 38, No. 2, Spring 1964.
497. Levin, F., "Spor s Nestorom," *VL*, No. 11, 1965, pp. 37-49.
498. Lobanov, M., "Feyerverk . . . ," *LG*, Dec. 17, 1964.
499. Lobanov, M., "Vnutrenniy i vneshniy chelovek," *MG*, No. 5, 1966, pp. 286-302.
500. Makarov, A., "Cherez pyat' let," *Znamya*, No. 7, 1966, pp. 201-219; No. 8, pp. 217-227; No. 9, pp. 207-225.
501. Makarov, A., "Fünf Jahre später: Wassili Axjonov, Ideen und Gestalten" (translation from the Russian version), *Kunst und Litteratur*, Vol. XIV, pp. 1146-1172, 1296-1309.
502. Makarov, A., *Pokoleniya i sud'by* (contains: Makarov, "Cherez pyat' let"), M, 1967.
503. Matuszewski, R., "W zwierciadle prasy literackiej," *Nowe drogi*, No. 16, 1962.
504. Meyer, P., "A Bibliography of Works by and about Vasilii Pavlovich Aksenov," *RLT*, No. 5, 1973.
505. Meyer, P., "A Bibliography of Works by and about Vasilii Pavlovich Aksenov," *10 Bibliographies of 20th Century Russian Literature* (F. Moody, ed.), Mich., 1977.

506. Meyer, P., "Aksenov and Soviet Literature of the 1950's and 1960's" (unpublished Ph.D. dissertation), Princeton University, 1971.
507. Meyer, P., "Aksenov, Vasilli Pav.," *The Modern Encyclopedia of Russian and Soviet Literature* (H.B. Weber, ed.), Vol. 1, p. 94.
508. Meyer, P., "Aksenov and Soviet Literature of the 1960's," *RLT*, No. 6, 1973.
509. Mezhenkov, V., *Strannaya proza*, 1971, pp. 189-203.
510. Mikhaylova, L., "Grubaya plot' i gore ot uma," *Znamya*, No. 11, 1963, pp. 203-216.
511. Mikhola, M.L., "Luettuani Aksjonovia," *Parnasso 22* (Helsinki), 1972, pp. 46-48.
512. Mitin, G., "Truba zovët," *LR*, Dec. 3, 1965, p. 17.
513. Möller, P.U., "Sovjetrussisk litteratur" (in) *Moderne Slavisk Litteratur* (H. Hertel and T. Liversager, eds.), Copenhagen, 1972.
514. Możejko, E., "Folklore, 'Narodnost'" and V. Aksjonov's Novelette 'Dikoj'," *Scando Slavica*, Vol. XVII, 1971.
515. Nagibin, Yu., "Svoyë i chuzhoye," *DN*, No. 7, 1959.
516. Nechayeva, L., "O chuvste pravdy," *MG*, No. 4, 1965, pp. 313-316.
517. Nikolin, E., "Polnoy dushoy," *Neva*, No. 7, 1963, pp. 171-176.
518. Ninov, A., "Gde nachinayetsya gorizont?," *Neva*, No. 10, 1966, pp. 171-178.
519. Ninov, A., "Yazyk rasskaza," *DN*, No. 4, 1966, pp. 257-66.
520. "The old and young in literature," *Survey*, Jan. 1963, pp. 23-30.
521. Ozerov, V., "Na boyevykh pozitsiyakh," *VL*, No. 3, 1963, pp. 3-9.
522. Permitin, Smirnov, "Lyubyashchim vzglyadom," *LR*, June 12, 1964, p. 19.
523. Pertsovskiy, V., "Sila dobra," *VL*, No. 11, 1963, pp. 21-44.
524. Pertsovskiy, V., "Osmysleniye zhizni," *VL*, No. 2, 1964, pp. 27-44.
525. Piekur, J., "Nekotoryye problemy khudozhestvennoy manery rannikh povestey Vasiliya Aksënova," *Zeszyty Naukowe Uniwersytetu Gdańskiego*, 1973.
526. Piskunov, V., "Conference on problems of Socialist Realism, A Survey," *Soviet Literature*, No. 7, 1967, pp. 142-51.
527. Portnov, V., "S kogo vy pishete portrety?", *Izvestiya*, Aug. 14, 1965, p. 5.
528. Povarov, S., "Poèziya prozy," *Omskaya pravda*, Dec. 17, 1964.
529. "Prasówki zagraniczne" (n.a.), *Życie literackie*, 45 (1379), 1978, p. 2.
530. Proffer, E.S. (article on Aksënov) in *The Third Wave: Russian Literature in Emmigration* (O. Matich and M. Heim, eds.), Ann Arbor, 1983, 300 p.
531. Radlow, D., "Lyublyu i nenavizhu," *Oktyabr'*, No. 10, 1969, pp. 197-202.
532. Rassadin, St., "Sila i slabost' molodosti," *VL*, Oct. 2, 1962, p. 3.
533. Ravnum, I., *Russisk Litteratur efter Stalin*, Copenhagen, 1974.
534. Romanets, M.V., *Problema gumanizma v sovremennom russkom rasskaze*, Khar'kov, 1969, pp. 18-19.
535. "Romans przegranego playboya" (n.a.), *Literature w świecie*, 1975, No. 50, p. 320.
536. Rybakov, Yu., "Kistochkin i drugiye," *LG*, June 15, 1965, p. 3.
537. Samarin, R., "The Provocateurs of Survey," *LG*, Apr. 18, 1963; translated in *Survey*, July 1963.
538. Sarnov, V., "Èto bylo nevozmozhno desyat' let nazad," *VL*, No. 7, 1964, pp. 31-36.
539. Semënov, G., "Pochti iz zapisnoy knigi," *Znamya*, No. 9, 1962.
540. Shcherbakov, "Geroy, kotoromu segodnya 20," *Teatr*, No. 24, 1963, p. 58.
541. Shcherbatova, G.A. (ed.), *Ob iskusstve seychas*, M, 1960.
542. Shcherbina, V., "Za otobrazheniye bogatstva deystvitel'nosti," *VL*, No. 6, 1962.
543. Shim, E., "Voprosy k samomu sebe," *Znamya*, No. 9, 1962.
544. Schaarschmidt, G.H., "Some Aspects of Pronominal Reference in Russian Prose" (with examples from Aksënov) (in) *The Structure and Semantics of the Literary Text: Struktura i semantika literaturnogo teksta* (M. Peter, ed.), Budapest, 1977.
545. Shneidman, N.N., *Literature and Ideology in Soviet Education*, Toronto, 1973.
546. Shneidman, N.N., *Soviet Literature in the 1970's*, Toronto, 1979.
547. Shubin, E.A., *Sovremennyy russkiy rasskaz*, L, 1974.

548. Skvortsov, L.A., "Zhargonnaya leksika v yazyke sovremennoy khudozhestvennoy literatury (v svyazi s dvumya redaktsiyami povesti Aksënova 'Apelsiny iz Marokko'," *Voprosy kul'tury rechi* (V.G. Kostromarov, ed.), Vol. 7, M, 1966.
549. Slonim, M., "European Notebook," *New York Times Book Review*, May 19, 1968.
550. Slonim, M., *Soviet Russian Literature*, NY, 1967.
551. Smolyakov, S., "O geroyakh vydumannykh," *Dal'niy Vostok*, No. 3, 1963, pp. 177-82.
552. Sokolov, V., "Chitatel' i literaturnyy protsess," *VL*, No. 1, 1965, pp. 44-47.
553. Solov'yëva, I., "Nachalo puti," *NM*, No. 9, 1959.
554. Steiniger, A., *Litteratur und Politik in der Sowjetunion nach Stalins Tod*, Weisbaden, 1965.
555. "Stripped of citizenship" (n.a.), *TLS*, Jan. 23, 1981.
556. Svetov, F., "Detali i sut'," *NM*, No. 4, 1966, pp. 262-65.
557. Svetov, F., "Geroy rasskaza," *VL*, No. 12, 1962, pp. 17-35.
558. Svetov, F., "O molodom geroye," *NM*, No. 5, 1967, pp. 218-32.
559. Svirsky, G., *A History of Post-War Soviet Writing*, Ann Arbor, 1981.
560. Svirskiy, G., *Na lobnom meste*, Lond., 1979.
561. Todorović, Ž., *Svetski pisci vaši učitelji*, Novi Sad, 1975.
562. Trifonova, T., "Dlya cheloveka i chelovechestva," *VL*, No. 6, 1961, pp. 12-35.
563. Tybjaerg Schacke, L., "Til konstitueringen af den indadrettede betydningsstruktur i Vasilij Aksenovs fortaelling 'Papa slozhi'," *Svantevit*, IV, No. 2.
564. Vayl', P., and Genis, A., "Kakimi my bol'she ne budem . . . : Roman Vasiliya Aksënova *Ozhog* i krizis russkoy intelligentsii," *NA*, Aug. 17, 1982.
565. Vayl', P., and Genis, A., "Literaturnyye mechtaniya. Ocherk russkoy prozy s kartinkami," *Chast' rechi*, No. 1, NY, 1980, pp. 204-33.
566. Vayl', P., and Genis, A., *Sovremennaya russkaya proza*, Ann Arbor, 1982.
567. Velengurin, N., "Velikoye i prostoye," *Kuban'*, No. 2, 1963, pp. 47-51.
568. Vinogradov, V.V., i drugiye, "Pochta Redaktora," *LG*, June 7, 1967, p. 5.
569. Vlasenko, A., "Pisateli o literaturnom masterstve," *Nash sovremennik*, No. 7, 1965, pp. 108-10.
570. Vlasenko, A., "Trud i kharakter," *Pisatel' i zhizn'*, vyp. 3, M, 1966.
571. Vlasenko, A., "Syuzhet i geroy," *Neva*, No. 8, 1963, pp. 171-80.
572. Vlasenko, A., "Trud—poèziya!", *Oktyabr'*, No. 12, 1964.
573. Voronov, V., "Chelovek—ryadom s toboy," *LG*, Oct. 20, 1962.
574. "Wassili Axjonow" (n.a.), *Moderne Sowjetische Prosa. Eine Übersicht und 22 Portratstudien*, Berlin, 1967.
575. Whitney, T. (ed.), *The New Writing in Russia*, Mich., 1964.
576. Winogradow, I., "Der Held unsere Zeit," *Kunst und Litteratur*, No. 10, 1962.
577. Woodward, K.L., "A Russian in New York," *Newsweek*, Dec. 8, 1980.
578. Zelinsky, K., "Russian Poetry Today," *Survey*, Jan. 1962.
579. Zholkovskiy, A., and Shcheglov, Yu., "K opisaniyu priyëma vyrazitel'nosti 'Var'irovaniye'," *Semiotika i Informatika* (Moscow), 9, 1977, p. 147.

CONTRIBUTORS

Briker, Boris— writer and literary critic, who has published several articles on contemporary Russian literature and a collection of short stories (in co-authorship with Anatoly Vishevsky), *Sobach'ye delo*, New York, 1983; at present, Ph.D. candidate in the Department of Slavic and East European Studies, The University of Alberta.

Busch, Robert L.— Professor and Chairman, Department of Slavic and East European Studies, The University of Alberta, the author of a number of articles on Russian Romanticism, the Russian psychological realistic novel and the poetry of O. Mandelshtam.

Dalgård, Per— author of articles published in Denmark on Russian nineteenth and twentieth century literature; he is also the author of a recently published book, *The Function of the Grotesque in Vasilij Aksenov*, Aarhus, 1982; a graduate from the University of Aarhus (Denmark); at present, a Ph.D. candidate at the Department of Comparative Literature, The University of Alberta.

Ètkind, Efim— distinguished and leading Russian scholar, former Professor at the Pedagogical Institute in Leningrad, at present Professor at Université Paris X Nanterre; he is the author of numerous articles in the fields of poetics, the theory of literature, the theory of translation, comparative and Russian literature; his publications include such books as *Poèziya i perevod*, Leningrad, 1963, *Forma kak soderzhaniye*, Würzburg, 1977, *Zapiski nezagovorshchika*, London, 1977, *Materiya stikha*, Paris, 1978.

Gorbanevskaya, Natal'ya—	Russian poetess, Associate Editor of *Kontinent*; several collections of her poetry have appeared in the West, the most recent of which are *Pereletaya snezhnuyu granitsu* (1979) and *Angel derevyannyy* (1983); she is widely published in the emigré and Western press and lives in Paris, France.
Johnson, D. Barton—	Professor of Russian Literature, Department of Germanic and Slavic Languages, University of California, Santa Barbara; Associate Editor of the well-known *Russian Literature Triquarterly*, edited by Carl R. Proffer and Ellendea Proffer; his publications include articles on modern Russian literature and the translation of Yuriy Lotman's *Analysis of the Poetic Text*, Ann Arbor, 1976.
Johnson, John J.—	well-known for his interests in the writings of V.P. Aksënov, he is the author of the first competent biography of Aksënov, which appeared as the Introduction to *The Steel Bird*, Ann Arbor, 1979.
Kolesnikoff, Nina—	Associate Professor in the Department of Russian, McMaster University, Hamilton, Ontario; her publications include articles on Polish and Russian literatures and the book *Bruno Jasieński. His Evolution from Futurism to Socialist Realism*, Waterloo, Laurier University Press, 1982.
Kustanovich, Konstantin—	has written articles on Yuriy Trifonov, Vasiliy Aksënov and Eduard Limonov; Mikhail Bakhtin's book *Formal'nyy metod v literaturovedenii* appeared under his editorship in "Serebryanyy vek," New York, 1982.
Kuznetsov, Eduard—	Soviet dissident and author of books based on his life experience: *Dnevniki* and *Mordovskiy maraphon*; his novel *Russkiy roman*

was published in 1983; member of the editorial board of *Kontinent*; now living in Israel.

Lauridsen, Inger— has published in Scandinavian periodicals and journals on Russian twentieth-century literature, especially Yuriy Trifonov; graduated from the University of Aarhus (Denmark); at present, Ph.D. candidate at the Department of Comparative Literature, The University of Alberta.

Maximov, Vladimir— writer and Editor-in-Chief of *Kontinent*; he was a popular author in the Soviet Union for his books *Zhiv chelovek, Shagi k gorizontu* and *My obzhivayem zemlyu*; forced to emigrate in 1974, he published in exile several important novels, such as *Sed'moy den' tvoreniya, Karantin*, the satirical pamphlet *Saga o nosorogakh*, and others; his prose has been translated into many languages; he lives permanently in Paris.

Meyer, Priscilla— is an Associate Professor of Russian at Wesleyan University; her publications include *Dostoevsky and Gogol*, Ann Arbor, 1979, co-edited with Stephen Rudy, "Aksenov and Soviet Literature of the 1960s," an interview with Vasiliy Aksënov; a bibliography of works by and about Vasiliy Aksënov in *Russian Literature Triquarterly*, 1973, v. II, no. 6, and many other articles on and translations of contemporary Russian writers.

Możejko, Edward— Ph.D. from Jagiellonian University of Cracow (Poland); Professor of Slavic and Comparative Literature, The University of Alberta; he has published articles on the literary avant-garde in Slavic countries and Russia (Russian literary Constructivism), the theory of literature and Soviet literature; his book, *Der Sozialistische Realismus. Theorie,*

Entwicklung und Versagen einer Literaturmethode was published by Bouvier in Bonn in 1977, appearing the same year in Danish and Norwegian.

Pogacar, Timothy— Ph.D. from the Department of Slavic Languages and Literatures at the University of Kansas, Lawrence, Kansas.

Vishevsky, Anatoly— writer who has published short stories in the Soviet Union and, since his emigration, in the United States; his collection of short stories (in co-authorship with Boris Briker), *Sobach'ye delo*, appeared in New York, 1983; Ph.D. from the Department of Slavic Languages and Literatures, The University of Kansas, Lawrence, Kansas.

Zholkovsky, Alexander— Professor, Department of Slavic Languages and Literatures, University of Southern California, Los Angeles; a prominent scholar and leading authority in the field of linguistics, poetics and modern Russian literature; his publications include over one hundred articles and books, some of them written in cooperation with Professor Yuriy Shcheglov.

OTHER SLAVICA BOOKS

American Contributions to the Eighth International Congress of Slavists (Zagreb and Ljubljana, Sept. 3-9, 1978), *Vol 1: Linguistics and Poetics*, ed. by Henrik Birnbaum, 1978; *Vol. 2: Literature*, ed. by Victor Terras, 1978

American Contributions to the Ninth International Congress of Slavists (Kiev 1983) *Vol. 1: Linguistics*, ed. by Michael S. Flier, 1983; *Vol. 2: Literature, Poetics, History*, ed. by Paul Debreczeny, 1983

Patricia M. Arant: *Russian for Reading*, 1981

Howard I. Aronson: *Georgian: A Reading Grammar*, 1982

James E. Augerot and Florin D. Popescu: *Modern Romanian*, 1983

John D. Basil: *The Mensheviks in the Revolution of 1917*, 1984

Henrik Birnbaum: *Lord Novgorod the Great Essays in the History and Culture of a Medieval City-State Part One: The Historical Background*, 1981

Henrik Birnbaum & Thomas Eekman, eds.: *Fiction and Drama in Eastern and Southeastern Europe: Evolution and Experiment in the Postwar Period*, 1980

Henrik Birnbaum and Peter T. Merrill: *Recent Advances in the Reconstruction of Common Slavic (1971-1982)*, 1985

Karen L. Black, ed.: *A Biobibliographical Handbook of Bulgarian Authors*, 1982

Marianna Bogojavlensky: *Russian Review Grammar*, 1982

Rodica C. Boțoman, Donald E. Corbin, E. Garrison Walters: *Îmi Place Limba Română/A Romanian Reader*, 1982

Gary L. Browning: *Workbook to Russian Root List*, 1985

Catherine V. Chvany and Richard D. Brecht, eds.: *Morphosyntax in Slavic*, 1980

Jozef Cíger-Hronský: *Jozef Mak* (a novel), translated from Slovak by Andrew Cincura, Afterword by Peter Petro, 1985

Frederick Columbus: *Introductory Workbook in Historical Phonology*, 1974

Gary Cox: *Tyrant and Victim in Dostoevsky*, 1984

R. G. A. de Bray: *Guide to the South Slavonic Languages (Guide to the Slavonic Languages, Third Edition, Revised and Expanded, Part 1)*, 1980

R. G. A. de Bray: *Guide to the West Slavonic Languages (Guide to the Slavonic Languages, Third Edition, Revised and Expanded, Part 2)*, 1980

OTHER SLAVICA BOOKS

R. G. A. de Bray: *Guide to the East Slavonic Languages (Guide to the Slavonic Languages, Third Edition, Revised and Expanded, Part 3)*, 1980

Bruce L. Derwing and Tom M. S. Priestly: *Reading Rules for Russian: A Systematic Approach to Russian Spelling and Pronunciation, with Notes on Dialectal and Stylistic Variation*, 1980

Dorothy Disterheft: *The Syntactic Development of the Infinitive in Indo-European*, 1980

Thomas Eekman and Dean S. Worth, eds.: *Russian Poetics Proceedings of the International Coloquium at UCLA, September 22-26, 1975*, 1983

James Elliott: *Russian for Trade Negotiations with the USSR*, 1981

Michael S. Flier and Richard D. Brecht, eds.: *Issues in Russian Morphosyntax*, 1985

Michael S. Flier and Alan Timberlake, eds.: *The Scope of Slavic Aspect*, 1986

John M. Foley, ed.: *Oral Traditional Literature A Festschrift for Albert Bates Lord*, 1981

Diana Greene: *Insidious Intent: An Interpretation of Fedor Sologub's* The Petty Demon, 1986

Charles E. Gribble, ed.: *Medieval Slavic Texts, Vol. 1, Old and Middle Russian Texts*, 1973

Charles E. Gribble: *Russian Root List with a Sketch of Word Formation, Second Edition*, 1982

Charles E. Gribble: *A Short Dictionary of 18th-Century Russian/Словарик Русского Языка 18-го Века*, 1976

Charles E. Gribble, ed.: *Studies Presented to Professor Roman Jakobson by His Students*, 1968

George J. Gutsche and Lauren G. Leighton, eds.: *New Perspectives on Nineteenth-Century Russian Prose*, 1982

Morris Halle, ed.: *Roman Jakobson: What He Taught Us*, 1983

William S. Hamilton: *Introduction to Russian Phonology and Word Structure*, 1980

Pierre R. Hart: *G. R. Derzhavin: A Poet's Progress*, 1978

Michael Heim: *Contemporary Czech*, 1982

Michael Heim, Zlata Meyerstein, and Dean Worth: *Readings in Czech*, 1985

M. Hubenova & others: *A Course in Modern Bulgarian, Vols. 1 and 2*, 1983

Martin E. Huld: *Basic Albanian Etymologies*, 1984

OTHER SLAVICA BOOKS

Roman Jakobson, with the assistance of Kathy Santilli: *Brain and Language   Cerebral Hemispheres and Linguistic Structure in Mutual Light*, 1980

Donald K. Jarvis and Elena D. Lifshitz: *Viewpoints: A Listening and Conversation Course in Russian, Third Edition*, 1985; plus *Instructor's Manual*

Leslie A. Johnson: *The Experience of Time in Crime and Punishment*, 1985

Raina Katzarova-Kukudova and Kiril Djenev: *Bulgarian Folk Dances*, 1976

Emily R. Klenin: *Animacy in Russian: A New Interpretation*, 1983

Andrej Kodjak, Krystyna Pomorska, and Kiril Taranovsky, eds.: *Alexander Puškin Symposium II*, 1980

Andrej Kodjak, Krystyna Pomorska, Stephen Rudy, eds.: *Myth in Literature*, 1985

Andrej Kodjak: *Pushkin's I. P. Belkin*, 1979

Andrej Kodjak, Michael J. Connolly, Krystyna Pomorska, eds.: *Structural Analysis of Narrative Texts (Conference Papers)*, 1980

Demetrius J. Koubourlis, ed.: *Topics in Slavic Phonology*, 1974

Richard L. Leed, Alexander D. Nakhimovsky, and Alice S. Nakhimovsky: *Beginning Russian, Vol. 1*, 1981; *Vol. 2*, 1982; plus a Teacher's Manual

Edgar H. Lehrman: *A Handbook to Eighty-Six of Chekhov's Stories in Russian*, 1985

Lauren Leighton, ed.: *Studies in Honor of Xenia Gąsiorowska*, 1983

Rado L. Lencek: *The Structure and History of the Slovene Language*, 1982

Jules F. Levin and Peter D. Haikalis, with Anatole A. Forostenko: *Reading Modern Russian*, 1979

Maurice I. Levin: *Russian Declension and Conjugation: A Structural Description with Exercises*, 1978

Alexander Lipson: *A Russian Course, Parts 1, 2, and 3*, 1981; *Teacher's Manual* by Stephen J. Molinsky, 1981

Yvonne R. Lockwood: *Text and Context   Folksong in a Bosnian Muslim Village*, 1983

Sophia Lubensky & Donald K. Jarvis, eds.: *Teaching, Learning, Acquiring Russian*, 1984

Horace G. Lunt: *Fundamentals of Russian*, 1982

Paul Macura: *Russian-English Botanical Dictionary*, 1982

Thomas G. Magner, ed.: *Slavic Linguistics and Language Teaching*, 1976

OTHER SLAVICA BOOKS

Vladimir Markov and Dean S. Worth, eds.: *From Los Angeles to Kiev Papers on the Occasion of the Ninth International Congress of Slavists*, 1983

Mateja Matejić and Dragan Milivojević: *An Anthology of Medieval Serbian Literature in English*, 1978

Peter J. Mayo: *The Morphology of Aspect in Seventeenth-Century Russian (Based on Texts of the Smutnoe Vremja)*, 1985

Vasa D. Mihailovich and Mateja Matejic: *A Comprehensive Bibliography of Yugoslav Literature in English, 1593-1980*, 1984

Edward Możejko: *Yordan Yovkov*, 1984

Alexander D. Nakhimovsky and Richard L. Leed: *Advanced Russian*, 1980

The Comprehensive Russian Grammar of A. A. Barsov/ Обстоятельная грамматика А. А. Барсова, Critical Edition by Lawrence W. Newman, 1980

Felix J. Oinas: *Essays on Russian Folklore and Mythology*, 1985

Hongor Oulanoff: *The Prose Fiction of Veniamin Kaverin*, 1976

Slava Paperno, Alexander D. Nakhimovsky, Alice S. Nakhimovsky, and Richard L. Leed: *Intermediate Russian: The Twelve Chairs*, 1985

Papers for the V. Congress of Southeast European Studies (Belgrade, September 1984), ed. by Kot K. Shangriladze, 1984

Ruth L. Pearce: *Russian For Expository Prose, Vol. 1 Introductory Course*, 1983; *Vol. 2 Advanced Course*, 1983

Gerald Pirog: *Aleksandr Blok's Итальянские Стихи Confrontation and Disillusionment*, 1983

Stanley J. Rabinowitz: *Sologub's Literary Children: Keys to a Symbolist's Prose*, 1980

Gilbert C. Rappaport: *Grammatical Function and Syntactic Structure: The Adverbial Participle of Russian*, 1984

Lester A. Rice: *Hungarian Morphological Irregularities*, 1970

David F. Robinson: *Lithuanian Reverse Dictionary*, 1976

Robert A. Rothstein and Halina Rothstein: *Polish Scholarly Prose A Humanities and Social Sciences Reader*, 1981

Don K. Rowney & G. Edward Orchard, eds.: *Russian and Slavic History*, 1977

Catherine Rudin: *Aspects of Bulgarian Syntax: Complementizers and WH Constructions, 1986*

Ernest A. Scatton: *Bulgarian Phonology*, 1975 (reprint: 1983)

Ernest A. Scatton: *A Reference Grammar of Modern Bulgarian*, 1984

OTHER SLAVICA BOOKS

William R. Schmalstieg: *Introduction to Old Church Slavic*, second edition, revised and expanded, 1983

R. D. Schupbach: *Lexical Specialization in Russian*, 1984

Peter Seyffert: *Soviet Literary Structuralism: Background Debate Issues*, 1985

Michael Shapiro: *Aspects of Russian Morphology, A Semiotic Investigation*, 1969

J. Thomas Shaw: *Pushkin A Concordance to the Poetry*, 1985

Theofanis G. Stavrou and Peter R. Weisensel: *Russian Travelers to the Christian East from the Twelfth to the Twentieth Century*, 1985

Gerald Stone and Dean S. Worth, eds.: *The Formation of the Slavonic Literary Languages, Proceedings of a Conference Held in Memory of Robert Auty and Anne Pennington at Oxford 6-11 July 1981*, 1985

Roland Sussex and J. C. Eade, eds.: *Culture and Nationalism in Nineteenth-Century Eastern Europe*, 1985

Oscar E. Swan: *First Year Polish*, second edition, revised and expanded, 1983

Charles E. Townsend: *Continuing With Russian*, 1981

Charles E. Townsend: *Czech Through Russian*, 1981

Charles E. Townsend: *The Memoirs of Princess Natal'ja Borisovna Dolgorukaja*, 1977

Charles E. Townsend: *Russian Word Formation*, corrected reprint, 1975 (1980)

Walter N. Vickery, ed.: *Aleksandr Blok Centennial Conference*, 1984

Daniel C. Waugh, ed. *Essays in Honor of A. A. Zimin*, 1985

Daniel C. Waugh: *The Great Turkes Defiance On the History of the Apocryphal Correspondence of the Ottoman Sultan in its Muscovite and Russian Variants*, 1978

Susan Wobst: *Russian Readings and Grammatical Terminology*, 1978

James B. Woodward: *The Symbolic Art of Gogol: Essays on His Short Fiction*, 1982

Dean S. Worth: *Origins of Russian Grammar Notes on the state of Russian philology before the advent of printed grammars*, 1983

JOURNALS:

Folia Slavica
International Journal of Slavic Linguistics and Poetics
Oral Tradition